Wissenschaftliche Untersuchungen
zum Neuen Testament · 2. Reihe

Herausgegeben von
Martin Hengel und Otfried Hofius

123

Petrus J. Gräbe

The Power of God
in Paul's Letters

Mohr Siebeck

PETRUS J. GRÄBE, born 1958; 1977–90 studied Philosophy, Greek and Theology at the University of Pretoria; 1987–88 research studies at the University of Münster; 1995 post-doctoral research in Munich, 1999 in Munich and Cambridge (UK); since 1989 lecturer of New Testament at the University of South Africa, presently Accociate Professor.

BS
2398
.G73
2000

Die Deutsche Bibliothek – CIP-Einheitsaufnahme

Gräbe, Petrus J.:
The power of God in Paul's letters / Petrus J. Gräbe. – Tübingen : Mohr Siebeck,
2000
   (Wissenschaftliche Untersuchungen zum Neuen Testament : Reihe 2 ; 123)
   ISBN 3-16-147372-8

© 2000 by J. C. B. Mohr (Paul Siebeck), P.O. Box 2040, D-72010 Tübingen.

The book was printed by Gulde-Druck in Tübingen on non-aging paper from Papier-fabrik Niefern and bound by Heinr. Koch in Tübingen.

Printed in Germany.

ISSN 0340-9570

To My Wife
Rachel

Acknowledgements

In its present form this work is a revised and extended version of my doctoral dissertation, "Δύναμις in the Sense of Power in the Main Pauline Letters", which was accepted by the Faculty of Theology, University of Pretoria, in November 1990. It is a privilege to express due acknowledgement and appreciation to the following people for their invaluable assistance in the completion of this study.

I would like to convey my sincere gratitude to Professor A B du Toit, who suggested this important topic to me, for his scholarly guidance.

Major portions of this monograph were completed during the year spent in residence at the "Westfälische Wilhelms-Universität" in Münster. I am especially indebted to Professor Karl Kertelge who, in many ways, showed personal interest in my work. During a sabbatical in Cambridge, Professor Graham Stanton offered valuable suggestions in the preparation of the final manuscript. I would also like to acknowledge Professor Christopher Rowland for his contribution to this research during a short visit to Oxford, as well as Professor Alexander Wedderburn, Professor Jörg Frey and Professor Ferdinand Hahn for their interest in this theme during my stay in Munich.

Furthermore, I would like to express my sincere appreciation to the "Association of Commonwealth Universities" (ACU) and the "German Academic Exchange Service" (DAAD) which made my research in Cambridge and Munich possible. I would also like to acknowledge my own institution, the University of South Africa (UNISA), which gave me the opportunity to complete this research project, and would like to convey my gratitude to Mrs Kay Du Plessis, Mr Willem Oliver and Rev Du Toit van der Merwe for their assistance in editing the manuscript and preparing the indexes.

Finally, I would like to thank Professor Martin Hengel for accepting this study in the series "Wissenschaftliche Untersuchungen zum Neuen Testament".

In appreciation of her constant encouragement and support, I dedicate this study to my wife, Rachel.

May 2000
Pretoria

Petrus Gräbe

Table of Contents

Section C: Theological Scope of the Concept of God's Power in the Pauline Letters

Introduction

The concept of God's power functions in key passages of Paul's letters and is intrinsically linked to his theology of the cross and its soteriological explication in his message of justification. Because this concept is so closely related to the message of the cross,[1] Paul often speaks of "power" in a paradoxical context[2] — compare for example the following two passages: In 1 Cor 1,18 Paul states that the message of the cross is *foolishness* to them that perish, but to us who are saved, it is the *power of God* (1 Cor 1,18); and in the context of his own apostolic ministry, he affirms that he will rather glory in his *weaknesses* (infirmities), that the *power of Christ* may rest upon him (2 Cor 12,9). Owing to the rhetorical function of alienation,[3] these paradoxical contexts have caught the attention of exegetes (especially as far as the relation between weakness and power in 2 Corinthians is concerned). Although "power" is generally assumed to be an important motif in Pauline theology (cf *inter alia* Forster [1950:178]: "Power ... *dúnamis* ... is a favourite word of St. Paul ..."; Nielsen 1980:140), the concept has *not yet been fully explored*.

For the concept of God's power, Paul *exclusively uses the Greek word* δύναμις. It is noteworthy that κράτος appears within the broader Corpus Paulinum only three times: Eph 1,19; 6,10 and in Col 1,11. In Eph 1,19 and Col 1,11 κράτος is used synonymously with δύναμις, while in Eph 6,10 it is (together with ἰσχύς) linked with the verb ἐνδυναμόω. Ἰσχύς occurs only three times in the Corpus Paulinum: synonymously with κράτος and δύναμις in Eph 1,19, as already mentioned in Eph 6,10 and in

---

[1] " ... die wohl der stärkste Ausdruck von Paradoxalität bei Paulus ist" (Hotze 1997:345).

[2] Broadly speaking, a paradox can be defined as a phenomenon which contradicts the general understanding of an issue. (Cf Hotze 1997:26: "Im weitesten Sinne läßt sich das Paradox definieren als *Phänomen, das dem landläufigen Vorverständnis von einer Sache widerspricht.*")

[3] Cf Lausberg (1982:39—41), referred to by Hotze (1997:35).

2 Thess 1,9, referring to the glory of the Lord's might (τῆς δόξης τῆς ἰσχύος αὐτοῦ). In Paul's letters δύναμις ("power") and ἐξουσία ("authority") also function quite differently. While δύναμις refers to the divine power of the crucified and exalted Lord, the Pauline use of ἐξουσία does not have a christological dimension (cf however 2 Cor 10,8; 13,10).[4]

It should be noted that the Greek term δύναμις occurs for a whole range of meanings in the Pauline letters: "ability"; "power"; "mighty deed"; "ruler"; "supernatural power"; "meaning" (cf Louw & Nida 1988b:67).[5] The present investigation is devoted to δύναμις in the sense of power — specifically with reference to *the power of God*.

Brief overview of the history of research

In 1927 Schmitz wrote an article on the concept δύναμις in Paul. His article bears the sub-title, "Ein Beitrag zum Wesen urchristlicher Begriffsbildung," and he sets himself the goal of pointing out the "religionsgeschichtliche Eigenart" of this concept. Schmitz's conclusions will be discussed in chapter 6.

During 1932 and 1935 the results of Grundmann's penetrating research into δύναμις were published. Up to the present day Grundmann has done the most extensive research on δύναμις, paying special attention to the religio-historical background of this concept.

Forster (1950) proposes two foci around which Paul's thinking about power revolves: His conviction that Jesus had risen and his own personal experiences as a missionary. A critical evaluation of this important issue will be given in section C of this monograph.

---

[4] Cf Scholtissek's comparison between Paul's use of ἐξουσία and δύναμις in his study, *Die Vollmacht Jesu* (1992:67—71).

[5] A few examples of passages in which δύναμις occurs for some of these meanings may be mentioned: "ability" — 2 Cor 1,8; 2 Cor 8,3; "mighty deed" (or, as Louw & Nida [1988a:681] put it] — "deed manifesting great power, with the implication of some supernatural force — 'mighty deed, miracle' ") — 1 Cor 12,10.28.29; Gal 3,5; "ruler" — Rom 8,38; "supernatural power" — 1 Cor 15,24 (it is also possible to interpret δύναμις in Rom 8,38 as meaning a supernatural power, cf Louw & Nida 1988a:479); "meaning" — 1 Cor 14,11 (cf also Nielsen 1980:140 note 13).

The different meanings of δύναμις are relatively far apart in semantic space. Only the meanings "power" and "mighty deed" belong to the same semantic domain (Louw & Nida 1988a:680—1; 1988b:67; cf also 1988a:ix emphasising the importance of the context to signal which of the various meanings may be involved).

Fascher (1959) published valuable information on δύναμις both in a profane as well as in a Christian context. He discusses the use of δύναμις in the New Testament, the Apostolic Fathers, Gnosticism magic and concludes with a section on the Christian power of the apostles and martyrs.

Both exegetical as well as religio-historical aspects receive attention in Karl Prümm's (1961a; 1961b) research on δύναμις. He not only focuses on δύναμις in the Greek-Hellenistic religion and philosophy, but also strives to render a contribution to a "*dynamis*-Theologie" (Prümm 1961b:643).

In 1980 two important essays on δύναμις appeared. i. Friedrich in his article in the "Exegetisches Wörterbuch zum Neuen Testament" discusses the appearance of δύναμις in the New Testament and the different meanings to which it is applied. He also refers to certain themes, namely God's δύναμις, the δύναμις of Christ, of the disciples, miracles, word and power, Spirit and power as well as supernatural powers ("Geistermächte"). ii. Nielsen wrote an informative article on "Paulus' Verwendung des Begriffes δύναμις". This article focuses on the implications that Paul's view of δύναμις has for a theology of the cross (cf the sub-title: "Eine Replik zur Kreuzestheologie").

Valuable contributions have more recently been made to the understanding of "weakness" and its relation to "power" in 2 Cor. In 1993 Ulrich Heckel's important dissertation on *Kraft in Schwachheit. Untersuchungen zu 2 Kor 10—13* was published. Timothy Savage made an important contribution to our understanding of Christian ministry with his monograph *Power through weakness. Paul's understanding of Christian ministry in 2 Corinthians* (1996). In 1998 Gruber's extensive work on *Herrlichkeit in Schwachheit. Eine Auslegung der Apologie des Zweiten Korintherbriefs 2 Kor 2,14—6,13* appeared.

Our understanding of the *pneumatological* dimension of power in Paul's theology has been broadened by Gordon Fee's *God's empowering presence. The Holy Spirit in the letters of Paul* (1994).[6]

The above-mentioned scholars made important contributions to our understanding of δύναμις in Pauline theology. Two observations can however be made:

---

[6] Cf also the literature on exegetical investigations of the paradoxical passages in Paul given by Hotze (1997:21—3).

i. As far as the older works are concerned I need to point out that progress in the field of linguistics has made the New Testament scholar of today sensitive to issues which were not so sharply distinguished in studies up to 1961.
ii. The more recent works (with the exception of Fee's study of Pauline pneumatology) focused primarily on the paradoxical relationship between weakness and power in *2 Corinthians*.

Methodological observations

Recognising the importance of both a synchronic and a diachronic study, these two should, however, not be confused. A diachronic study is important, since it provides the only background against which the specific nuances Paul attached to his use of δύναμις can be distinguished. In order to understand the function of power in Pauline theology, the point of departure must, however, be the *pericopes* in which δύναμις occurs in Paul's letters. The intended contribution of this study is to lay special emphasis on the Pauline use of δύναμις and to do it mainly from an exegetical viewpoint through a responsible exegetical investigation of the different pericopes in which the concept of power occurs in the Pauline letters. This procedure has not been followed yet. The nature of Friedrich's study, as a contribution to an exegetical lexicon, does not allow such an intensive study of the different pericopes in which δύναμις occurs, while Nielsen and Savage deal with specific aspects of δύναμις/power in Paul, namely the implications for a theology of the cross (Nielsen) and for Christian ministry (Savage).

Section A is devoted to a *lexico- and conceptual-historical survey of* δύναμις. Attention is paid to the Hellenistic (profane Greek) use of δύναμις, to the Old Testament background concerning the concept of power in Paul's letters and to concepts of power in early Judaism, Philo and Qumran. The purpose of this section is not to provide an exhaustive investigation into the concept of power in these contexts, but to establish a few relationships in order to cast light on power in Paul's letters. A lexico- and conceptual-historical investigation of δύναμις is also meaningful in the sense that it gives the reader an idea of the relevance of this concept (e g as power of salvation in early Judaism and Hellenism) without implying any direct influence on Paul. As this lexico- and conceptual-historical aspect of "power" has been dealt with most extensively in existing studies on δύναμις, special attention will be paid to the results of these enquiries. However, the present writer wishes to endorse Eichholz's (1985:227) statement:

" 'Entscheidend ist nicht die Begriffsgeschichte, sondern der *Kontext*' ... Die Vorgeschichte des Begriffs kann nur in Grenzen hilfreich sein, weil der jeweilige Kontext bei Paulus ein anderer ist und dieser der eigentliche Verstehenschlüssel sein muß."[7]

Many of the pericopes in the Pauline letters in which δύναμις occurs, are pericopes which confront the exegete with numerous problems of interpretation. It is, therefore, not strange that entire dissertations and monographs have been devoted to some of these pericopes or even sub-pericopes.[8]

The purpose of the *exegetical section (section B)* is to provide a responsible exegetical overview of the pericopes that constitute the context in which the concept of power has to be interpreted. The reader will observe that throughout this section the writer has applied a fairly strict pattern. After locating a pericope within the macrocontext of the letter in which it occurs, its structure is analysed. A discourse analysis proves to be helpful in this regard, although it has not been considered necessary in chapters 8, 9 and 11. As a first step in analysing the structure, all pericopes have been divided into colons (used in the sense of a syntactic unit, comprising an independent verbal and nominal element [cf Louw 1976:77—8]). One colon can be divided into several commata (subordinate phrases). Colons may also be grouped together in "clusters". The structural analysis is followed by an exegetical overview of the pericope, focusing on the immediate context in which δύναμις occurs. The length and nature of the discussion will determine whether or not a conclusion will be added.

As "power" in Rom 9,17 occurs in a quotation from the Old Testament, the reader is referred to the section dealing with the use of

---

[7] " 'Crucial is not the history of a concept, but its *context*' ... The history of a concept has only limited value, because the specific Pauline contexts are different and these should be the real interpretative key" (freely translated:PJG).

[8] Cf for example Lang (1973); Smith (1983). Betz (1972), McClelland (1980) and Zmijewski (1978) may also be mentioned in this regard.

δύναμις in the Old Testament (Septuagint). The context in which 1 Cor 6,14 occurs, does not seem to justify a detailed discussion of this passage in the exegetical section. In the discussion of God's resurrection power (chapter 24.3.2) this passage will however be dealt with.

In the light of the exegetical study, it is clear that the ways in which the concept of power functions in specific pericopes in Paul's letters are related to one another. In Section C these pericopes will be grouped together in the discussion of certain themes. To emphasise the fact that the way this grouping has been done has emerged from a thorough exegetical investigation and has not been decided upon beforehand the pericopes in section B will not be grouped but will be arranged chronologically.[9]

The purpose of *section C* is to *distinguish the nuances* present when Paul relates the concept of God's power to specific themes and to integrate the results with *Pauline theology* in a broader sense. A theological-christological as well as a pneumatological emphasis has been distinguished. Paul's ministry within the christological perspective on weakness and power will also be discussed.

The purpose of this section is not to provide a "scheme" into which all the passages in which the concept of power occurs, can be fitted. The themes discussed in this section emerged from an intensive exegetical study of the relevant passages and reveal the emphases in Paul's understanding of power. It is perhaps in this regard that the weaknesses of previous studies of δύναμις are most clearly evident. (It will, e g, become clear from the following discussion that Forster affirms that there are two foci around which Paul's thinking about power revolves, namely the conviction that Jesus was risen and his own personal experiences as a missionary. This view is highly inadequate.)

In the ensuing discussion it will be emphasised that the concept of power is intimately related to various other crucial themes in Paul's theology, for example: "righteousness" (Rom 1,16—17, 1 Cor 1,24.30); "sanctification", "redemption" (1 Cor 1,30); "hope" (Rom 15,13); "faith" (1 Cor 2,5); "the life of Jesus" (2 Cor 4,10.11); "grace" (2 Cor 12,9); "immortality" (ἀφθαρσία), "glory" (δόξα) (1 Cor 15,42.43); "kingdom of God" (1 Cor 4,20) (cf Fascher 1959:437—8; Friedrich 1980:861—2;

---

[9] For a recent discussion of Pauline chronology, cf Söding (1997:3—30). Extensive reference to literature on this subject is also given in this essay (cf note 1 on page 3).

Forster 1950:180; Nielsen 1980:140—1; Prümm 1961b:647.649.657—8. 676—7; Schmitz 1927:164). Although this work focuses on the main Pauline letters,[10] an overview is also presented of the way in which the concept of the power of God functions in the rest of the Corpus Paulinum. This study is also placed within the context of the New Testament as a whole, taking into account the motif of the power of God in Luke (as an example from the synoptic tradition),[11] Acts as well as in Revelation. The overview of this broader context makes it possible to distinguish more clearly the *specific Pauline interpretation* of the power of God.

---

[10] Romans, 1 & 2 Corinthians, Galatians.

[11] Luke has been selected as the concept of power ($\delta\acute{v}\nu\alpha\mu\iota\varsigma$) occurs most in this Gospel.

A Lexico- and Conceptual-historical Overview
of the Concept of Power

Chapter 1

The Hellenistic (profane Greek) use of δύναμις

1.1 All areas of life — especially physical

Δύναμις (in the sense of "power" or "might")[1] was used in the Greek milieu over a very broad spectrum, including almost all areas of life — especially the physical (cf Fascher 1959:415—6).[2] According to Plato's Republic the δυνάμεις are a genus of being (γένος τι τῶν ὄντων) which enables us, gives us power (Fascher 1959:416). To this belong the sensual organs of seeing and hearing (Pl Resp 477c). Of these powers the most powerful δύναμις is knowledge (ἐπιστήμη πασῶν δυνάμεων ἐρρομενεστάτη [Pl Resp 477e]).

Aristotle affirms that every visible body has a "... gestaltende oder empfindende Kraft oder beides", πᾶν σῶμα αἰσθητὸν ἔχει δύναμιν ποιητικὴν ἢ ἄμφω (Aristot Cael 1,7 [Fascher 1959:416]).[3] He also portrays coldness as power (δύναμις γὰρ τίς ἐστιν ἡ ψυγρότης; Probl 7,5.)

Plants have healing powers, which are also called δυνάμεις. Galen (Περὶ κράσεως καὶ δυνάμεως τῶν ἁπτῶν φαρμάκων 3,2) distinguishes about 60 different kinds of healing plants. While still exploring the sphere of the physical powers attributed to medicine, one seems to be entering the sphere of magic when one learns that coral can save one from danger in

---

[1] For a comparison of the use of δύναμις and ἐξουσία in the Greek literature of antiquity, cf Scholtissek 1993:81—5.

[2] Cf also Grundmann (1935:288): "Bei Übersicht über die Verwendung von δύναμις war deutlich geworden, daß im ganzen menschlichen Leben, ebenso aber auch im Leben des κόσμος δύναμις wirksam gefunden wird." He continues: "Das führt nun im Laufe der griechischen und hellenistischen Entwicklung des Nachdenkens über die Welt und ihr Geheimnis dazu, die δύναμις immer mehr zum Weltprinzip werden zu lassen."

[3] In this passage, however, δύναμις may perhaps not mean "power", but "capability". (Cf Liddell & Scott [1968:1285] who translate παθητικὴ δύναμις as "capable of feeling".)

battle and bears in itself an ἀποτρεπτικὴ δύναμις, an averting power against drought and hail (Fascher 1959:417).

1.2 Δύναμις as world principle

In the philosophy of the Pythagorean, Philolaos, one already finds a clear development in this direction. "World principle" is the number ten as δύναμις ἰσχύουσα. Alongside Plato's affirmation "ἐπιστήμη is δύναμις", comes that of the Pythagorean that the δεκάς is δύναμις.[4]

In the philosophy of *inter alia* Melissos and Thales the juxtaposition of philosophy and religion, original substance and God is evident. However, between these there is no mediation through a personalistic creation concept. It is difficult to determine whether a word like δύναμις in ancient texts refers to a mere "principle" or to a divine being as power, penetrating the whole cosmos.[5]

Ekphantos was of the opinion that visible things have three characteristic features: μέγεθος, σχῆμα and δύναμις. According to Hippolytus (Refut 1,15) he regards a θεία δύναμις, which he portrays as reason and soul, as the origin of movement (Diels 1966:442). Ekphantos, therefore, equals the δύναμις with the *nous* or "world soul" like the Stoics. In the same way as the natural philosophers, however, he relates the origin of the world to the divine (Fascher 1959:418—9).

The tendency increased to make δύναμις an absolute cosmic principle. In the philosophies of Aristotle and the Stoics the *nous* represented this principle. Only in Poseidonius δύναμις became a true cosmic principle. In his philosophy Poseidonius erected a whole system of powers which fashions the world and operates in it, whether in the macrocosm or the microcosm, and which is based upon the δύναμις ζωτική, the original power of all being, which "... inwardly holds the world together" (Grundmann 1964:287). Poseidonius is an independent philosopher worthy

---

[4] Cf Fascher 1959:417: "... die δεκάς ist allgemeiner, sinnlich wahrnehmbarer Ausdruck von δύναμις schlechthin, die eben nur als δύναμις ἰσχύουσα, d.h. sich in Kraftwirkungen äußernde Macht 'gesehen' werden kann".

[5] Regarding the Stoics, Fascher (1959:418) however remarks: "Klar liegt die Sache bei den Stoikern, wenn die mit der Weltkraft identifizierte Gottheit den Weltstoff gestaltet, während sie die unsichtbare, die Welt bewegende, aber aus sich selbst entstandene u. sich selbst bewegende Kraft ist."

to be ranked with Aristotle and Chrysippus. Chrysippus teaches that the world is to be explained in terms of concept, Aristotle explains it in terms of reason and Poseidonius in terms of power (cf Reinhardt, *Poseidonius*, quoted in Grundmann 1964:287).

1.3 Δύναμις as religious concept

Although the emphasis fell on philosophy in the preceding discussion, it has been pointed out that in ancient times philosophy and theology could not be separated from one another. From the philosophical viewpoint the cosmic principle and God are identical. Because of this neutral concept of God, the Greek philosophers seldom referred to the power of God (Grundmann 1964:289).

Δύναμις is used as attribute to various Greek gods.[6] It is possible for one God to unite in himself different δυνάμεις. The supreme divinity unites all power in himself. (Aelius Aristides says in his Zeus speech that he is creator and founder of all; the one who bears all essentialities and powers in himself.)

The philosophers consider the principle δύναμις as θεῖος or θεός. According to the devout people who believed in gods the worshipped Person has δύναμις or δυνάμεις (cf Fascher 1959:420).

1.4 Magic and healing

Both in the philosophical work of Hellenism and in the popular thinking expressed in magic, the world is conceived as a manifestation of the forces working in and by and on it. All occurrence is comprised in these forces. To do anything, one must participate in them and know them. The whole point of magic is participation in the forces of the cosmos (Grundmann 1964:288).

---

[6] Fascher (1959:419) points out that when in Homerici Hymni 3,117 "... der Rinderdiebstahl des kaum geborenen Hermes die Begründung erfährt: δύναμις δὲ οἱ ἔπλετο πολλή, so soll offenbar werden, daß dieser Gott von Anfang an auf einem Gebiet 'Kraft' entfaltet, das ihm hernach als sein Ressort zugewiesen wird, da ja für alle Lebensgebiete Götter oder Dämonen als helfende oder hemmende Mächte mitwirken".

In the early phase of Greek thought there is no centralised "power" as godhead, but power is divided between different bearers and is ascribed in later times to demons as power divided in different manifestations (Nilsson 1941:205).[7] Fascher (1959:422) is of the opinion that it is only since Poseidonius, who explained the world in terms of power and also contributed to the dissolution of the cosmos in magical fields of power that the door was opened to occultism in the Greek world and that occult thought at the same time became amenable to science as "philosophy".

The religious use of the concept of power very seldom occurs in Stoic philosophy. The original faith in the power which pervades everything had been pushed into the background until it returned as the magic δύναμις during the religious "Umwälzung der Spätzeit" (Schmitz 1927:154).

As far as the Graeco-Roman world is concerned, the word "power" (δύναμις) was technical in the language of religion, superstition and magic, and was one of the most common and characteristic terms in the language of pagan devotion. "Power" was what the devotees respected and worshipped; any exhibition of "power" was thought to have its cause in something that was divine (Ramsey 1915:118).

In the great Parisian Magical Papyrus one reads of the bear star: ἀρκτικὴ δύναμις πάντα ποιοῦσα. The δυνάμεις in plants and stones are not only active as medicine, but are also active in weather magic. Plutarch (Symp 4,2,1) was of the opinion that an onion, despite its smallness, does not flee from the lightning, but has a power that works against it, like a fig and the skin of a seal (Fascher 1959:422).

In Iamblichus Myst (II,1) we have an express depiction of the demonic forces. He describes their origin in the words: λέγω τοίνυν δαίμονας μὲν κατὰ τὰς γεννητικὰς καὶ δημιουργικὰς τῶν θεῶν δυνάμεις ἐν τῇ πορρωτάτῃ τῆς προόδου ἀποτελευτήσει καὶ τῶν ἐσχάτων διαμερισμῶν παράγεσθαι ... . There are, therefore, powers in the world which constitute a great nexus of power, a single, supreme power of which the different demonic powers are emanations (Grundmann 1964:289).

In the light of this total picture, Iamblichus portrays the magician as follows: Knowing the cosmic, divine and demonic forces and their interconnections, the magician can mediate between them for the good or detriment of others. The position of the magician, however, does not

---

[7] Nilsson (1941:206) also mentions that the "... Daimones sind die Form, durch die sich in der altgriechischen Religion der Glaube an die Kraft offenbart".

exclude the possibility that the gods, who stand alongside the demons or are identified with them, might intervene directly with acts of power, especially to help or to heal. In the Greek Hellenistic world Asclepius especially is recognised to be a god of healing. The healing miracles of Epidaurus may serve as an example (cf Klauck 1995:130—9). In the Imuthes-Asclepius papyrus, in which Imuthes is identified with Asclepius, the wonderful power of the god is extolled and one reads of ... ἡ τοῦ θεοῦ δύναμις σωτήριος (Grundmann 1964:289).

1.5 The question of a power of salvation

The dissolution of the cosmos into the forces that rule and affect it has profound consequences for the position of man. As these forces are hidden from man, and his knowledge or ignorance determines his being, man stands outside these forces and must strive to participate in them. Against this background, the question of salvation arises: How can man attain the power which will lift him above the fate of mortality, or, described in Hellenistic terms, which will redeem him from the bondage of matter, and thus make him immortal? Grundmann (1964:289) mentions that a comprehensive answer to this question of salvation is given in the thirteenth tractate of the Corpus Hermeticum, in the λόγος παλιγγενεσίας. The situation of man is described in the twelve τιμωρίαι: ἄγνοια, λύπη, ἀκρασία ... . In man's situation of being lost and controlled by these twelve τιμωρίαι, which are related to the zodiac, the question of a power which can liberate and save is posed. This saving power consists in the ten saving forces which enter into man and effect the γένεσις τῆς θεότητος. Man's deification is brought about by these δυνάμεις which enter into the person taking part in the mystery. It is for this reason, according to Grundmann (1964:290), that the mystagogue greets the initiate: χαῖρε λοιπόν, ὦ τέκνον, ἀνακαθαιρόμενος ταῖς τοῦ θεοῦ δυνάμεσιν εἰς συνάρθρωσιν τοῦ λόγου (Corpus Hermeticum XIII,7 f).

In the introduction to the Mithras Liturgy,[8] δύναμις is the power which is needed for the heavenly journey and the vision of God. It is imparted through the initiation which effects deification (Grundmann 1964:290).

---

[8] Cf μύσται τῆς ἡμετέρας δυνάμεως ταύτης ἦν ὁ μέγας θεὸς Ἥλιος Μίθρας ἐκέλευσέν μοι μεταδοθῆναι ... ὅπως ἐγὼ μόνος αἰτητὴς οὐρανὸν βαίνω καὶ κατοπτεύω πάντα (Parisian Magical Papyrus IV,478 ff; [Grundmann 1964:290]).

In the first tractate of the Corpus Hermeticum, in Poimandres, the question of salvation rises again because of man's situation. The initiate prays: ἐνδυνάμωσόν με (I,32). Endowed with γνῶσις (for γνῶσις is the saving power) the initiate is ὑπ' αὐτοῦ (sc λόγου) δυναμωθείς (I,27). What δυναμοῦν with gnosis accomplishes through the λόγος is the deification attained by the incorporation of the initiate into the divine system of forces as the δύναμις. After the journey through the girdle of the planets, in which he sets aside the qualities which bring about mortality, he attains ἐπὶ τὴν ὀγδοαδικὴν φύσιν τὴν ἰδίαν δύναμιν ἔχων καὶ ὑμνεῖ σὺν τοῖς οὖσι τὸν πατέρα ... καὶ ὁμοιωθεὶς τοῖς συνοῦσιν ἀκούει καί τινων δυνάμεων ὑπὲρ τὴν ὀγδοαδικὴν φύσιν οὐσῶν φωνῇ τινι ἰδίᾳ ὑμνουσῶν τὸν θεόν. καὶ τότε τάξει ἀνέρχονται πρὸς τὸν πατέρα καὶ αὐτοὶ εἰς δυνάμεις ἑαυτοὺς παραδιδόασι καὶ δυνάμεις γενόμενοι ἐν θεῷ γίνονται. τοῦτο ἔστι τὸ ἀγαθὸν τέλος τοῖς γνῶσιν ἐσχηκόσι, θεωθῆναι (I,26 [Grundmann 1964:290; cf also Fascher 1959:42]). The saving process is here taken up into the cosmic system of forces. The hermetic God is pure power — the believer also becomes power.[9]

The Greek concept of power is based entirely on the idea of a natural force which, imparted in different ways, controls, moves and determines the cosmos, and which has its origin in widespread primitive notions of Mana and Orenda (Grundmann 1964:290).

---

[9] Cf Nilsson 1950:577: "Der hermetische Gott ist die reine Kraft, der Kraftbegriff; auch der Gläubige wird zur Kraft (I 26). So wird es ausgesprochen, und so tritt Gott in der religiösen Erfahrung hervor."

Chapter 2

Old Testament Background
(with special reference to the use of δύναμις
in the sense of power in the Septuagint)[1]

2.1 Introduction

In Greek translations of the Old Testament the term δύναμις is used for approximately twenty-five different Hebrew words. At the same time many of these twenty-five terms are sometimes translated by other Greek terms than δύναμις (Fascher 1959:427).

In about 120 cases, δύναμις in the sense of an "army" is used as translational equivalent for the Hebrew word צבא. These cases mainly occur in the older stories of the Old Testament, dealing with Israel's army. Also Yahweh has his armies. He is a God with military power, which defeats Israel's enemies (Ps 67 [68],29: δύναμις for עז in the sense of power [cf Fascher 1959:427—8]).

In formal passages in prophetic discourse (Hos 12,6; Amos 3,13; 5,14.16; 6,14; Jer 5,14), also in 1 Kings 19,10.14, an old Elijah saying, and in the call of the praying Psalmist (Ps 80 [79],5.15.20, in LXX also v 8) Yahweh is called הוה אלהים צבאות or הצבאות אלהי יהוה. The Septuagint translates in Am 6,14 (codex Vaticanus) and Ps 79 (80) κύριος τῶν δυνάμεων (elsewhere, however, κύριος [ὁ θεός] ὁ παντοκράτωρ); in a few places a loan-word is simply built with Greek letters: σαβαώθ (e g 1 Kings 17,45 — Fascher 1959:428).

In the following study attention will be focused on uses of δύναμις in the Septuagint which shed light on the Pauline use of this word. The present writer has, however, considered it necessary to broaden the scope of this

---

[1] The 1982 edition of the Septuagint text edited by Alfred Rahlfs has been used for this investigation.

investigation in order to include also the dimension of power of the Old Testament message concerning the spirit of God (even though the word δύναμις does not always occur).

2.2 The theological use of δύναμις in the Septuagint

It may be said that the Pauline use of δύναμις is essentially theological (cf the discussion from chapter 7 onwards). Septuagint passages in which δύναμις is connected to God are, therefore, especially relevant to this study.

Especially in the later books of the Septuagint the phrase δύναμις θεοῦ occurs as a *set phrase*. Compare:

Wisdom of Solomon 7,25:   ἀτμὶς γάρ ἐστιν τῆς τοῦ θεοῦ δυνάμεως ...

2 Mac 3,24:   ... ὥστε πάντας τοὺς κατατολμήσαντας συνελθεῖν κατα-πλαγέντας τὴν τοῦ θεοῦ δύναμιν ...

2 Mac 9,8:   ... φανερὰν τοῦ θεοῦ πᾶσιν τὴν δύναμιν ἐνδεικνύμενος

(Cf also Job 37,14: στῆθι νουθετοῦ δύναμιν κυρίου)

Although the phrase δύναμις θεοῦ does not occur in the rest of the Old Testament, δύναμις is frequently related to God. It is remarkable that the greatest percentage of passages in which δύναμις is related to God are *passages in which God is addressed* in prayer, petition and praise. In the following passages *God's δύναμις is celebrated* in prayer: Deut 3,24; 1 Chron 29,11; Job 11,20; 12,13; Ps 20 (21),2.14; 58 (59),17; 62 (63),3; 65 (66),3; 67 (68),29; 144 (145),4.6.11[A]; Wisdom of Solomon 12,15.17; 3 Mac 6,13.

Two themes that can be distinguished in this regard specifically need to be pointed out, namely: 1) Praise of the Lord's power as it was manifested during the exodus; 2) The focusing on God as the power of those who trust in him.

2.2.1 In praise of the Lord's power as it was manifested during the exodus

For the Israelites the δύναμις of Yahweh is not a principle discovered through theoretical reflection, but a historical reality. The concept of God's power occurs in prayers and confessions also in the later writings (cf Judith 13,11 — Fascher 1959:430). As contrasted with the gods of the surrounding world, the God of the Old Testament is the God of history. The destiny of Israel is determined at the very beginning of its history by an historical event κατ' ἐξοχήν, by the Exodus from Egypt and the deliverance at the Red Sea. The concept of power constantly recurs in this connection (Grundmann 1964:291).

It must, however, be mentioned that whereas the Masoretic text uses נב and עז in this connection, the Septuagint almost always has ἰσχύς, while δύναμις seldom occurs (Grundmann 1964:291 note 33). Ex 9,16, referred to by Paul in Rom 9,17, reads in the Septuagint text edited by Rahlfs: ἵνα ἐνδείξωμαι ἐν σοὶ τὴν ἰσχύν μου ... . It is, however, noteworthy that codex Alexandrinus instead of ἰσχύν, reads δύναμιν.

The Lord's power (δύναμις) manifested in the exodus is also a recurring theme in prayer (cf Neh 1,10; Bar 2,11; 3 Mac 2,6 [see Rom 9,17]). This event marking the beginning of the history of Israel was also the substance of its religion and led to its historical and personalistic concept of God. Grundmann (1964:292) correctly affirms that the view of power is interwoven with this concept. Of special significance in this respect, are the words from the lips of Moses in Deut 3,24: Κύριε κύριε σὺ ἤρξω δεῖξαι τῷ σῷ θεράποντι τὴν ἰσχύν σου καὶ τὴν δύναμίν σου καὶ τὴν χεῖρα τὴν κραταιὰν καὶ τὸν βραχίονα τὸν ὑψηλόν· τίς γάρ ἐστιν θεὸς ἐν τῷ οὐρανῷ ἢ ἐπὶ τῆς γῆς, ὅστις ποιήσει καθὰ σὺ ἐποίησας καὶ κατὰ τὴν ἰσχύν σου. At a historically decisive hour the power of God proved itself.

The unique and incomparable power of Yahweh is to be declared to all nations. The historical awareness of the Old Testament, which is based on the act at the beginning of history, includes faith in the further deployment of the power of Yahweh in history. For this reason, the history of Israel reveals the nation's continual resort to the power and assistance of Yahweh when needed in times of affliction (cf for example 2 Esdras 11,10; Neh 1,10; Judith 9,8; 13,11; 3 Mac 6,13; Is 10,33 — cf Grundmann 1964:292). God's power shapes and fashions history, according to his own will and purpose.

2.2.2 God as the power of those who trust in him

In the same way in which the power of Yahweh created the world and still maintains it, it also shapes the destinies of individual human beings (cf Grundmann 1935:294). The superior power of Yahweh is extolled, for example, in Job 12,13: ... παρ' αὐτῷ σοφία καὶ δύναμις. The writers of the Old Testament share the conviction that in every national or individual need, crisis or difficulty, the people of Yahweh should turn to him and his helping power. God is the one who gives his people power and strength. In Deut 8,17—18 man is warned against boasting in his own power and is urged to remember that it is the Lord who gives him the ability to produce wealth (μὴ εἴπῃς ἐν τῇ καρδίᾳ σου Ἡ ἰσχύς μου καὶ τὸ κράτος τῆς χειρός μου ἐποίησέν μοι τὴν δύναμιν τὴν μεγάλην ταύτην· καὶ μνησθήσῃ κυρίου τοῦ θεοῦ σου, ὅτι αὐτός σοι δίδωσιν ἰσχὺν τοῦ ποιῆσαι δύναμιν καὶ ἵνα στήσῃ τὴν διαθήκην αὐτοῦ ...). In Ps 83 (84),6—8 those whose strength is in the Lord and who have set their hearts on pilgrimage are said to be blessed ... they go from strength to strength (πορεύσονται ἐκ δυνάμεως εἰς δύναμιν [v 8]). With confidence the Psalmist may say: "God is our refuge and strength" (Ps 45 [46],2: ὁ θεὸς ἡμῶν καταφυγὴ καὶ δύναμις).[2]

The theme of God as the power of those who trust in him needs to be emphasised as this conviction is also shared by Paul and is an important aspect of his understanding of δύναμις.

See for example:

2 Kings 22,32—33:	τίς ἰσχυρὸς πλὴν κυρίου;
	καὶ τίς κτίστης ἔσται πλὴν τοῦ θεοῦ ἡμῶν;
	ὁ ἰσχυρὸς ὁ κραταιῶν με δυνάμει ...
Ps 137 (138),3:	ἐν ᾗ ἂν ἡμέρᾳ ἐπικαλέσωμαί σε, ταχὺ
	ἐπάκουσόν μου·
	πολυωρήσεις με ἐν ψυχῇ μου ἐν δυνάμει.
139 (140),8:	κύριε κύριε δύναμις τῆς σωτηρίας μου,
Hab 3,19:	κύριος ὁ θεὸς δύναμίς μου
Dan (Theodotion) 2,23:	σοφίαν ... καὶ δύναμιν δέδωκάς μοι ...
(Cf also Zach 4,6:	Οὐκ ἐν δυνάμει μεγάλῃ οὐδὲ ἐν ἰσχύι, ἀλλ' ἢ
	ἐν πνεύματί μου, λέγει κύριος παντοκράτωρ.)

---

[2] Cf Prümm 1961b:646: "Der Beter des Alten Testamentes wußte wohl, daß Hoffnung und Vertrauen, die Grundsäulen des Gebetes, nicht nur auf dem Erbarmen, sondern auch auf der Macht Gottes fußen."

2.3 Δύναμις related to glory (δόξα), wisdom (σοφία), and salvation (σωτηρία)

In the following study it will be pointed out that Paul relates δύναμις (i a) to δόξα and σοφία. It is interesting to note that this already occurs in the Septuagint. Compare:

Job 11,20[A]:	παρ᾿ αὐτῷ γὰρ σοφία καὶ δύναμις
Job 12,13:	παρ᾿ αὐτῷ σοφία καὶ δύναμις
Dan (Theodotion) 2,23:	σοφίαν ... καὶ δύναμιν δέδωκάς μοι ...
Ps 62 (63),3:	τοῦ ἰδεῖν τὴν δύναμίν σου καὶ τὴν δόξαν σου.

Paul prominently relates δύναμις θεοῦ to σωτηρία, as the following study will point out. Although there is a great difference between σωτηρία in the Old Testament and in the Pauline letters, the attention may be drawn to passages such as:

Ps 20 (21),2:	κύριε, ἐν τῇ δυνάμει σου εὐφρανθήσεται ὁ βασιλεὺς καὶ ἐπὶ τῷ σωτηρίῳ σου ἀγαλλιάσεται σφόδρα.
Ps 139 (140),8:	κύριε κύριε δύναμις τῆς σωτηρίας μου
3 Mac 6,13:	ἔντιμε δύναμιν ἔχων ἐπὶ σωτηρίᾳ Ιακωβ γένους

2.4 The dimension of power in the Old Testament message concerning the Spirit of God

In the ensuing study of δύναμις in the main Pauline letters it will become increasingly clear that δύναμις is essentially a pneumatological category (cf especially chapter 24). This aspect of δύναμις cannot, however, be fully understood without appreciating the dimension of power in the Old Testament message about the יהוה רוח.[3]

2.4.1 The רוח representing God or his character

This is an anthropomorphic use of the רוח, referring to God's presence, his character or simply God himself. In the creation context, Yahweh's רוח is the planning and executing dimension of God's being with wisdom and executing power. It is also God's רוח that completed the entire exodus process (cf Is 63,10 [Ma 1999:208]).

---

[3] Cf Westermann (1981:223): "Man kann nicht verstehen, was im NT Pneuma heißt, wenn man nicht die Geschichte des Wortes ruah im AT kennt."

2.4.2 The רוח as the power of God enabling individuals to perform a specific task

2.4.2.1 The leaders

The religio-historical background of the רוח among Israel's national leaders is to be found in the ancient Near Eastern royal ideology that the king is either divine (Egypt), demi-god (as in the Mesopotamian king list), or God-designated. The king or chosen leader is considered to have divinely endowed superhuman qualities. In the early Israelite traditions the leaders are characterised by superhuman or physical powers (e g the judges and Saul — Ma 1999:205).

In the earlier stages of the history of רוח (in the sense of "spirit") it was seen as a dynamic power coming over a person and enabling him for a short period of time to perform a certain task. This was especially the case in the period of the charismatic leadership in Israel (Albertz & Westermann 1976:743). It is noteworthy that this specific use of "spirit" from the earlier period of the Old Testament usage also occurs in the New Testament. This is the case where the elusive character of the work of the Spirit is focused upon, as for instance in Jesus' conversation with Nicodemus in John 3,8.[4] The most significant task of the רוח יהוה is the empowerment for a specific task of those who would otherwise not have been able to perform this task. In the Pauline letters the miraculous change of lives as well as the empowerment of those who is weak in themselves are also ascribed to the Spirit (1 Cor 1,25—29; 2 Cor 12,9—10; cf Vosloo 1983:63).

With the introduction of the kingship in Israel a drastic change in the concept of the רוח יהוה occurred. Instead of a dynamic power there emerged a more static concept: a gift resting on the anointed of Yahweh equipping him for his task. The Spirit embodies a specific form of Yahweh's abiding with his people, רוח is therefore associated with Yahweh's blessing (Albertz & Westermann 1976:750).

The leadership's endowment of the רוח also has moral and religious consequences. The main task of the future ideal king (Is 11,1—3a) is the administration of righteousness and justice in the community. Although "might" is part of the royal endowment, the future king is portrayed in his

---

[4] Westermann (1981:229) affirms: "Der Geist ist eine wunderbar wirkende Kraft, deren Woher und Wohin im Dunkel bleibt. Ein Zeichen dafür ist, daß sie dort etwas bewirkt, wo es keine nachweisbare Verfügungsgewalt gibt."

spiritual piety ("fear of the Lord", Is 11,3a). Yahweh promises the "spirit of justice" (Is 28,6) to the one who presides in a court of justice (Ma 1999:206).

2.4.2.2 The רוח as the source of prophetism

In 1 Sam 10,10 and 19,20 (e g) the presence of the רוח among earlier prophets is characterised by ecstatic behaviour. Pre-exilic Isaianic texts have, on the other hand, almost no reference to the prophetic spirit. The exilic period however evidences a sudden surge of prophetic references. In this stage the frequent pairing between "word" and the "spirit" replaces the link between the רוח and ecstatic behaviour. The prophetic nature of the Servant's task (cf Is 42,1—4) is evidence of this resurgent prophetic interest. The postexilic period also characterises the coming age of restoration with God's promise of the spirit and the accompanying prophetic word (Is 59,21). The perpetuity and wide availability of the word and the spirit ensures Yahweh's covenantal presence in the community (Ma 1999:206—7).

2.4.2.3 The future king of salvation

The רוח יהוה will also rest on the future king of salvation, the Messiah, empowering him for his specific mission.

Is 42,1: Here is my servant ...
I have put my spirit on him ...

Is 11,1—2: Then a branch will grow from
the stock of Jesse ...
On him the spirit of the LORD will rest:
a spirit of wisdom and understanding,
a spirit of counsel and power,
a spirit of knowledge and fear of the
LORD;

Is 61,1: The spirit of the Lord God is
upon me
because the LORD has anointed me;
he has sent me to announce good
news to the humble ...

It is noteworthy that in Is 42,1 a contrast is brought forward by the word
רוח: Not the king is any longer bearer of the spirit, but the servant. The
spirit is taken away from the political institution of the kingship and
assigned to the activity of one who is weak in himself — a servant.

This usage is taken up and carried further by Trito-Isaiah in the form of
an intended paradox. Is 61,1 clearly alludes to the anointing of the king in 1
Sam 16,13. It is, however, said that the Spirit of Yahweh now no longer
operates in the context of royal power, but in the context of the
proclamation of good news to the humble.

In Is 11,1 traditional language of the kingship sounds unchanged when
it is said that the spirit of the Lord will rest on a branch from the royal
stock. This is, however, not the case in the following description of the
activity of the king in the time of salvation. In Is 11,2 completely different
activities are ascribed to the spirit. "Spirit" has become an abstract concept
(cf Westermann 1981:228).

2.4.3 The רוח יהוה and creation as well as recreation

The רוח אלהים in Gen 1,2 is *God's creative power* in action.[5] Ps 104,30
reveals that man lives due to God's creative power (רוח) and by his רוח
God maintains his creation. God's creative power is represented by his רוח
(Vos 1984:81).

It is noteworthy that in almost every case in exilic and postexilic
texts רוח occurs with the first person pronominal suffix. רוח most
frequently occurs in the framework of prophetic announcements of
salvation. In exilic and postexilic promises of salvation the gift of the spirit
is promised not only to individuals, but to the whole nation (Ezek 36,27;
37,14; 39,29; cf 11,19; 18,31; 36,26: Joel 3,1—5; Is 32,15; 44,3; 59,21;
Hg 2,5). The activity of the spirit in this context is essentially a *recreative
activity*.

The verbs שפך (Ezek 39,29; Joel 3,1.2), יצק (Is 44,3) and ערה nifal (Is
32,15) cause one to think of רוח as a type of fluid. The image of the
blessing of rain may have had an influence on these expressions (Albertz &
Westermann 1976:751).

The promise of the eschatological giving of the Spirit to the whole
nation of God is developed most extensively in Ezekiel. The recreative

---

[5] For a detailed discussion of different ways to interpret רוח אלהים in Gen 1,2, cf Vos
(1984:80).

activity functions in Ezekiel in the context of Israel as God's unfaithful partner. Despite God's faithfulness, Israel is incapable of obeying and knowing God. It is in this context that Ezekiel talks of Israel's heart of stone (Ezek 36,26). The glory of God is at stake. He acts in order to hallow his name, which Israel has profaned among the nations (Ezek 36,23). God's recreative activity commences with ritual purification (Ezek 36,25). After this ritual purification follows the renewal of the "inner man" (cf Ezek 11,19). A radical change of heart has to take place. לב is an inclusive concept. It not only includes the centre of the life of experience, but also the mind and the will. What Israel needs is a new heart and a new spirit (Ezek 36,26). Yahweh brings about this recreation through his רוח (Ezek 36,27). *The* רוח *is a manifestation of Yahweh's recreative power.*

Yahweh's recreative activity has profound consequences for the existence of his people. In Ezek 37 (áfter Ezek 36) the implications of this recreation for Israel's earthly existence is investigated. Israel mourns: "Our bones are dry, our hope is gone, and we are cut off" (Ezek 37,11). The loss of all vitality is evident from this cry. In Ezekiel's prophetic vision man's weakness stands in contrast to God's power (Ezek 37,3). God is going to revive the dry bones. Ezekiel uses the term רוח to describe this radical revival. Yahweh's רוח indeed represents his recreative power (Vos 1984:95—8).

In Is 44,1—5 רוח is the divine power of blessing ("Segenskraft" — Albertz & Westermann 1976:752).[6] As water in the desert miraculously brings forth new life (cf Is 41,19), the רוח יהוה will bring the seemingly dead people to new life and vitality (Vos 1984:98).

Joel 3,1—5[7] is of great importance to the relationship between the רוח and the people of Yahweh within an eschatological context. In the light of God's deeds of salvation Joel prophesies that Israel will know that God is present in their midst and that he and no other is the Lord their God. Joel 3,1—5 expounds the full meaning of this confession of the presence of Yahweh in the midst of his people. Viewed from a cosmic perspective the future is filled with new vitality and power through the outpouring of

---

[6] It is noteworthy that רוח and ברכה are used in Is 44,3 as parallel concepts (cf Vos 1984:98).

[7] According to the Masoretic text printed in Biblica Hebraica Stuttgartensia this pericope is Joel 3,1—5. In most modern translations, however, this passage is printed as Joel 2,28—32.

Yahweh's רוח. Just as Yahweh gave new life to the cosmos through the outpouring of the rain (cf Joel 2,24), he will give his people new vital power through the outpouring of his spirit (cf Vos 1984:99—100). As vital power, רוח stands in a fundamental opposition to the frailness of the בשׂר (cf Is 31,3). Through the recreation brought about by the outpouring of the spirit the relation to God has become completely new (Wolff 1969:78—9). "Spirit" in this context refers to God in relation to mankind, communicating with and revealing himself to his creatures (Allen 1976:98).

Chapter 3

Concepts of power in early Judaism

3.1 Introduction

Awareness of the event at the beginning of the history of Israel as a peculiar demonstration of the power of God persisted in early Judaism and was actually strengthened during the Maccabean wars in which, at a time of national danger, faith was rekindled in the powerful saving act of Yahweh at the commencement of Israel's history (cf 1 Mac 4,9—11; 3 Mac 2,6; Grundmann 1964:294)[1].

In the Rabbinical period the great doxology in 1 Chron 29,11—12, which magnifies the power of Yahweh (σοὶ, κύριε, ἡ μεγαλωσύνη καὶ ἡ δύναμις), is characteristically explained as follows: "Rabbi Shela says: 'Thine, Yahweh, is the greatness', refers to the work of creation, of which it is said that '... he doeth great things past finding out; yea, and wonders without number' [Job 9,10]; 'and the power', refers to the Exodus from Egypt, of which it is said that 'Israel saw the great hand which the Lord displayed against Egypt' [Ex. 14,31]" (B Berakot 58a).

In early Judaism the connection is, therefore, maintained between belief in Yahweh and history. The same is also true of the connection between the belief in Yahweh and creation. We find here the Old Testament view of the creation of the world by the Word of Yahweh as the instrument of his power. Compare the parallelism of Word and power in TgIs 48,13: "With my Word I have established the earth, and with my power I have suspended the heavens." The Old Testament association of belief in Yahweh with the view of power is maintained. The individual can rely on this power of Yahweh. In Mek Ex 15,2 we read: " 'My power', that is, thou art a support and strength for all the dwellers upon earth." We are

---

[1] Frequent use of Grundmann's penetrating research has been made in this chapter.

obviously dealing here with the personal power with which Yahweh
supports men and allies himself with them.

3.2 Eschatological emphases

A line of development becomes noticeable which is particularly important
in the New Testament: the emphasis on the eschatological deployment of
the power of God. There are intimations of this in the Old Testament (cf
inter alia Is 2,19; 40,10; Ezek 20,33). The experience that many things
take place in this world that God does not will, gives rise to the hope that
God will demonstrate his power in a last great conflict, destroying his
opponents and saving those who belong to him. The righteous, therefore,
wait for God to reveal himself in his power and to establish his dominion
definitely (cf e g the Greek Book of Henoch 1,4).

Together with this demonstration of eschatological power, early
Judaism includes a belief which is not so apparent in the Old Testament but
which is to be found in the Hellenistic Greek World, namely, an essential
belief in the power of demons represented in Judaism by Satan. Grundmann
(1964:295) points out that the eschatological exercise of God's power is
basically an overthrow of demonic powers. Between God and humanity
forces interpose themselves which fight partly against God and partly for
him — the forces of angels and demons. These bear different names, for
example: ἀρχαί, κυριότητες, ἐκλεκτοί, ἐξουσίαι, θρόνοι and also δυνάμεις.

The pseudo-epigraphical writings refer to natural forces personified as
angels (cf En 61,10: powers which are on the dry land and above the water;
cf also En 82,8 and 4 Esdras 6,6). We read in B Pesachim 118a that
Gabriel reigns over fire and Jurqemi over hail. In En 40,9 an angel which
controls all forces is mentioned. These powers and forces are intermediate
beings between God and man which rule over the realm between heaven
and earth. One part of these forces and powers belongs to God and
constitutes his host, compare En 61,1, the Jewish portion of the Parisian
Magical Papyrus (IV, 3050f) and also Corpus Hermeticum I,26. The other
section of these powers belongs to Beliar or Satan, who rules men by means
of them. Human existence is the battlefield between angels and demons,
between God and Satan.

The impact of oriental influences on Judaism is evident. A significant
distinction between Judaism and the Hellenistic development of ideas of the

demonic must, however, not be overlooked: In Hellenism we find the expression of forces present in the world which constitute a great nexus of power, a supreme power of which spirits are emanations. Behind this conception stands a neutral view of God. In Judaism we are dealing with magnitudes which are authorised and created by God. Behind this conception a theistic view is to be found. This distinction also applies to Hellenistic Judaism in which the supremacy of God is safeguarded.

3.3 Power and the essence of God

Despite the presence of angelic and demonic conceptions, the supremacy of God as the Creator and Lord of the world is maintained in Judaism. The essence of God is found in his power. As the name of God retreats into the background in Judaism, being replaced by paraphrases, one of these descriptions is "power" (Grundmann 1964:297). Jesus uses this before the Sanhedrin in Jerusalem[2] (Mt 26,64; Mk 14,62). In the Targums "power" is one of the terms used when God speaks of himself (cf *inter alia* TgO Deut 33,26: "And my power is in the highest heaven"; TgJer 16,19b translates the Hebrew "to thee" by "to hear thy power". This is no hypostatisation of the concept of power, but a paraphrase of the name of God and the divine "I". The fact that the concept of power could be used in this way is evidence of the extent to which the essence of God consists in his power according to the view of Judaism.

3.4 The question of saving power in early Judaism

When one bears Rom 1,16 in mind, it is interesting to note that rabbinical literature related the Torah to the power of Yahweh.[3] עוז and תורה are directly equated on the exegetical basis of Ps 29,11. Strength, power refers

---

[2] Cf also the cry of Jesus on the cross in GPt 19: ἡ δύναμις μου, ἡ δύναμις μου.

[3] Michel (1978:72), however, correctly observes that in the New Testament, "... [d]er Ausgangspunkt der *'Kraft Gottes'* ist nicht, wie man annehmen könnte, der Vergleich mit der Tora des Mose, sondern die Christologie [Röm 1,16 weist auf 1,3 zurück]. Die Kraft der Auferweckung teilt sich durch den Boten dem Evangelium mit".

to the Torah.[4] The Torah is the bond that unites Israel, which maintains it as people of God and brings them the coming salvation.[5]

---

[4] In Mek Ex 15,30.50b we read (in the translation of Grundmann [1932:86]): "Du hast in deiner Stärke geführt, d.i. im Verdienst der Tora, die sie in der Zukunft empfangen werden, und es ist deine Stärke nichts anderes als die Tora, denn es steht geschrieben: Jahwe gibt Stärke seinem Volk." (Cf also Mek Ex 15,2; 18,1; Sif Nm 6,24.)

[5] Cf Mek Ex 15,26.54b: "Und wozu ist eine Belehrung also: 'Ich, Jahwe, bin dein Arzt? ['] Es hat zu Mose der Heilige, gepriesen sei er, gesagt: Sage den Israeliten: Die Worte der Tora, die ich euch gegeben habe, sie sind Heilung für euch, sie sind Leben für euch ... Rabbi Jizchak sagt: ... ich, Jahwe, bin dein Arzt in der kommenden Welt" (quoted from Grundmann 1932:86).

Chapter 4

Philo

Grundmann (1964:297), following Bréhier, points out that what Rabbinic Judaism avoided, namely, making power into an independent hypostasis in consequence of the growing emphasis on the divine transcendence and the consequent shunning of the name of Yahweh, is found in the Hellenistic Judaism of Philo.

Different characteristics of God were bound together by Philo under the concept of δύναμις.[1] Just as the wisdom of God may act as mediating hypostasis between God and world (Wisdom of Solomon 7,25 ff: ἀτμὶς ἐστιν τῆς τοῦ θεοῦ δυνάμεως ... μία δὲ οὖσα πάντα δύναται ...), Philo can say: θεὸς δ᾽ ἡ ἀνωτάτω καὶ μεγίστη δύναμις ὢν οὐδενός ἐστι χρεῖος (VitMos 1,111). Although the powers are separated from God and put under the Logos, he still remains ἡνίοχος τῶν δυνάμεων (Fug 101).

Since according to the Wisdom of Solomon, the wisdom of God embodies δύναμις, Philo's Logos as ἡνίοχος τῶν δυνάμεων is the mediator of God (as ἀνωτάτω καὶ μεγίστη δύναμις). Just as in Plato (Tim 41a/c) the creator of the universe calls on his assistants to create mortal beings μιμούμενοι τὴν ἐμὴν δύναμιν, Philo says: διαλέγεται ... ὁ τῶν ὅλων πατὴρ ταῖς ἑαυτοῦ δυνάμεσι, αἷς τὸ θνητὸν ἡμῶν τῆς ψυχῆς μέρος ἔδωκε διαπλάττειν (Fug 69 [Fascher 1959:433]).

In Rabbinic Judaism God was — even in his perfect transcendence — still a living person. In the Hellenised Judaism of Philo, however, he is pure being in this perfect transcendence (Grundmann 1964:297—8). It was because the Hellenisation of Judaism in Philo had to a large extent Hellenised the concept of God that the power of God could itself become a hypostasis.

---

[1] Cf Fascher 1959:432: "Es ist Philos Verdienst ... die in der Tradition des AT unverbunden nebeneinanderstehenden Eigenschaften Gottes unter dem Begriff der D. [= δύναμις] zusammengefaßt zu haben."

The relationship between God and the powers is defined in such a way that on the one side God in his unity with them is supreme power (the Jewish element in Philo's view of God, cf VitMos 1,111). Yet on the other side the powers are independent of God and God withdraws behind them ... τὸν ἀνωτάτω εἶναι θεόν, ὃς ὑπερκέκυφε τὰς δυνάμεις ἑαυτοῦ καὶ χωρὶς αὐτῶν ὁρώμενος καὶ ἐν αὐταῖς ἐμφαινόμενος (Sacr 60). The powers distinct from God are linked with the *Logos*, the ἡνίοχος τῶν δυνάμεων (Fug 101) which God ἐκπεπλήρωκεν ὅλον δι' ὅλων ἀσωμάτοις δυνάμεσιν (Som I,62). As hypostases of God they belong to the eternal world of God (Grundmann 1964:298).

The δυνάμεις divide into two main powers, the δύναμις ποιητική and the δύναμις βασιλική. With these powers are linked the names of God according to their efficacy. According to the ποιητική, καθ' ἣν ἔθηκε καὶ ἐποίησε καὶ διεκόσμησε τόδε τὸ πᾶν, he is called θεός; according to the βασιλική, ᾗ τῶν γενομένων ἄρχει καὶ σὺν δίκῃ βεβαίως ἐπικρατεῖ, he is called κύριος (VitMos II,99). The power hypostases are, therefore, the power which creates and directs the world. As Philo's view of God receives an ethical trait from the biblical conception of God, so, too, does his view of power (cf Grundmann 1964:298).

It may be affirmed, that the roots of the Philonic view of power lie partly in Judaism (the ethical traits and expositions, the thought of a power which creates and directs the world), and partly in the Hellenistic Greek world (the autonomy of the power of God in relation to the powers as hypostases, the severance of the Old Testament concept of power from history). Philo himself draws attention to the Platonic notion of ideas as one of the sources of his teaching (cf ConfLing 172). Grundmann (1964:299) correctly observes that of itself this is inadequate to explain the central position of the powers in Philo and his system. This central position of power is plain in statements like the following: συνέχεσθαι μὲν τόδε τὸ πᾶν ἀοράτοις δυνάμεσιν, ἃς ἀπὸ γῆς ἐσχάτων ἄχρις οὐρανοῦ περάτων ὁ δημιουργὸς ἀπέτεινε (MigrAbr 181). ... πανταχοῦ δέ, ὅτι τὰς δυνάμεις αὐτου διὰ γῆς καὶ ὕδατος ἀέρος τε καὶ οὐρανοῦ τείνας μέρος οὐδὲν ἔρημον ἀπολέλοιπε τοῦ κόσμου (ConfLing 136). The world is regarded as a great nexus of divine powers which create and sustain its life and being. This teaching is based upon the philosophy of Poseidonius. In Philo's view of power, Hellenistic philosophy unites with the Jewish view of God (Grundmann 1964:299).

Chapter 5

Qumran and the power of God

From the vision of the new birth (Hodajoth III,9 f)[1] it is clear that the renewal of man to a God-pleasing *geber* is regarded as the wonderful act of God, grounded in his power (*g^eburah*: Kosmala 1959:220—39). The concept of the new man, the right man of God, the *geber*, had already been fully developed amongst the Essenes and had its roots in the poetic books of the Old Testament. The renewal of man is only a part of the renewing events of the end times, as all beings will be renewed (Hodajoth XI,13 f). This act of renewal is already happening, as the end time has already begun. The author of the Hodajoth has experienced renewal as the work of God in his own person. The fact of the new birth he has described in his vision (Hodajoth III,6—12). Again and again he confesses that God in his mercy and through his power has effected this decisive event.[2]

The power of God is, indeed, an important theme in the Psalms. He does justice to the individual through his power (cf Ps 54), he rules over the people in his power (cf Ps 66,7). He who trusts in God (Ps 71,1), knows that God will save him, the Psalmist confesses that God's saving acts will always be upon his lips (Ps 71,15) and he prays that God will not forsake him while he extols his mighty arm to future generations. Towards the end

---

[1] Cf also IV,30—33 (translated by Kosmala [1959:221]): "Denn nicht dem (schwachen), Menschen ist Gerechtigkeit eigen, nicht dem Menschenkind die Vollendung des Weges — dem höchsten Gott (allein) gehören alle Werke der Gerechtigkeit. Und was den Weg des Menschen betrifft, so kann er nur durch den Geist festgerichtet werden, welchen Gott für ihn geschaffen hat, um den Menschenkindern den Weg vollkommen zu machen, damit sie erkennen alle seine Taten durch die Stärke seiner Kraft (*b^ekoah g^eburato*) und die Größe seines Erbarmes über alle Kinder seines Wohlgefallens."

[2] "Du hast ein Wunder mit Staub vollbracht und am Lehmgebilde hast du deine Kraft erwiesen *[higbarta]* ... und mich in deinen Wunderwerken belehrt. ... darum will ich singen über deine Gnaden- und Krafterweisungen *[g^eburot]* ..." (Hodajoth XI,3 ff; translated by Kosmala [1959:220]).

of the book of Job the power of God and its unfolding in his works becomes an important theme. He is not only the source of all physical strength (cf Job 39,19), but with him alone is true wisdom and strength, counsel and understanding (Job 12,13 — Kosmala 1959:222).

The piousness of the Psalms and the book of Job profoundly influenced the Essene thought which developed it further. Something new emerges here amongst the Essenes: Man's knowledge of God and his profound secrets are made possible by the power of God (Kosmala 1959:222). Already Daniel confesses in his prayer (2,20—23) that wisdom and might belong to God, that he reveals deep mysteries; he knows what is in the darkness and the light dwells with him. Daniel thanks and praises him because he has given him wisdom and might (*g^eburah*) and has made known to him the revelation he has prayed for. The wisdom with which the Essenes faithfully know God's works, is the "... mighty wisdom which trusts in all the deeds of God" (1 QS 4,3 — Vermes 1975:76; Kosmala 1959:222). "... His might is the support of my right hand", are the words which open the Book of Discipline (1 QS 11,5 [Vermes 1975:72; Kosmala 1959:222]). The new man *(geber)* is the effect of the power *(g^eburah)* of God, and by the power of God (Hodajoth IX,25—27), he lives his life in the knowledge of God and in the dedication towards God. Already in the Hodajoth (IV,31 f) the Spirit and power of God coordinate and are in fact identical.

With reference to 2 Cor 12,9 and 10, Kosmala (1959:223) is of the opinion that this Pauline passage is completely in agreement with Essene thought. The question arises, however, whether Kosmala sufficiently takes into account the specific emphasis in 2 Cor 12,9. Braun (1966a:199) correctly observed that it is to be questioned whether Qumran — as Paul in 2 Cor 12,10 — would find power dialectic *in* weakness. Kosmala (1959:224) however maintains:

"In den vorangehenden Abschnitten haben wir gesehen, daß die christliche Lehre vom neuen Menschen durch die Kraft Gottes im Grunde essenisch ist, *wenn man von der Verkündigung des Messias Jesus absieht*, die jedoch keine wesentliche Züge der alten Lehre abgewandelt hat" (emphasis: PJG).

Contradictory to Kosmala, we must, however, emphasise that the starting point for the understanding of the Pauline concept of power (δύναμις) is to be found in the "message of the cross" (1 Cor 1,18; cf also 1,24) and in the power of the resurrection (cf 6,14; 15,43). For the correct understanding of the power of God in Pauline theology it is, therefore, *impossible* "... von der Verkündigung des Messias Jesus abzusehen".

Chapter 6

Concluding remarks

Against which lexico-historical background must the Pauline use of δύναμις be seen? Albrecht Dieterich ([1923] 1966:46) is of the opinion that the concept of power in a passage such as Rom 1,16 is used in the same way as in the Mithras Luturgy: δύναμις means the dedication which mediates strength for the heavenly journey, for the vision of God and for deification (cf Grundmann 1964:309).[1]

In addition to his reference to the Mithras Liturgy, Johannes Weiß ([1910] 1970:26) refers to the astrologist, Vettius Valens:

> "Der Astrologe Vettius Valens braucht δύναμις = ἀγωγή ... Wie also Röm 1₁₆ δύναμις εἰς σωτηρίαν eine kraftvolle, erfolgreiche 'Anweisung z. Heil' bedeutet, so wäre hier das Kreuz Christi geradezu als ein gewaltiges, erprobtes Mittel gedacht, das Gott den σωζόμενοι verliehen, um sie aus der Macht der Dämonen zu befreien."

Richard Reitzenstein (*Die hellenistischen Mysterienreligionen*, 214, quoted by Schmitz [1927:156—7]) comments on ἐν ἀποδείξει πνεύματος καὶ δυνάμεως (1 Cor 2,4) by referring to ἐνδυνάμωσόν in Corpus Hermeticum I,32 and affirms that "... diese Mitteilung einer δύναμις an den Prediger schon im hellenistischen Glauben notwendiges Erfordernis ist".

---

[1] Dieterich ([1923] 1966:46—7 note 1) affirms: "Wie das Wort [δύναμις] bei den griechischen Ärzten längst die Heilkraft der Arzneien and dann die Arzneien selbst bezeichnet, so später alle 'Heilkraft' der Zaubersprüche und Zauberaktionen, der Gebete und der religiösen Rituale und dann alle diese Dinge selbst ... Es ist häufig ... fast so viel als 'Weihe', etwas dasselbe, was wir mit 'Sakrament' ausdrücken."

In his book, "Vom göttlichen Fluidum nach ägyptischer Anschauung", Pressigke also argues for a Hellenistic background of "power" in early Christendom.[2] In his succeeding publication, "Die Gotteskraft der frühchristlichen Zeit", Preisigke (1922:1) emphasises that the main source for the early Christian concept of the power of God is to be found in Egypt — this is, however, not the only source.[3]

Schmitz (1927:157) also points to the importance of taking into account the appropriate history of religions background. In this connection he (1927:157—8) distinguishes two lines of thought, into which the New Testament δύναμις sayings may be fitted: on the one hand the prophetic history of salvation line of the Old Testament, as it is also effective in Early Judaism; on the other hand the magic mystical line of the world of Hellenistic piousness, which also reached across into Diaspora Judaism.

According to Schmitz (1927:163.165) the religio-historical peculiarity of the Pauline δύναμις sayings is to be found in their salvation historical and pneumatic character. It is therefore the prophetic salvation historical line of the Old Testament and early Judaistic concept of power which Paul develops (1927:166).[4]

On the other hand, Windisch (1934:191 ff) is of the opinion that Jesus and Paul, because of their δυνάμεις, are to be reckoned religio-historically

---

[2] "Die Vorstellung von der strömenden Gotteskraft, die vom Urgotte als dem Urquell aller Dinge stammt und in die Leiber aller Götter und Menschen weitergegeben wird ... diese uralte Vorstellung hatte sich ... so tief in die breiten Massen des Volkes hineingesenkt, daß sie in der Frühzeit des Christentums überall durch die dünne christliche Oberschicht hindurchbricht" (Preisigke 1920:57).

[3] "Erneut muß ich hierbei vorweg betonen, daß in Ägypten keinesfalls der alleinige Urquell für die frühchristliche Anschauung [der Gotteskraft] zu suchen ist, wohl aber der Hauptquell."

[4] Schmitz (1927:166—7) elaborates on his point of view by pointing out that "... das *Gleichgewichts*verhältnis zwischen der Gegenständlichkeit des Heilsgeschehens und seiner eben dadurch konstituierten Nichtgegenständlichkeit [ ] beim alttestamentlichen Kraftbegriff noch nicht zu voller Erfüllung gelangt [ist], während es im paulinischen Kraftbegriff seine pneumatische Erfüllung gefunden hat. Dieser Sachverhalt äußert sich darin, daß die *paradoxe Spannung*, die den Kraftbegriff des Apostels durchdringt, in den alttestamentlichen Kraftaussagen sich erst anbahnt. Diese paradoxe Spannung ist neben der Nichtgegenständlichkeit und der heilsgeschichtlichen Bestimmtheit ein drittes Kennzeichen seiner religionsgeschichtlichen Eigenart, durch das sich diese in ihrem *Erfüllungs*charakter erst voll abhebt von aller Religionsgeschichte, auch der Religionsgeschichte Israels".

Fascher (1959:438—9) also observes that in the New Testament δύναμις keeps its Old Testament character, which is simultaneously both historic and eschatologic, now only concentrated on the work of Jesus of Nazareth.

as θεῖοι ἄνθρωποι.[5] Against this view of Windisch, Fascher (1959:439) however remarks that the eschatological orientation of the δύναμις concept by Jesus and Paul distinguishes them from this category.

From the preceding discussion it is evident that in the research on δύναμις, the history of religions background has been dealt with fairly extensively. One of the greatest shortcomings of these studies is the neglect of the realisation that the lexical unit δύναμις occurs for a whole range of meanings (cf introductory discussion to this study). δύναμις with the meaning "power", therefore does not necessarily have the same religio-historical background as δύναμις with the meaning "mighty deed, miracle" (often used in the plural: δυνάμεις).[6]

In Paul's use of δύναμις the Hellenistic influence can be observed in a passage such as Rom 1,20, which is only to be understood against the background of a Hellenistically influenced Jewish apocalyptic tradition (cf chapter 18). This, however, does not mean that Paul is necessarily dependent on a Greek concept of God. The motif of creation actually points to an Old Testament-Jewish background to his preaching (cf Kertelge 1983:39).

As asserted by Schmitz (1927) and Fascher (1959), referred to in the preceding discussion (cf also Prümm 1961b:646—7; Combrink 1969:45), the lexico-historical background of Paul's use of δύναμις is to be found mainly in the Old Testament.

---

[5] On the issue of the Θεῖος ἀνήρ, cf Klauck 1995:145—6.

[6] The question arises whether Paul has not been strongly influenced by Hellenism, especially in his thaumatology. Does one find here the Christian variation of the θεῖος ἀνήρ notion? The attention may especially be drawn to Rom 15,19 and 2 Cor 12,12.

In these passages one finds a fixed concept ("einen festen Begriff"). In his article, "Zeichen und Wunder. Die prophetische Legitimation und ihre Geschichte", Stolz (1972:125—44) investigates the meaning and function of σημεῖα καὶ τέρατα in the Old Testament. He concludes that this fixed concept points to "... die unmittelbare Erfahrung göttlicher Gegenwart". According to Stolz, during their divine services the Pauline congregations experienced the immediate power of the Exalted through the activities of the Holy Spirit. These manifestations as guarantee ("Verbürgung") of the Lordship of Christ could be described as "signs and wonders".

In Paul it appears as if two lines of thought converge: 1) δυνάμεις as prophetic authorization, and 2) the miraculous Hellenistic powers. Paul must have known the Hellenistic use and took a critical look at it from the viewpoint of the "message of the cross". From this perspective everything is seen in relative terms. For Paul the δυνάμεις are not the main issue.

It is now appropriate to proceed with the exegetical section in which the lexico-historical background of δύναμις will also be touched upon in the discussion of Paul's use of δύναμις in specific pericopes.

Section B:

An Exegetical Investigation
of the Concept of God's Power in Paul's Letters

Chapter 7

1 Corinthians 1,18.24; 2,4.5

7.1 Location within the macrocontext of 1 Corinthians

1 Cor can be divided into the following sections:

1,1—3	Letter-opening: senders, recipients, salutation
1,4—9	Thanksgiving
1,10—6,20	IN RESPONSE TO REPORTS
1,10—4,21	A church divided — internally and against Paul
5,1—6,20	Immorality and litigation: text cases of the crisis of authority and gospel[1]
7,1—16,12	IN RESPONSE TO THE CORINTHIAN LETTER
7,1—40	Marriage and related matters
8,1—11,1	Food sacrificed to idols
11,2—14,40	Problems related to public worship and the gifts of grace
11,2—16	Women and men in worship
11,17—34	Abuse of the Lord's supper
12,1—14,40	Spiritual gifts and spiritual people
15	The resurrection as the foundation of faith and of the Christian hope

---

[1] According to Fee (1987,21). Cf Barrett (1968:28): 1 Cor 1,10—6,20: "News from Corinth" (a) "Wisdom and Division at Corinth i.10—iv.21".

However, Bruce (1971), Conzelmann (1981), Fascher (1980), Klauck (1984) Lang (1986) and Wolff (1996) regard 1,10—4,21 as the first main section of this letter (cf also Schrage 1991:90), headlined by Bruce (1971:25): "Paul deals with the report received from Chloe's people", while Conzelmann *et al* summarise this section as dealing with the divisions in Corinth. (For an illuminating discussion of the relationship between wisdom and divisions in Corinth [1 Cor 1—4], see Polhill [1983:325—37].)

As 1 Cor 5:1—6,20 also conveys Paul's response to reports he has received, it seems better to regard 1,10—6,20 as the first main section.

16,1—12   About the collection

16,13—24   CONCLUDING MATTERS
16,13—18   Concluding exhortations
16,19—24   Closing: greetings, the holy kiss, valediction
             (Lategan 1985:74; Fee 1987:21—3).

1 Corinthians 1,10—4,21 may further be divided in the following way:

1,10—17   Admonition to unanimity
1,18—2,5   The message about the crucified Christ is the power and
             wisdom of God, but foolishness and weakness to the world.
             This is illustrated by the nature of the congregation in
             Corinth, as well as by Paul's ministry.
2,6—16   The gospel as God's secret wisdom
3,1—17   Divisions in the church and the correction of a false view
             of church and ministry
3,18—23   In criticism of false wisdom and self-glorification
4,1—21   Paul and the Corinthian church
             (cf Wolff 1996:VIII; Fee 1987:21—3; Lang 1986; Lategan
             1985:73—4; Klauck 1984:13—4)

The issue of the demarcation of this pericope is touched upon in 7.2.1.

7.2 Discourse analysis: 1 Corinthians 1,18—2,5

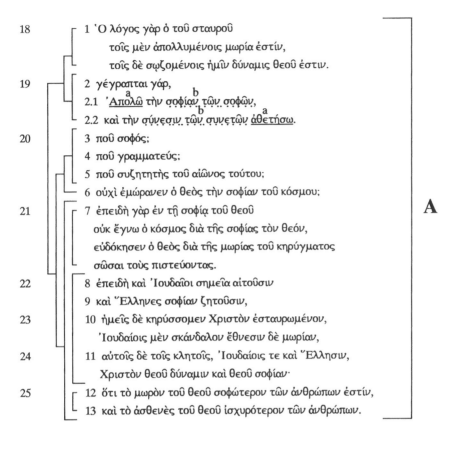

18   1 Ὁ λόγος γὰρ ὁ τοῦ σταυροῦ
        τοῖς μὲν ἀπολλυμένοις μωρία ἐστίν,
        τοῖς δὲ σῳζομένοις ἡμῖν δύναμις θεοῦ ἐστιν.

19   2 γέγραπται γάρ,
     2.1 Ἀπολῶ τὴν σοφίαν τῶν σοφῶν,
     2.2 καὶ τὴν σύνεσιν τῶν συνετῶν ἀθετήσω.

20   3 ποῦ σοφός;
     4 ποῦ γραμματεύς;
     5 ποῦ συζητητὴς τοῦ αἰῶνος τούτου;
     6 οὐχὶ ἐμώρανεν ὁ θεὸς τὴν σοφίαν τοῦ κόσμου;

21   7 ἐπειδὴ γὰρ ἐν τῇ σοφίᾳ τοῦ θεοῦ   A
        οὐκ ἔγνω ὁ κόσμος διὰ τῆς σοφίας τὸν θεόν,
        εὐδόκησεν ὁ θεὸς διὰ τῆς μωρίας τοῦ κηρύγματος
        σῶσαι τοὺς πιστεύοντας.

22   8 ἐπειδὴ καὶ Ἰουδαῖοι σημεῖα αἰτοῦσιν
     9 καὶ Ἕλληνες σοφίαν ζητοῦσιν,

23   10 ἡμεῖς δὲ κηρύσσομεν Χριστὸν ἐσταυρωμένον,
        Ἰουδαίοις μὲν σκάνδαλον ἔθνεσιν δὲ μωρίαν,

24   11 αὐτοῖς δὲ τοῖς κλητοῖς, Ἰουδαίοις τε καὶ Ἕλλησιν,
        Χριστὸν θεοῦ δύναμιν καὶ θεοῦ σοφίαν·

25   12 ὅτι τὸ μωρὸν τοῦ θεοῦ σοφώτερον τῶν ἀνθρώπων ἐστίν,
     13 καὶ τὸ ἀσθενὲς τοῦ θεοῦ ἰσχυρότερον τῶν ἀνθρώπων.

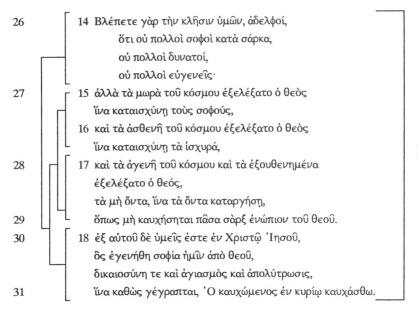

26   14 Βλέπετε γὰρ τὴν κλῆσιν ὑμῶν, ἀδελφοί,
          ὅτι οὐ πολλοὶ σοφοὶ κατὰ σάρκα,
          οὐ πολλοὶ δυνατοί,
          οὐ πολλοὶ εὐγενεῖς·

27   15 ἀλλὰ τὰ μωρὰ τοῦ κόσμου ἐξελέξατο ὁ θεὸς
          ἵνα καταισχύνῃ τοὺς σοφούς,
        16 καὶ τὰ ἀσθενῆ τοῦ κόσμου ἐξελέξατο ὁ θεὸς
          ἵνα καταισχύνῃ τὰ ἰσχυρά,

28   17 καὶ τὰ ἀγενῆ τοῦ κόσμου καὶ τὰ ἐξουθενημένα   **B**
          ἐξελέξατο ὁ θεός,
          τὰ μὴ ὄντα, ἵνα τὰ ὄντα καταργήσῃ,

29   ὅπως μὴ καυχήσηται πᾶσα σὰρξ ἐνώπιον τοῦ θεοῦ.

30   18 ἐξ αὐτοῦ δὲ ὑμεῖς ἐστε ἐν Χριστῷ Ἰησοῦ,
          ὃς ἐγενήθη σοφία ἡμῖν ἀπὸ θεοῦ,
          δικαιοσύνη τε καὶ ἁγιασμὸς καὶ ἀπολύτρωσις,

31   ἵνα καθὼς γέγραπται, Ὁ καυχώμενος ἐν κυρίῳ καυχάσθω.

Chapter 2

1   19 Κἀγὼ ἐλθὼν πρὸς ὑμᾶς, ἀδελφοί,
          ἦλθον οὐ καθ' ὑπεροχὴν λόγου ἢ σοφίας
          καταγγέλλων ὑμῖν τὸ μυστήριον τοῦ θεοῦ.

2   20 οὐ γὰρ ἔκρινά τι εἰδέναι ἐν ὑμῖν
          εἰ μὴ Ἰησοῦν Χριστὸν καὶ τοῦτον ἐσταυρωμένον.   **C**

3   21 κἀγὼ ἐν ἀσθενείᾳ καὶ ἐν φόβῳ
          καὶ ἐν τρόμῳ πολλῷ ἐγενόμην πρὸς ὑμᾶς,

4   22 καὶ ὁ λόγος μου καὶ τὸ κήρυγμά μου οὐκ ἐν πειθοῖ σοφίας
          ἀλλ' ἐν ἀποδείξει πνεύματος καὶ δυνάμεως,

5   ἵνα ἡ πίστις ὑμῶν μὴ ᾖ ἐν σοφίᾳ ἀνθρώπων ἀλλ' ἐν δυνάμει θεοῦ.

Headings of the pericope and sub-pericopes

Pericope heading:

The message about the crucified Christ is the power and wisdom of God, but foolishness and weakness to the world. This is illustrated by the (nature of the) congregation in Corinth as well as by Paul's ministry.

Sub-pericope A:

The message about the cross, the crucified Christ is the power and wisdom of God, but foolishness and weakness to the world.

Sub-pericope B:

You, brothers, are proof of the fact that God has chosen what is foolish and weak in the opinion of the world to shame the wise and the strong. Christ Jesus has become for us the wisdom of God. Boasting is, therefore, excluded.

Sub-pericope C:

My message concerned only the crucified Jesus Christ and was given not with wise words but despite my own weakness with a demonstration of the Spirit's power.

7.2.1 A few notes on the structure of this pericope with special reference to actants and structural markers

The present pericope is introduced by the thesis-like statement of 1 Cor 1,18 (cf 7.4.2.1). In 1 Cor 2,6 a new pericope is introduced by the phrase σοφίαν δὲ λαλοῦμεν ... . The internal cohesion within this pericope is illustrated by the structural markers and actants occurring throughout this pericope (cf the discourse analysis [7.2] as well as the following discussion).

7.2.1.1 Structural markers (and actants) occurring throughout this pericope

δύναμις

1,18	δύναμις
1,24	δύναμιν

2,4   δυνάμεως
2,5   ἐν δυνάμει

θεός
1,18   θεοῦ
1,21   θεοῦ ... θεόν, θεός
1,24   θεοῦ ... θεοῦ
1,25   θεοῦ, θεοῦ
1,27   θεός, θεός
1,28   θεός
1,29   θεοῦ
1,30   (αὐτοῦ), θεοῦ
2,1   θεοῦ
2,5   θεοῦ

Jesus Christ
1,23   Χριστόν
1,24   Χριστόν
1,30   ἐν Χριστῷ Ἰησοῦ, (ὅς)
1,31   (κυρίῳ)
2,2   Ἰησοῦν Χριστόν, (τοῦτον)

Cross/crucified
1,18   τοῦ σταυροῦ
1,23   ἐσταυρωμένον
2,2   ἐσταυρωμένον

Word/preaching/message
1,18   λόγος
1,21   κηρύγματος
1,23   κηρύσσομεν
2,1   καταγγέλλων
2,4   λόγος ... κήρυγμά

Wisdom/wise — foolishness
1,18   μωρία
1,19   σοφίαν ... σοφῶν; σύνεσιν ... συνετῶν

1,20	σοφός, (γραμματεύς), (συζητητής), ἐμώρανεν ... σοφίαν
1,21	ἐν τῇ σοφίᾳ, σοφίας, μωρίας
1,23	μωρίαν (σκάνδαλον is here used almost synonymously)
1,24	σοφίαν
1,25	μωρὸν ... σοφώτερον

1,26	σοφοί (δυνατοί and εὐγενεῖς are semantically closely related to σοφοί in this verse)
1,27	μωρὰ ... σοφούς
1,30	σοφία
2,1	σοφίας
2,4	σοφίας
2,5	σοφίᾳ

Structural markers referring to weakness

1,25	ἀσθενές
1,27	ἀσθενῆ
2,3	ἀσθενείᾳ

(Cf also the relevant structural markers marked in the discourse analysis.)

World/man/this age

1,20	αἰῶνος τούτου ... κόσμου
1,21	κόσμος
2,25	ἀνθρώπων, ἀνθρώπων
1,27	κόσμου, κόσμου, κόσμου
2,5	ἀνθρώπων

Faith/believes

1,21	πιστεύοντας
2,5	πίστις

7.2.1.2 Structural markers/actants occurring only in specific parts of this pericope

Jews/Gentiles

1,22	Ἰουδαῖοι ... Ἕλληνες
1,23	Ἰουδαίοις ... ἔθνεσιν
1,24	Ἰουδαίοις ... Ἕλλησιν

καυχᾶσθαι
1,29   καυχήσηται
1,31   καυχώμενος ... καυχάσθω

Expressions referring to Paul's coming to the Corinthians
2,1   ἐλθὼν πρὸς ὑμᾶς
2,3   ἐγενόμην πρὸς ὑμᾶς
Note also   κλητοῖς (1,24)
            κλῆσιν (1,26)

7.2.1.3 Division into sub-pericopes

1 Cor 1,18—2,5 may be divided into three sub-pericopes.

A   1 Cor 1,18—25, dealing with the crucified Christ as the power (and wisdom) of God in the context of the conflict between Godly and worldly foolishness and wisdom, weakness and power.

B   In 1 Cor 1,26—31 the second person plural is introduced. "Boasting" (cf καυχήσηται — v 29; καυχάσθω — v 31) is the new theme that is introduced here.

C   In 1 Cor 2,1—5 Paul's coming to the Corinthians (cf ἐλθὼν πρὸς ὑμᾶς — 2,1; ἐγενόμην πρὸς ὑμᾶς — 2,3) as well as his preaching ministry (cf λόγου, καταγγέλλων — 2,1; ὁ λόγος μου, τὸ κήρυγμά μου, λόγοις — 2,4) is mentioned for the first time.

7.3 Textual criticism

1 Cor 1,24: The reading of papyrus 46, also supported by Clement of Alexandria, in which the nominative forms instead of the accusatives Χριστὸν ... δύναμιν ... σοφίαν appear, can not be accepted due to the very slender manuscript evidence.

1 Cor 2,4: In this verse the exegete encounters a very difficult text-critical problem. Metzger (1994:481) points out that of the eleven different variant readings in this passage, those which read ἀνθρωπίνης before or after σοφίας (the second corrector of codex Sinaiticus, codex Alexandrinus, codex Ephraemi, codex P, codex Ψ, as well as the minuscule manuscripts 81, 614, 1962, 2495, the Byzantine manuscript ...) are obviously secondary. If the word were original, there is no good reason why it would have been deleted. It has the appearance of an explanatory gloss inserted by copyists in order to identify more exactly the nuance attaching to σοφίας.

The text printed in the twenty-seventh edition of Nestle-Aland reflects the text of the original scribe of codex Sinaiticus (despite certain negligible variations), codex Vaticanus, codex Claromontanus, the minuscule manuscripts 33, 1175, 1506, 1739, 1881 and a few others, the "Stuttgart Vulgate" as well as the Syriac Peshitta (although exhibiting certain negligible variations). The difficulty with this reading (cf Fee 1987:88) is the word πειθοῖς, an adjective found in no other passage in all of Greek literature. Fee (1987:88) agrees with Zuntz that the reading of p⁴⁶ F G, πειθοῖς σοφίας, alone makes sense of how the various corruptions arose. The ς at the end of πειθοῖς is a result of the simple corruption of doubling the initial σ of σοφίας. The λόγοις was then added, also on the analogy of verse 13, to make sense of what had now become an adjective. This position seems acceptable for the following two reasons (cf Fee 1987:88):

— This reading is unquestionably the "lectio difficilior" and more easily explains how the others came about than vice versa. It is very difficult to account for the "omission" of λόγοις on any grounds; and in this case it would need to have happened twice, once in the ancestors of papyrus 46 and codices F and G respectively.
— The complete absence of the word πειθός in the entire Greek tradition is difficult to explain. The regular adjective πιθανός is common. The noun πειθώ, however, is plentiful in this tradition. Given the fact that Paul is here reflecting so much of the language of this tradition, a Pauline creation seems less likely than a scribal corruption. Thus the text would read: καὶ ὁ λόγος μου καὶ τὸ κήρυγμά μου οὐκ ἐν πειθοῖ σοφίας ἀλλ' ἐν ἀποδείξει πνεύματος καὶ δυνάμεως ... .

7.4 An exegetical overview

7.4.1 Introduction

Johann Weiß ([1910] 1970:24) has already pointed to the close connection between this pericope (1 Cor 1,18—2,5) and 1 Cor 1,17. Verse 18 serves as foundation for both Paul's standpoint in verse 17 and for this pericope as a whole.[2] In 1 Corinthians 1,18—25; 1,26—31 and 2,1—5 Paul supplies the reason for his unwillingness to proclaim the gospel ἐν σοφίᾳ λόγου (v 17) [cf Rolf Baumann (1968:80)]. Against this "proclamation in wisdom", so highly regarded by the Corinthians, Paul sets the very centre of the gospel: "... the word of the cross".[3] A christology of the cross has predominance over a christology constructed under the sign of σοφία.[4] The apostle Paul carefully delineates the differences between God's wisdom and the wisdom of the world. The wisdom of the world will not find God because God's power has been manifested in a most unlikely way — a way sure to cause sneers and humiliation in every age — Christ nailed to the cross (Marshall-Green 1988:683).

The theme discussed in this pericope is very closely related to the strife between the different groups in Corinth — the exponents of these groups practise worldly wisdom and deny the wisdom of God, revealed in the cross of Christ. Paul exposes the search for wisdom as the most profound ground for the division in the Corinthian church (Lang 1986:27).

In his letter to the Romans, Paul formulates the centre of his theology in the concept of justification by faith. In 1 Corinthians the concept of the "theology of the cross" prevails.[5]

The theocentricity of Paul's theology is clearly emphasised in this pericope. God has taken the initiative to reconcile the world with himself (2 Cor 5,19). This message, which Paul expresses in Romans and Galatians in the language of his doctrine of justification, is expressed within the Corinthian context in the language of the theology of the cross (Lang 1986:28).

---

[2] Cf Weiß (1910) 1970:24: "Denn V.17 (Entleerung des Kreuzes Christi) wird im Grunde genommen erst in 2₅ wirklich erläutert, wozu alles Vorhergehende nur als Vorbereitung dient."

[3] Eichholz (1985:57) remarks: "Spricht Paulus in 1,18 vom 'Wort vom Kreuz', so meint er das Evangelium in einer bestimmten *Zuspitzung* oder auch in einer für ihn charakteristischen *Abbreviatur*."

[4] Stuhlmacher (1976:511) correctly remarks: "Bei der Verkündigung des Kreuzes geht es um das ganze der paulinischen Theologie, und zwar in gesetzes- und weisheitskritischer Zuspitzung."

[5] The relation between Paul's theology of the cross in 1 Cor and his message of justification (developed in Rom and Gl) is discussed in chapter 23.2.1.

The pericope 1 Cor 1,18—2,5 is of crucial importance within the Corpus Paulinum.[6] A very important relationship exists between 1 Cor 1,18 and Rom 1,16—17, as well as between 1 Cor 1,21 and Rom 1,18—2,29. The rejection of wisdom as an instrument of salvation parallels the rejection of the law and justification through works of the law as instruments of salvation in Rom 1,16—3,31.

The polemical tendency in this pericope arises from the fact that Paul not only proclaims the word of the cross as an instrument of salvation, but links the cross with an extended rejection of earthly wisdom as a way of obtaining salvation.[7] Salvation by a cross is illogical by all standards of human reason and thus becomes God's final "no" to all human attempts at self-salvation (Polhill 1983:329). Apart from the polemical tendencies, the fundamental character of this pericope must also be recognised. Paul's discussion takes place within a broad horizon: It is the wisdom *of the world* that he denounces; He views himself in opposition to humankind in its totality, Jews and Gentiles alike. In 1 Cor 1,18—25 no personal address of the Corinthians can be found (cf Wilckens 1959:221).

Cross and resurrection belong together in the theology of Paul, yet in the context of this pericope Paul focuses on the cross. The issue at stake between Paul and the Corinthians was the question concerning the way in which the resurrected Lord is present in the congregation: either only as glorified conquerer or as the exalted who is at the same time the crucified.[8]

This pericope (especially 1 Cor 1,18—25) is carefully structured. Explicit and implicit counter sentences relating to the notions of wisdom and folly occur throughout this text. Chiastic constructions, parallelisms

---

[6] Cf Baumann (1968:81): "Auch formal ist V.18—25 ein Text, in dem uns 'wichtigste Sätze und Entscheidungen paulinischer Theologie in äußerster Gedrängtheit' begegnen."

[7] Peterson (1951:98—9) comments on the antithesis in 1 Cor 1,18—31: "... die in diesen in sich geschlossenen Ausführungen vorgenommene Gegenüberstellung der christlichen Weisheit gegenüber einer andern Weisheit scheint mir stilistisch im Rahmen jüdischer Tradition formuliert worden zu sein. Vor allem sind die Übereinstimmungen mit der Homilie auf die Weisheit in Baruch: 3,9—4,4 sehr beachtenswert, nur dass für den Juden das Gesetz die Weisheit ist, die aller irdischen Weisheit entgegengestellt wird, während für Paulus an die Stelle des Gesetzes Christus getreten ist, sonst aber erstrecken sich die Übereinstimmungen bis in die Einzelheiten der Formulierungen hinein".

[8] Cf Lang (1986:28): "... es geht um die Frage, ob das Kreuz nur ein Durchgangsstadium zur Herrlichkeit bildet oder ob es eine grundlegende und bleibende Bedeutung für den Christusglauben besitzt".

and rhetorical questions contribute to the rhetorical effect of this passage (Klauck 1984:24).

7.4.2 Sub-pericope A (1 Cor 1,18—25)

7.4.2.1 1 Corinthians 1,18—19

Paul starts his discussion by stating his fundamental thesis concerning the confrontation of man by the gospel. The word of the cross (the message about the crucified Jesus Christ) can be seen in its opposite effect: To "... those who are perishing", it is foolishness, but to those who "... are being saved" (i e to the believers) it is the power of God (Lang 1986:28). The soteriological scope of Paul's argument is clear. It is as if Paul asks in this passage: "What is the saving δύναμις, the word of the cross or the sophia?" (cf Baumann 1968:82). As counter-expression for μωρία, Paul does not write the expected σοφία. Schmithals explains this by affirming that this statement by Paul is to be understood as a shift of the Corinthian sophia question to a soteriological level.[9] Paul's statement makes it clear that the gospel is not only a theoretical doctrine, but the effective power of God unto salvation for all who believe (Rom 1,16).[10]

1 Cor 1,18 has a clear "thesis-character" (cf Wilckens 1959:6). The profound meaning of this thesis is discussed in 1,19—25 within the context of Jews and Gentiles. This thesis is further explained in the following two passages: with reference to the way and structure of God's "election" in the grounding of the congregation (1,26—31) and with reference to the way and structure of the apostle's proclamation through which the congregation was constituted (2,1—5).

Johannes Weiß ([1910] 1970:25) speaks of a "powerful antithetical parallelismus membrorum" in verse 18. The fact that the second part of this "parallelismus membrorum" is qualified by θεοῦ, that μωρία and δύναμις θεοῦ function on two totally different levels and that Paul through ἡμῖν draws the Corinthians from the beginning into the group of "... those who

---

[9] "Paulus zeigt auf, daß nicht die in Korinth so hoch geschätzte 'Weisheitsrede', sondern das Wort vom Kreuz Gotteskraft zur Rettung ist" (referred to by Baumann 1968:86).

[10] Cf Lang 1986:29. Schrage (1991:173—4) emphasises that the power of the message of the cross is not an aesthetic, moral or psychological power — it is the power *of* God (δύναμις Θεοῦ).

are being saved" (Baumann 1968:83), indicate that Paul's thesis emphasises this second part of the parallelism. The *eschatological judgement of God* becomes evident in people's reaction to the word of the cross. The participles ἀπολλυμένοις and σῳζομένοις point to this eschatological interpretation.[11] This passage emphasises the present decision between salvation and doom in the light of the word of the cross.[12]

In verse 19 Paul bases his view that God rejected the wisdom of the world as way of salvation on a quotation from Is 29,14 (LXX). He applies what had been said of the wise men of Israel, to the wise men of the world (Lang 1986:29).

7.4.2.2 1 Corinthians 1,20—25

By further alluding to words of the prophet Isaiah (19,12; 33,18), Paul shows that in Scripture God has already predicted the rejection of the wise. The three rhetorical questions (ποῦ ...) assume a negative answer.[13] The notions "wise man", "scholar" and "philosopher" serve as reference to both Jewish and Greek teachers of wisdom. Neither the Jewish scholars of Scripture, nor the Greek philosophers acknowledged the divine plan of salvation. With reference to Is 44,25, Paul argues that through Christ God has turned the wisdom of the world ("this world" 1 Cor 2,6; 3,19) into

---

[11] Cf Baumann (1968:84):"'Ἀπολλυσθαι bezeichnet im Gegensatz zu σῷζεσθαι und zur ζωὴ αἰώνιος besonders bei Paulus und Johannes 'ein definitives Scheitern', 'das ewige Versinken im Hades'. In ähnlicher Weise sind bei Paulus σῷζω und σωτηρία 'offenbar bewußt auf das Verhältnis des Menschen zu Gott beschränkt' und meinen 'das zukünftige Endheil'."

[12] Müller (1966:247—8) formulates: "In der Predigt vom Kreuze trifft das menschlich-*gegenwärtige* auf das göttlich-eschatologische Urteil. Dem λόγος τοῦ σταυροῦ eignet *eschatologisch-kritische Mächtigkeit*."

[13] Conzelmann (1981:61) mentions that through the length of the third rhetorical question "entsteht eine Steigerung in der dreifachen Anaphora".

foolishness. With the concepts of "wisdom" and "foolishness" colon 6 causes a dialectical tension to arise (Klauck 1984:24).[14]

In verse 21 Paul explains why God has chosen such a paradoxical way for the salvation of man. It seems as if the best possible interpretation of this passage is against the background of the parallel passage in Rom 1,18—23.[15] Paul avails himself in Rom 1 and 1 Cor 1 of thoughts and ideas from the Jewish-Hellenistic tradition of wisdom in which wisdom is regarded as God's helper in creation and the world is regarded as the creation of wisdom of God (cf Wisdom of Solomon 9,9) (Lang 1986:29—30).[16]

The new initiative God has taken is contrary to the expectations of Jews and Gentiles.[17] The Greeks' search for wisdom may refer to the philosophical quest for truth as well as the reaching out to religious knowledge in mystery-faith and Gnosis.

Whether ἡμεῖς (v 23) refers to Paul and the other early Christian preachers (Klauck 1984:25) or to the church as the new community of those called as saints (1,2) (Lang 1986:30) or to the σῳζόμενοι in verse 18 (Conzelmann 1981:67) is not of crucial importance to the meaning of this

---

[14] An interesting glimpse of the *history of effect* ("Wirkungsgeschichte") of this passage is found in the way in which Justin Martyr contrasts the *power of God* with *human wisdom*. In his first apology Justin refutes the accusation brought against Christians that they are atheists (chapters 1—29). In chapters 30—60 proof from the Old Testament is used to show that Jesus is really the Son of God and not a magician (cf Skarsaune 1988:473). It is within this context that Justin stresses the contrast between human wisdom and the power of God.

In I Apol 14,5 Justin affirms that "… brief and concise utterances fell from him, *for he was no sophist, but his word was the power of God*" (translation: Roberts and Donaldson MDCCCLXVII:18 — οὐ γὰρ σοφιστὴς ὑπῆρχεν, ἀλλὰ δύναμις θεοῦ ὁ λόγος αὐτοῦ ἦν [Greek text: Blunt 1911:22]).

I Apol 60,11: "… so that you may understand that these things are *not the effect of human wisdom*, but are *uttered by the power of God* [ὡς συνεῖναι οὐ σοφίᾳ ἀνθρωπείᾳ ταῦτα γεγονέναι, ἀλλὰ δυνάμει θεοῦ λέγεσθαι]".

[15] Cf *inter alia*: Conzelmann (1981:64—5); Klauck (1984:24), referring to Rom 1,19—25; Lang (1986:29—30).

[16] Klauck (1984:24) affirms: "An sich wäre es der Welt möglich, zur Erkenntnis Gottes zu gelangen, weil sie in der von Gottes Weisheit durchwirkten Schöpfung ihren Existenzraum hat [vorausgesetzt ist die Mitwirkung der personifizierten Weisheit bei den Schöpfungswerken in der frühjüdischen Weisheitstheologie]. Aber diese theoretische Möglichkeit wurde nicht genutzt."

[17] Klauck (1984:25) observes that Paul's statement about the Jews is probably made "… von der Messiasfrage her, was auch die nähe zur synoptischen Zeichenforderung erklärt: Vom *Messias* erwartet man ein machtvolles Beglaubigungswunder".

verse. Against the background of Deut 21, 22 and 23 in which it is stated that anyone hanged is accursed in the sight of God, it is clear why the message of a crucified Christ is a stumbling block to the Jews (cf also 5 Moses 21,23). (Although the Christ-title is often used merely as a noun, Klauck [1984:25] argues that the messianic components in this passage can still be observed.) A crucified[18] Son of God also stands in sharp contrast to the Graeco-Roman picture of God. Lucian, for example, sneers at the Christians who foolishly honour a fallen Sophist as their God (Klauck 1984:25).

Against the sombre background portrayed by verses 22—23, verse 24 expresses the confession of those who accepted the message of the cross (Baumann 1968:106). Verse 21 affirms that God, through the foolishness of the kerygma, saves those who *believe*. In verse 24 it is stated that only those who are *called*[19] are capable of recognising who the crucified Christ really is. In their encounter with the unbelieving world, the believers recognise that their faith remains a gift of God, a result of God's calling (Baumann 1968:107).

The death of Christ on the cross nullifies the social classification and grouping so important at that time; "in Christ" Jews and Gentiles, slaves and free men, men and women have the same religious value and responsibility (Gal 3,28). To those whom God has called, the gospel is God's power and God's wisdom. "Power" and "wisdom" must also be seen in the light of what has been said of Jews and Greeks in verse 23. The Jews also praise the power and wisdom of God. What is new in what Paul has said, is his *focus on the cross of Christ* (Lang 1986:31).

Celine Mangan (1980:32) has pointed out that the linking of wisdom and power in the Old Testament and in the intertestamental literature occurred in texts where the activity of God was very much in evidence. It was clear that he was in control and could turn the tables on those who

---

[18] Müller (1966:266—7) points to the meaning of the perfect participle ἐσταυρωμένος: "Gemäß der Eigenart griechischer Perfektbildungen ist das prädikativ und appositiv dem apellativum χριστός beigegebene partic. perf. pass. ἐσταυρωμένος weit davon entfernt, den gekreuzigten Messias Jesus nur in einem rückblickenden Sinne ins Auge zu fassen."

[19] For a discussion of the meaning of the phrase αὐτοῖς δὲ τοῖς κλητοῖς, see Baumann (1968:107—8). The meaning of this passage is clear (in the words of Baumann): "Jedenfalls hebt Paulus darauf ab, daß nur die Gemeinde der Glaubenden, die Christen als 'der Anfang einer neuen erlösten Menschheit' ... erfahren haben und bekennen können, was für sie der gekreuzigte Christus ist."

regarded themselves as powerful. "The great insight of Paul was to realise that the *same* powerful wisdom of God which was active in the past in great feats of creation and of salvation, was now present in a man broken on a cross" (Mangan 1980:32).

The relationship between the cross and the resurrection of Christ is of pivotal importance. To those who believe God confirmed Christ's mission through the resurrection from the dead. Through the resurrection the cross became the symbol of God's wisdom and his power over sin and death (Lang 1986:31).[20] The crucified Christ (in principle identical to the word of the cross) is God's saving action to those who believe (cf v 18).[21] The θεοῦ σοφία must also be understood in this soteriological sense.

In verse 24 the reader finds the thought which has already been expected in verse 18: σοφία. Paul first had to destroy the Corinthian notion of wisdom through his proclamation of the *cross* before he could use this thought without the fear of being misunderstood. Therefore, instead of σοφία he uses δύναμις θεοῦ in 1,18, a thought which is also awarded primary importance in 1,24. The theocentric dimension of this passage needs to be emphasised.[22] From the acceptance of the message of the cross something is born which has eluded the world: the knowledge *of God* in the wisdom *of God* through the wisdom *of God* (1,21); this wisdom of God confronts man in the *cross of Christ*, the believer accepts this as his salvation in *Christ* (1,30). This perspective allows us to fully understand the phrase σῶσαι τοὺς πιστεύοντας (v 21).[23] The power and wisdom of God,

---

[20] A hint of the theological presupposition, which enables the *apostle to portray the cross of Christ as sign of divine power* in 1 Cor 1,23—24, is to be found in 2 Cor 13,4a: καὶ γὰρ ἐσταυρώθη ἐξ ἀσθενείας, ἀλλὰ ζῇ ἐκ δυνάμεως θεοῦ. Cf 1 Cor 6,14: ὁ δὲ θεὸς καὶ τὸν κύριον ἤγειρεν καὶ ἡμᾶς ἐξεγερεῖ διὰ τῆς δυνάμεως αὐτοῦ. "*Der gekreuzigte Christus kann von Paulus insofern als Macht Gottes verkündigt werden, als an ihm die Macht des totenerweckenden Gottes zur Wirkung kam*" (emphasis:PJG) (Müller 1966:267—8).

[21] "Er ist für sie Kraft Gottes schlechthin" (Baumann 1968:109).

[22] Cf Wilckens (1959:38): "Auf dieser θεοῦ ... kommt ihm alles an ... ."

[23] "Gottes 'aktive Initiative' ist es allein, die ihre Rettung wirkt (vgl. 1,30 ἐξ αὐτοῦ), die Rettung derer, die mitten in ihrer Torheit von ihm gerufen sind" (Wilckens 1959:39).

hidden behind the weakness and foolishness of the cross, can only be perceived through faith.[24]

The profound truths Paul has just stated are further underlined in verse 25. Within the context of a *theologia crucis* — and only within this context — Paul also uses the concepts "wise" and "strong" (Klauck 1984:25).

7.4.3 Sub-pericope B (1 Cor 1,26—31)

We have seen, therefore, that Paul broadens the horizon of his argument so as to connect the rejection of his message of the cross (and its substitution by a doctrine of wisdom acceptable to the Corinthians) with the world's negative reaction to this "kerygma". The congregation and the way it was founded serve as proof for the Pauline thesis that in the cross of Christ God frustrated the wisdom of the world. This is illustrated by Paul in the following two sub-pericopes (1 Cor 1,26—31; 2,1—5) (Klauck 1984:25—6).

On the literary level, this sub-pericope (1,26—31) is very carefully structured. The words reflecting the main themes, are combined in groups of three or four. In verse 26 Paul mentions three groups to which the Corinthian Christians did not belong: the representatives of worldly education (σοφοὶ κατὰ σάρκα), those who wielded power politically (δυνατοί) and those who were of royal descent (εὐγενεῖς). The almost precise parallel way in which colons 15—17 are structured, should be noted. The Old Testament background becomes very prominent towards the end of this passage where we find a greatly condensed citation. Two important Biblical themes seem to form the background of 1 Cor 1,26—31: the time Israel spent in the wilderness and God's incomprehensible election. The most profound purpose of God's action as described in verses 27—28 is to render impossible any boastfulness on the side of man. During the time in the wilderness Israel was solely dependent on God and in Deut

---

[24] "Darum ist der Glaube and das Wort vom Kreuz das Ende aller Ideologie und jeder Weltanschauung, die das Offenbarungshandeln des unsichtbaren Gottes ablehnt" (Lang 1986:32).

Grundmann (1935:306) pointed out the great difference between our passage and the description of Simon Magnus as ἡ δύναμις τοῦ θεοῦ ἡ μεγάλη (Acts 8,10): "… das eine Mal [ist] δύναμις der magisch substantielle Kraftbegriff [ ], das andere Mal aber der Ausdruck der in der Geschichte überwindend wirkenden und sie zu einem Ziel gestaltenden Kraft …". Stuhlmacher (1966:345) views Christ, the eschatological Ruler as the "… Verkörperung der Heilsmacht und Geschichtsgewalt Gottes".

7,7—8 it is stated that the Lord chose Israel not because they were more numerous than any other nation, for they were the smallest of all nations. It was because the Lord loved them and stood by his oath to their forefathers that he delivered Israel with his strong hand. The theme of the fall of the high and the lifting up of the humble by God, a theme widely distributed throughout the ancient world (cf Job 12,17—24; Lk 1,52), is also part of the background of this passage (Klauck 1984:26).

Verse 30 focuses on the pivotal role of God. The new existence of the believers may indeed be termed as being in Christ Jesus.[25] This "being in Christ Jesus" has its deepest ground in God (ἐξ αὐτοῦ).[26] In colon 23 Jesus Christ's role in the salvation of the congregation is both confessed and praised.[27] The phrase σοφία ἡμῖν ἀπὸ θεοῦ is mentioned first as this was the theme in 1,18—25. This wisdom of God (contrasted to wisdom according to worldly standards) is mentioned with reference to the salvation of man. The three closely associated ideas δικαιοσύνη, ἁγιασμός, ἀπολύτρωσις stand here as an expression for the whole event of salvation (Lang 1986:34).[28]

Righteousness as the result of justification, God-given holiness and redemption are mediated through the Christ-event.[29] Verse 24 states that "... Christ is the power of God and the wisdom of God"; in the present verse (v 30) Paul says that "... Christ Jesus has become for us wisdom from God ... righteousness, holiness and redemption". Both statements are connected with dative constructions: αὐτοῖς δὲ τοῖς κλητοῖς (v 24), ἡμῖν (v 30). In this way both the origin, as well as the direction of the salvation events are portrayed: from God, in Christ, for us (Conzelmann 1981:73).[30]

---

[25] "... ein Dasein haben in Christus Jesus" (Klauck 1984:27).

[26] "Das Sein 'in Christus' ist eine geprägte Formel [vgl. Phil 2,5], mit der Paulus das Einbezogenwerden des ganzen Menschen mit Leib, Seele und Geist in das Heilsgeschehen von Kreuz und Auferweckung Jesu Christi umfassend beschreibt" (Lang 1986:34).

[27] J Weiss ([1910] 1970:40) describes these christological statements as the "... großen Schlagworte der Erlösungs-Religion".

[28] The reaction of the reader on reading this confession is poignantly described by Weiss ([1910] 1970:40): "Er beugte sich unter dem Eindruck: Wie Großes hat der Herr an uns getan! Was waren wir und was sind wir heute!"

[29] It is widely assumed that a baptismal confession may have inspired this expression: Cf *inter alia*: Klauck (1984:27); Lang (1986:34).

[30] Conzelmann continues: "Und es ist angedeutet, daß es sich nicht um allgemeine Seinsbestimmungen über Christus handelt ..., sondern um die Auslegung des Kreuzes."

In verse 31 Paul stresses again the point he has already made in verse 29 by alluding to Jer 9,22—23, a passage in which God warns man against boasting of having wisdom, power and riches. Paul uses this citation in his argument by inserting the phrase ἐν κυρίῳ referring to Christ. To boast in the Lord is the opposite of human boasting in the own capabilities and strengths, as it refers to glorying in the cross (Gal 6,14) and in weakness (2 Cor 11,30) (Lang 1986:34).

Under the heading "Humankind in the Encounter with the Gospel",[31] Georg Eichholz (1985:55—61) examines 1 Cor 1,18—31 with the purpose of illuminating the way in which humanity is seen in Pauline theology. The gospel as the message of the cross is the apocalypse of humankind — on the one hand it is "... foolishness to those who are perishing", on the other hand "... to us who are being saved it is the power of God". The gospel is God's decision for humankind, God's yes to them. Specifically as the message of the cross, it is God's saving power to humankind. It is saving power to those who believe (1 Cor 1,21, cf also Rom 1,16). When people are encountered by the gospel, they have, however, already a pre-understanding of God. In this pre-understanding humankind is not uniform, but as Jew and Greek typically differentiated. God encounters humankind, both Jew and Greek alike in the cross of Jesus Christ. He is different from the way in which people have envisaged him.[32] Paul repeatedly stresses weakness as the legitimate way in which God encounters us, in which God's power is hidden. Only God's grace triumphs over all weakness, triumphs in all weakness.[33] This theme, explicitly stated in 2 Cor 12,9—10; 13,3—4, has already been expressed, though implicitly, in 1 Cor 1,18—31.

7.4.4 Sub-pericope C (1 Cor 2,1—5)

7.4.4.1 Introduction

There is a very close relationship between 1 Cor 2,1—5 and 1,26—31. It has already been pointed out that 1 Cor 2,1—5 may be seen as a second illustration of Paul's thesis, that God in the event on the cross denied the

---

[31] "Der Mensch in der Begegnung mit dem Evangelium."

[32] "Der wirkliche Gott ist eine einzige Überraschung für den Menschen ... Die Schwachheit des Kreuzes gewinnt ... *übergreifende kritische Funktion*, trifft mit dem Juden auch den Griechen bzw. den Gnostiker" (Eichholz 1985:59—60).

[33] "Gottes königliches Handeln, sein nur noch als Gnade zu begreifendes Tun" (Eichholz 1985:60).

wisdom of the world (Klauck 1984:26). In 1 Cor 1,26—31 the same subject matter is in view, firstly from the perspective of the congregation, how they ought to see themselves; then from the perspective of the apostle, how he understood his conduct and mission in Corinth (Klauck 1984:27—8).

7.4.4.2 1 Corinthians 2,1—3

In his presentation of the "mystery of God" to the Corinthians Paul did not avail himself of sophisticated rhetorical techniques, nor did he try to persuade the Corinthians by means of rational philosophical arguments.[34] Talbert (1987:5) points out the contrast with Socrates' description of the spell which the funeral orator's account of Athens' great past cast upon him: "As I listen, the spell falls upon me, I feel that I have become at the moment a greater, nobler, finer man, and this feeling persists for three or four days' (Pl Menex 235A—C). In this statement Paul perhaps alludes to the other preachers in Corinth.

The resurrection of Christ is an essential part of the Pauline message (cf 1 Cor 15,1—5). In Corinth Paul preached the resurrection and second coming of the Lord. His whole message receives however its special emphasis and meaning within the *context of the cross*. In the centre of Paul's message about Christ stands the message of the Crucified (cf Gal 3,1 — Lang 1986:36). It is possible that in this specific situation of the Corinthians it had to be stressed that the presence of the glorified Lord through his Spirit is not to be separated from his vicarious death on the cross. Paul clearly regards the glorified Lord, who works through his Spirit, and the earthly Jesus, who died on the cross, as one and the same person.

Paul's decision to preach Christ and him crucified is grounded in the fundamental structure of his theology and is bound to his existence as suffering apostle (cf 4,9—13). In biblical language, fear and trembling represent phenomena which go hand in hand with epiphany and revelation (Ex 20,18) (cf Klauck 1984:28). Paul saw his whole apostolic service as

---

[34] It has been proposed that the failure of Paul's preaching in Athens, where he availed himself of philosophical language, led him to the opposite conduct (as described in 1 Cor 2,3) (cf Klauck 1984:28).

following Christ — also in his suffering (cf 2 Cor 4,7—15).[35] A purely psychological interpretation of this verse certainly has to be rejected.[36]

7.4.4.3 1 Corinthians 2,4—5

Paul stresses the fact that in his missionary activity (in his message and preaching) he did not avail himself of sophisticated rhetorical techniques as was the case with propagandists of worldly wisdom (cf 1 Thess 2,3—6). Despite the textcritical difficulties encountered in this verse, the essential meaning is clear. The original text was probably: "... not in the persuasion of wisdom" (which was then lengthened in different ways — cf 7.3). Next to this negative phrase, the expression "... in demonstration of Spirit and of power" represented a formal parallel and underlined the contradiction between worldly and Godly wisdom. Instead of a link between the power and wisdom of God (1,24), we encounter the concepts "Spirit and power". In the Old Testament and Early Judaism the Spirit and the power of God were already revealed as closely-related concepts (cf chapter 2.4).

The confirmation of the truth of Paul's message is neither the result of nor demanded by logical premises, as in the case of a skilled orator (this would have been faith grounded on the foundation of the wisdom of man), but is brought about by God himself. From the perspective of a sociological interpretation Lim (1987:145—7) has pointed out that in 2 Cor 1,1—5 Paul uses terminology which was part of the rhetorical tradition and appears to be distinguishing himself from the other preachers who were circulating in the Corinthian church. In 1 Cor 2,4, when Paul writes καὶ ὁ λόγος μου καὶ τὸ κήρυγμά μου οὐκ ἐν πειθοῖ σοφίας ἀλλ' ἐν ἀποδείξει πνεύματος καὶ δυνάμεως, he appears to be rejecting that specific, studied art of persuasive speech which was practised by orators and rhetoricians of the Graeco-Roman world and by at least some of the Corinthian preachers.

Lim (1987:147) also mentions that although ἀπόδειξις is a *hapax legomenon* in the New Testament, it occurs frequently as a technical term in rhetoric and represents a demonstration or cogent proof of argument on the ground of generally accepted premises. By employing it with πνεύματος and δυνάμεως, Paul uses ἀπόδειξις in a way that is different from and

---

[35] "Wie die Predigt des Apostels nach Inhalt und Form ganz vom Kreuz geprägt war, so entsprach auch sein äußeres Auftreten dem Wort vom Kreuz" (Lang 1986:36).

[36] For a discussion of the different commentators holding this view, cf Baumann (1968:166 note 85).

counter to the rhetorical meaning of the term. His word and his preaching are based upon a demonstration, not of the rhetorical kind, but of the Spirit and of power. This demonstration does not consist of arguments based upon generally-accepted truths, but upon the divine conviction of the Spirit and power (cf 1 Cor 4,20).

To what does Paul refer with his phrase, ἐν ἀποδείξει πνεύματος καὶ δυνάμεως? Many commentators regard 1 Cor 2,4 as a reference to miracles.[37] Passages such as Gal 3,5, 2 Cor 12,12, Rom 15,19 and Heb 2,4 are then related to 1 Cor 2,4. This interpretation is, however, rejected by several scholars on the basis of 1 Cor 1,22 and due to the specific situation in Corinth at that time (cf Polhill 1983:331; Baumann 1968:166 note 86). Baumann (1968:167) argues that the "... demonstration of the Spirit and of power" is to be seen in ἡ πίστις ὑμῶν, but then with specific reference to an external, visible event, namely the founding of the believing congregation in Corinth. Klauck (1984:28) also argues that the fact that there were believers in Corinth is both result and proof of the powerful working of the Spirit. Wilckens (1959:50—1) points to the importance of recognising the contrasting motives in this passage: σοφία and πνεῦμα and δύναμις.[38]

These interpretations of Baumann, Klauck and Wilckens have correctly pointed out the main emphasis of this passage. Paul does not elaborate on

---

[37] "... das zuletzt unbegründbare und daher unbeweisbare Kerygma schafft sich einen eigenen 'Beweis', indem Gott in Christus Jesus sich in ihm 'in der Weise von Gaben oder Vermögen' offenbart, so daß Kerygma und 'Gaben', Kerygma und 'Zeichen und Wunder' zusammengehören" (Baumann 1968:166 quotes from Schlier *Kerygma und Sophia*: 224).

[38] He also discusses the meaning of the phrase ἐν ἀποδείξει πνεύματος καὶ δυνάμεως in this perspective: "Der Beweis der Sophia hat seine Überzeugungskraft darin, daß es die Weisheit der Menschen selbst ist, die hier überzeugt. Der Beweis des Geistes und der Kraft dagegen hat seine Überzeugungskraft darin, daß es Gottes Macht ist, die sich erweist. Der Gegensatz σοφία — δύναμις impliziert also ein Gegegeneinanderstehen von Welt und Gott. Das erstaunliche aber ist dies, daß es inmitten der Welt die πίστις gibt, die nicht in der Weltweisheit, sondern in der Macht Gottes begründet ist. Diese hat die Gestalt der 'Schwachheit'; sie ist schwach eben darin, daß sie sich nicht von der Welt — und darum auch nicht von sich selbst — sondern einzig von Gott überzeugen läßt. Und in dieser Schwachheit erweist sich Gottes Kraft als Macht, indem sie nämlich als sie selbst (und d.h. als πνεῦμα θεοῦ) in den Schwachen wohnt ... ."

the meaning of "a demonstration of the Spirit's power"[39] because this is not essential to his argument in this passage. It seems to me, however, that the argument, according to which a reference to miracles is totally excluded on account of Paul's statement in 1 Cor 1,22, is not conclusive.[40] Nielsen (1980:154) correctly observes that it is clear from this passage that the δύναμις of God has a visible effect (cf ἀποδείξει — 1 Cor 2,4). The charismatic-thaumaturgical dimension of δύναμις should, therefore, not be excluded.

In verse 5 the contradiction between σοφία ἀνθρώπων = τοῦ κόσμου and δύναμις θεοῦ, which already played an important role in 1 Cor 1,20—25, is explicitly stated again. The reason for Paul's mode of conduct, described in the preceding verses is confirmed: "... so that your faith might not rest on men's wisdom, but on God's power" (cf Conzelmann 1981:77).

7.5 Conclusion

This pericope focuses upon the soteriological dimension of δύναμις. In a thematic statement Paul affirms in 1 Cor 1,18 that the message of the cross is foolishness to those who are perishing, but to those who are being saved it is the power of God. Verse 24 affirms that to those whom God has called, Christ is the power of God and the wisdom of God.

The preceding discussion has underlined the following perspectives on Paul's use of δύναμις in this pericope:

i   The *theocentricity* of Paul's thought: God has taken the initiative to reconcile the world with himself (cf 2 Cor 5,19). The message of the cross

---

[39] Correctly translated in this way by the New International Version: The genitive signifies that a close relation exists between ἀπόδειξις and πνεῦμα. With καί another qualification is added to πνεῦμα. πνεῦμα and δύναμις must be seen as a unity because of their coherence. The power which exists in the Spirit is the contents of the ἀπόδειξις. Paul, therefore, refers here to a demonstration of the power which exists in the Spirit — or, "a demonstration of the Spirit's power" (NIV).

The genitives πνεύματος καὶ δυνάμεως refer to the contents of the preceding noun (ἀπόδειξις).

[40] The immediate connection of Paul's statements in 1,22 with 2,4 does not seem to be uncomplicated. Due to the difference in character and scope of his argumentation in these two sub-pericopes, Paul's argumentation can certainly not be seen as functioning on exactly the same level in both cases.

is the power of *God* (v 18) ... the (crucified [v 23]) Christ is the power of *God* (v 24).

ii   Within a soteriological context Paul's theological use of δύναμις (δύναμις θεοῦ, 1,18; cf 1,24) is interpreted *christologically*. In 1,23.24.30.31 and 2,2 the supreme centrality of Christ in the whole process of salvation becomes very clear.

iii   Paul's central thesis in this pericope is that God has frustrated the wisdom of the world in the cross of Christ and yet the message about the cross of Christ is the δύναμις of God.

iv   The preaching ministry of Paul stood in the sign of the cross, both with regard to its content as well as the way in which it was conducted. He did not rely on his own wise and persuasive words to make his message effective, but relied on the power of God which he interprets *pneumatologically* (1 Cor 2,4—5). Since the message about the crucified Christ is *contrary to the wisdom of this world* it can only be believed and thus be God's δύναμις through the powerful activity of the Spirit. The charismatic-thaumaturgical dimension of the δύναμις of the Spirit is here not to be excluded.

v   The use of δύναμις in 1 Cor 2,4—5 has important consequences for the discussion about *theologia crucis* and *theologia gloriae* in Pauline theology. Δύναμις (including a possible charismatic-thaumaturgical dimension) occurs here *in the context of* Paul's ministry which stands under the sign of the cross of Christ. 1 Cor 2,4—5 is, however, not compatible with a concept of the theology of the cross in which power always occurs *as* or *concealed in* weakness (Nielsen 1980:154; cf also Hübner 1987:2726—9). (This issue will be discussed in more detail in chapter 25: "Paul's ministry within the christological perspective on weakness and power" — cf especially 25.2.)

vi   The *Trinitarian* view on δύναμις presented by this pericope is therefore evidently clear: The message about the crucified *Christ* is the power of *God*. This message of Paul was brought with a demonstration of the power of the *Spirit* so that the Corinthians' faith might not rest on people's wisdom, but on God's power.

Chapter 8

1 Corinthians 4,19 and 20

Like the previous pericope, 1 Cor 4,1—21 also belongs to the first main section of this letter (after the prologue), dealing with reports Paul has received (i e 1,10—6,21) and concludes the first part of this main section (1,10—4,21), dealing with a divided church (Fee 1987:21; Wolff 1996:91). The theme of the sub-pericope in which 1 Cor 4,19—20 occurs (1 Cor 4,14—21) deals with the relationship between Paul and the Corinthians (cf *inter alia* Barrett 1968:28; Bruce 1971:26; Conzelmann 1981:6; Fee 1987:21; Lang 1986:66; Lietzmann-Kümmel 1969:1), while the theme of apostolic authority is also prominent (Klauck 1984:40; Wolff 1996:91 portrays 4,14—21 as the "... fatherly authority of the apostle").

The frequent appearance of words relating to Paul's coming to the Corinthians in verses 18—21 is noteworthy: ἐρχομένου (v 18), ἐλεύσομαι (v 19); ἔλθω (v 21).[1] When he comes to the Corinthians, Paul states he will find out not only how the arrogant people in Corinth are talking (τὸν λόγον τῶν πεφυσιωμένων), but also what power they have (τὴν δύναμιν). Some members of the church, who belittled his authority, revealed themselves as quite arrogant (literally "inflated"), suggesting that Paul would not dare to

---

[1] In his commentary on 1 Cor 4,17—21 Klauck (1984:40) gives a description of "... [d]as einfache Grundmuster der ... *Reiseankündigung*" which reoccurs in more or fewer details in the Pauline letters: (a) Herewith I write to you (4,14) ... (b) send you in the meantime my co-worker ... (c) hope, however, to come to you soon. The function of this "Reiseankündigung" is to thematise the question concerning the presence of the apostle in the congregation and the exercise of his authority. The ideal situation is Paul's *personal* presence in the congregation. The announcement of his planned visit is, therefore, the climax. Paul can, however, also send a *co-worker* as substitute/deputy, a faithful person from the most intimate circle of co-workers, for example Timothy, who came to faith through him and was with him in Corinth when the church was being founded there. Paul is, however, consistent with the Hellenistic theory of letters, also fully represented by his *letter*.

come and face the gradually mounting opposition because of fear and would therefore not send Timothy (Bruce [1971] 1980:52, Klauck 1984:41). These Christians in Corinth (perhaps due to their pneumatic gifts or their "gnosis" [cf 1,5; 8,1—2.10—11; 13,28; 14,6]) probably asserted that they had already attained the promised reigning with Christ, and already possessed the things to come (Schnackenburg 1961:202). Against this assertion the apostle stresses that the reign of God reveals itself not in words, but in divine power.[2] Paul states that when he comes, he will approach them in a powerful way and test their ministry (Conzelmann 1981:120). As to the distinction between λόγος and δύναμις, note 1 Thess 1,5: "... our gospel came to you not simply with words, but also with power, with the Holy Spirit and with deep conviction".

In verse 20 Paul grounds his (planned) mode of conduct in the essence of God's kingdom.[3] Verse 20 does not want to give an exhaustive definition, but states an essential trait which is important in this situation (Conzelmann 1981:120).

The expression ἐν λόγῳ is viewed negatively here in connection with the arrogant talk of Paul's opponents and may be linked with the words of wisdom of this world (cf for example 1 Cor 1,20) (Lang 1986:68). It also seems as if Paul's opponents relied very much on their rhetorical skills (Klauck 1984:41). The crucial factor in Paul's view is not rhetorical

---

[2] The talk of these "puffed up" people (cf verse 6) is illustrated ironically in v 8 and in the solemn and shaming sentences of the apostle in vv 9—13. They must have said (e g): "We already have all we want; we have already become rich. We have become kings without the apostles" (v 8a). Exactly this last expression (βασιλεύειν) is taken up by Paul when he says: "How I wish that you really had become kings so that we might be kings with you!" (v 8b). However, then Paul portrays how the apostles (who are actually in the first place called to reign with Christ) are despised, how they suffer and are persecuted (vv 9—13). It is therefore, not yet time for "reigning" and glory, but time to follow the way of the cross ("die Zeit der Kreuzesnachfolge").

Schnackenburg (1961:202—3) emphasises that ἡ βασιλεία τοῦ θεοῦ in v 20 may not be interpreted in a sense referring to the future. There is no contradiction with vv 8—13:
"Beide Gesichtspunkte haben ihr Recht: Die apostolische Existenz und Erfahrung beweist, daß die offenbare Gottesherrschaft und die Mitherrschaft mit Christus [vgl. auch 6, 2 f.!] noch nicht da sind; gleichwohl offenbart sich die Gottesherrschaft schon jetzt in der Kraft des Gottesgeistes [vgl. 2,1—5; daran dürfte Paulus konkret bei ἐν δυνάμει denken]."

[3] "An den Gegensatz von Wort [lógos] und Kraft [dynamis] schließt der Apostel begründend eine sentenzartige Aussage über das Reich Gottes an" (Lang 1986:68).

capability, so highly valued in the Greek world, but the manifestation of divine power.[4] Paul has already stated in 1 Cor 2,4—5 to what extent this δύναμις is at work in him and it is the presence of this δύναμις that he will investigate at his next visit.

It is well-known that the expression ἡ βασιλεία τοῦ θεοῦ occurs very seldom in Pauline literature. This eschatological concept is mostly understood as a future reality.[5] 1 Cor 4,20 and Rom 14,17 ("For the kingdom of God is not a matter of eating and drinking, but of righteousness, peace and joy in the Holy Spirit ...") serve as illustrations of the fact that Paul can also speak of the kingdom as a present reality.[6] The power with which the kingdom of God works, is the power of the Holy Spirit (cf Rom 14,17), by which God's purpose is put into effect and the future anticipated in the present (Barrett 1968:118; cf also Bruce [1971] 1980:52).

In her discussion of the kingdom of God and the kingdom of Christ in it's present and future dimensions, M-T Wacker (1985:43) mentions that Paul explicitly thematises this question in 1 Cor 15,24—28: With the resurrection of Christ a time has begun in which Christ reigns as king and prepares the world for the kingship of his Father, which is still to come. The present is qualified as the time of the reign of Christ, in which the power of sin is already broken through his death. Life in the reality of the kingdom of God, which has already dawned, is possible. However, at the same time life is still tainted by the temporariness and suffering of this uncompleted world (2 Thess 1,5).[7]

When mentioning the kingdom of God in 1 Cor 4,20, Paul points to the tension in the "basileia"-concept. Although the full manifestation of God's eschatological kingdom still lies in future, the apostle — and with

---

[4] "Denn δύναμις ist der Erweis der Gottesherrschaft ..." (Fascher 1980:154).

[5] For a discussion of the problem concerning the future/present dimensions of this passage, cf Nielsen (1980:155—6). The following passages point to ἡ βασιλεία τοῦ θεοῦ as a future reality: 1 Cor 6,9—10; Gal 5,21; 1 Thess 2,12; 2 Thess 1,5. Cf also 1 Cor 15,24.

[6] Kümmel (against Lietzmann) in Lietzmann (1969:22) comments on this passage: "ἡ βασιλεία τοῦ θεοῦ, gewöhnlich bei Paulus rein eschatologisch angesehen ... gilt hier wie Col 1₁₃4₁₁ und in der völlig parallelen Stelle Rom 14₁₇ als in der Gemeinde Christi sich bereits offenbarend." Cf also Barrett (1968:118); Lang (1986:68).

[7] Luz (1980:490) argues that ἡ βασιλεία τοῦ θεοῦ has remained an expression of the proclamation of Jesus in the New Testament letters and therefore seldom occurs. Paul interprets the christological basis and soteriological scope of the eschatological kingdom of God as δικαιοσύνη θεοῦ. Referring to 1 Cor 4,20, he draws the attention to Mk 9,1.

him the whole early church — experienced powerful manifestations of this kingdom already in the present through the work of God's Spirit (cf 2,4 — Schnackenburg 1961:203). Paul's use of the expression ἡ βασιλεία τοῦ θεοῦ indicates that his eschatology may indeed be characterised as an "already — not yet" (cf Nielsen 1980:155). There exists a very profound relation between the Spirit and the kingdom of God. The Spirit not only guarantees the full inheritance; he is himself the beginning and first part of that inheritance. That is why Paul can describe the kingdom in terms of the Christian's present experience of the Spirit: "The kingdom of God is not a matter of eating and drinking, but of righteousness, peace and joy in the Holy Spirit" (Rom 14,17); it does not consist in talk but in the power of the Holy Spirit (1 Cor 4,20; cf Dunn 1970—71:36).

1 Cor 4,20 indeed combines the "already of the eschatological events" with the concept of power (δύναμις) (Nielsen 1980:156).

Chapter 9

1 Corinthians 5,4

The pericope 1 Cor 5,1—13 introduces the second part (5,1—6,20) of the first main section (1,10—6,20) of 1 Corinthians (cf discussion under 7.1). 1 Cor 5,1—6,20 deals with immoral deeds in the congregation. 1 Cor 5,1—5 forms the first sub-pericope of this pericope (5,1—13)[1] and may be regarded as the immediate context within which δύναμις is used in 1 Cor 5,4.

The section 1 Cor 5,1—6,20 commences without a connecting particle and covers different cases of immorality in the Corinthian congregation. The theme of sexual immorality is very prominent in the pericopes 1 Cor 5,1—13 and 6,12—20 while 6,1—11 treats the problem of lawsuits among believers. Without suggesting any direct connection with the Corinthian striving after wisdom in chapters 1—4, the cases referred to in chapters 5 and 6 clearly show how little reason the Corinthians have to be proud of their "wisdom".[2]

The Jew of Old Testament times viewed sexual immorality (πορνεία) as the main sin of the heathen and regarded it as the result of the worship of their idols. In the Jewish-Hellenistic wisdom tradition the connection between idol worship and moral depravity is a common theme (Wisdom of Solomon 14). Early Christianity also rejected sexual immorality as an offence against the holiness of God's church (cf 1 Cor 6,9; Gal 5,19). 1 Cor 5,1—5 is concerned with a very severe case of sexual immorality — unheard of even amongst the heathen. Extraordinary disciplinary measures

---

[1] 1 Cor 5,1—13 is regarded as the first pericope (of the section 1 Cor 5,1—6,20) dealing with "The case of the incestuous man" (Fee 1987:21). Cf also (*inter alia*) Fascher (1980:VIII); Klauck (1984:41); Lang (1986:69); Wolff (1996:98).

[2] "Ging es dem Apostel in den Kapiteln 1—4 vorwiegend um die *Einheit* der Gemeinde, so legt er in dem neuen Hauptteil den Nachdruck auf die *Heiligkeit* der Gemeinde" (Lang 1986:69; cf Klauck 1984:41—2).

are, therefore, required.[3] The procedure, recommended by the apostle, must be seen against the background of the people of God in the Old Testament. When a severe sin is committed in Israel the whole community is concerned, because the covenant relationship between God and his people is affected. The sinner's exclusion from the Old Testament congregation and his execution is interpreted by Israel as an act which once more normalises this relationship. Lev 18,8 and 20,11 pronounce the death sentence upon that person who partakes in sexual intercourse with his father's wife (cf also Deut 17,5—7).

Paul also understands the Christian congregation as a unity from the perspective of the "body of Christ" and not merely as a totality of individuals. As someone bound by the law of Christ (Gal 6,2) Paul does not proceed according to the letter of the Old Testament law, but brings God's act of salvation in Christ into consideration. Despite Paul's strict advice, his main concern is still the salvation of the evildoer.[4] Paul proceeds according to the principle which applies to the bad missionary in 1 Cor 3,15: "... the doer will be saved, but only as one escaping through the flames" (cf Lang 1986:71).

Hans Conzelmann (1981:124; cf also Fee 1987:206—7) pointed out the following possibilities of connecting the constituent phrases of verses 4 and 5:

1   ἐν τῷ ὀνόματι belongs to συναχθέντων ὑμῶν, σὺν τῇ δυνάμει belongs to παραδοῦναι.

2   Both belong to συναχθέντων ὑμῶν.

3   Both belong to παραδοῦναι.

4   Both belong to both.

5   ἐν τῷ ὀνόματι belongs to παραδοῦναι, σὺν τῇ δυνάμει belongs to the participal sentence.

6   ἐν τῷ ὀνόματι belongs to κέκρικα, σὺν τῇ δυνάμει belongs to συναχθέντων ὑμῶν.

---

[3] The evildoer's exclusion from the congregation is not merely a juridical action, but in the words of Lang (1986:70): "... eine gottesdienstliche Handlung nach dem heiligen Gottesrecht, die in den Bereich von Segen und Fluch gehört".

[4] "Wie kann man sein Pneuma retten, damit es am 'Gerichtstag' gerettet werde? *Das ist des Apostels eigentliche Frage und Sorge!*" (Fascher 1980:158).

Paul's demand to hand the evildoer over to Satan is dependent on the main verb κέκρικα (cf Lang 1986:71). The authorising formula ἐν τῷ ὀνόματι τοῦ κυρίου {ἡμῶν} 'Ιησοῦ is, however, according to Lang, preferably not to be connected with the gathering of the congregation (with which it may also be linked, cf Mt 18,20), but with the central act of handing over to Satan. The sentence in between ("Zwischensatz") then describes the liturgical congregation as the place at, and occasion on which the handing over should take place.

Although the present writer agrees with Lang that Paul's demand to hand the evildoer over to Satan is dependent on the main verb κέκρικα, the most unforced way of connecting the immediate constituent parts of verses 4 and 5 seems to be:

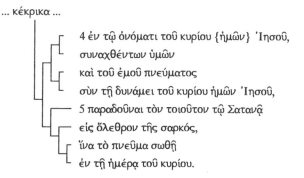

... κέκρικα ...

4 ἐν τῷ ὀνόματι τοῦ κυρίου {ἡμῶν} 'Ιησοῦ,

συναχθέντων ὑμῶν

καὶ τοῦ ἐμοῦ πνεύματος

σὺν τῇ δυνάμει τοῦ κυρίου ἡμῶν 'Ιησοῦ,

5 παραδοῦναι τὸν τοιοῦτον τῷ Σατανᾷ

εἰς ὄλεθρον τῆς σαρκός,

ἵνα τὸ πνεῦμα σωθῇ

ἐν τῇ ἡμέρᾳ τοῦ κυρίου.

Conzelmann (1981:124) speaks of a "sacred pneumatic act of judgment" against the evildoer. It would however be wrong to portray this statement of Paul's simply as an example of the magical world view of the apostle (cf Fascher 1980:160). In the liturgical gathering of the congregation, the praying congregation may be aware of the presence of the exalted Lord with the power of his Spirit in their midst and ought to hand over the evildoer to Satan in his Name (cf 1 Tim 1,20) (Lang 1986:71).[5] The

---

[5] Klauck (1984:42) has pointed to the "briefspezifische Formulierung" which we encounter in verses 3—5. The acknowledging of this letter style will prevent the mistake made by earlier commentators, "... die von einer geheimnisvoll-magischen geistigen Fernwirkung sprechen". Verse 5 "... beinhaltet eine Fluch- und Bannformel im Rahmen einer dualistischen Weltsicht". The evildoer is excluded from the congregation in which the Spirit of God is actively present and falls prey to evil powers lurking outside. "Sie haben Macht über den Menschen, verursachen Krankheit und vorzeitigen Tod [Ijob]. Paulus denkt an eine Art Strafwunder (vgl. Apg 5[1—11]), dessen letztes Ziel die endzeitliche Rettung des Bestraften darstellt (vgl. 3[15])".

miraculous power of Jesus is present within the gathering of the congregation, through prayer (cf Lietzmann-Kümmel 1969:23). Acts 5,5.10 and 13,11 can be cited as passages within the New Testament to be compared with 1 Cor 5,4.[6] The power of Christ is needed to protect the upbuilding of the community, which is threatened by the evildoer (cf Grundmann 1935:313).

How must Paul's reference to *the power of our Lord Jesus* be understood within this context? Instructing the Corinthian congregation on the action to be taken against the immoral member of the congregation, Paul strongly emphasises the role to be played by the *gathered* congregation[7] (even including himself "in spirit"). The gathered congregation together with Paul's presence in spirit, however, needs the presence of the power of our Lord Jesus in order to hand the evildoer over to Satan. Grundmann (1935:313) mentions within this context that the power which Paul exercises in his apostolic activity, is the power of Christ, and it is not he, but Christ, who disposes of it. By referring to the presence of the power of Christ Paul underlines the sincerity of the procedure to be adopted.

Although it almost seems as if the power of Christ is hypostatised in this passage, this is not the case.[8] The presence of the power of Christ is the presence of Christ with his power. The *reality* of the presence of the Lord within the gathering of the congregation is underlined by referring to the presence of the power of Jesus. Within the context of Pauline theology (and the way in which it is expressed in 1 Corinthians), it is certainly correct to associate the presence of the exalted Lord with the power of his *Spirit* in the midst of the praying congregation (cf Lang 1986:71).[9]

---

[6] Cf also Actus Petri (Vercellenses) 2,15,32; Acta Johannis 41f; Acta Thomae 6; Acta Johannis 86 and Ign Eph 13,1 (Lietzmann-Kümmel 1969:23).

[7] "Zu beachten ist, daß die Disziplinargewalt nicht bestimmten Beamten, sondern der ganzen Gemeinde zugesprochen wird ..." (Lietzmann-Kümmel 1969:23).

[8] Grundmann (1932:104 note 12) refers to rabbinical usage in this regard: "Derartige Ausdrucksweise ist dem Paulus nahegelegt durch den Sprachgebrauch der Umwelt. Charakteristisch ist dafür Targ. Onk. Deut. 33,26: 'und meine Kraft ist im höchsten Himmel'. An eine Hypostase ist im Sprachgebrauch des Targumisten nicht zu denken, sondern um den Gottesnamen zu vermeiden, setzt er seine Eigenschaften dafür [cf. Jer. 16,19b 'zu dir', beim Targumisten 'um zu hören deine Kraft']. Dieser Sprachgebrauch liegt bei Paulus vor."

[9] Referring to 1 Cor 2,4—5 and 4,19—20 Fee (1987:206) affirms that the term "power" is a reference to the Spirit, who is dynamically present among them when they are together.

Chapter 10

1 Corinthians 15,43

10.1 Location within the macrocontext of 1 Corinthians

The pericope, 1 Cor 15,42—49, which focuses on the resurrected body must be seen against the context of 1 Cor 15, dealing with the resurrection of believers (cf Conzelmann 1981:300—55; Fee 1987:23; Klauck 1984: 107.118—20; Lang 1986:208, 234—38; Lietzmann-Kümmel 1969:76. 84—6; Wolff 1996:X).

1 Cor 15 can be divided into the following sections:

15,1—11   The resurrection of Christ as the foundation of Paul's argumentation.
15,12—34   The certainty of resurrection.
15,35—49   The nature of the resurrection and the way in which it will take place.
15,50—58   The assurance of triumph (cf Fee 1987:23; Lang 1986:207—41; Wolff 1996:349—426).

The section 15,35—49 consists of two pericopes: 15,35—41, dealing with the different kinds of bodies in the old creation, and 15,42—49 dealing with the new resurrection body. The pericope 15,42—49 is introduced by the phrase, οὕτως καί ... . Internal cohesion binding the pericope together as a coherent unit is illustrated by the repeated occurrence of structural markers as well as the neat structure of this pericope (cf discourse analysis and discussion under 10.2.1).

10.2 Discourse analysis: 1 Corinthians 15,42—49

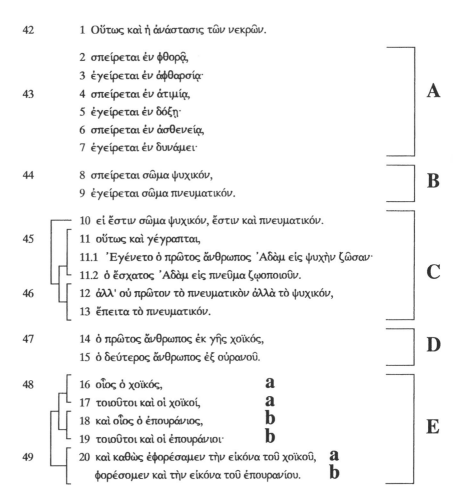

42   1 Οὕτως καὶ ἡ ἀνάστασις τῶν νεκρῶν.

      2 σπείρεται ἐν φθορᾷ,

      3 ἐγείρεται ἐν ἀφθαρσίᾳ·

43   4 σπείρεται ἐν ἀτιμίᾳ,   **A**

      5 ἐγείρεται ἐν δόξῃ·

      6 σπείρεται ἐν ἀσθενείᾳ,

      7 ἐγείρεται ἐν δυνάμει·

44   8 σπείρεται σῶμα ψυχικόν,   **B**

      9 ἐγείρεται σῶμα πνευματικόν.

      10 εἰ ἔστιν σῶμα ψυχικόν, ἔστιν καὶ πνευματικόν.

45   11 οὕτως καὶ γέγραπται,

      11.1 Ἐγένετο ὁ πρῶτος ἄνθρωπος Ἀδὰμ εἰς ψυχὴν ζῶσαν·

      11.2 ὁ ἔσχατος Ἀδὰμ εἰς πνεῦμα ζῳοποιοῦν.   **C**

46   12 ἀλλ' οὐ πρῶτον τὸ πνευματικὸν ἀλλὰ τὸ ψυχικόν,

      13 ἔπειτα τὸ πνευματικόν.

47   14 ὁ πρῶτος ἄνθρωπος ἐκ γῆς χοϊκός,   **D**

      15 ὁ δεύτερος ἄνθρωπος ἐξ οὐρανοῦ.

48   16 οἷος ὁ χοϊκός,   **a**

      17 τοιοῦτοι καὶ οἱ χοϊκοί,   **a**

      18 καὶ οἷος ὁ ἐπουράνιος,   **b**   **E**

      19 τοιοῦτοι καὶ οἱ ἐπουράνιοι·   **b**

49   20 καὶ καθὼς ἐφορέσαμεν τὴν εἰκόνα τοῦ χοϊκοῦ,   **a**

      φορέσομεν καὶ τὴν εἰκόνα τοῦ ἐπουρανίου.   **b**

10.2.1 A few notes on the structure of the pericope

1 Cor 15,42—49 constitutes a very neatly-structured pericope. Colon 1 serves as the heading of the whole pericope. Colons 2—7 must be grouped together due to the alternate use of σπείρεται and ἐγείρεται followed by ἐν + the dative.

Colons 8—9 fulfil the function of a hinge between 2—7 and 10—13. σπείρεται and ἐγείρεται relate to 2—7 while σῶμα ψυχικόν and σῶμα πνευματικόν relate to 10—13.

The contrast between σῶμα ψυχικόν, ψυχήν and πνευματικόν, πνεῦμα is typical of colons 10—13. Colon 11 provides proof from Scripture for colon 10 (as well as a christological affirmation) while colons 12—13 comment on the Scriptural proof and christological affirmation (note the occurence of πρῶτος/ἔσχατος, πρῶτον/ἔπειτα. The actants πρῶτος ἄνθρωπος Ἀδάμ and ἔσχατος Ἀδάμ newly occur on the scene.

Colons 14—15 function as a hinge between 10—13 and 16—20: πρῶτος/δεύτερος relate to the previous colon group, while χοϊκός/οὐρανοῦ relate to the following colon group.

The contrast between χοϊκός (χοϊκοί, χοϊκοῦ) and οὐρανοῦ (ἐπουράνιος, ἐπουράνιοι, ἐπουρανίου) is the main feature of colon group E (colons 16—20).

Note the following groups of contrasts:

Colon groups A and B:

σπείρεται	γείρεται
ἐν φθορᾷ	ἐν ἀφθαρσίᾳ
ἐν ἀτιμίᾳ	ἐν δόξῃ
ἐν ἀσθενείᾳ	ἐν δυνάμει
σῶμα ψυχικόν	σῶμα πνευματικόν

The contrast between σῶμα ψυχικόν and σῶμα πνευματικόν is then expounded by the contrast between ὁ πρῶτος ἄνθρωπος Ἀδάμ and ὁ ἔσχατος Ἀδάμ. In colon groups CDE the following contrast occurs:

ὁ πρῶτος ἄνθρωπος Ἀδάμ	ὁ ἔσχατος Ἀδάμ
Ἐγένετο ὁ ... εἰς ψυχὴν ζῶσαν	... εἰς πνεῦμα ζῳοποιοῦν
(οὐ πνευματικὸν) ἀλλὰ τὸ ψυχικόν	τὸ πνευματικόν
ἐκ γῆς χοϊκός	ἐξ οὐρανοῦ

ὁ χοϊκός/οἱ χοϊκοί　　　　　　　　　ὁ ἐπουράνιος/οἱ ἐπουράνιοι
ἐφορέσαμεν τὴν εἰκόνα τοῦ χοϊκοῦ (aor)　　φορέσομεν καὶ τὴν εἰκόνα
　　　　　　　　　　　　　　　　τοῦ ἐπουρανίου (fut)

Note the way in which the contrast between πνευματικόν and ψυχικόν is accentuated in colons 12—13 (οὐ πρῶτον τὸ πνευματικὸν ἀλλὰ ... ἔπειτα τὸ πνευματικόν). Colon 20 deserves special emphasis: 1. For the first time in this pericope the first person singular occurs. 2. The contrast between the two parts of this colon is accentuated by the difference in tense (ἐφορέσαμεν: aor; φορέσομεν: fut).

It may be said that the general (impersonal) affirmations of A and B are expounded in C and D by the reference to the first and the second Adam. Impersonal consequences are drawn in the first part of E (colons 16—17) and the personal application is found in colon 20.

10.3 An exegetical overview

Although verse 42 introduces a new pericope, it is clear that this pericope must be read against the background of 1 Cor 15,35—41.[1] Paul emphasises the overall difference between the resurrected body and the earthly body. The old creation is characterised as being transitory, weak and imperfect. The new creation is fundamentally different.[2] By using the present tense, Paul expresses this profound difference. In three short, rhetorically formulated antitheses Paul contrasts the essence of the old and the new creation (vv 42—43, followed by 44a & b), with the view on man in this and in the coming world.[3] The same God who creates life from death in the old creation is also at work in the eschatological resurrection.

---

[1] "Die alte Schöpfung, in der Gott immer wieder so mannigfaltige Leiber schafft, faßt Paulus nun als Analogie und Gleichnis für die neue Schöpfung" (Lang 1986:234).

[2] "Soll die neue Schöpfung ewigen Bestand haben und der vollendeten Gottesherrschaft entsprechen, so muß sie verschieden sein von der alten Welt [vgl. Offb 21]" (Lang 1986:234).

[3] "Aus seinen bisherigen Ausführungen zieht Paulus in Form eines kunstvollen antithetischen Parallelismus membrorum die Folgerung für die eschatologische Schöpfung ..." (Wolff 1982:198).

In verse 42 the image of sowing from the metaphor of the seed (cf 15,37—38) is applied to man. Often the metaphor of "being sown" is limited to the burial of the dead body, or the creation of earthly man; it may, however, also be seen as a broader reference to the whole of life with death as its end (cf Klauck 1986:118). The profound discontinuity between what is perishable and what is imperishable can not be bridged by a natural evolution, but only by the miraculous creative power of God. The passive form of the verb is to be seen as a divine passive. Ἀφθαρσία played an important role in late Hellenistic times and was known to Paul through Hellenistic Judaism (cf Rom 2,8).[4] Δόξα is a reference to the eschatological glory of the resurrection, in contrast to feeble, earthly man. (The contrast to "glory" is ἀτιμία — dishonour.)[5]

The antithesis σπείρεται ἐν ἀσθενείᾳ, ἐγείρεται ἐν δυνάμει, receives special emphasis due to its position at the end of colon group A. It seems as if the essence of the contrast at stake in this series of antitheses may in a certain sense be found in the contrast between ἀσθένεια and δύναμις. Over and against the weakness of earthly existence, Paul emphasises the power of the resurrection body.[6] Δύναμις is often used in relation to πνεῦμα (God's creative Spirit) (Lang 1986:234).[7] God, who raised Christ from the dead, will also raise the mortal bodies of the believers through his Spirit who lives in them (Rom 8,11).[8]

In verse 44 the answer to the question of verse 35 is given (Wolff 1982:199). Verse 44 may be seen as the goal of the preceding series of

---

[4] Wolff (1982:199) refers in this regard to 4 Mac 9,22; 17,12 and 4 Esdras 7,96. In this passage (with reference to 2 Bar 51,3—10) he translates δόξα with the words "Glanz, Pracht".

[5] Or as Lang (1986:234) affirms: "Unansehnlichkeit im Sinn von Jämmerlichkeit." He sees here a reference to man in his "… Anfälligkeit und Versuchlichkeit, der der Herrlichkeit Gottes ermangelt [Röm 3,23]".

[6] This broader interpretation by Wolff (1982:199) of weakness in this passage as "… Schwachheit der irdischen Existenzweise" is to be preferred to the interpretation of Lang (1986:234): "Gemeint ist der Mensch, der Anfechtungen, Krankheit und Leiden ausgesetzt ist und der das Gute nicht zu tun vermag, das er will [Röm 7,19]." The aspects mentioned by Lang certainly form part of the weakness of human existence. Fee (1987:785) correctly points out that "weakness" is a word that particularly recurs in 2 Cor 10—13 to describe not only the body, but Paul's whole present existence. Its opposite, "power", in this case (1 Cor 15,43) emphasises its resurrection rather than its permanent heavenly state.

[7] Cf chapter 24.

[8] He also points to Rom 1,4 in this context. (The question whether πνεῦμα ἁγιοσύνης actually refers to the Holy Spirit is discussed in chapter 16.3.)

antitheses.[9] In the New Testament ψυχικός refers to this world and what belongs to it, in contrast to the other world, which is marked by the πνεῦμα (Wolff 1982:199). 1 Cor 2,13—14 and 3,1—3 show that Paul can use ψυχικός and χοϊκός synonymously. In the same way he can use χοϊκός instead of ψυχικός in 15,46—49. The antithesis ψυχικός-πνευματικός is not really gnostic, but occurs also in the context of Jewish Wisdom (Wolff 1982:199 especially note 272; cf also Ja 3,15).

The *pneuma* is already a reality in the believer "... as a deposit, guaranteeing what is to come" (2 Cor 5,5; 1,22; cf also Rom 8,23). In the Spirit the guarantee for the continuity between the present and future existence of man is given (cf 6,14.19; Rom 8,11). In the light of the Pauline understanding of the Spirit this may even be formulated more specifically: through the activity of the risen Lord, already experienced by the believers.[10] The crucial factor for the continuity between the old and the new creation is the wonderful power of the God who remains true to his plan of creation and his promises (Lang 1986:235).

Paul strongly emphasises the aspect of a spiritual body by repeating the word σῶμα three times in verse 44.[11] From God's creative power, as it has previously been put forward, he concludes:[12] If there is a natural perishable body, there is also a heavenly, imperishable body.[13]

The thesis of verse 44c (colon 10), which is logically already present in the corresponding antitheses in verses 42b—44b (colons 2—9) is motivated by Paul from the Old Testament as well as christologically (Lang

---

[9] "Die vierte Antithese (V. 44a) faßt die drei vorausgehenden zusammen im Blick auf die Leiblichkeit ..." (Lang 1986:234).

[10] Wolff (1982:199) emphasises that "... πνευματικός hier nicht substanzhaft verstanden ist ... Der pneumatische Auferstehungsleib ist als durch und durch vom göttlichen Geist beherrschter Leib nach V. 45 eine Schöpfung Christi, der 'lebendigmachender Geist' ist". Cf also Wolff 1982:200, see note 274.

[11] This emphasis has probably been caused by the absence in Corinth of this concept of a spiritual body. Wolff (1982:200) draws the attention to the fact that Paul also dissociates himself from the very realistic expectation of the resurrection in the rabbinical witnesses: "Nach Gen. rabba 28 zu 6,7 schafft Gott den Auferstehungsleib aus dem untersten Wirbel des Rückgrats, weil dieser unzerstörbar ist ... ."

[12] Lietzmann-Kümmel (1969:84) consider v 44b not as a conclusion from what has been said thus far, but as a thesis being proved in the following verses.

[13] Klauck (1986:119) remarks that the conditional sentence of verse 44c may be an allusion to Jesus' resurrection as the only example thus far for the realised transition "... von psychischer zu pneumatischer Leiblichkeit".

1986:235). He quotes from Gen 2,7.[14] With the important additions πρῶτος and 'Αδάμ he contrasts this citation with Christ as the last Adam.[15] Adam was subjected to temporariness. Ψυχή must be interpreted against the background of verses 42b—43. Paul's formulation of this verse reflects his belief that temporariness is a reality since creation.[16] The imperfection of the present world (Adam, the first man) is seen as opposed to the eschatological new creation. The second part of the verse, although crucial to the argumentation here, no longer belongs to the citation. However, this is not discernable from the way in which this passage has been formulated, as the predicate occurs in the first part of the verse (cf also Rom 10,6—7).

To the citation from Scripture Paul relates, therefore, a christological affirmation as the consequence of the divine plan of salvation according to the Adam-Christ typology: The last Adam became *a life-giving Spirit* (Lang 1986:235). Paul focuses here on the resurrected, exalted Jesus Christ, who is active through his Spirit. By calling Christ the ἔσχατος Adam, his *eschatological* importance is accentuated. The resurrection of Jesus is not

---

[14] Conzelmann (1981:337—8) points out how Gen 2,7 (LXX) has been altered by Paul and the meaning, therefore, completely changed: 1. By adding πρῶτος "man" is interpreted typologically. 2. By adding "Adam", "... sein Characker [ist] als 'Urmensch' angedeutet". 3. Through the antithesis ψυχή—πνεῦμα which is not present in the Old Testament text, Adam occurs as antitype. This thought is then developed further. Conzelmann also remarks that Paul stands within an already existing exegetical tradition. This exegesis can not be deduced from the Old Testament, nor is it Paul's own creation. "Allerdings formt er seine Tradition nach seiner eigenen Christologie und Eschatologie selbständig um."

[15] As to the religio-historical background to Paul's exegesis, cf for example: Conzelmann (1981:338—42); Klauck (1984:119); Lietzmann-Kümmel (1967:84—6); Wolff (1982:202—3, see especially note 286 for further references).

Wolff (1982:202) remarks: "*Philon*, De opificio mundi 134 f., unterscheidet bei der Exegese von Gen. 2,7 den 'jetzt gebildeten Menschen' von dem 'früher nach dem Bild Gottes gewordenen' (Gen. 1,27). Viele Ausleger sehen in dieser Unterscheidung den Hintergrund der paulinischen Polemik. Dies ist aber kaum zutreffend ... ." He correctly points out that Paul formulates in v 46 in the neutrum and not in the masculine. Heavenly man is not understood eschatologically by Philo. Paul does not refer to Gen 1,27 at all, while Philo portrays the man of Gen 1,27 as an intelligent entity, as pure idea. It must be agreed with Wolff that due to the few witnesses other than Philo and the uncertainty of their dates of origin it is difficult to conclude that "... eine mythologische Vorstellung zweier sich gegensätzlich gegenüberstehender Urmenschen in neutestamentlicher Zeit bekannt und verbreitet war. Aus Philons Schrifttum läßt sich das jedenfalls kaum zwingend belegen".

[16] Wolff (1982:201, cf also note 278). In Rom 5,12 death is seen as a result of sin. Both perspectives are also to be found in the Old Testament (cf Wolff 1973:170—5).

seen as an isolated event, but as an event with profound consequences for the believer: The Resurrected is creatively active in his pneumatic existence — or even more accurately: Through him God is, in accordance to Gen 1,2, active as creator (cf v 22). Christ is then understood as the eschatological creative mediator. In this way Christ is contrasted to Adam, the creature.[17]

10.4 Conclusion

In this pericope the eschatological new creation is contrasted with the imperfection of the present world. Δύναμις together with δόξα and ἀφθαρσία *belongs to this eschatological new creation.*

The fundamental breach between the present earthly existence and the eschatological new creation can only be bridged by God's wonderful creative power (cf the divine passives, vv 42b—44a). The motive of "reviving/live-giving", therefore, plays a crucial part in this pericope expressed by words such as ἀνάστασις (v 42), ἐγείρεται (vv 42.43.44), ζῳοποιοῦν (v 45).

This pericope specifically focuses on one aspect of the eschatological new creation: the σῶμα πνευματικόν. The fourth antithesis (v 44a) summarises the three preceding ones (Lang 1986:234). The pneumatic resurrected body is according to verse 45a creation of Christ, who is *a life-giving spirit*. Paul focuses here on the resurrected, exalted Jesus Christ, who is active through his Spirit. In the present the Spirit anticipates the future glory.

---

[17] Wolff (1982:201) correctly points to the significance of the present participle ζῳοποιοῦν: "Paulus weiß, daß der lebenschaffende Geist des Kyrios bereits in der Gegenwart wirkt [2. Kor 3,6.17 f; Kommentar dazu ist 2. Kor 4,8 ff; vgl. ferner 2. Kor 5,17]; das Pneuma wirkt in der Gegenwart auf die kommende Herrlichkeit hin, die sich wiederum ganz dem Pneuma verdankt."

Chapter 11

1 Corinthians 15,56

The use of δύναμις in 1 Cor 15,56 is unique in the main Pauline letters, because it is the only case in which δύναμις (in the sense of power) is not related to God, Jesus Christ (the "gospel", the "message of the cross") or the Holy Spirit, as Paul speaks here of ἡ ... δύναμις τῆς ἁμαρτίας ὁ νόμος.

This expression of Paul occurs in a context, as already pointed out in the preceding chapter, dealing with the resurrection of believers (1 Cor 15:1—58). The climax of the pericope, 1 Cor 15,50—58, is reached with verse 55: "Where, o death, is your victory?
Where, o death, is your sting?"[1]

The final words of the taunt in verse 55 apparently touch on a theological cord that must be given a moment's hearing. By using a step-parallelism, Paul moves from the final line of the Hosea "quotation" to a brief compendium of his own theology as to the relationship of sin and the law to death. Not only has death been overcome by resurrection; but "mutatis mutandis" so have the enemies that have brought death to all — sin and the law (Fee 1987:805).[2]

---

[1] Scholars such as J Weiss, W Bousset and Moffat have argued that this verse is a gloss, either by Paul himself at a later time or by a later editor. (Cf also the conjecture by Straatman mentioned in the textcritical apparatus of Nestle-Aland [twenty-seventh edition].) This view can not be accepted. Verse 56 is "... durchaus paulinisch formuliert und widerspricht nicht dem Gedankengang" (Wolff 1982:209).

[2] Cf Lang (1986:241): "... nun zeigt er [Paulus:PJG] hier mit zwei knappen, thesenartigen Sätzen an, daß nach seiner Theologie die Totenauferstehung nicht von Sünde und Gesetz und von der Rechtfertigung durch den stellvertretenden Sühnetod Christi getrennt werden kann".

Paul formulates in verses 55b—56:

ποῦ σου, θάνατε, τὸ κέντρον·
τὸ δὲ κέντρον τοῦ θανάτου ἡ ἁμαρτία,
ἡ δὲ δύναμις τῆς ἁμαρτίας ὁ νόμος·[3]

In the theology of Paul sin is the deadly poison[4] that has lead to death (Fee 1987:805). Despite the fact that this word group has not occurred frequently in the letter to describe the Corinthian behavioural aberrations, there can be no question that Paul considered their actions sinful and in need of divine forgiveness. The word occurs with greater frequency in chapter 15. The reason Christ died is "... for our sins" (v 3) and "... if Christ has not been raised ... you are still in your sins" (v 17). In verse 34 the Corinthians are urged to "... stop sinning". The full explication of this sentence emerges in Paul's letter to the Romans.[5]

In the gentile community, addressed by this letter, the relationship of sin to the law has not seemed to emerge as a problem.[6] The essential matters that surface in a thoroughgoing way in Galatians, and are spelled out at length in Romans, had been essential to Paul's theology long before the Judaising controversy erupted (in the form in which we know it from Galatians). Its point is simple, and is spelled out in detail in Rom 7: The relationship of law to sin is that the former is what gives the latter its power. In Rom 5,13 Paul explains that sin is not taken into account when there is no law. The law not only makes sin observable as sin, but also, and more significantly, demonstrates that one's actions are finally against God, and thus lead to condemnation (cf 2 Cor 3,6). The law, which is good, functions as the agent of sin because it either leads to pride of achievement, on the one hand, or reveals the depth of one's depravity and rebellion

---

[3] Note the chiastic construction of verses 55b and 56a: ... θάνατε ... κέντρον ... κέντρον ... θανάτου ... .

[4] The word κέντρον is used of a "goad" (Acts 26,14; Pr 16,3) and may be so intended by the LXX translator. It is also used of the sting of insects (4 Mac 14,19) and scorpions (Rev 9,10) and is probably the sense that Paul is picking up here (Fee 1987:805; cf also Lang 1986:241).

[5] Klauck (1984:122) mentions that one has to say, "... daß Paulus in änigmatischer Kürze, als Chiffre nur, einen Gedankengang hinwirft, mit dem er sich schon länger beschäftigt hat und den er im Römerbrief erst entfalten wird".

[6] "Ein Nomismus der Korinther ist im Brief ... nicht nachzuweisen" (Wolff 1982:209).

against God, on the other. In either case it becomes death-dealing instead of life-giving.

Paul's point in this theological aside is that death is not simply the result of decay through normal human processes. It is the result of the deadly poison, sin itself, which became all the more energised in our lives through acquaintance with the law. Hence, in exulting in Christ's victory over death, Paul is reminded that that victory is the *final* triumph over the sin that brought death into the world, and over the law that has emboldened sin. But since both sin and the law have already been overcome in the cross, this compendium prefaces a final doxology[7] that thanks God for present "victory" as well (cf Fee 1987:806—7).

11.1 Conclusion

1 Cor 15,56 has profound implications for our study of Paul's use of δύναμις especially in a soteriological context.[8] In the final section of this study (chapter 23.2) Paul's use of δύναμις in 1 Cor 15,56 will be related to other passages such as (*inter alia*) 1 Cor 1,18.

---

[7] This doxology is found in v 57.

[8] The issue of "Paul and the law" has just been touched upon in the discussion of 1 Cor 15,56. A more detailed treatment of this issue lies beyond the scope of this study. For some recent literature on this subject, cf Fee (1987:806 note 47).

Chapter 12

2 Corinthians 4,7

12.1 Introduction

A very *close relation* exists between 2 Cor 4,7—5,10 and the preceding pericope, 3,4—4,6.[1] Phrases consisting of ἔχειν and a demonstrative pronoun occur prominently throughout both pericopes.

3,4	... δὲ τοιαύτην ἔχομεν ...
3,12	Ἔχοντες οὖν τοιαύτην ...
4,1	... ἔχοντες τὴν ... ταύτην ...
4,7	Ἔχομεν δὲ τὸν ... τοῦτον ...
4,13	ἔχοντες δὲ τὸ αὐτό ...

Words and phrases pertaining to confidence, boldness, not losing heart ... also *connect* these two pericopes

3,4	Πεποίθησιν δὲ τοιαύτην ἔχομεν ...
3,12	Ἔχοντες οὖν τοιαύτην ἐλπίδα πολλῇ παρρησίᾳ χρώμεθα
4,1	Διὰ τοῦτο, ἔχοντες τὴν διακονίαν ταύτην ... οὐκ ἐγκακοῦμεν
4,16	Διὸ οὐκ ἐγκακοῦμεν ...
5,6	Θαρροῦντες οὖν ...
5,8	θαρροῦμεν ...

Despite the close relation between 2 Cor 3,4—4,6 and 4,7—5,10, the present writer is of the opinion that we have to do with two separate pericopes. The pericope 2 Cor 3,4—4,6 is introduced by the phrase πεποίθησιν δὲ τοιαύτην ἔχομεν. Internal cohesion within this pericope is

---

[1] This broader context will therefore be taken into account in the concluding section (12.5).

evident from the structural markers occurring throughout it (cf 12.3 & 12.3.1). Beginning in 4,7 another and special subject is present, initially formulated as the suffering of apostles (4,8—9), then enlarged to the topic of mortality (4,11) and thereafter further extended to include the situation of all believers (4,18—5,10) (Furnish 1984:277). The words εἰδότες οὖν clearly introduce a new pericope in 5,11.

12.2 Location within the macrocontext of 2 Corinthians 1—9[2]

2 Cor 1—9 can be divided as follows:

1,1—2	Letter-opening: sender(s), recipients, salutation
1,3—7	Thanksgiving
1,8—11	Body-opening: Paul's adventures
1,12—2,13	*Assurances of concern*
1,12—2,4	Paul's cancelled visit and the "tearful letter"
2,5—11	Forgiveness for the transgressor
2,12—13	Beginning of the account of Titus' arrival
2,14—17,4	*Defence of the apostolic ministry*
2,14—13,3	Introduction
3,4—4,6	Ministers of a new covenant of glory
4,7—5,10	"We have this treasure in jars of clay to show that this all-surpassing power is from God and not from us" — reflections on Paul's apostolic ministry, beset with afflictions, but accomplished with confidence and commitment within the perspective of the eschatological fulfilment.
5,11—6,2	The apostolic office as service of reconciliation
6,3—10	A commendable ministry in the midst of many afflictions by the power of God

---

[2] The majority of exegetes today assume that 2 Corinthians comprises two (or perhaps three) letters: chapters 1—9 and 10—13 (or 1—8.9.10—13). An argumentation of the question of the unity of 2 Corinthians falls beyond the scope of this study. Thrall (1994:3—49) offers an extensive discussion and a useful survey of major critical theories (pp 47—9). Considerations in favour of the unity of the letter are discussed by Lambrecht (1999:9). The reader is also referred to the in-depth discussion by Bieringer (1994:67—179).

6,11—7,4   Apostolic appeal

7,5—16   *Titus' return*

8,1—9,15   *The collection for the church in Jerusalem*
                 (cf Furnish 1984:xi & xii; Klauck 1986:13—4; Lam-
                 brecht 1999:10—1; Lang 1986; Lategan 1985:87—8;
                 Windisch [1924] 1970:xi; Thrall 1994:xiii—xiv)

The pericope 4,7—5,10 forms part of the larger section (2 Cor 2,14—7,4)
in which Paul defends his *apostolic ministry*.

12.3 Discourse analysis: 2 Corinthians 4,7—5,10

Chapter 4

7   1   Ἔχομεν δὲ τὸν θησαυρὸν τοῦτον ἐν ὀστρακίνοις σκεύεσιν,
         ἵνα ἡ ὑπερβολὴ τῆς δυνάμεως ᾖ τοῦ θεοῦ καὶ μὴ ἐξ ἡμῶν·
8   2   ἐν παντὶ θλιβόμενοι
     3   ἀλλ' οὐ στενοχωρούμενοι,
     4   ἀπορούμενοι
     5   ἀλλ' οὐκ ἐξαπορούμενοι,
9   6   διωκόμενοι
     7   ἀλλ' οὐκ ἐγκαταλειπόμενοι,
     8   καταβαλλόμενοι   A
     9   ἀλλ' οὐκ ἀπολλύμενοι,
10   10 πάντοτε τὴν νέκρωσιν τοῦ Ἰησοῦ ἐν τῷ σώματι περιφέροντες,
         ἵνα καὶ ἡ ζωὴ τοῦ Ἰησοῦ ἐν τῷ σώματι ἡμῶν φανερωθῇ.
11   11 ἀεὶ γὰρ ἡμεῖς οἱ ζῶντες εἰς θάνατον παραδιδόμεθα διὰ Ἰησοῦν,
         ἵνα καὶ ἡ ζωὴ τοῦ Ἰησοῦ φανερωθῇ ἐν τῇ θνητῇ σαρκὶ ἡμῶν.
12   12 ὥστε ὁ θάνατος ἐν ἡμῖν ἐνεργεῖται,
     13 ἡ δὲ ζωὴ ἐν ὑμῖν.

13 14 ἔχοντες δὲ τὸ αὐτὸ πνεῦμα τῆς πίστεως, κατὰ τὸ γεγραμμένον,

'Επίστευσα, διὸ ἐλάλησα,

καὶ ἡμεῖς πιστεύομεν, διὸ καὶ λαλοῦμεν,

14 εἰδότες ὅτι ὁ ἐγείρας τὸν κύριον 'Ιησοῦν καὶ ἡμᾶς σὺν 'Ιησοῦ ἐγερεῖ   B

καὶ παραστήσει σὺν ὑμῖν.

15 15 τὰ γὰρ πάντα δι' ὑμᾶς,

ἵνα ἡ χάρις πλεονάσασα διὰ τῶν πλειόνων τὴν εὐχαριστίαν περισσεύσῃ

εἰς τὴν δόξαν τοῦ θεοῦ.

16 16 Διὸ οὐκ ἐγκακοῦμεν,

17 ἀλλ' εἰ καὶ ὁ ἔξω ἡμῶν ἄνθρωπος διαφθείρεται,

ἀλλ' ὁ ἔσω ἡμῶν ἀνακαινοῦται ἡμέρᾳ καὶ ἡμέρᾳ.

17 18 τὸ γὰρ παραυτίκα ἐλαφρὸν τῆς θλίψεως ἡμῶν   C

καθ' ὑπερβολὴν εἰς ὑπερβολὴν αἰώνιον βάρος δόξης κατεργάζεται ἡμῖν,

18 19 μὴ σκοπούντων ἡμῶν τὰ βλεπόμενα ἀλλὰ τὰ μὴ βλεπόμενα·

20 τὰ γὰρ βλεπόμενα πρόσκαιρα,

21 τὰ δὲ μὴ βλεπόμενα αἰώνια.

Chapter 5

1 22 Οἴδαμεν γὰρ ὅτι ἐὰν ἡ ἐπίγειος ἡμῶν οἰκία τοῦ σκήνους καταλυθῇ,

οἰκοδομὴν ἐκ θεοῦ ἔχομεν

οἰκίαν ἀχειροποίητον αἰώνιον ἐν τοῖς οὐρανοῖς.

2 23 καὶ γὰρ ἐν τούτῳ στενάζομεν,

τὸ οἰκητήριον ἡμῶν τὸ ἐξ οὐρανοῦ ἐπενδύσασθαι ἐπιποθοῦντες,

3 24 εἴ γε καὶ ἐνδυσάμενοι   D

οὐ γυμνοὶ εὑρεθησόμεθα.

4 25 καὶ γὰρ οἱ ὄντες ἐν τῷ σκήνει στενάζομεν βαρούμενοι,

ἐφ' ᾧ οὐ θέλομεν ἐκδύσασθαι ἀλλ' ἐπενδύσασθαι,

ἵνα καταποθῇ τὸ θνητὸν ὑπὸ τῆς ζωῆς.

5 26 ὁ δὲ κατεργασάμενος ἡμᾶς εἰς αὐτὸ τοῦτο θεός,

ὁ δοὺς ἡμῖν τὸν ἀρραβῶνα τοῦ πνεύματος.

6   27 Θαρροῦντες οὖν πάντοτε
        καὶ εἰδότες ὅτι ἐνδημοῦντες ἐν τῷ σώματι
        ἐκδημοῦμεν ἀπὸ τοῦ κυρίου,

7   28 διὰ πίστεως γὰρ περιπατοῦμεν
        οὐ διὰ εἴδους -

8   29 θαρροῦμεν
        30 δὲ καὶ εὐδοκοῦμεν μᾶλλον ἐκδημῆσαι ἐκ τοῦ σώματος   **E**
        καὶ ἐνδημῆσαι πρὸς τὸν κύριον.

9   31 διὸ καὶ φιλοτιμούμεθα,
        εἴτε ἐνδημοῦντες εἴτε ἐκδημοῦντες,
        εὐάρεστοι αὐτῷ εἶναι.

10   32 τοὺς γὰρ πάντας ἡμᾶς φανερωθῆναι
        δεῖ ἔμπροσθεν τοῦ βήματος τοῦ Χριστοῦ,
        ἵνα κομίσηται ἕκαστος τὰ διὰ τοῦ σώματος πρὸς ἃ ἔπραξεν,
        εἴτε ἀγαθὸν εἴτε φαῦλον.

Headings of the pericope and sub-pericopes

Pericope heading: "We have this treasure in jars of clay to show that this all-surpassing power is from God and not from us" — reflections on Paul's apostolic ministry beset with afflictions, but accomplished with confidence and commitment within the perspective of the eschatological fulfilment.

Sub-pericope A: "We have this treasure in jars of clay to show that this all-surpassing power is from God and not from us" — a ministry beset with hardships interpreted from the perspective of the death and resurrection of Jesus.

Sub-pericopes B: Speaking by faith on the ground of the certainty of the resurrection.

Sub-pericope C: We do not lose heart: Renewal day by day despite the fact that we are wasting away. The eschatological perspective.

Sub-pericope D: The heavenly dwelling — certainty and sighing.

Sub-pericope E: Confidence and commitment — an eschatological perspective: The confidence of a life lived by faith and committed to pleasing the Lord.

12.3.1 A few notes pertaining to the structure of 2 Corinthians 4,7—5,10 with special reference to actants and structural markers

Actants and structural markers occurring throughout the pericope:

God

4,7	τοῦ θεοῦ
4,15	τοῦ θεοῦ
5,1	θεοῦ
5,5	θεός

Jesus Christ

4,10	τοῦ ᾽Ιησοῦ
4,11	᾽Ιησοῦν
4,11	τοῦ ᾽Ιησοῦ
4,14	τὸν κύριον ᾽Ιησοῦν ...᾽Ιησοῦ
5,6	τοῦ κυρίου
5,8	τὸν κύριον
5,9	αὐτῷ
5,10	τοῦ Χριστοῦ

Holy Spirit

4,13	πνεῦμα
5,5	τὸν ἀρραβῶνα τοῦ πνεύματος

Glory

4,15	δόξαν
4,17	δόξης

The above-mentioned structural markers are also important structural markers of the previous pericope (3,4—4,6).

Faith

4,13	πίστεως
4,13	᾽Επίστευσα
4,13	πιστεύομεν

5,7   πίστεως
ὑπερβολή

4,7   ὑπερβολή
4,17   ὑπερβολὴν εἰς ὑπερβολήν

Constructions with ἀλλά are also noteworthy:

4,8 & 9   ἐν παντὶ θλιβόμενοι ἀλλ' οὐ στενοχωρούμενοι,
            ἀπορούμενοι ἀλλ' οὐκ ἐξαπορούμενοι,
            διωκόμενοι ἀλλ' οὐκ ἐγκαταλειπόμενοι,
            καταβαλλόμενοι ἀλλ' οὐκ ἀπολλύμενοι

4,16   Διὸ οὐκ ἐγκακοῦμεν,
            ἀλλ' εἰ καὶ ὁ ἔξω ἡμῶν ἄνθρωπος διαφθείρεται,
            ἀλλ' ὁ ἔσω ἡμῶν ἀνακαινοῦται ἡμέρα καὶ ἡμέρα.

Note the following *contrasting notions* which occur successively in the
different sub-pericopes:

(i)   *Treasure* (θησαυρόν) in *jars of clay* (ἐν ὀστρακίνοις σκεύεσιν) (4,7)

(ii)   *Death*   *life*
        νέκρωσιν   ζωή (4,10)
        οἱ ζῶντες   θάνατον (4,11)
        ζωή   θνητῇ (4,11)
        θάνατος   ζωή (4,12)

(iii)   *Outer person is wasting away ... inner is being renewed*
        ὁ ἔξω ... ἄνθρωπος διαφθείρεται ... ὁ ἔσω ... ἀνακαινοῦται (4,16)

(iv)   *Light and momentary troubles ... fulness of eternal glory*
        τὸ ... παραυτίκα ἐλαφρὸν τῆς θλίψεως ... αἰώνιον βάρος δόξης

(v)   *The seen ...*   *the unseen*
        τὰ βλεπόμενα   τὰ μὴ βλεπόμενα (4,18)
        τὰ βλεπόμενα   μὴ βλεπόμενα (4,18)

(vi)   *Momentary/temporary ... eternal*
        παραυτίκα   αἰώνιον (4,17)
        πρόσκαιρα   αἰώνια (4,18)

In 5,1—5 the following concepts play a very important role:

(vii) (a) *House, dwelling, tent, building*

in connection with earthly ...	heavenly:
ἡ ἐπίγειος ... οἰκία τοῦ σκήνους ...	οἰκοδομὴν ἐκ θεοῦ ... οἰκίαν ἀχειροποίητον αἰώνιον ἐν τοῖς οὐρανοῖς (5,1)
τὸ οἰκητήριον ... τὸ ἐξ οὐρανοῦ	

(b) *Be unclothed* ...

	put on, wear, be (fully) clothed
ἐκδυσάμενοι (5,3)	ἐπενδύσασθαι (5,2)
ἐκδύσασθαι (5,4)	ἐπενδύσασθαι (5,4)

(Note the prominent occurrence of στενάζομεν within this sub-pericope: 5,2.4.)

(viii) *Be at home* ...   *be away from home*

ἐνδημοῦντες	ἐκδημοῦμεν (5,6)
ἐνδημῆσαι	ἐκδημῆσαι (5,8)
ἐνδημοῦντες	ἐκδημοῦντες (5,9)

(ix) *Body* ...   *Lord* (in connection with ἐκδημεῖν/ἐνδημεῖν)

σώματι	κυρίου (5,6)
σώματος	τὸν κύριον (5,8)

"Christ" and "body" also occur in 5,10 (not in connection with ἐκδημεῖν/ἐνδημεῖν)

Χριστοῦ	σώματος

(x) *Faith* ...   *Sight*

πίστεως	εἴδους

The ἵνα-*phrases* also play an important role within this pericope:

4,7: ... ἵνα ἡ ὑπερβολὴ τῆς δυνάμεως ᾖ τοῦ θεοῦ ...

4,10: .. ἵνα καὶ ἡ ζωὴ τοῦ Ἰησοῦ ἐν τῷ σώματι ἡμῶν φανερωθῇ.

4,11: ... ἵνα καὶ ἡ ζωὴ τοῦ Ἰησοῦ φανερωθῇ ἐν τῇ θνητῇ σαρκὶ ἡμῶν.

  (Note the parallelism as well as chiastic construction:

  ἐν τῷ σώματι ἡμῶν φανερωθῇ [4,10]

  φανερωθῇ ἐν τῇ θνητῇ σαρκὶ ἡμῶν [4,11])

4,15: ... ἵνα ἡ χάρις πλεονάσασα ...

(Lambrecht [1986:123] correctly mentions that all of these purpose clauses possess something of a "conclusion". They point to the purpose and consequence of a particular situation, attitude and activity. Cf also verse 12, introduced by ὥστε.)

5,4:   ... ἵνα καταποθῇ τὸ θνητὸν ὑπὸ τῆς ζωῆς

5,10:   ... ἵνα κομίσηται ἕκαστος ...

The *double expression of confidence* within the last sub-pericope is also noteworthy:

Θαρροῦντες (5,6)

θαρροῦμεν (5,8)

Note also the important relation between *present* and *future* in this pericope:

Verses 7—11 deal with the paradoxical fact that, notwithstanding the appearance to the contrary (persecution, oppression fear, the wasting away of the body, death), the very life of Jesus is already breaking through and manifesting itself in the present.

In verses 13—14 it is stated that Paul is proclaiming the gospel now because he possesses the same Spirit of faith (as the psalmist) and because he believes in our *future* resurrection. We are confronted here with an eschatological motivation. With its ἵνα-clause verse 15 likewise opens a further eschatological horizon: the increasing praise and thanksgiving to the glory of God. It is, therefore, also the future which underscores the present; it is also hope to live a resurrection life later, with Christ and fellow-believers, and not only the paradoxical experience of life in the midst of dying, which supports the apostle in his present suffering ministry (Lambrecht 1986:126).

12.4 An exegetical overview

12.4.1 Introduction

The meaning of this pericope can only be grasped fully if it is seen against the background of the very close connection with the previous pericope (cf Lambrecht 1986:122—3). The attention has already been drawn to the structural markers linking these two pericopes. At the same time 2 Cor 4,7—5,10 is an integral part of the discussion of apostolic service opened in 2,14.

12.4.2 Sub-pericope A (2 Cor 4,7—12)

Paul acknowledges that his sufferings and those of his apostolic associates might be (and probably have been) taken by some as invalidating their claim to be ministers of a new covenant of surpassing glory (3,7—4,6). In 4,7—12 Paul interprets these mortal adversities as an integral and appropriate part of true apostleship (cf Patte 1987:49). He continues with a reiteration of the boldness of his apostolate (v 16) and comments on the nature and meaning of Christian hope in general.

2 Cor 4,7 states *the thesis* of this pericope. The image used by Paul ("jars of clay"), had wide currency in the ancient world, not only in the apostle's own Jewish tradition but also in the literature of the broader Hellenistic society, both Greek and Roman (cf *inter alia* Furnish 1984:253). Pottery vessels are cheap but fragile, and therefore they are of no enduring value (cf Bishop 1971:3—5). Within this context Paul is using the image of a jar of clay to describe his mortal existence and that of his apostolic associates, their humanity as it is subject to the ravages of time and adversity (vv 8—9), their ἔξω ἄνθρωπος that "is being wasted away" (v 16). With this metaphor Paul seems to focus on two aspects: Because he contrasts these "jars of clay" with the "treasure" they contain, it seems clear, firstly that he has in mind the great value of the one and the trifling value of the other. Secondly, the frailty and vulnerability to breakage and destruction must be equally in view, because it is precisely the mortality of this earthly existence that is emphasised in the following verses.[3] The idea we find in ἐν ὀστρακίνοις σκεύεσιν (4,7) seems to be taken up in a number of expressions: ἐν τῷ σώματι (ἡμῶν) (v 10), ἐν τῇ θνητῇ σαρκὶ ἡμῶν (v 11) and ἐν ἡμῖν (v 12) (Lambrecht 1986:125; 1999:71).

It is to be noted that as much as Paul could share the general Hellenistic view about human mortality (which was equally at home in the Jewish tradition), his intention in this pericope is not to contrast "our

---

[3] Cf Klauck 1986:45: "Die zerbrechlichen [wörtlich: 'irdenen'] Gefäße sind ein Hinweis auf die Hinfälligkeit des Menschen, der aus Lehm von der Erde gebildet wurde [Gen 2[7]; Jes 64[7]]." A similar statement as Paul's is to be found in Sen Dial 6,11,3 (quoted by Klauck 1986:45).

On the background to the imagery of "earthenware containers", cf Thrall (1994:322—4).

mortal body" with "our immortal soul". In accordance with his Jewish heritage, the apostle regards the body, mortal as it is, as a constituent part of the total human being (Furnish 1984:279).

The treasure mentioned by Paul in verse 7 is the ministry of the new covenant with everything associated with it: the proclamation of the gospel, the knowledge, the glory, the transformation, the illumination of the heart. These are all building blocks of a *theologia gloriae*, summarised by the expression ὑπερβολὴ τῆς δυνάμεως (Klauck 1986:44—5; cf also Lambrecht 1986:135).

An interesting view is that of Hanson (1987:43—4) who interprets "the treasure" in this context by relating it (with reference to Mt 19,21 and Lk 12,34) to the teaching of Jesus:

> "In Jesus' teaching, then, the treasure is the kingdom, and in Paul's thought the treasure is the knowledge of God in Christ attainable by the coming of the kingdom through the life, death, and resurrection of Jesus Christ ... it seems to me by no means beyond the bounds of possibility that as Paul wrote the fourth chapter of Second Corinthians he had in mind a corpus of dominical teaching known to him by oral tradition, and that he is transposing into the conditions of the new age, after the death and resurrection of the Messiah, the teaching that was originally given by Jesus to his disciples to prepare them for the coming of the kingdom."

The main point Paul wants to make in 4,7 is that the frailty of the apostles is a demonstration of the essential point, *"... that this all-surpassing power might be seen to be[4] God's[5] and not from us"*. Earlier in this same letter Paul has mentioned that the recent threat to his life experienced in Asia had taught him not to rely on self, but on *God* (1,9), and here one sees that realization now formulated as a principle applicable to apostolic service in general. The same principle is apparent in 12,9b, in another form in 3,5—6 ("... not that we are competent to claim anything for ourselves, but our competence comes from God. He has made us competent ..."), and again

---

[4] Thrall (1994:324 n 923) points out that there is support for the sense "might be seen to be" (Greek: ᾖ). Logically speaking the plain "might be" cannot be what Paul intends.

[5] *Lambrecht* (1999:71—2) prefers the translation "God's" and not "from God".

in 13,4b, in which verse Paul contrasts the weakness of the apostles with the power of God, at the same time affirming an important relation between the two (cf 2 Cor 4,7). In both 2 Cor 13 and 2 Cor 4 (vv 10—11) the weakness of the apostles is related to the weakness of Christ seen in his crucifixion (Furnish 1984:279).

The intimate connection between the true nature of the gospel and the manner in which it is borne in Paul's theology is also evident in this passage (cf Lambrecht 1986:124—5.136—42). Paul's interpretation of the meaning of the adversities by which apostles are beset, is dependent upon his understanding of the gospel they preach. The gospel is God's "power for salvation" (Rom 1,16) present in "the message of the cross" (1 Cor 1,18.24). Therefore Paul had written in an earlier letter that the weakness, fear, and trembling with which he had brought the gospel to Corinth in the first place had allowed a full "demonstration of the Spirit's power", that the Corinthians' faith "might not rest on men's wisdom, but on God's power" (1 Cor 2,3—5).[6]

The catalogue of hardships in 4,8—9 (to be compared with similar catalogues in 6,4c—5; 11,23b—29; 12,10; Rom 8,35; 1 Cor 4,9—13) has been formulated into a series of antitheses, and these serve to illustrate not just the weakness of apostles but *how that weakness discloses the incomparable power of God.* The distance in meaning between both halves of these antitheses is very close (cf especially v 8b where the same verb stem in used: ἀπορούμενοι ... οὐκ ἐξαπορούμενοι). The question arises how these antitheses have to be interpreted. Of importance here is the broader context: The contrasts in verses 8—9 are taken up and given theological grounding in verses 10—11. The most natural interpretation is therefore, to suppose that, whilst the first half of each contrast corresponds to the death of Jesus, the second half corresponds to the manifestation of Jesus' life, which is a revelation of the transcendent power of God. In the midst of

---

[6] Hübner (1993:222) points to the Old Testament background of this passage and refers specifically to Old Testament prophets (e g Jr) who had to suffer, because of the message God gave them to proclaim.

weakness and dying the apostle experienced much victory, power and glory (Thrall 1994:330—1).[7]

Although Stoic statements[8] may formally appear to be very close to Paul's, the presuppositions and intentions which underlie Paul's list of hardships in 4,8—9 are quite different. He does not share the Stoic ideal of training oneself to look upon afflictions as insignificant and inconsequential. Paul does not speak of "happiness" in the midst of adversity (Epictetus) or of remaining "invincible" in the face of hardships (Plutarch), but rather of being comforted in his afflictions (1,4—7; 7,6—13) and rescued from them (1,10).

For Epictetus, "It is difficulties that show what men are" (I.xxiv.1), because difficulties must be met and overcome with the disciplined power of reason and with courage. For Paul, however, difficulties must be met and borne with *faith*. When there is faith, hardships and difficulties become an occasion for the disclosure of God. Within the perspective of the fundamental conception which underlies Paul's catalogues of hardships, these difficulties disclose not "what men are" but "… *that this all-surpassing power is God's and not from us*".

Various examples of hardship lists may also be found in the literature of apocalyptic Judaism as Schrage (1974:143—6) has pointed out.[9] These are, in general, recitals of the present tribulations endured by the righteous as they wait, hoping for eschatological deliverance from their suffering and for divine retribution against their oppressors (e g 1 En 103,9—15; 1 QH 9,6—7; 2 En 66,6; Furnish 1984:282). It is true that because of the theological presuppositions, ethical concerns and general eschatological perspective, these Jewish lists bear a greater resemblance to Paul's lists than to those of the Stoics (cf Lambrecht 1999:77). In 1 QH 9,3 ff for example, the psalmist praises God for the consolation which comes from the manifestation of God's divine grace and power in the midst of suffering.

---

[7] Margaret Thrall (1994:331) refers here to Lambrecht (1986:131). She discusses various interpretations of these antitheses (Rissi, Bultmann and Theobald) where there is a tendency to assert that what is changed is not the situation, but simply the sufferer's attitude towards it (e g in Bultmann's view). Thrall correctly affirms that to say power is found within a situation of weakness is not to say that power *is* weakness. The "visibility" of those aspects of Paul's experience which he attributed to the power of God may not be eliminated.

[8] Cf *inter alia* Furnish (1984:281) where Seneca and Plutarch amongst others are quoted.

[9] He mentions i a: 2 En 66,6 and Jub 23,13.

Elsewhere, he is even able to attribute the violence perpetrated against him to God's will, "… that Thou mayest be glorified/by the judgment of the wicked,/and manifest Thy might through me" (1 QH 2,23—25). Barré (1975:516) points out that nowhere, neither in the Qumran hymns nor in the New Testament, can one find a clearer expression of God's causative involvement with the suffering of the persecuted just man than in this passage. (Cf also 1 QH 5,25: "… to manifest Thy might within me".)

The distinctiveness of the Pauline conception must, however, be noted, because the Qumran hymns do not actually speak of the manifestation of God's power in and through suffering as such. As Furnish (1984:282—3) has pointed out, they rather associate suffering closely with God's judgement of those who inflict suffering on the righteous (e g 1 QH 2,23—25) and with God's protection, consolation, and assurances of ultimate deliverance from suffering (e g 1 QH 5,18—19; 9,13.25—26) (cf also Schrage 1974:146—7).

In the final analysis the distinctiveness of Paul's message is to be found in the way in which he interprets his afflictions from the perspective of the gospel which centres on the death and resurrection of Jesus. Paul is oppressed and persecuted, and his body bears many signs of the killing of Jesus. But this is the means of communicating life. Paul's sufferings prove that the life he has, is not his own but belongs to Jesus. His vocation is to enact the pattern of death and resurrection over and over again. The purpose is to absorb affliction, destruction and death, to complete what is lacking of the sufferings of Christ, so as to communicate power, life, the Spirit (Young & Ford 1987:129).

The negative half of the list of antitheses is summarised in verses 10—11 by "death", the positive through "life". Paul interprets the suffering he has to endure in his ministry of proclaiming the gospel as a participation in Jesus' suffering on the cross (cf 2 Cor 1,5). Christ's resurrected life gives him, however, power in the present to endure everything and hope for salvation in the midst of very dark circumstances (cf Klauck 1986:45—6).

The paradox which has been in view since verse 7 — God's power disclosed in the midst of weakness — is sharpened in verse 10b, where Paul states that the "carrying about of the death of Jesus" is for the purpose of revealing his "life". ἡ ζωὴ τοῦ Ἰησοῦ in this context refers to the resurrection life of Jesus (contra Murphy-O'Connor 1988:545).[10] Because of his emphasis on the cross, Paul speaks in this passage about the life of *Jesus* — although he refers to Christ's resurrection life (Klauck 1986:45). When in verses 10, 11 and 14 Paul simply refers to Christ as "Jesus", it looks as if he draws a parallel between his own suffering and hardships and those endured by the earthly Jesus as distinguished from the risen and glorified Lord. The expressions "the life of Jesus" in verses 10b and 11b and "the Lord Jesus" in verse 14 indicate that for Paul the earthly Jesus is not separated from the glorified Christ (Lambrecht 1986:125).

The "*all-surpassing power*" of God (v 7) is manifested above all in God's resurrection of Jesus from the dead (v 14). To be a bearer of Christ's death is to be a bearer of his resurrection too, and that means being an agent for the disclosure of God's power to save. Here Paul is referring specifically to apostles as participants in and bearers of the death and life of Jesus, because his subject here is the meaning and character of the apostolic ministry. Paul writes elsewhere in the same way about all believers as participants in Christ's suffering and death (e g, 1,5—7; 1 Thess 1,6—7), and therefore also bearers of his life — not only in their hope for resurrection with him (e g, Rom 6,5.8; 8,17; Phil 3,10—11) but in their present existence in faith (e g Rom 6,4; Gal 2,19). The manifestation, even now within the community of faith, of the resurrection power of God is seen in the present letter (and even pericope) when the apostle writes of a deposit, guaranteeing what is to come proffered through the Spirit (1,22; 5,5), and of the transformation (3,18), renewal (4,16), and new creation (5,17) which signal the presence of the day of salvation (6,2) (Furnish 1984:283—4).

With παραδιδόμεθα in verse 11 Paul takes up a central word from the passion tradition (Klauck 1986:46). The point of verse 10 is repeated and intensified in verse 11. When Paul writes that apostles "... are always being given over to death" even as they live, he is not thinking of the natural process of ageing (cf Sen Ep xxiv,19: "... we die every day"),[11] but of the adversities which apostles must bear by reason of their serving the gospel,

---

[10] Although a fuller christological title is normally used when Christ's suffering (e g 1,5) and death (e g Rom 6,3; 1 Cor 2,2; Gal 3,1) are in view, the present passage is not the only exception (cf 1 Thess 4,14 and Gal 6,17) (Furnish 1984:256). "Thus Jesus in this context means exactly what is usually meant by the title Christ" (Kramer 1966:200).

[11] Cited by Furnish (1984:284).

"for Jesus' sake".[12] In 12,10 the same point is stressed: The apostle's sufferings are "for Christ's sake" (ὑπὲρ χριστοῦ) in the sense that they are the manifestation of his suffering and death and thus a proclamation of the gospel. The distinctiveness of Paul's thought is seen especially in the purpose-clause of verse 11b which, like the one it parallels in verse 10b, refers to the manifestation of the *resurrection life of Jesus* (and thus of the *all-surpassing power of God* [cf Tannehill 1967:84]), in and through the weakness, suffering, and death of Jesus borne by the apostles. In verse 14 Paul writes of an ultimate resurrection with Jesus, but here (v 11) the reference is first of all to the disclosure of God's power in the apostles' present mortal existence (in our mortal body [cf 6,9 "dying, and yet we live ..."]).

The paradox of death and life is articulated in another way in verse 12, where Paul contrasts "death ... at work" in the apostles with the "life ... at work" in the congregation. The formulation of the paradox here intends to bring out a point Paul stresses repeatedly in 2 Cor 1—9, namely, that the exercise of his ministry is for the sake of those to whom he is an apostle.[13]

> " 'We have this treasure in earthen vessels'. Not earthly fame, but a mirroring of the radiance of God — that is what lies at the heart of Paul's understanding of the apostolic task, and that is what he has been trying to show up to now. But this takes place in the context of a creation which is groaning and travailing, a world under God's wrath, a church in the midst of affliction ... and an apostle constrained by his bodily frame and earthly weaknesses. For Paul, however, this constraint is itself something to exult in; for it shows that his power is derived from God and not from his own resources" (Young & Ford 1987:128).

---

[12] "Die Apostelleiden sind wie die Leiden eines jeden Christen Nachvollzug der Leiden Jesu, und sie ergeben sich als Folge aus der Ausführung eines Auftrags" (Klauck 1986:46).

[13] "Die Leiden, die der Missionar auf sich nimmt um der Verkündigung willen, schaffen Leben für diejenigen, die durch die Predigt zum Glauben kommen ..." (Klauck 1986:46).

12.4.3 Sub-pericope B (2 Cor 4,13-15)

Paul's ministry, which brings him suffering — but life to the congregation — is confirmed by the Spirit, the source of faith.[14] Courage to speak out despite adversity is also the point in 2 Cor 4,13, which also supports the statement about apostolic boldness Paul has already made and will make again. (The reader is referred to the discussion of words and phrases pertaining to confidence, boldness ... in 2 Cor 3,4—4,6 and 4,7—5,10 above [cf the introduction to this chapter].) That 2 Cor 4,13 does not fit loosely in its context (as Windisch asserted)[15] is confirmed by the phrase ἔχοντες δὲ τὸ αὐτό which places this verse in a certain relationship with 3,12; 4,1 and 4,7 (cf introduction). In the midst of distress the persecuted apostle speaks from the power and confidence of faith established by the new covenant and proclaims the gospel in the knowledge of the future resurrection at Christ's *parousia* (cf Lang 1986:282).

What has just been said in verse 12 and the previous verses, is a reality that can only be grasped in faith, the realization of which is still to come, as the traditional sentence of faith in verse 14 affirms. This sentence is enframed by a citation from Scripture (LXX Ps 115) in verse 13 and a doxological view in verse 15, which forms an *inclusio* with verse 7: ὑπερβολὴ τῆς δυνάμεως ... τὴν εὐχαριστίαν περισσεύσῃ.[16]

The affirmation of the resurrection faith in verse 14 shows that for Paul

---

[14] Does the phrase πνεῦμα τῆς πίστεως refer to the Holy Spirit or is πνεῦμα used here as it is in the phrase "spirit of gentleness" in 1 Cor 4,21, Gal 6,1 and does it need to be interpreted as a "disposition" or "impulse", as suggested by Hughes (1962:147 note 15)? As this phrase is used nowhere else by Paul, a definite decision is very difficult to make. Two arguments may be presented for the first possibility: (i) A close connection between "faith" and the Spirit occurs often in the Pauline letters: 1 Cor 12,9 (although faith here, portrayed as a gift of the Spirit has a more restricted meaning), Rom 8,14—16; Gal 3,2.5.14; 5,5; cf 1 Cor 2,4-5; 1 Thess 1,5-7 (cf Collange 1972:162). (ii) The reference to the Spirit in the present verse is in accordance with what Paul has written earlier about the Spirit's work (3,3.6.8.17.18) and with what he will shortly reiterate about the Spirit's presence (5,5; cf 1,22) (Furnish 1984:258, 286). Cf also Klauck (1986:46-7) and Lang (1986:282).

Bultmann (1976:123), however, comments: "... das πνεῦμα bezeichnet im Grunde die Art und Weise des Glaubens ...".

[15] "Von den drei Absätzen des Abschn. 4₁₇₋₁₈ scheint dies Mittelstück [4,13—15:PJG] etwas aus dem Zusammenhang herauszufallen ..." (Windisch [1924] 1970:147).

[16] "... Übermaß der Kraft — überreiche Gnade ..." (Klauck 1986:46).

the new life already disclosed and effective for believers in the present (cf vv 10—12) is not their own spiritual possession.[17] In verse 14a Paul identifies the object of faith (and thus the source of apostolic boldness) as the God "... who raised the Lord Jesus from the dead" and who "... will also raise us with Jesus". To this resurrection credo, Paul has added a comment about God's presentation of "us with you" (v 14b). This being together with his converts in the presence of the Lord will be the crowning evidence not only of the authenticity of their faith but also of the authenticity of those by whom they have come to faith (cf 1,14; Phil 2,16; 1 Thess 2,19).

The notion already implicit in this passage, that dying and being raised again lead the believer into the presence of God, is explicated in more detail in 5,1—10 (Klauck 1986:47).

The comment in verse 15 that "... all this is for your benefit" both expands on "with you" in verse 14 and introduces the conclusion of Paul's supporting argument (vv 13—15) for the statement of verse 12 (cf Bultmann 1976:125). In verse 15 the loftiest goal of Paul's missionary activity is given. It is stated how grace proceeds from God, reaches more and more people through the preaching of the gospel and returns to God in the form of a prayer of thanksgiving. By this reaction to God's grace, the glory of the new covenant comes to the fore as a spontaneous response to exalt him alone (cf Klauck 1986:47).

12.4.4 Sub-pericope C (2 Cor 4,16—18)

The introductory words to 4,16 resume 4,1 in concentrated form, but bear the full impact of the discussion in 4,7—15 (cf Klauck 1986:48). The distinction between the "inner" and "outer person" (NIV: "outwardly ... inwardly") is formally comparable to that between a physical body and the "mind" or "soul" that inhabits it, a distinction commonly made in the Hellenistic world. The one visible and mortal, the other invisible but immortal, the "true" person (Philo) "hidden" within the "container" that covers it (Marcus Aurelius; cf 4,7).[18] Paul, however, means one and the

---

17 This life, states Bultmann (1976:125), "... [steht] außer ihm [ ] in Christus und vor ihm in der Auferstehung, und ... [ist] ihm eigen [ ] im Glauben". (Cf v 13; 5,7.)

18 For further information about the Hellenistic background of these terms, cf Furnish (1984:261.289).

same person in his/her personal unity,[19] viewed however from a different perspective. The "outer person" is that aspect of one's humanity which is subject to the various assaults and hardships of historical existence (4,8—9) and which, because of its vulnerability to these, may be likened to "jars of clay" (4,7). While it is illegitimate to identify the "outer person" in this passage with the old person of Rom 6,6, it is legitimate to identify the "inner person" (v 16) with the "new creation" in 2 Cor 5,17, and, therefore with the description in Rom 6 of those who have been set free from sin to be "... alive to God in Christ Jesus" (v 11). The hallmark of the inner person is a *life transformed by the resurrection life of Jesus through which God's own incomparable power is present and manifest* (4,7.10—12). This inner person (as Furnish [1984:289] poignantly points out) is the "I" of Gal 2,20 who by faith has grasped the reality of the new life in Christ.

The way in which the apostles are "outwardly wasting away" has been described in the catalogue of hardships (vv 8—9). In the light of verse 16 this "wasting away" is not confined to certain crises, but is part of the whole apostolic ministry.[20] It is a striking but thoroughly Pauline conviction that this "inner person" which has been made new is itself "renewed day by day". The same idea expressed in the imperative is present in Rom 12,2. The use of the imperative in Rom 12,2 and the expression "day by day" in the present verse require us to associate this renewal with a repeated act of faith whereby "the life of Jesus" is received and appropriated in the believer's life over and over again (Furnish 1984:290).

Seneca can also write admiringly of the man who is able to be "unterrified in the midst of dangers" and "happy in adversity" because he "passes through every experience as if it were of small account" (Ep xli,4—5; cf Epict I.ix. 16—17). This is possible, according to Seneca, because of the "peculiar property" of man which is "the soul, and reason brought to perfection in the soul". In Paul's view, however, it is not the inherent rationality of human nature that allows adversity to be endured, but only "faith and hope", which in the midst of adversity point beyond and ahead of themselves to God. Verse 17 accents the hope in describing the

---

[19] "personale Ganzheit" (Klauck 1986:48).

[20] Klauck (1986:48) points to the paradigmatic dimension of these Pauline statements: "Prinzipiell kann sich jeder Christ darin wiedererkennen." The renewal of the inner person may be compared with the transformation of 3,18, "... Erneuerung bedeutet Realisierung der neuen Schöpfung [5[17]], ist Neuschöpfung im Vollzug, ist Rettungstat Gottes".

present afflictions as only preliminary to the coming glory. This theme was already a common theme of apocalyptic Judaism (cf 2 Bar 48,50). By emphasising the disproportionate "eternal glory that far outweighs them all" in relation to the light and momentary troubles, Paul does not appear to regard the hoped-for "glory" as a reward for enduring so much distress. The subject of κατεργάζεται is παραυτίκα ἐλαφρὸν τῆς θλίψεως ἡμῶν. It is God who is at work in and through the present affliction (NIV: "troubles") to bring about "... an eternal glory that far outweighs them all" as its eventual and lasting fruit (Furnish 1984:290—1).[21]

It is noteworthy that Paul uses ὑπερβολή in verse 7 in connection with the *power of God* (τῆς δυνάμεως ... τοῦ θεοῦ) and in verse 17 in connection with *eternal fullness of glory* (αἰώνιον βάρος δόξης).

The new life is not visible, it can not be empirically demonstrated. It can only be grasped in faith. In verse 18 leading motifs of this pericope are finally brought together. To the category of what can be seen may be assigned: the outward person, the present sufferings, temporariness, the earthly vessel, the veiled face, the letter that kills and Jesus' sufferings of death. To the category of the unseen belong: the inward person, salvation in the midst of sufferings, the eternal and lasting, the valuable treasure, the heart and the Spirit as well as the life of Jesus (Klauck 1986:48).

Furnish (1984:288—301) considers 2 Cor 4,16—5,5 as one sub-pericope. He argues that the overall theme of these eight verses is the contrast between what is of preliminary significance only and what is of absolute significance. This contrast is expressed in various interrelated ways in virtually every sentence of the paragraph: *outwardly/inwardly*, 4,16; *light and momentary/eternal ... that far outweighs them all*, 4,17; *seen/unseen*, 4,18; *temporary/eternal*, 4,18; *earthly/in heaven*, 5,1—2; *tent/building from God*, 5,1; *destroyed/eternal*, 5,1; *naked/clothed*, 5,2—4; *mortal/life*, 5,4. Paul's comments here continue to be directed at the subject of the apostolic ministry and specifically at the question of how the hardships he and his associates experience are serving that ministry, rather than invalidating it.

---

[21] This view of Paul, which concerns the hardships mentioned in verses 8—9 "... hat nur dann Sinn, wenn man erkennt, daß sich in der Not die überreiche Herrlichkeit des neubundlichen Dienstes durchsetzt" (Klauck 1986:48).

There can be no doubt that a close relationship exists between 5,1—5 and the preceding sub-pericope. Two factors have, however, contributed to the decision to regard 5,1—5 as a separate sub-pericope:
(i) The prominent introductory phrase οἴδαμεν γάρ (cf 4,7 Ἔχομεν δέ; 4,16 διὸ οὐκ ἐγκακοῦμεν ... [4,13 ἔχοντες δὲ ... πιστεύομεν ... λαλοῦμεν]); and
(ii) as pointed out in the discourse analysis important structural markers occur in 5,1—5, which do not occur in 4,16—18. It may, however, be fully agreed with Lang (1986:283) that 2 Cor 4,16—18 constitutes the basis for 5,1—10.

12.4.5 Sub-pericope D (2 Cor 5,1—5)

For the correct interpretation of 2 Cor 5,1—10 it is most important to appreciate the way these verses fit into their context in 4,7—18 and, beyond this pericope, into the whole discussion of apostolic service which began in 2,14.[22]

In 2 Cor 5,1—10 Paul's exposition of the hidden glory of his ministry reaches a climax. While 3,4—4,6 focuses on the present aspect of the glory of the ministry of the new covenant and 4,7—18 emphasises its hiddenness, 5,1—10 looks forward to the ultimate fulfilment which has not yet been reached. To the hardships that Paul may have to face, also belongs the possibility that he may die in the near future. Even in this event God in his power and glory will still accomplish his goal, because even death can not separate the apostle from the reality of the resurrection (cf Klauck 1986:52).

2 Cor 5,1—10 may be regarded as the climactic supporting statement for the expression of apostolic confidence in 4,16a.[23] The context makes it clear that ἡ ἐπίγειος ἡμῶν οἰκία τοῦ σκήνους is to be identified with ὁ ἔξω ἡμῶν ἄνθρωπος (4,16b) with "our mortal body" (4,11), "our body" (4,10) and with "jars of clay" (4,7). The house metaphor is primary here. (It is carried forward in the second part of the verse, "a building ... an eternal house", and in verse 2, "our ... dwelling".) ἡ ἐπίγειος ἡμῶν οἰκία is

---

[22] For a discussion of the history of interpretation of 2 Cor 5,1—10, see Lang (1973).

[23] Furnish (1984:293) views only 5,1 (which he regards as part of the sub-pericope 4,16—5,1) as the climactic supporting statement for 4,16. Cf, however, Θαρροῦντες in 5,6.

qualified further by τοῦ σκήνους to emphasise that it is impermanent and collapsible. In many other Hellenistic religions and philosophical texts tent imagery is employed to describe the mortal body as distinguished from the immortal soul which inhabits it until it "collapses".[24] Nothing in this verse indicates that Paul is making such a distinction and this dualistic concept can not be accommodated within his thought.[25] The image of the οἰκία τοῦ σκήνους like that of the "jars of clay" (4,7) focuses on the vulnerability of one's mortal existence.

In verses 1—5 there is a description of the sighing of the believers who have received the Spirit as a deposit guaranteeing what is to come and the consequent longing to be clothed with the heavenly dwelling.[26] The question behind 5,1 is: How can Paul say "we do not lose heart" (v 16a) in the face of death itself? Death is understood here as the culmination of suffering and as constituting the most serious challenge to the boldness Paul has claimed for his apostolate.[27]

Paul affirms with certainty (οἴδαμεν receives special emphasis due to its position in the sentence), that "... we have a building from God, an eternal house in heaven, not built by human hands". In the Jewish and early Christian apocalyptic traditions the house or building of God is associated, first, with the temple of the new eschatological Jerusalem (e g 2 Bar 4,3) and then, by extension, with the new Jerusalem itself, which awaits the righteous as their proper destiny (e g 2 Esdras 10,40—57; 1 En 39,4; 41,2) (cf Lang 1973:182—5). In 2 Esdras 10,53—55 the "building" metaphor is used to describe the eschatological age, the glory and the vastness of what God has prepared for his people. If Paul is using the metaphor in a similar way in 2 Cor 5,1, it would be a further description of what he has referred

---

[24] For a discussion of the relevant texts, see Furnish (1984:264). Cf also Lang (1986:286). He points out that already in the Old Testament (Is 38,12) and in the Hellenistic Jewdom (Wisdom of Solomon 9,15) the body is portrayed as a tent.

[25] "Die Aussage über den Menschen in ¹ weist, wie manches in diesem Abschnitt, Berührungspunkte mit griechischen Dualismus auf, bleibt aber insgesamt eingebunden in eine einheitliche biblische Sicht" (Klauck 1986:49).

[26] "Die zeitliche Begrenztheit der gegenwärtigen Bedrängnis, die ein Übergewicht an Herrlichkeit erwirkt (4,17), ist ein Hinweis auf die kommende Vollendung, wie sich andererseits die *Vollendungshoffnung* bereits jetzt *als Kraft im Leiden* auswirkt" (Lang 1986:285; emphasis:PJG).

[27] Within this context, Paul's image of the "... destruction of this earthly tent we live in", probably refers to death in the sense described above. For a discussion of other interpretations of this phrase, cf *inter alia* Furnish (1984:293) and Lang (1986:286—7).

to more generally as the "... absolutely incomparable, eternal abundance of glory"[28] which awaits those who endure the afflictions of this world (4,17). It would be another and more graphic reference to the realm of the unseen and eternal to which believers are oriented even as they exist in the present realm of the visible and the transitory (4,18). A consideration of the parallels between the present passage and Phil 3,12—21 enhances the plausibility of this interpretation of the building metaphor. There are both verbal and material parallelisms between these passages (Furnish 1984:295; Lang 1973). The heavenly dwelling of 2 Cor 5,1, no less than the heavenly commonwealth of Phil 3,20, may be an image for the new age. Not even death, the final proof of mortality, need cause apostles to "lose heart" (4,16a), for they, like all believers, know that their true home is in heaven.

Lang (1986:286) stresses, however, that the connection of the image of a house with that of being clothed (cf 1 Cor 15,49), refers to the new eschatological body. Furnish (1984:296) on the other hand correctly points out that the subject here in 2 Corinthians is not "embodiment" or the time and nature of bodily transformation. Here the issue is the meaning of mortality, and in particular the meaning of apostolic sufferings. A broader eschatological (versus a narrowly anthropological) interpretation of this sub-pericope (and pericope), therefore, seems to do justice to this text.

In the preceding verses Paul has been arguing that hardships and the wasting away of the ἔξω ἄνθρωπος do not destroy the confidence of apostles, because they share the general Christian conviction that beyond the "... earthly tent we live in ... we have a building from God, an eternal house in heaven" (2 Cor 5,1).

In 5,2—5 the argument is now extended by the addition of a reference to the "sighing" which characterises mortal existence, and a comment about its meaning. The best commentary on verses 2—5 is found in Rom 8,18—27 (Furnish 1984:295; Collange 1972:202). In Rom 8,23.26 the sighing (στενάζομεν, v 23; στεναγμοῖς, v 26), which characterises mortal existence and its weakness, is specifically associated with the Spirit's presence as the "first fruits" of redemption. This interpretation of the sighing of mortal existence is fully applicable to the thought in 2 Cor 5,2—5 and is in accordance with its broader context in 4,7—5,10. Here, too, Paul has argued that sufferings are preliminary to the eternal glory

---

[28] Furnish's (1984:294) translation of 2 Cor 4,17.

(4,17; cf Rom 8,17), that faith is guided by what is not seen (4,18, cf Rom 8,24—25), and that God's presence through the Spirit provides assurance of what is to come (5,5; cf Rom 8,23). It may be agreed with Furnish (1984:295—6) that given these parallels, one is surely warranted in concluding that the association of mortal *sighing* with the Spirit's presence, which is explicit in Rom 8, is implicit in 2 Cor 5.[29]

Certain difficulties in the interpretation of this passage may be ascribed to the overlapping of three images: the body as a house, the body as a garment, and in verses 6—9 a comparison from the imagery of "being at home" — "being away"/"being absent — being present" (cf Klauck 1986:49). The clothing metaphor which first emerges in verse 2 must, therefore, be interpreted in association with the metaphor of a "dwelling" with which it is combined ("... clothed with our heavenly dwelling", 2 Cor 5,2).

As already stated above, the issue in this pericope is the meaning of mortality, and in particular the meaning of apostolic sufferings (not "embodiment" or the time and nature of bodily transformation). In this context, therefore, the longing to be "clothed with our heavenly dwelling" (v 2) must have a more general sense, not restricted to the longing for a spiritual body. It must be the longing for the fulfilment of salvation, the longing for what Paul will describe in Rom 8,21 as "... the glorious freedom of the children of God". The reference in verse 4 to the mortal being "... swallowed up by life" should in this context also be understood more generally than the similar phrase in 1 Cor 15,54. In the latter, "... death ... swallowed up in victory" has the narrower meaning: the mortality (of the body) dissolved by immortality. But in verse 4 "... what is mortal ... swallowed up by life", means "... all that pertains to one's mortal

---

[29] "Das Seufzen der Christen ist Ausdruck des 'Noch nicht' der eschatologischen Vollendung infolge des Geistempfangs." Also with reference to Rom 8, Lang (1986:287) comments that this "sighing" "... ist ... nicht Ausdruck der Todessehnsucht oder eines allgemeinen Weltschmerzes, sondern die folge der Hoffnung auf die Vollendung durch die Erstlingsgabe des Geistes [Röm 8,23]".

existence ... overcome when salvation shall be complete" (Furnish 1984:296—7).[30]

For the understanding of this passage a glance at Paul's use of the word ἐνδύεσθαι may be fruitful. In 1 Cor 15,53 it is used as a metaphor for the eschatological transformation of the body. This verb is used several times for "putting on" Christ (Gal 3,27; Rom 13,14) or Christ's armour (1 Thess 5,8; Rom 13,12; cf Eph 6,11.14). Furnish (1984:297) comments that in these passages, doubtlessly influenced by the language of the early Christian baptismal liturgy (cf Gal 3,27), Paul is thinking of a moral transformation of the individual in his or her earthly existence, not of a future metaphysical transformation (cf Col 3,9—10, 12—14 and Eph 4,22—24, where the "new nature" with which believers are clothed is also understood as a present moral transformation). This being "clothed" stands for the reception of the Spirit by faith (e g Gal 3,2.5) and for the inception through the Spirit's working of the new life in Christ (e g Rom 7,6). Given the context of the present passage (2 Cor 4,16—5,5), it would appear that the longing "... to be clothed with our heavenly dwelling" (v 2; v 4, that "... what is mortal may be swallowed up by life") is the longing for the fulfilment of that salvation which has already been inaugurated in the believer (symbolised by baptism) (cf also Lang 1973:187—8). The meaning of the compound verb ἐπενδύεσθαι (used in vv 2 and 4) as "be fully clothed" (suggested by Newman [1971:67]) fully suits this interpretation.

---

[30] While endorsing the view that Paul's focus is different in 1 Cor 15 and 2 Cor 4—5 (1 Cor 15 drives home the necessity for bodily transformation; 2 Cor 4—5 works out the implications of apostolic suffering), Gillman (1988:441) has correctly pointed out that these two themes are not mutually exclusive, but do interface with each other in the respective letters. Apostolic suffering introduced already in 1 Cor 4,9—13 also seems to be briefly signalled in 15,30—32 as a personal testament to the future resurrection, which is in question. Transformation, explicit in 2 Cor 3,18 (cf 4,16) where it is depicted as gradually taking place in earthly life, is implicit as an operative assumption underlying the line of argument in 2 Cor 5,1—5.

What does Paul mean by using the aorist participle ἐνδυσάμενοι?[31] It seems likely that the reference is to the clothing with Christ, symbolised by baptism. (Cf Gal 3,27: "… for all you who were baptised into Christ have clothed yourselves with Christ".) Thus, the aorist participle in verse 3 would match the two aorist participles of verse 5 which are associated with the coming of the Spirit (cf Furnish 1984:297; Collange 1972:218; Thrall 1962:92—3).

Contrary to Barrett's (1973:153) criticism, this interpretation does not hamper the explanation of the use of ἐπενδύσασθαι in verse 2.[32] Verse 3 represents an extension of the primary metaphor: to "clothe oneself" with Christ at baptism is to receive the Spirit as a "deposit, [guaranteeing what is to come]" on the fullness of salvation (v 5; 1,22; cf Rom 8,23) and to long to "be fully clothed" with a heavenly dwelling is to long for the fulfilment of what has already been inaugurated (Furnish 1984:297—8).

When interpreting Paul's use of γυμνοί in 2 Cor 5,3 one must be careful not to interpret this passage according to the model of 1 Cor 15,35—58 since, as has already been pointed out, the subject in 2 Cor 4,7—5,10 is not "embodiment" as it had been in 1 Cor 15,35—58. The meaning of 2 Cor 5,3 must, therefore, be determined primarily on the basis of the discussion of apostolic suffering (of which it forms a part).

It has already been determined that ἐνδυσάμενοι (v 3) probably refers to the putting on of Christ by the believer as symbolised by baptism. In this context nakedness would most naturally refer to neither the "nakedness of

---

[31] While the Nestle-text prior to the twenty-sixth edition read ἐνδυσάμενοι, the twenty-sixth and twenty-seventh editions read ἐκδυσάμενοι. It has been asserted (cf Metzger 1994:511) that internal considerations decisively favour the latter reading, for with ἐνδυσάμενοι the apostle's statement is banal and even tautologous, whereas with ἐκδυσάμενοι it is characteristically vivid and paradoxical. (The reading ἐκλυσάμενοι [codexes F and G] probably arose through palaeographical confusion).

In this study the personal view of Metzger (1994:511), contrary to that of the committee, has been adopted, namely, that due to its superior external support the reading ἐνδυσάμενοι should be adopted, while the reading ἐκδυσάμενοι may be seen as an early alteration introduced to avoid apparent tautology. (The reading ἐνδυσάμενοι is supported by papyrus 46, codex Sinaiticus, codex Vaticanus, codex Ephraemi, codex Claromontanus, codex Ψ, codex 0243, the Majority text, a part of the Old Latin and Vulgate versions, all the Syriac as well as all the Coptic versions and by Clement of Alexandria. ἐκδυσάμενοι is read by only the original scribe of codex Claromontanus, Old Latin manuscripts a and f [alteration due to a corrector], as well as by Tertullian and Speculum [Pseudo-Augustine]).

[32] Barrett asserts that the interpretation adopted here "… leaves the *put on over* [ἐπενδύσασθαι] of verse 2 unexplained".

the soul" at death, nor to the nakedness of moral shame and guilt (which are not being discussed here), but to alienation from Christ, to have in some way denied one's baptism (cf Collange 1972:215—8.225).

Paul interrupts his comments about the longing to "be fully clothed" with the fullness of salvation in order to interject a remark which is implicitly polemical. He warns that what has been affirmed about the coming salvation presupposes that those who have once been clothed with Christ will not be found alienated from him — "naked" — when they appear before their Judge. Both the fact and the form of this interjection suggest that Paul has reason to think that there are some in Corinth who will not be able to meet this condition. These are people who have been orientated only to "what is seen" (4,18); but when their disguises are revealed, they will be exposed for what they are "found naked". According to this interpretation of verse 3, the comment of verse 4 that "... we do not wish to be unclothed but to be clothed", would be a statement of resolve — and therefore an implicit appeal to the readers — to remain faithful to the gospel of Christ.

The theocentricity of Paul's thought again comes to the fore in the last verse of this sub-pericope. In 4,16a we find an affirmation of continuing confidence; in 5,5 an affirmation about God, the ultimate source of that confidence. God is the one "who has prepared[33] us for this very purpose", for the life which shall engulf our mortality (v 4) by giving us "... the Spirit as a deposit guaranteeing what is to come".[34]

In verse 5 Paul exposes that the receiving of the Spirit is the basis on which the knowledge and conduct described in verses 1—4 rests. As in 1,22 the Spirit is depicted as the deposit guaranteeing the eschatological fulfilment (cf the affirmation concerning the "firstfruits of the Spirit" in Rom 8,23).

---

[33] It seems as if "prepare"/"equip" is a better translation for κατεργάζεσθαι in this passage as "made" (NIV). Cf Newman (1971:97); Furnish (1984:270—1). Louw and Nida (1988:684) also translate this phrase in 2 Cor 5,5: "... God who has prepared us for this".

[34] "Für den Empfang dieser neuen Seinsweise hat Gott ihn vorbereitet durch eine 'Anzahlung' (1[22]), die im Geist besteht ..." (Klauck 1986:50).

The aorist participles (κατεργασάμενος ... δούς corresponding to ἐνδυσάμενοι in v 3) point to a decisive moment in the past, the coming to faith in Christ, symbolised by baptism.[35]

The emphasis on the role of the Spirit in Christian life generally, and for apostles specifically as they endure countless hardships for the sake of the gospel, is fully in harmony with Paul's earlier description of the apostolic vocation as a "ministry of the Spirit" (3,8). The Spirit brings about the transformation ἀπὸ δόξης εἰς δόξαν (3,18) as well as the inward renewal day by day (4,16). The same Spirit will bring about the eschatological fulfilment (Klauck 1986:51).

12.4.6 Sub-pericope E (2 Cor 5,6—10)

The close connection between this sub-pericope and the pericope as a whole (beginning with 2 Cor 4,7) is of the utmost importance for the correct interpretation of 2 Cor 5,6—10. The same basic line of thought expressed by the various antitheses throughout the pericope is also to be observed here. The issue of apostolic confidence in the face of the many hardships endured by the apostle throughout his apostolic ministry (cf 4,8—9) is also the main point of this sub-pericope. (The expression of confidence at the beginning of this paragraph, reformulates the declaration of apostolic boldness in 4,16a).

As was the case with the previous sub-pericope, 5,6—10 supplies us with the reason for apostolic confidence (and Christian faith in general) even when our earthly existence is threatened. Paul's affirmation in these two sub-pericopes may indeed be described as: "Die Vollendungshoffnung als Kraft im Leiden" (Lang 1986:284).

Within 2 Cor 5,6—10 the antithesis of "being at home" and "being away" plays a leading role (cf Klauck 1986:51). In verses 6—10 the longing "... to be clothed with our heavenly dwelling" (2 Cor 5,4) is now extended to the immediate personal fellowship with Christ in the *eschaton*. As baptised believers the Christians are already "in Christ" and identify themselves with the exalted Lord (4,18). Life in the earthly body, however,

---

[35] Bultmann (1976:141) comments: "Was aber nach Paulus diese Deutung der Sehnsucht ... erlaubt, das ist nach V.₅ der ἀρραβὼν τοῦ πνεύματος. Dieser wird in der Taufe geschenkt; die Taufe aber empfängt nur der Glaubende."

still implies a being away from the Lord as complete fellowship with Christ is not yet possible (cf Lang 1986:288).[36] The exclusive contrast in Paul's metaphor (either "away from home" or "at home") is to be interpreted in a relative sense (Lang 1986:289).[37] Verse 7 supplies a clue to the correct interpretation of verse 6 by stating that our present Christian life is lived by faith. Although the believers already behold the "Lord's glory" (3,18), they do not yet "see face to face" (1 Cor 13,12).[38]

For Paul, the crucial point is the orientation of one's life. This is what is conveyed by the antithesis of verse 7, that believers are guided by what is believed, not by what is seen[39] (which is simply a repetition of what has been emphasised already in 4,18). By pointing to Gal 2,20, Furnish (1984:302) stresses that Paul in our present verse is contrasting two modes of existence in *this* age. The contrast in verse 7 is not between faith as the mode of one's present existence (in this age) and "seeing" as the mode of one's existence in the age to come.[40]

Paul's hope of fulfilment is not crushed by the present hardships, it is actually kindled by them. He compares his present life, accompanied by many sufferings, with his being with Christ (cf Klauck 1986:51). The knowledge of the "not yet" of full fellowship with Christ (v 6) kindles the

---

[36] Although this is the only text in the Bible in which this idea is portrayed by the notion of "being at home" and "being away from home", "... die gemeinte Sache ist jedoch in der Struktur der paulinischen Eschatologie enthalten, insofern die Christen als 'neue Geschöpfe' zwar schon mit Gott versöhnt, aber noch nicht aus dem todverfallenen Leib erlöst sind [Röm 5,8—10; 8,23]" (Lang 1986:288).

[37] Cf also Klauck 1986:51: "Es geht um ein Mehr oder Weniger."

[38] "Der V. 7 unterscheidet also die jetzige Existenz im Glauben von der zukünftigen Existenz in der vollendeten Gottesherrschaft" (Lang 1986:289).

[39] It has often been pointed out that εἶδος must be understood in a passive sense (Furnish 1986:273: "appearance"). Klauck (1986:51) comments that εἶδος can never be used in an active sense. Newman (1971:52) however, mentions both "sight" and "seeing" as translational equivalents for εἶδος, while Louw and Nida (1988:277) state that it is possible to interpret the phrase διὰ πίστεως γὰρ περιπατοῦμεν οὐ διὰ εἴδους (2 Cor 5,7) in two ways: "our life is a matter of faith and not of seeing" or to interpret εἶδος as meaning "what is seen".

[40] However the present writer agrees with the following interpretation put forward by Lang (1986:289): "Die Deutung von V. 7 auf die unterschiedlichen Lebenseinstellungen in der Gegenwart gemäß 4,18 ... wird der Gegenüberstellung von Gegenwart und Zukunft nicht gerecht." This statement is in line with Paul's argumentation in this pericope in which the eschatological motif comes more and more to the fore.

longing to leave the earthly body in order to be able to be fully with the Lord.[41]

In verse 9 it is evident that the final hope has consequences for one's earthly life. It is a matter of utmost importance to please the Lord in all situations. According to Paul, the only important question is whether one's service as an apostle (or as any ordinary believer) is finally adjudged "acceptable" to the Lord (Furnish 1984:304). The expressions "at home or away from home" correspond with the phrases: "whether we are awake or asleep" (1 Thess 5,10) and "whether we live or die" (Rom 14,8) (Lang 1986:289).[42]

The desire to lead a life which would please the Lord is essential because all must appear before the judgement seat of Christ. What Paul says in verse 10 about the ultimate accountability of all believers is designed to support the appeal which is implicit in verse 9.

The receiving of the Spirit, which enables a new life, places the Christians who are still subjected to temptations in a position of responsibility before God. The image of the judgement seat of Christ (of God: Rom 4,10) clearly refers to the eschatological judgement which Christ will carry out on behalf of God at his *parousia* (cf Acts 17,31; Rom 2,6.16; 14,10; 1 Cor 3,13—15; 4,4—5) (cf Lang 1986:290).

Every one will "... receive what is due to him for the things done" through the body,[43] "whether good or bad". The phrase διὰ τοῦ σώματος may also be understood temporarily (cf NIV: "... while in the body" [i e during his earthly life]). It must be pointed out, however, that Paul's vision of the final judgement is also based upon his confidence to be clothed with "... the righteousness of God" (v 21) bestowed in Christ and of being able then to "... be with the Lord forever" (v 18; cf 1 Thess 4,17).

This discussion may be concluded with a few notes on Pauline eschatology in the light of 2 Cor 5,1—10: In the centre of Paul's theology stands God's act of salvation through the cross and the resurrection of Jesus Christ. The apostle considers the cross and the resurrection as

---

[41] "Die Verben [in v 8:PJG] beschreiben jetzt die Bewegung hin zum zukünftigen Ziel der unmittelbaren Gemeinschaft mit Christus ..." (Lang 1986:289).

[42] "Der angstfreie Eifer, dem Herrn zu dienen, kennt nicht nur keine Todesfurcht mehr, sondern in ihm schweigt sogar auch die Sehnsucht nach dem Tode" (Bultmann 1976:144).

[43] "... das Organ des Wirkens und der Kommunikation in der Welt" (Lang 1986:290).

"eschatological events". The cross and the resurrection of Christ relate both to God's previous acts of salvation portrayed in the Old Testament revelation as well as to God's future creative activity in the fulfilment. In his Son God has sent the eschatological bringer of salvation in whom all promises of God have come to fulfilment (2 Cor 1,20). This, however, still stands under the affirmation of 12,9 that *God's power* is made perfect in *weakness*. The creation of salvation remains God's act solely and not the work of man (cf 4,7), to be grasped in faith. In Paul's view the certainty of final redemption and complete fellowship with the Lord rests in God's gift of reconciliation in Christ and in the firstfruits of the Spirit (cf Rom 5,8—11; 8,23). The members of the new creation, therefore, live in the present as believers "in Christ"; they are, however, not at home with the Lord yet (cf Lang 1986:290—1).

12.5 Summary and conclusion

Paul and his associates are ministers of a new covenant, instituted in and with Christ's death (2 Cor 3,7—18). Therefore, he can understand the gospel as "the word of the cross". God's eschatological power is made present and effective for salvation in Christ's death (1 Cor 1,18; cf Rom 1,16—17). Through Christ the old covenant has come to an end, and through him a new covenant, inscribed on human hearts by the Spirit, has been given as the power and the promise of life.

Paul's ministry, endowed with God's all-surpassing power (4,7), may be defined in terms of the "new covenant" (καινῆς διαθήκης — 3,6), in terms of the "Spirit" (τοῦ πνεύματος — 3,8), in terms of "righteousness" (τῆς δικαιοσύνης — 3,9), and as "that which lasts" (τὸ μένον — 3,11).

In 1 Cor 1,18 Paul portrays the gospel as ὁ λόγος ... ὁ τοῦ σταυροῦ and in 1 Cor 2,2 he describes the contents of his message as Ἰησοῦν Χριστὸν καὶ τοῦτον ἐσταυρωμένον. Yet, in 2 Cor 4,4 Paul can refer to the gospel of the glory of Christ (τοῦ εὐαγγελίου δόξης τοῦ Χριστοῦ) without contradicting himself. For Paul, it is precisely as the crucified one that Christ is "the Lord of glory" (1 Cor 2,8). In passages such as 2 Cor 4,7—12; 12,9—10 and 13,4, Paul reflects on this paradox and articulates the implications of the paradox for his own apostolic role and for the Corinthians' faith and life.

He acknowledges that his sufferings and those of his apostolic associates might have been (and probably have been) taken by some as invalidating their claim to be ministers of a new covenant of surpassing glory (3,7—4,6). In 4,7—15 Paul interprets these mortal adversities as an integral and appropriate part of the apostleship (4,7—15). The thesis of the pericope (4,7—5,10) is stated in 4,7. By contrasting "jars of clay" with the "treasure" they contain, Paul stresses the great value of the one and the trifling value of the other as well as the frailty and vulnerability to breakage and destruction of the jars of clay. The precious treasure he mentions, is the ministry of the new covenant with everything pertaining to it: the proclamation of the gospel, the knowledge, the glory, the transformation, the enlightenment of the heart.

The main point Paul wants to make in 4,7 is that the frailty of the apostles is a demonstration of the vital issue "... that this all-surpassing power is God's and not from us". In 13,4b, just as here (v 7), he contrasts the weakness of apostles with the power of God, at the same time affirming an important relation between the two. Paul's interpretation of the meaning of the adversities by which apostles are beset is dependent upon his understanding of the gospel they preach. The gospel is God's "power for salvation" (Rom 1,16) present in "the message of the cross" (1 Cor 1,18.24). Therefore, Paul had written in an earlier letter, the weakness, fear and trembling with which he had brought the gospel to Corinth in the first place had allowed a full "... demonstration of the Spirit's power", that the Corinthians' faith "... might not rest on men's wisdom, but on God's power" (1 Cor 2,3—5). The way in which he describes affliction and God's power anticipates 12,9—10: God's grace is sufficient, power is perfected in weakness.

On the one hand Paul interprets the sufferings he endures while serving the gospel as participation in Jesus' sufferings on the cross (cf 2 Cor 1,5). On the other hand the *resurrection life provides the vital power to endure everything in the light of the eschatological hope.* The paradox which has been in view since verse 7 (God's power disclosed through weakness) is, therefore, sharpened in verse 10b, where Paul states that the "carrying about of the death of Jesus" is for the purpose of revealing his "life" (ἡ ζωή τοῦ Ἰησοῦ: the resurrection life of Jesus). A fundamental concept in Paul's thought emerges in the purpose clause of verse 11b which, like the one it parallels in verse 10b, refers to the manifestation of the *resurrection life of Jesus* (and thus of the *all-surpassing power of God*), precisely in and through the weakness, suffering, and death of Jesus borne by the apostles.[44]

On a very profound level Paul is aware of his union with Christ. In view of texts such as 2 Cor 1,5; 13,4; Gal 6,17 and Phil 3,10—11 Paul's carrying in his body the putting to death of Jesus and the twofold mention of Jesus' life manifested in the apostle are to be interpreted in terms of participation, the effect of his *union with Christ*. At its deepest roots apostolic suffering goes back to that participation. The consequence of that union is therefore the fact that in Paul's suffering Christ manifests himself (Lambrecht 1999:77—8).

Δύναμις is, therefore, used in this context in which the *tensions* of the apostolic ministry (and of Christian life in general) are so clearly portrayed. On the first level of interpretation δύναμις refers to Paul's *apostolic ministry*. This apostolic ministry is, however, based on the very *heart of the gospel*. This is the reason why many of the affirmations in these two pericopes bear relevance to daily Christian life.

On the second level of interpretation δύναμις therefore also refers here to the *most profound power enabling Christian existence as such*. Christian existence with all its tensions, so profoundly explicated in this passage, is in desperate need of *God's power*. "But we have this treasure in jars of clay to show that the all-surpassing power is God's and not from us" (2 Cor 4,7).

God's power is connected most intimately with the *resurrection life of Jesus* (cf 4,7b.10b.11b). The gospel is, however, God's "power for salvation" (Rom 1,16) present in "the message of the cross" (1 Cor 1,18.24). God's power is made perfect in weakness (2 Cor 12,9). The context makes it clear that this power is a *reality* in the present, a reality to a life lived in *faith*. At the same time an *eschatological* orientation belongs to the very structure of this new life (cf Lambrecht 1994:335—49). Within this context the vital role of the *Spirit* must be discerned. Through the Spirit the power (δύναμις) coming from God is a reality in the present. At the same time the Spirit creates in the believer a longing for the eschatological

---

[44] Schröter (1996:691) underlines the importance of 2 Cor 4,7—12 as a passage which gives us insight into central aspects of Paul's thought. The implications of the Christ event stretch far beyond the doctrine of the justification of sinners: "Für Paulus stellen sich Tod und Auferstehung Christi als ein Vorgang dar, der auch die Existenz der καινὴ κτίσις prägt."

fulfilment — a fulfilment of which the Spirit himself is the guarantee (ἀρραβών — 2 Cor 5,5).

A treasure in jars of clay? This is in accordance with the structure of the gospel itself, a gospel which centres around the cross and resurrection of Jesus Christ, a gospel which points man away from himself to God "... *to show that this all-surpassing power is God's and not from us"* (2 Cor 4,7).

Chapter 13

2 Corinthians 6,7

13.1 Location within the macrocontext of 2 Corinthians as well as delimitation of the pericope

The pericope, 2 Cor 6,3—10 forms part of a larger section of 2 Cor (2,14—6,10) in which Paul comments on his apostolic service. This pericope, therefore, forms part of the same larger section of 2 Cor as the pericope discussed in the previous chapter. The reader is especially referred to 12.1 where the macrocontext has been discussed in more detail.[1]

---

[1] Commentators do not agree concerning the exact extent of this section. The views of a few commentators may be mentioned:

Bultmann (1976:164—76):
5_{20}—6_{10}: *Die Ausübung der Verkündigung*
5_{20}—6_2: Die Verkündigung als eschatologisches Geschehen
6_{3-10}: Der Apostel in der Kraft des eschatologischen Geschehens

Furnish (1984:xii):
Appeals, 5,20—9,15
Reconciliation with God, 5,20—6,10
The Appeal Proper, 5,20—6,2
The Appeal Supported, 6,3—10

Klauck (1986:52—6)
Paulus im Dienst der Versöhnung
Vorläufiger Rückblick: 5^{11-13}
Neue Schöpfung: 5^{14-17}
Die Ansage der vollzogenen Versöhnung: 5^{18-21}
Die Zeit der Gnade: 6^{1-2}
Die Zeit der Bewährung: 6^{3-10}

Lang (1986:293—306):
Das Angebot des Heils durch den apostolischen Dienst
Das Apostelamt als Dienst der Versöhnung 5,11—6,2
Die Bewährung des Paulus im apostolischen Dienst 6,3—10

2 Cor 6,3—10 may syntactically be linked to παρακαλοῦμεν (v 1) due to its participial constructions (Lang 1986:304). Διδόντες (v 3), however, may simply be another instance of Paul's use of a participle instead of a finite verb.

Although it is difficult to decide between these two options διδόντες has been viewed in this study as a participle used instead of a finite verb (cf Furnish 1984:342). ἀλλ' relates verse 4a (comma 1.3) to verse 3. The relation to verses 4b—10 (commata 1.4—32) is emphasised by the fact that ἐν and ὡς (occurring already in comma 1.3) prominently function in commata 1.4—32 (cf discourse analysis). Paul presents in this pericope *a catalogue of the hardships* he had to endure. 2 Cor 6,1—2 seemingly does not fit well into this context.

This whole pericope consists of only one colon. A new colon (and also a new pericope) is introduced in verse 11 by the phrase: Τὸ στόμα ἡμῶν ἀνέῳγεν ... .

Lambrecht (1999:v—vi.10—1):
PAUL'S APOSTLESHIP (2,14—7,4)
As Ministers of God (6,1—10)

Thrall (1994:xiii):
DEFENCE OF THE APOSTOLIC MINISTRY (2,14—7,4)
Paul's ministry: further considerations (5,11—7,4)
Beginning of direct appeal and further defence of apostolic conduct (6,1—13)

Windisch ([1924] 1970:XI):
Verherrlichung des apostolischen Amtes und Rechtfertigung der apostolischen Amtsführung zur Herstellung eines guten Einvernehmens mit der Gemeinde 2_{14}—7_4.

13.2 Discourse analysis: 2 Corinthians 6,3—10

A commendable ministry in the midst of many afflictions by the power of God

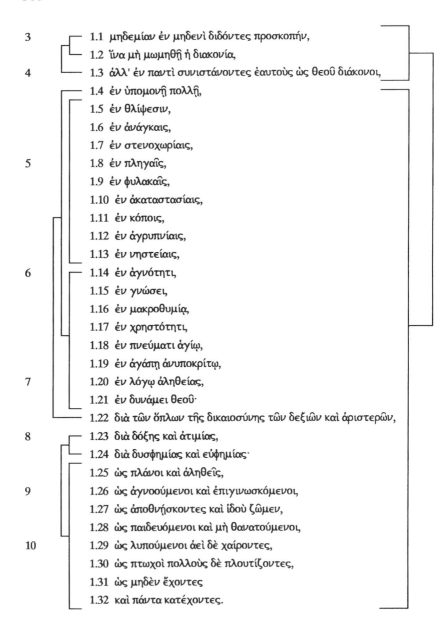

3   1.1 μηδεμίαν ἐν μηδενὶ διδόντες προσκοπήν,

    1.2 ἵνα μὴ μωμηθῇ ἡ διακονία,

4   1.3 ἀλλ' ἐν παντὶ συνιστάνοντες ἑαυτοὺς ὡς θεοῦ διάκονοι,

    1.4 ἐν ὑπομονῇ πολλῇ,

    1.5 ἐν θλίψεσιν,

    1.6 ἐν ἀνάγκαις,

    1.7 ἐν στενοχωρίαις,

5   1.8 ἐν πληγαῖς,

    1.9 ἐν φυλακαῖς,

    1.10 ἐν ἀκαταστασίαις,

    1.11 ἐν κόποις,

    1.12 ἐν ἀγρυπνίαις,

    1.13 ἐν νηστείαις,

6   1.14 ἐν ἁγνότητι,

    1.15 ἐν γνώσει,

    1.16 ἐν μακροθυμίᾳ,

    1.17 ἐν χρηστότητι,

    1.18 ἐν πνεύματι ἁγίῳ,

    1.19 ἐν ἀγάπῃ ἀνυποκρίτῳ,

7   1.20 ἐν λόγῳ ἀληθείας,

    1.21 ἐν δυνάμει θεοῦ·

    1.22 διὰ τῶν ὅπλων τῆς δικαιοσύνης τῶν δεξιῶν καὶ ἀριστερῶν,

8   1.23 διὰ δόξης καὶ ἀτιμίας,

    1.24 διὰ δυσφημίας καὶ εὐφημίας·

    1.25 ὡς πλάνοι καὶ ἀληθεῖς,

9   1.26 ὡς ἀγνοούμενοι καὶ ἐπιγινωσκόμενοι,

    1.27 ὡς ἀποθνῄσκοντες καὶ ἰδοὺ ζῶμεν,

    1.28 ὡς παιδευόμενοι καὶ μὴ θανατούμενοι,

10   1.29 ὡς λυπούμενοι ἀεὶ δὲ χαίροντες,

    1.30 ὡς πτωχοὶ πολλοὺς δὲ πλουτίζοντες,

    1.31 ὡς μηδὲν ἔχοντες

    1.32 καὶ πάντα κατέχοντες.

13.2.1 A few notes pertaining to the structure of this pericope

In verses 3 and 4a (commata 1.1—3) we find the thematic heading.[2] The catalogue is introduced by the phrase ἐν ὑπομονῇ πολλῇ, followed by the listing of the situations in which the apostle exercised great endurance. Here the reader encounters three groups, consisting of three phrases each, every phrase introduced by ἐν and in the plural form (the singular ἐν ὑπομονῇ πολλῇ relates to the singular ἐν-phrases in 6,6—7ab [commata 1.14—21]). The first four phrases of verse 6 are constructed in the following way: ἐν + noun. The last two phrases and the first of verse 7 are extended by the addition of an adjective, while the last consists of two nouns. In this way Paul emphasises ἐν πνεύματι ἁγίῳ, ἐν ἀγάπῃ ἀνυποκρίτῳ, ἐν λόγῳ ἀληθείας and both the climax and summary are expressed by ἐν δυνάμει θεοῦ.

In verses 7c (1.22) and 8ab (1.23—24) there are three phrases which are introduced by the preposition διά. The first strings together a series of genitives, while the second and third present two sets of contrasting words (Furnish 1984:356). The second and third phrases relate to the phrases introduced by ὡς (vv 8c—10 [1.25—31]) where this contrasting style is continued. Semantically it is clear that the first διά-phrase (v 7c) relates to the preceding group of ἐν-phrases.

It is also to be observed that from 8c onwards (ὡς πλάνοι ...) adjectives and participles occur instead of nouns.

The hardships mentioned in verses 4—5 are opposed by the "powers" in verses 6—7 which enabled Paul to stand fast/conquer in the midst of suffering (cf Friedrich 1963a:42).[3]

13.3 An exegetical overview

In 2 Cor 6,3—10 the apostolic ministry is portrayed in the style of the so-called "catalogue of hardships", in the same way as in 4,8—9; 11,23—29 and 1 Cor 4,11—13. The fact that Paul exults in his sufferings, which

---

[2] "Die Verse 3 und 4a ... stellen die Bewährung des Paulus als Diener Gottes heraus" (Lang 1986:304).

[3] "Die Gruppen $_{4c—5}$ und $_{6—7}$ bilden also eine Anthithese, während in $_{8—10}$ die einzelnen Glieder Antithesen sind" (Bultmann 1976:170).

resulted from following the way of the cross, distinguishes him from his opponents, who took pride in external things (5,12) (cf Lang 1986:304). The literary form of the catalogue of hardships is a loose, often antithetically constructed list of hardships in which the wise or godly man proves himself. This form is encountered in both Greek literature (Dio Chrysostomus, Or VIII,15 ff) and Jewish apocalyptic writings (cf 2 En 66,6).[4]

The apostle offers a brief resumé of the "credentials" on which the authority of his apostolate is based. These credentials are introduced in 6,3—4a and enumerated in the rhetorically impressive 6,4b—10. In verses 4b—5 Paul commends his apostolate for its endurance through many adversities, in 6—7b for its working in the power of God, in 7c—8b for its having the weapons of righteousness and in 8c—10 by contrasting the worldly perception of the apostolate with the view held by those who are "in Christ" (Furnish 1984:349). It is clear that Paul does not view the apostles as fighters for virtues, but as instruments of God who know that in the midst of hardships they are borne by God's power and God's Spirit (cf Lang 1986:305).[5]

Paul knows that his critics constantly keep his life under close scrutiny. Should he fail in his personal life, the trustworthiness of the message of reconciliation, with which he has been entrusted by God, would be questioned; his personal failure would become an obstacle to the faith of those to whom he has preached. His self-recommendation can not be misunderstood any more, when one takes into account that he exults in the abundance of daily sufferings, in the midst of which the new life becomes manifest (cf Klauck 1986:58).

Verses 3—4a serve as an introduction to the rest of the pericope. The comment in verse 3 about putting "... no stumbling block in anyone's path, so that our ministry will not be discredited", complements the comment in 5,12 that Paul wants the Corinthians to be able to be proud of his apostolate. The reference to self-recommendation in v 4a seems to pick up the rejection of the same in 5,12. What was rejected was the pretentious

---

[4] "Paulus lehnt sich an diese Form an, stellt sie aber inhaltlich ganz in den Dienst seiner Christologie" (Lang 1986:304).

[5] Bultmann (1976:171) summarises 2 Cor 6,3—10: "Das Ganze ist eine Charakteristik des apostolischen Dienstes in der Kraft des eschatologischen Geschehens parallel zu 4_{7-12} ... ."

boasting of external things (ecstatic experiences and the like) by his rivals. What Paul offers instead are "credentials" of a different order, in keeping with the life of "ministers of God" (Furnish 1984:354).

The position of ἐν ὑπομονῇ πολλῇ at the beginning of three groups of three terms each, all in the plural and all prefaced by ἐν (listed in vv 4c and 5), stresses the importance of "great endurance" within this context.[6] Like ὑπομονῇ, the concepts in commata 1.5—7 remind us of the *eschatos*. In apocalyptic texts, these concepts occur in the context of the end-time trials and tribulations of the just, which Paul applies to his ministry. He views his ministry in the light of the nearby *parousia*.

In commata 1.8—10 hardships endured at the hands of others[7] are mentioned and in commata 1.11—13 mention is made of phenomena accompanying Paul's exhausting missionary activity.

Within the list of hardships, the reader suddenly encounters a small list of virtues (cf 6,4 ἐν ὑπομονῇ πολλῇ). Of these eight expressions (connected with ἐν) the last, ἐν δυνάμει θεοῦ, provides an apt summary. The Pauline apostolate is commended as an agency through which God's power is made manifest and in which the Holy Spirit is at work (Nielsen 1980:148—50). Paul identifies close ties between three of the first four terms and the Spirit: γνῶσις is one of the gifts of the Spirit (cf 1 Cor 12,8), while μακροθυμία and χρηστότης as well as ἀγάπη are included among the fruit of the Spirit (Gal 5,22). These are not only "... moral characteristics of Paul's behaviour" as Barrett (1973:186) suggested, they represent the special gifts and powers which are present where the community of faith and individual believers are open to the guidance of the Holy Spirit (Furnish 1984:335). Paul sees the Spirit as fostering the virtues he lists, and the virtues themselves as evidence of the Spirit's inward operation. He defends his own ministry as the διακονία τοῦ πνεύματος (3,8) (Thrall 1994:460).[8]

---

[6] "Die Standhaftigkeit in ⁴ᵇ ist das Vorzeichen, das vor der folgenden Liste steht" (Klauck 1986:58).

[7] "... politische Gefährdungen, die von Behörden oder von der aufgehetzten Volksmenge ausgehen" (Klauck 1986:58).

[8] "Die vorbildlichen Verhaltensweisen, die Paulus in den Bewährungsproben an den Tag legt, werden auf die tragenden Kräfte zurückgeführt. Sie kann man verschieden umschreiben. Man kann Liebe dazu sagen ... Man kann Wirkungen des Geistes darin erkennen [vgl. 3³·⁶·¹⁸; 5⁵]. Man kann schließlich alles auf die Dynamik zurückführen, die von Gott ausgeht" (Klauck 1986:58—9).

It is noteworthy that Paul recognises a link between ἐν λόγῳ ἀληθείας in verse 7 and ἐν δυνάμει θεοῦ. He considers the gospel he preaches to be "the word of truth". The translation of the NIV (and RSV), "in truthful speech", must be viewed as less probable.[9] The reader's attention should also be drawn to 1 Cor 1,18, where "the word of the cross" is associated with God's power (cf also 1 Cor 2,4; 1 Thess 1,5). In Eph 1,13 and Col 1,5 "the word of truth" is specifically identified as "the gospel" (cf 2 Tim 2,15). The absence of the articles in verse 7 is no argument against the same meaning here, because the anarthrous phrase is derived from the Septuagint, where "the words of truth" refer to God's word delivered to his people (Ps 118 [119],43.160). Compare also "the word of life" (λόγον ζωῆς) in Phil 2,16; Gal 2,5.14 ("the truth of the gospel") and 2 Cor 4,2 (where "the truth" refers to "the word of God"). The power of God is a frequent and important Pauline topic, and the apostle emphasises it particularly in this letter (cf 4,7). Young and Ford (1987:239) affirm: "*In 2 Corinthians ... the leading concept is that of power*" (my emphasis).[10] Similarly δύναμις θεοῦ is likened to the gospel in Rom 1,16 (Furnish 1984:345—6).

The description of Paul's message as the word of truth may be intended to cut polemically against Paul's rivals, whom he views as "... peddling the word of God for profit" (2,17) and "... distorting the word of God" (4,2). Collange (1972:296) has pointed out that the word "truth" often appears in polemical contexts in 2 Cor. "For Paul, *the word of truth* is nothing else than 'the word of reconciliation' [5,19], and thus 'the word of the cross' [1 Cor 1,18] through which God's power is present as redeeming and renewing love [2 Cor 5,14 ff]" (Furnish 1984:356).[11]

It may appear as if the divine power is concealed by the personal weakness of the apostle. This is, however, not the case. Paul's preaching occurred with a demonstration of the Spirit's power (1 Cor 2,4; cf 1 Thess 1,5). Friedrich (1963a:47—8) correctly affirms that in the context of 2 Cor

---

[9] Bultmann (1976:173) comments: "... schwerlich ist das wahre, ehrliche Wort gemeint, sondern λόγος ἀληθείας technisch = das Evangelium ...".

[10] Also Thrall (1994:461) remarks that Paul here alludes "... to one of the dominant themes of the letter, i.e., the effectiveness of divine power in situations of human weakness".

[11] Cf Lang (1986:305): "Die Kraft Gottes wird in Wort und Geist durch die Apostel wirksam (1. Kor 2,4)."

6,7 where the δύναμις θεοῦ is mentioned next to λόγος ἀληθείας, the reference is in the first place to miracles which happened through God's messengers (Rom 15,19; 2 Cor 12,12). Word and sign (or miracle) belonged together in early Christendom. It was not only preached, but the preaching was accompanied by signs of God's power, with the result that people were healed inwardly and outwardly.

In verse 7c apostles are commended as warriors for the kingdom of God, fully armed with the weapons of righteousness. The force of the genitive τῆς δικαιοσύνης is probably not "... having weapons to defend righteousness" but "... having weapons that God's righteousness has provided" (Furnish 1984:346; cf Bultmann 1976:174).[12] Weapons in both the right and the left hand refer to weapons for attack and defence, sword and shield. The image of an armed soldier has its origin in prophetic and wisdom imagery, dealing with God's eschatological judgement.[13]

Paul recognises a close link between righteousness and the Spirit. In 3,8.9 he refers successively to ἡ διακονία τοῦ πνεύματος and ἡ διακονία τῆς δικαιοσύνης. Compare also Rom 14,17 and Gal 5,5. As far as content is concerned, there is a close relationship between verse 7c and verses 6—7b.[14] Their "weapons of righteousness" are another sign that Paul and his co-workers have been fully equipped by God to do battle for the gospel in the world (Furnish 1984:357).

In verse 8 Paul uses two pairs of contrasting expressions to portray the positive and negative reactions to the apostolic preaching: He remains true to his commission, in spite of "glory and dishonour", "bad report" (cf also 1 Cor 4:12—13) or "good report" (cf Gal 4,14) (Lang 1986:305).[15]

Verses 8c—10 are characterised by a marked change in style. By using antithetic expressions concerning the apostles, Paul focuses on the paradoxical character of his apostolic ministry. The glory of his ministry exists in its lowness and sufferings (Lang 1986:305—6). The judgement of the world is opposed to the judgement of God.

---

[12] The genitive may be regarded as a genitive of origin.
[13] Klauck (1986:59) refers to Is 59,17 and Wisd 5,17—20.
[14] Friedrich (1963a:48) correctly mentions that the first διά-phrase "... gehört ... in gewisser Weise noch zum Vorhergehenden", while the next two διά-phrases "... durch ihre gegensätzlichen Aussagen bereits zur vierten Strophe überleiten". Cf also Windisch ([1924] 1970:206).
[15] Note the chiastic construction:
διὰ δόξης καὶ ἀτιμίας, διὰ δυσφημίας καὶ εὐφημίας.

There is an interesting relation between the dialectic nature of "seen" and "unseen" in 2 Cor 4,18 and 2 Cor 6,8c—9. The first sentences of the antitheses in 8c—9 propose a negative feature which seems to be visible. The following sentences state positively a truth present in a deeper dimension of life. This apparent contradiction only serves to emphasise two sides of one reality (cf Klauck 1986:59).

The description of a true Stoic as one who is "happy" despite the fact that he might be "sick ... in danger ... dying" (Epict II.xix.24), is no parallel to these verses at all.[16] Paul's statements are formulated as antitheses: The apostles are perceived in one way according to the false judgement of the world, but in quite another way in the light of the true judgement of those who are in Christ (Furnish 1984:357).

The apologetic function of this whole apostolic resumé is especially clear in the final antitheses. Paul seems to be aware of certain charges being laid by those who are contesting the validity of his apostleship. The first antithesis (ὡς πλάνοι καὶ ἀληθεῖς) may refer to the issue of his visit which had been cancelled (cf 1,15—2,2) (Furnish 1984:357—8). The Jews persecuted Paul because of his message of freedom from the law and furthermore his Jewish and Christian opponents considered him an impostor.[17]

In the second antithesis (ὡς ἀγνοούμενοι καὶ ἐπιγινωσκόμενοι) Paul acknowledges that his apostolate has no worldly status (cf 1 Cor 4,13). The lack of worldly fame was a popular topic for reflection among the Stoics (cf Sen Ep XXXI, 10; Epict IV viii.35; Marcus Aurelius VII,67). Paul's thought here is, however, unlike Seneca's (Ep XXXIX,14), that one's virtue will ultimately be known to the world, even if only after one's death. The point is that Paul and his colleagues are already fully known, even though not to the world at large (Furnish 1984:358). They are unknown in the eyes of men, but well known to God and in the congregation. This passage not only refers to the issue of acquaintance, but also to the issue of acknowledgement and appreciation: men who are not acknowledged by the world at large, but are appreciated by the congregation as people commissioned by God (cf Lang 1986:306).

---

[16] Contra Windisch [1924]1970:207: "Eine volle Parallele liefert ... die stoische Diatribe, vgl. Epictet Diss. II 19₂₄... ."

[17] "Vom Standpunkt der Menschen aus werden die Apostel als Verführer beurteilt, in Wirklichkeit vertreten sie die Wahrheit Gottes, die nur der Glaube erkennt" (Lang 1986:306).

The following two anthitheses take up the contrast between life and death in 4,10—12 and seem to have been constructed on the basis of the Septuagint Ps 117 (118),17—18. Verse 9b (ὡς ἀποθνῇσκοντες καὶ ἰδοὺ ζῶμεν) epitomises the theme of Paul's discussion of apostleship in 4,7—5,10. The apostles are bearers of "the death of Jesus" in order that "the life of Jesus", the resurrection power of God, may be disclosed in their mortal bodies (cf 4,7—11) (Furnish 1984:358; Lang 1986:306). The fourth antithesis (παιδευόμενοι καὶ μὴ θανατούμενοι) is to be interpreted in the same way. For Paul the suffering of the apostles is a means of God's self-disclosure (cf 4,7—12). It is not a sign that Paul's apostolic ministry is invalid, as some critics obviously think, but that it is true to its divine commission.

In the present letter especially, Paul acknowledges the sorrow he has felt (even because of the Corinthians themselves [2,1]). But here in the fifth antithesis (ὡς λυπούμενοι ἀεὶ δὲ χαίροντες) he is thinking in more general terms.[18]

In the sixth antithesis the world's perception of the apostles can not be contradicted. With respect to material goods, the apostles were impoverished. The theme of poverty is often present in contemporary descriptions of the lives of the Cynic and Stoic philosophers. It is possible that Paul's rivals in Corinth tried to interpret his poverty and his unwillingness to ask help from the local church as a tacit admission that he lacks apostolic authority (cf 1 Cor 9,1—18; 2 Cor 11,7—11). But Paul's statement that his apostolate, though materially "poor" is "making many rich", has no clear parallels in the descriptions of the Cynic and Stoic philosophers. It is frequently said that they have moral and spiritual riches despite their lack of worldly goods, but their enrichment of others is not a special theme. For Paul, however, this is the essence of apostleship: its bringing of the "riches" of salvation (see Rom 10,12; 11,12) to the world (2 Cor 2,14—16; 4,6; 5,13b; cf Rom 1,11; 1 Cor 1,5 ...) (Furnish 1984:359).

The elements of the final antithesis are closely related in meaning: The apostles are perceived by the world as μηδὲν ἔχοντες, but by those who are in Christ as πάντα κατέχοντες. The "have" formulas in the context may

---

[18] "Beständige Freude mitten in schweren Prüfungen ist biblisch gesehen ein Wesensmerkmal des Frommen, der auf Gott vertraut" (Klauck 1986:59—60).

provide a clue to what Paul possesses: confidence (3,4), hope (3,12), this ministry (4,1), this treasure (4,7), faith (4,13), a building from God, an eternal house in heaven (5,1). He who possesses these things has been made rich by God (Klauck 1986:60).

Mealand (1976:278—9) has compared Pseudo Crates Epectetus 7 (ἔχοντες μηδὲν πάντ᾽ ἔχομεν) with 2 Cor 6,10c (ὡς μηδὲν ἔχοντες καὶ πάντα κατέχοντες). The phrase in question is probably a commonplace and unlikely to have been coined by the author of the Cynic Epistles. Mealand correctly affirms that Paul uses occasional ideas and sentences of this kind, but builds them into a theological framework, which is quite different from that of the philosophers. For example, Paul builds the Stoic and Cynic concept of independence into a theology of dependence on divine grace. So in 2 Cor 6 Paul speaks of both the grace and power of God, and of the capacity to make others "rich", thus incorporating an old commonplace into a new faith.

13.4 Conclusion

In this passage Paul focuses on the apostolic ministry from a specific point of view: He explains in which way the apostolic ministry was conducted: "We put no stumbling block in anyone's path, so that our ministry will not be discredited. Rather as servants of God we commend ourselves in every way ..." (2 Cor 6,3—4a).

The hardships accompanying the apostolic ministry are accentuated in this pericope as having an important function. In stressing the hardships, Paul diverts the attention from the apostles and their own competence and focuses on God and his power. God himself is the ultimate source of power which can enable the apostolic ministry to function. This apostolic ministry, conducted ἐν δυνάμει θεοῦ, stands under the sign of "the word of truth", "the message of the cross" (1 Cor 1,18), "the gospel" (Rom 1,16). Paul's apostolic ministry, which finds its sole aim in the proclamation of the gospel, which is the power of God (Rom 1,16), avails itself of the weapons that God's righteousness has provided (διὰ τῶν ὅπλων τῆς δικαιοσύνης ... [2 Cor 6,7 — cf Rom 1,17]).

The way in which God's power is realised in the apostolic ministry is explained pneumatologically (ἐν πνεύματι ἁγίῳ). In the midst of considerable hardships the apostolic ministry is conducted with great endurance (ἐν ὑπομονῇ πολλῇ), in purity (ἐν ἁγνότητι), with knowledge (ἐν γνώσει) with patience (ἐν μακροθυμίᾳ), and with kindness (ἐν χρηστότητι). There is special emphasis on the fact that this ministry is conducted in unfeigned love (ἐν ἀγάπῃ ἀνυποκρίτῳ). Paul's ministry is characterised by both the gifts (here γνῶσις is mentioned (cf 1 Cor 12,8) and the fruits of the Spirit (ἀγάπη, μακροθυμία, χρηστότης — cf Gal 5,22).

Verses 8—10 provide an important key to the understanding of God's power in Paul's ministry. These verses reveal the way in which Paul interprets the power of God in the light of his theology of the cross. The judgement of the world is contrasted with the judgement of God. The apostles are perceived in one way according to the false judgement of the world, but in quite another way in terms of the true judgement of those who are in Christ.

Chapter 14

2 Corinthians 12,9

14.1 Location within the macrocontext of 2 Corinthians 10—13[1]

The structure of 2 Cor 10—13 may be set out schematically as follows:

10,1—13,10	*LETTER BODY*
10,1—18	PAUL'S DEFENCE OF HIS APOSTOLIC AUTHORITY
11,1—15	THE FALSE APOSTLES
11,16—12,13	A FOOL'S SPEECH
11,16—12,10	Paul is determined to boast about his weaknesses so that the power of Christ may come to dwell in him
12,11—13	Epilogue
12,14—13,10	RENEWAL AND CONCLUSION OF PAUL'S APPEAL TO THE CORINTHIANS; HIS IMPENDING THIRD VISIT
12,14—21	Expressions of concern
13,1—10	Body-closing: warning and admonition
13,1—4	*Paul's third visit and his weakness and power as an apostle*
13,5—10	*Pastoral care and pastoral authority*
13,11—14	*CLOSING*: greetings, the holy kiss, valediction (cf Lategan 1985:88; Furnish 1984:xii; Klauck 1986:77—104; Lambrecht 1999:11; Lang 1986)[2]

---

[1] New Testament scholars fully agree on the fact that 2 Cor 10—13 forms a separate unity within 2 Cor and therefore constitutes the macrocontext against which the pericope under discussion must be interpreted. On the issue of the unity of 2 Cor, cf chapter 12.2 note 2.

[2] For a rhetorical analysis of 2 Cor 10—13, cf Sundermann 1996.

The pericope 2 Cor 11,16—12,10 forms part of the section 2 Cor 11,16—12,13 in which Paul's ironical self-recommendation is very prominent. With strong irony Paul defends his apostolic authority (cf Loubser 1980:303).[3] (The demarcation of this pericope is discussed in 14.2.1.)

14.2 Discourse analysis: 2 Corinthians 11,16-12,10

Chapter 11

16	1 Πάλιν λέγω, μή τίς με δόξῃ ἄφρονα εἶναι·	
	2 εἰ δὲ μήγε, κἂν ὡς ἄφρονα δέξασθέ με,	
	ἵνα κἀγὼ μικρόν τι καυχήσωμαι.	
17	3 ὃ λαλῶ οὐ κατὰ κύριον λαλῶ,	**A**
	ἀλλ' ὡς ἐν ἀφροσύνῃ, ἐν ταύτῃ τῇ ὑποστάσει τῆς καυχήσεως.	
18	4 ἐπεὶ πολλοὶ καυχῶνται κατὰ σάρκα,	
	κἀγὼ καυχήσομαι.	
19	5 ἡδέως γὰρ ἀνέχεσθε τῶν ἀφρόνων φρόνιμοι ὄντες·	
20	6 ἀνέχεσθε γὰρ εἴ τις ὑμᾶς καταδουλοῖ,	
	7 (ἀνέχεσθε) εἴ τις κατεσθίει,	
	8 (ἀνέχεσθε) εἴ τις λαμβάνει,	**B**
	9 (ἀνέχεσθε) εἴ τις ἐπαίρεται,	
	10 (ἀνέχεσθε) εἴ τις εἰς πρόσωπον ὑμᾶς δέρει.	
21	11 κατὰ ἀτιμίαν λέγω, ὡς ὅτι ἡμεῖς ἠσθενήκαμεν·	
	12 ἐν ᾧ δ' ἄν τις τολμᾷ, ἐν ἀφροσύνῃ λέγω, τολμῶ κἀγώ.	
22	13 Ἑβραῖοί εἰσιν;	
	14 κἀγώ.	
	15 Ἰσραηλῖταί εἰσιν;	
	16 κἀγώ.	**C**
	17 σπέρμα Ἀβραάμ εἰσιν;	

---

[3] There is no consensus among New Testament scholars about the exact demarcation of this section, cf Bultmann (1976:6): "10_{12}—12_{18}: Die τόλμα des Paulus"; Furnish (1984:xii): "A Fool's Speech, 11,1—12,13"; Klauck (1986:86): "Die 'Narrenrede': 11^{16}—12^{13}"; Lang (1986:334): "Der Selbstruhm des Apostels wider Willen 11,1—12,13"; Windisch ([1924] 1970): "Törichte Selbstverherrlichung zur vernichtenden Abwehr der Gegner und zur Rechtfertigung der eigenen Person 11_1—12_{13}." Zmijewski (1978) regards our pericope as part of the larger section 2 Corinthians 11,1—12,10, "die paulinische 'Narrenrede' ".

18 κἀγώ.

23   19 διάκονοι Χριστοῦ εἰσιν;

20 παραφρονῶν λαλῶ, ὑπὲρ ἐγώ·

21 ἐν κόποις περισσοτέρως,

22 ἐν φυλακαῖς περισσοτέρως,

23 ἐν πληγαῖς ὑπερβαλλόντως,

24 ἐν θανάτοις πολλάκις·

24   25 ὑπὸ Ἰουδαίων πεντάκις τεσσαράκοντα παρὰ μίαν ἔλαβον,

25   26 τρὶς ἐραβδίσθην,

27 ἅπαξ ἐλιθάσθην,

28 τρὶς ἐναυάγησα,

29 νυχθήμερον ἐν τῷ βυθῷ πεποίηκα·   C

26   30 ὁδοιπορίαις πολλάκις,

31 κινδύνοις ποταμῶν,

32 κινδύνοις λῃστῶν,

33 κινδύνοις ἐκ γένους,

34 κινδύνοις ἐξ ἐθνῶν,

35 κινδύνοις ἐν πόλει,

36 κινδύνοις ἐν ἐρημίᾳ,

37 κινδύνοις ἐν θαλάσσῃ,

38 κινδύνοις ἐν ψευδαδέλφοις,

27   39 κόπῳ καὶ μόχθῳ,

40 ἐν ἀγρυπνίαις πολλάκις,

41 ἐν λιμῷ καὶ δίψει,

42 ἐν νηστείαις πολλάκις,

43 ἐν ψύχει καὶ γυμνότητι·

28   44 χωρὶς τῶν παρεκτὸς ἡ ἐπίστασίς μοι ἡ καθ' ἡμέραν,

ἡ μέριμνα πασῶν τῶν ἐκκλησιῶν.

29   45 τίς ἀσθενεῖ, καὶ οὐκ ἀσθενῶ;

46 τίς σκανδαλίζεται, καὶ οὐκ ἐγὼ πυροῦμαι;

30   47 Εἰ καυχᾶσθαι δεῖ, τὰ τῆς ἀσθενείας μου καυχήσομαι.

31   48 ὁ θεὸς καὶ πατὴρ τοῦ κυρίου Ἰησοῦ οἶδεν,
      ὁ ὢν εὐλογητὸς εἰς τοὺς αἰῶνας,
      ὅτι οὐ ψεύδομαι.

32   49 ἐν Δαμασκῷ ὁ ἐθνάρχης Ἀρέτα τοῦ βασιλέως
      ἐφρούρει τὴν πόλιν Δαμασκηνῶν πιάσαι με,

33   50 καὶ διὰ θυρίδος ἐν σαργάνῃ ἐχαλάσθην διὰ τοῦ τείχους
      51 καὶ ἐξέφυγον τὰς χεῖρας αὐτοῦ.

D

Chapter 12

1   52 Καυχᾶσθαι δεῖ·
     53 οὐ συμφέρον μέν,
     54 ἐλεύσομαι δὲ εἰς ὀπτασίας καὶ ἀποκαλύψεις κυρίου.

2   55.1 οἶδα ἄνθρωπον ἐν Χριστῷ πρὸ ἐτῶν δεκατεσσάρων -

        ┌───┐
        │ 56 εἴτε ἐν σώματι οὐκ οἶδα,   │
        │ 57 εἴτε ἐκτὸς τοῦ σώματος οὐκ οἶδα,   │
        │ 58 ὁ θεὸς οἶδεν -   │
        └───┘

        55.2 ἁρπαγέντα τὸν τοιοῦτον ἕως τρίτου οὐρανοῦ.

E

3   59.1 καὶ οἶδα τὸν τοιοῦτον ἄνθρωπον -

        ┌───┐
        │ 60 εἴτε ἐν σώματι   │
        │ 61 εἴτε χωρὶς τοῦ σώματος οὐκ οἶδα,   │
        │ 62 ὁ θεὸς οἶδεν -   │
        └───┘

4   59.2 ὅτι ἡρπάγη εἰς τὸν παράδεισον
        63 καὶ ἤκουσεν ἄρρητα ῥήματα ἃ οὐκ ἐξὸν ἀνθρώπῳ λαλῆσαι.

5   64 ὑπὲρ τοῦ τοιούτου καυχήσομαι,
     65 ὑπὲρ δὲ ἐμαυτοῦ οὐ καυχήσομαι
       εἰ μὴ ἐν ταῖς ἀσθενείαις {μου}.

F

6   66 ἐὰν γὰρ θελήσω καυχήσασθαι, οὐκ ἔσομαι ἄφρων,
     67 ἀλήθειαν γὰρ ἐρῶ·
     68 φείδομαι δέ,
       μή τις εἰς ἐμὲ λογίσηται ὑπὲρ ὃ βλέπει με ἢ ἀκούει {τι} ἐξ ἐμοῦ

7   69 καὶ τῇ ὑπερβολῇ τῶν ἀποκαλύψεων.
       διό, ἵνα μὴ ὑπεραίρωμαι,
       ἐδόθη μοι σκόλοψ τῇ σαρκί, ἄγγελος Σατανᾶ,
       ἵνα με κολαφίζῃ,
       ἵνα μὴ ὑπεραίρωμαι.
8   70 ὑπὲρ τούτου τρὶς τὸν κύριον παρεκάλεσα
       ἵνα ἀποστῇ ἀπ' ἐμοῦ·   G
9   71 καὶ εἴρηκέν μοι,
       71.1 'Αρκεῖ σοι ἡ χάρις μου·
       72 ἡ γὰρ δύναμις ἐν ἀσθενείᾳ τελεῖται.
       73 ἥδιστα οὖν μᾶλλον καυχήσομαι ἐν ταῖς ἀσθενείαις μου,
       ἵνα ἐπισκηνώσῃ ἐπ' ἐμὲ ἡ δύναμις τοῦ Χριστοῦ.

10   74 διὸ εὐδοκῶ
       ἐν ἀσθενείαις, ἐν ὕβρεσιν, ἐν ἀνάγκαις,   H
       ἐν διωγμοῖς καὶ στενοχωρίαις, ὑπὲρ Χριστοῦ·
       75 ὅταν γὰρ ἀσθενῶ, τότε δυνατός εἰμι.

14.2.1 A few notes pertaining to the structure of this pericope

The present pericope is introduced by the introductory formula, πάλιν λέγω. The line of thought is interrupted between 12,10 and 12,11. A new pericope is introduced by γέγονα ἄφρων in verse 11.

The following structural markers occur throughout this pericope and, therefore, bind it together:

Verbs indicating Paul's boasting

καυχήσωμαι (11,16); καυχήσεως (11,17); καυχῶνται (11,18); καυχήσομαι (11,18); (τολμᾷ [11,21]; τολμῶ [11,21]); καυχᾶσθαι (11,30); καυχήσομαι (11,30); Καυχᾶσθαι (12,1); καυχήσομαι (12,5); καυχήσομαι (12,5); καυχήσασθαι (12,6); καυχήσομαι (12,9); (εὐδοκῶ [12,10]).

Weakness/being weak

ἠσθενήκαμεν (11,21); ἀσθενεῖ (11,28), ἀσθενῶ (11,28); ἀσθενείας (11,30); ἀσθενείαις (12,5); ἀσθενείᾳ (12,9), ἀσθενείαις (12,9); ἀσθενείαις (12,10), ἀσθενῶ (12,10).

Verbs indicating Paul's boasting have already occurred earlier, namely in 2 Cor 10—11. This is an indication of the close relationship between this pericope and its broader context. *The motif of weakness, however, appears for the first time in this pericope and the relationship between the two motifs is of great importance for the interpretation of this passage.*

Note the close correspondence between the lists of hardships (dative constructions) in 12,10 and 11,23 (colons 21—24), 11,25d—27 (νυχθήμερον ἐν τῷ βυθῷ πεποίηκα ... ἐν ψύχει καὶ γυμνότητι).

Although this pericope comprises various sub-pericopes, the interpretation of 11,16—12,10 as a unit has important consequences. It will be pointed out in the following discussion that the *tension* that exists between the most dominant motifs that occur throughout this pericope, namely the motifs of *boasting* and of *weakness*, is resolved towards the end of this pericope. The phrase which holds the *key* to the solution of this tension is to be found in the δύναμις τοῦ Χριστοῦ (12,9). To understand the full meaning of Paul's affirmation here (2 Cor 12,9), it must be viewed against the background of the pericope as a whole (and not only in the context of 2 Cor 12,1—9).

Relation of sub-pericopes to one another

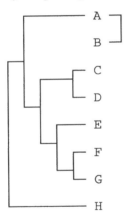

This whole pericope is dominated by the boasting which Paul has had to resort to unwillingly because of pressure brought to bear upon him by his opponents.

In sub-pericope B we find an ironic motivation for the boasting, which is elaborated in sub-pericopes C—H.

The contents of Paul's boasting is expressed in sub-pericopes C—G. There is a clear break between sub-pericopes D and E. Important structural markers and actants occur in sub-pericope E which do not occur in sub-pericope D. Sub-pericopes C and D are, however, closely related to each other, with regard to both content and structure. In sub-pericope C the content of Paul's *boasting* is expressed. Towards the end of this sub-pericope the important motif of *weakness* is introduced. In the first colon of sub-pericope D these motifs (boasting and weakness) are related to each other:

Εἰ καυχᾶσθαι δεῖ, τὰ τῆς ἀσθενείας μου καυχήσομαι

In sub-pericopes F and G the reader encounters an elaboration and interpretation of the events described by Paul in sub-pericope E.

In sub-pericope H the conclusion is put forward which Paul has reached in the course of the argumentation in the preceding sub-pericopes.

This leads to the conclusion that this pericope has a climactic structure.

14.3 Textual criticism: 2 Corinthians 12,9

The second corrector of codex Sinaiticus, codex Alexandrinus, the second corrector of codex Claromontanus, codex Ψ and 0243 as well as the Majority text, all the Syriac versions and five or more witnesses in Bohairic, read ἡ γὰρ δύναμις μου. The possessive pronoun which is (seemingly) absent from papyrus 46, and was left out by the original scribe of codex Sinaiticus, codex Vaticanus, the original scribe of codex Claromontanus, codices F and G, all the Latin witnesses, all the Sahidic versions, five or more witnesses in Bohairic and the Latin version of Irenaeus, seems to have been added by copyists for the sake of perspicuity (Metzger 1994:517). External evidence also tips the scale in favour of the reading without the possessive pronoun.

The second corrector of codices Sinaiticus and Claromontanus, codex Ψ, codex 0243 and the Majority text read τελειουται. On the basis of external support (the original scribe of codex Sinaiticus, codex Alexandrinus, codex Vaticanus, the original scribe of codex Claromontanus as well as codices F and G) the reading τελεῖται should be preferred. It is possible that a copyist made use of an alternative form which was better known to him.

μου in the phrase, ἐν ταῖς ἀσθενείαις μου, is omitted by codex Vaticanus, minuscule manuscripts 6, 81, 1175 (original scribe), 1739, a few other Greek manuscripts, the Syriac Harclensis, the Bohairic versions as well as by Irenaeus. However, μov appears in the following codices: Sinaiticus, Alexandrinus, Claromontanus, F, G, Ψ, the Majority text, all the Latin versions as well as in the Syriac Peshitta. Although μov is omitted by codex Vaticanus, it is present in several important manuscripts from different families. On the basis of external support the reading with μov is to be preferred.

14.4 An exegetical overview: Christ's power in 2 Corinthians 12,9

14.4.1 Introduction

In 2 Cor 10—13 Paul touches on two important themes:

— His response to receiving news about the growing intensity of attacks on his apostolate in Corinth.
— Anticipation of his third visit to the congregation (Furnish 1984:459).

The pericope under discussion deals with the first theme (cf McCant 1988:553). In the final pericope of chapter 10 (vv 12—18) Paul is critical of those who, by recommending themselves to and claiming a certain authority over the Corinthian congregation, have encroached upon his apostolic jurisdiction.[4] This criticism is sharpened in 11,1—12,13 (Furnish 1984:498). (However, the present writer has decided that a new pericope commences with 11,16 as this passage is introduced by a clear introductory

---

[4] Georgi views Paul's opponents as Jewish Christian missionaries, who are theologically characterised by a θεῖος ἀνήρ piety (cf Betz 1969:304). He (1964:295—6) points to the close relation between the view Paul's opponents had of Christ and their conduct: "Rühmte sich Paulus seiner Leiden, so die Gegner ihrer geistlichen Erfahrungen und Machttaten und sahen sie im Gegensatz zu Paulus als Beweise für die Echtheit und Lebendigkeit ihrer Christusrepräsentation an. Ebenso wie nach Paulus die Macht des Christus in der Schwachheit zur Vollendung kommt [12,9], müssen sie der Überzeugung gewesen sein, daß die Macht des Christus in den Machttaten seiner Boten gegenwärtig ist ... Die gegnerischen Pneumatiker mußten sich den Gottesmännern der Vergangenheit, die die Grenzen des Menschlichen überspielt und durchbrochen hatten, besonders dann nahe fühlen, wenn ihnen ekstatische Erlebnisse vergönnt waren."
Schmithals (1956:199.205), however, stresses the *Gnostic* presuppositions with which Paul's opponents operated.

formula [πάλιν λέγω] and important structural markers occur in this pericope which do not occur in the preceding verses, cf 14.2.1.)

Paul deliberately (but nonetheless reluctantly) adopts the procedure of his rivals and boasts of his own credentials.[5] He has just quoted Scripture against boasting of this sort (10,17—18), but he feels constrained to do it in order to regain the confidence of the congregation.

Although verses 17—18 may be regarded as parenthetical, they fulfil an important function in this context. This passage supports Paul's appeal in verse 16 by explaining that he was forced to boast by those who opposed his apostleship (v 18; cf v 12). Verses 17—18 also explain why he must regard all boasting as essentially foolish — to boast is to speak not "... as the Lord would" (v 17), but "... in the way the world does".

As elsewhere, Paul refers to his opponents in veiled language, here simply as πολλοί (cf 2,17). This oblique reference (cf also vv 4.13.20.21b) aims at diminishing their stature in the eyes of the Corinthians[6] (Furnish 1984:511).

The main support for the renewed appeal in verse 16 is presented in verses 19—21a. The irony of Paul's statement about the Corinthians in verse 19 turns it into the sharpest criticism.[7] It is clear that Paul believes that his rivals have tyrannised and exploited the congregation (Furnish 1984:512).

After a lengthy prologue, Paul launches at last (pericopes C—F) into the "foolish" boasting with which he has been so reluctant to become involved. The phrases ἐν ἀφροσύνῃ λέγω (v 21b) and παραφρονῶν (v 23) make his self-consciousness apparent. He has been forced to these tactics by his rivals in Corinth, who have made extravagant claims for themselves while at the same time impugning the authority of the Pauline apostolate (cf 11,18.21b—23; 12,1a). One may infer from Paul's response to those

---

[5] A helpful discussion of Paul's boasting in 2 Cor 10—13 is presented by Lambrecht 1996:325—46.

[6] Cf Zmijewski (1978:202): "Wie so oft, wenn Paulus über seine Gegner Negativ-Abwertendes sagen will, bedient er sich auch hier bewußt einer 'verhüllenden' Redeweise, um dadurch die Gegner noch stärker zu treffen ... ."

[7] Zmijewski (1978:230) describes the function of the irony in verses 19 to 21a: "Die Ironie weist an den genannten Stellen auch unterschiedliche Intensitätsgrade auf. Sie erscheint in V.19 mehr als witzige Satire, in V.20 eher als groteske Parodie, in V.21a als unsinnig 'verfremdende' Selbstkarikatur."

claims that the rival apostles (a) took special pride in their Jewish heritage, (b) pointed to various specific accomplishments as evidence that they were Christ's true ministers, and (c) boasted of being the recipients of extraordinary visions and revelations. Paul counters each of his rivals' claims: (a) he is also of Jewish stock (11,22); (b) his career as an apostle distinguishes him as a better minister of Christ than his rivals are (11,23—29); and (c) extraordinary religious experiences are not unknown to him (12,1—4). Contrary to his rivals, however, Paul affirms in 11,30—33 and 12,5—10 that he would boast only about his weaknesses.

With 2 Cor 12,7 Paul moves to his crowning antithesis. After he has refused to boast of visions and revelations, he turns instead to the memory of humiliation: σκόλοψ τῇ σαρκί (v 7). Critics differ widely concerning the exact nature of the thorn. (An investigation into Paul's σκόλοψ τῇ σαρκί falls beyond the scope of this study.)[8] The central point of the narrative is, however, unaffected by the nature of the thorn. The point is, as Forbes (1986:21) correctly affirms, the answer given by God to Paul's threefold prayer in 12,8—9.

Paul is, therefore, not really matching the claims of his rivals, although he appears to start out in this way in 11,22. He ends up parodying the claims of his rivals, much as he had in 10,12: In contrast to the boasts of those who claim to have special apostolic powers and religious insights, Paul offers a long list of sufferings (11,23c—29) (Furnish 1984:532—3).[9] On his description of his extraordinary experience in 12,1—4,[10] follows 12,5—10 in which Paul explicitly states (as in 11,30—33) that his boasting is a boasting in weaknesses. This perspective reveals the distinguishing marks of the true apostle.

In Hellenistic thought δύναμις refers to a power, a sign of the god — in the case of Asclepius — a power that brings healing (ἡ τοῦ θεοῦ δύναμις

---

[8] It does seem most probable that Paul refers to a form of personal suffering in his body (cf Heininger 1997:258 and for a critique of the thesis that the "thorn in the flesh" refers to his sufferings, Heckel 1993a:69—80).

Lambrecht (1999:205) concludes: "All in all, those who read 2 Cor 12,7 more realistically are inclined to see in the 'thorn' a physical disability such as a speech impediment or an eye ailment, while those who regard both 'thorn' and 'angel of Satan' more spiritually think rather of persecutions and opposition."

[9] What follows on Paul's ὑπὲρ ἐγώ in verse 23 "... sind ja keine solchen Vorzüge deren sich die Gegner rühmen, sondern sind im Grunde schon die ἀσθένεια von V.$_{30}$, also der paradoxe Erweis der δύναμις von 4$_{7ff}$"(Bultmann 1976:217).

[10] On "Paul's Journey to Paradise" (2 Cor 12,2—4), cf Thrall 1996:347—63.

σωτηρίος). Healings were regarded as epiphanies of the divine power (ἐπιφανείαι δυνάμεως).[11] Should a healing *not* take place, it is a sign of the god's powerlessness.[12] Against this background the word in 2 Cor 12,9a gains profile. The expectation of the readers is disappointed — corrected: the healing does not take place. Despite the fact that the healing does not take place, δύναμις is still there, it is made perfect in weakness (ἐν ἀσθενείᾳ) (cf Heininger 1997:261—2).

There is an important logic behind Paul's insight in this passage (cf Savage 1996:167). Had he not been humbled by the thorn in the flesh he would have been tempted to boast of his divine visions as though they were his own achievement and might have used them to exalt himself (cf the phrase ἵνα μὴ ὑπεραίρωμαι, which appears twice in 12,7). Where there is pride and arrogance there cannot be divine power.

This principle occurs throughout the Old Testament. Very often those who enjoyed the most dramatic manifestations of divine power, were those of the greatest humility (cf Abraham [Gen 18,7], Moses [Ex 3,11], Gideon [Judg 6,15] and David [1 Sam 18,23]). God "... dwells with the contrite and lowly of spirit" (Is 57,15) and "... is near the broken hearted" (Ps 34,18). This principle is carried over into Judaism, where the rabbis taught that it was with humble men that God was pleased to dwell.[13]

The Corinthians were evaluating Paul according to the self-exalting standards of their secular environment. It is therefore not surprising that they were dismayed by his humility — his "weakness". Paul however turned their logic on its head: It was his *weakness* which not only affirmed his position as a minister of Christ, but also assured that his labours would be accompanied by divine power (Savage 1996:187—8).

Since the appearance of H D Betz's "Der Apostel Paulus und die sokratische Tradition", scholarly attention to Paul's "boasting" in 2 Cor 10—12 has focused on the question of literary form (Forbes 1986:1).[14]

---

[11] P Oxy 1381,215—8 in a song of praise to Imuthes-Asclepius, cf Heininger (1997:261).

[12] Cf W 36 Herzog (quoted by Heininger 1997:261): "Kephisias von X., Fuß. Dieser lachte über die Kuren des Asklepios und sagte: Wenn der Gott sagt, er habe Lahme geheilt, so lügt er; denn wenn er die Kraft dazu hättte [εἰ δύναμιν ε(ἶχε)], warum hat er dann nicht den Hephaistos geheilt." Kephisias of course had to pay for his *hybris* and his foot became cripple. After he had asked the god many times for forgiveness, he was healed.

[13] For specific references, cf Savage 1996:167—8.

[14] "Was uns in Kap. 10—13 vorliegt, ist ein Fragment einer sehr bewußt und kunstvoll komponierten 'Apologie' in Briefform" (Betz 1972:14).

Within this *apologia* Paul makes use of another literary form: the foolish discourse.[15]

Profound criticism has been levelled against this interpretation by Christopher Forbes (1986:1). He mentions that one weakness of this mode of interpretation is that it does not do justice to the very clear evidence that Paul is responding to his opponents in kind. If others are boasting, like fools, then so, like a fool, will he. One would therefore expect that Paul's methods would mirror those of his opponents, though ironically. Forbes adds that the "apology" is too diverse a form, if it is a form in any strict sense of the word at all, to give us close exegetical control of the passage.

The work of Zmijewski from which I have already quoted above and in which a detailed literary analysis of the "Narrenrede" is given, drew almost exclusively from modern, rather than ancient literary theory. Forbes (1986:30) mentions that it is to be doubted whether this really brings us any closer to understanding Paul in his own environment. (It must be conceded that this is a legitimate point of criticism against this study of Zmijewski, which is, however, in many other respects an excellent work.)

In his article, "Comparison, self-praise and irony: Paul's boasting and the conventions of Hellenistic rhetoric", Forbes offers a careful analysis of comparison in rhetorical argument, followed by the conventions relating to self-praise, and the conditions applying to its acceptability. He also considers the various forms of irony considered proper for the public speaker and the traditional characterisation of the "ironic man". In applying this material to the close analysis of the "boasting" passage in 2 Cor 10—12, Forbes (1986:2) suggests that Paul, responding to the opponents' characterisation of him as inconsistent, and hence as a flatterer, and to the invidious comparisons of his opponents, attacks the whole convention of self-advertisement by means of a remarkably subtle and forceful parody of its methods. He characterises his opponents as pretentious and fraudulent,

---

[15] Cf Betz (1972:79): "Die Rolle des 'Narren' ist ... aus dem griechischen und römischen Mimus und aus der Komödie als die des närrischen Prahlers und Aufschneiders bekannt."

while laying before the Corinthian congregation a powerful statement of his own apostolic position and authority.[16]

14.4.2 The Lord's answer to Paul's pleading

It is necessary at this stage to focus more sharply on the Lord's answer to Paul's pleading and Paul's subsequent reaction (2 Cor 12,9-10). The Lord's answer to Paul's pleading, ἀρκεῖ σοι ἡ χάρις μου,[17] is motivated in a significant way: ἡ γὰρ δύναμις ἐν ἀσθενείᾳ τελεῖται. This word of the Lord can be traced back directly to the exalted Lord and constitutes the centre of chapters 10—13, around which other thoughts may be grouped concentrically. It contains the three leading theological motifs, namely grace (χάρις), power (δύναμις) and weakness (ἀσθένεια) (Klauck 1986:94-5).

The statement that "power is made perfect in weakness" constitutes the "Magna Charta christlicher Existenz" (Klauck 1986:95). The power of Christ wants to make its dwelling in Paul's broken existence. This is why Paul refrains from boasting of anything except his "weakness", his

---

[16] In a study of 2 Cor 12,7—10, H D Betz (1969:288—305) portrays this passage as "... eine Christus-Aretalogie bei Paulus". Betz affirms that seen from the perspective of form criticism we have in verses 7 to 10 "... ein 'Heilungswunder' vor uns, das im Stile einer Aretalogie vorgetragen ist". In the context of the so-called fool's narrative "... kann eine solche Aretalogie nur als Parodie angesprochen werden" (1969:289).

In this study Betz finds affirmation for Georgi's thesis that Paul's opponents in 2 Corinthians are Jewish Christian missionaries "... die theologisch durch eine θεῖος ἀνήρ-Frömmigkeit geprägt sind" (1969:304).

When referring to this part of the "fool's narrative" in his study, Betz (1969:305) points to the theological geniality of Paul: "... gegen eine als 'Heilungswunder' erfahrene Verweigerung der Heilung, zusammen mit der Offenbaring eines erklärenden Logions des erhöhten Christus, läßt sich im religionsgeschichtlichen Horizont der θεῖος ἀνήρ-Frömmigkeit nichts mehr einwenden."

However, despite Betz's argumentation, the whole thrust of this passage makes its categorisation as a "Heilungswunder" unconvincing.

[17] Bultmann (1976:228) comments: "Das Sich-Begnügen ist wirklich ein Genug-Haben. Es liegt also keine Resignation vor wie Dtn 3₂₃ ff." (God's answer to Moses' request to enter the promised land). He also points to the great difference between this passage and Stoic parallels: "Der Unterschied ... liegt in der verschiedenen Auffassung der menschlichen ἀσθένεια und der göttlichen δύναμις."

humiliations and sufferings.[18] They are to him the surest marks of his commendation by the suffering Messiah (Forbes 1986:21).[19] From Paul's point of view the decisive demonstration of the truth of this oracular pronouncement is Christ himself, "... crucified in weakness, yet He lives by God's power" (2 Cor 13,4a; cf 1 Cor 1,18.22—24).

It is important to bear in mind that the understanding of the crucifixion as the event in which Christ proved radically "weak", forms the background to Paul's whole discussion. O'Collins (1971:532-3) correctly pointed out that in the case of the crucifixion and resurrection, weakness and power constitute an inseparable unity. By raising Christ, God's power was effective and manifested in the face of that ultimate "weakness" which the crucifixion meant. The apostolic ministry undertaken on Christ's behalf also involves participation in this weakness and power of Calvary and Easter. Paul himself boasts of that "weakness" which, by aligning him with Christ's death, brings him to experience the power of the resurrection. The "thorn in the flesh" and further "weakness" fail, therefore, to serve as evidence that Paul does not count as a true apostle.

In the same way it may be said that apostolic authority is the authority of the gospel itself. The gospel is the message of the "foolishness" and "weakness" of God himself (1 Cor 1,18-25) and the true apostle embodies that foolishness and weakness. His life and work bear the marks of the death of Christ: the physical sufferings and the social stigmata enumerated in the "catalogues of hardships". The pattern is not confined to the apostle, but it is pre-eminently exemplified in him (contra O'Collins 1971:533-5). His congregations are to imitate him in his "weakness" as he imitates Christ. The power of the gospel in the person of the apostle is the eschatological power of God, revealed "in weakness" (Forbes 1986:22).

---

[18] Paul's boasting of his weaknesses is a quite extraordinary paradox. Forbes (1986:22) mentions that in Philo, for example, it is human weakness that most effectively reduces boasting by reminding man of his proper place in relation to God. In this paradox Paul is, however, saying fundamental things about the nature of his understanding of both apostolic authority and life "in Christ" generally.

[19] McCant (1988:570) also points to the christological level of meaning of this passage: "The catchwords ἀσθένεια and δύναμις in 12,9-10 and 13,4 assure a christological understanding of his [i e Paul's] apostolate. He so identifies with Christ that the 'sufferings of Christ are ours' (2 Cor 1.18). In Corinth Paul's message was the foolishness of 'the word of the Cross' (1 Cor 1.18) and 'Christ crucified' (1 Cor 1.23; 2.2) in a context of weakness. Paul carries 'in the body the dying of Jesus' and this earthen vessel is 'delivered over to the death of Jesus' (2 Cor 4.10-1)."

The words of the Lord which Paul quotes in 2 Cor 12:9 are *a special formulation of the gospel itself: salvation, one's only true sufficiency, is by God's grace and in God's power* (cf 3,5; 8,9; Rom 1,16) (Furnish 1984:550-1).

In his letters Paul normally attributes power (δύναμις) to God or to the Spirit. This is the only passage where he speaks of the δύναμις τοῦ Χριστοῦ. Ebner (1991:187) emphasises that the "power of Christ" in 2 Cor 12,9 does not mean God's resurrection power — as is the case when Paul connects δύναμις with God. Paul speaks here in a *paradoxical sense* of the δύναμις Christi, and refers to the weakness and powerlessness of Christ on the cross. The broader context of 2 Corinthians, however, does not seem to justify such a distinction between the power of God and of Christ. Throughout this letter Paul interprets the power of God in the light of *both* the crucifixion and resurrection of Christ.

The distinction between Paul's weakness and the power of Christ is very evident in 12,9. The Lord says to Paul: "My grace is sufficient for you, for power is made perfect in weakness." Paul then draws the conclusion: "I will all the more gladly boast of my weaknesses, that the power of Christ may rest upon me."[20] This distinction between Christ and Paul himself, however, disappears in the paradoxical language of 12,10b: "... for when I am weak, then I am strong". Paradoxical language intends to be provocative. A paradox mentions only the antithesis and does not offer a complete presentation of the case, and is, therefore, never absolute. Weakness is not strength. The paradox ought to lead to reflection; by reflection the discerning listener or reader should find the solution (Lambrecht 1999:208).

How should the relation between weakness and power then be understood? Bultmann (1976:229) affirms:

"So ist die ἀσθένεια die Bedingung für die Realisierung der δύναμις wie der Tod die Bedingung für das φανερωθῆναι der ζωή τοῦ Ἰησοῦ 4₁₀f.; vgl.4₁₆ und 4₇: Ἔχομεν δὲ τὸν θησαυρὸν τοῦτον ἐν ὀστρακίνοις σκεύεσιν, ἵνα ἡ ὑπερβολὴ τῆς δυνάμεως ᾖ τοῦ θεοῦ καὶ μὴ ἐξ ἡμῶν."

---

[20] Quotation from the RSV.

O'Collins (1971:536) objects to the view that "weakness" is a precondition for "power" by pointing out that Paul's words both in 2 Cor 12,9—10 and elsewhere indicate the *simultaneousness* of weakness and power. When he was with the Corinthians "... in weakness and fear, and with much trembling" his message was characterised by a "... demonstration of the Spirit's power".

These two views of the relation of "weakness" and "power" (i e weakness as the condition for the realisation of δύναμις [Bultmann] and the interpretation stressing the simultaneousness of weakness and power [O'Collins]) do not necessarily exclude one another when one bears in mind that this relation must be interpreted against the background of the structure of the gospel which centres round the cross and resurrection of Jesus Christ.

Weakness belongs to the earthly sphere[21] — δύναμις refers to *God's power* with the nuance in this context of the resurrection power of Christ.[22] Weakness is a precondition for power in the same way in which salvation can only be obtained by man in Pauline theology when he acknowledges his complete incompetence and just accepts in faith what Christ has done for him. But weakness and power also occur simultaneously when man in his weakness finds himself "... lost in the grace, protection, and power of Christ" (Black 1984:156—7). Therefore, the Lord can say that his power is *made perfect* (τελεῖται; cf Louw & Nida 1988:747) in weakness.[23]

The close relation between χάρις and δύναμις in 2 Cor 12,9 is of great importance for the present study.[24] Bultmann (1976:229) is of the opinion that it is due to the *Hellenistic* concept of χάρις, that Paul can understand God's calling and grace as a power directing the whole of life.

John Nolland (1986:31) has, however, pointed out that the notion of a power given by God is present in *Jewish* usage of χάρις and affirms that

---

[21] Cf Zmijewski 1978:383: "Wie die unbestimmte Singularform anzeigt, bezeichnet ἀσθένεια hier generell die ganze *irdisch-menschliche Existenz* in ihrer 'Schwachheit'."

[22] Cf Zmijewski (1978:383—4): "Es wurde bereits herausgestellt, daß die δύναμις Gottes wesentlich 'Auferstehungskraft' bedeutet. Diese nähere Kennzeichnung der δύναμις ergibt sich aber für Paulus [wie überhaupt für das Neue Testament] *nicht auf Grund von theoretischen Überlegungen, sondern auf Grund des göttlichen Heilshandelns, d.h. konkret: des Christusgeschehens. Die Gültigkeit des paradoxen Gesetzes wird in Kreuz und Auferstehung Christi faßbar* [vgl. 2 Kor 13,4; Röm 1,4; Phil 3,10 u.ö.]" [emphasis:PJG].

[23] The present tense passive form underlining the "... Allgemeingültigkeit der Aussage" (Zmijewski 1978:383).

[24] "χάρις and δύναμις sind hier wesentlich gleichbedeutend, wie denn V.₉ an Stelle der χάρις des κύριος die δύναμις τοῦ Χριστοῦ tritt ..." (Bultmann 1976:229).

there is no need to look to late Hellenistic sources to establish the provenance that does justice to that stand of New Testament usage of χάρις in which the word is seen to designate a tangible power at work in the believer. The semantic background of the word χάρις comprises a surprising identification of "weakness" with "power".[25]

In verse 10a one sees Paul boasting of (actually delighting in) his weaknesses "for Christ's sake". This second catalogue of hardships (v 10b) is much shorter than the one in 11,23b—29 (and those in 4,8—9; 6,4c—5), and the adversities listed are much more general.

Both catalogues of hardships fulfil the same function in the composition of this pericope. The longer catalogue leads to the conclusion only to "... boast of the things that show my weaknesses" (11,30). The shorter catalogue leads to the same conclusion. This conclusion has now, however, obtained another dimension in the light of the Lord's answer in 12,9, expressed by the ἴνα-phrase: "... that the power of Christ may come to dwell in me" (cf Louw & Nida 1988b:731—2).

The main point of the oracle Paul had received (v 9a), is reiterated in verse 10b, now formulated as an expression of the apostle's own deep conviction (Furnish 1984:551).[26] The paradox of power and weakness receives special emphasis in this passage. Windisch ([1924)] 1970:394) is of the opinion that "power" in verse 10a refers to the *patience*, with which Paul endured all the suffering. This interpretation can however not be accepted, as δύναμις in this passage refers primarily to the *power of Christ* in Paul's ministry, which is emphasised by his weaknesses.

The paradox with which Paul is working here is profound, and it must not be misunderstood. He is not saying that "weakness is power" as Philo is when he refers to Moses and the people of Israel who because of their weakness were sheltered from harm by the providence of God (*Moses* 1,69). Nor does Paul mean that he lives in the confidence that the weak will themselves be clothed with power, displacing the mighty from their seats (as, e g, in Hannah's song, 1 Sam 2,1—10; cf Lk 1,46—55). He is saying,

---

[25] Cf Loubser (1980:228). Pop (1962:365) also pointed in this direction by recognising in χάρις an emphasis on the active character of grace: "... 'mijn genade' is het totaal van het genadig handelen Gods gelijk het de mens Paulus wordt toebedeeld. Er ligt nadruk op het actieve karakter van Gods genadig-zijn ... De genade van de Heer is hier het inbegrip van alles wat de Heer met Paulus gedaan heeft, doet en doen zal".

[26] "Wir erleben in der sprachlichen Gestaltung die Internalisierung des christlichen Grundgesetzes, seine existentielle Aneignung durch Paulus, mit" (Klauck 1986:95).

rather, that the weaknesses which continue to characterise his life as an apostle provide the opportunity for the effective working of the power of the crucified Christ to be perfected in his ministry (cf Furnish 1984:551—2). These weaknesses point away from the apostle and his own abilities to the *power of Christ*.[27]

In the light of the preceding discussion it is now clear why the statement could be made earlier (14.2.1) that the solution of the tension between two of the most dominant motifs in this pericope, "boasting" and "weakness" is found in the δύναμις τοῦ Χριστοῦ. Paul's weaknesses are necessary for participation in the δύναμις τοῦ Χριστοῦ, just as the *crucified* Christ experienced God's *resurrection power* (2 Cor 13,4). Viewed from this perspective, ἀσθένεια is the hallmark of true apostleship, allowing Paul to say: Εἰ καυχᾶσθαι δεῖ, τὰ τῆς ἀσθενείας μου καυχήσομαι (2 Cor 11,30).

---

[27] "In der Leidensexistenz des Apostels kommt die Kraft Christi voll zur Wirkung, weil hier nicht der Mensch seine eigene Kraft demonstriert" (Lang 1986:350).

Chapter 15

2 Corinthians 13,4

15.1 Location within the macrocontext of 2 Corinthians 10—13

The pericope, 2 Cor 13,1—4, is part of that section of 2 Cor 10—13 dealing with Paul's impending third visit to Corinth (2 Cor 12,14—13,10; cf Loubser 1980:294.325—6; Klauck 1986:97). Paul's apostolic authority is an issue throughout 2 Cor 10—13 (cf Hughes 1962:VIII). In the pericope under discussion an admonition and threat are expressed (cf Barrett 1973:326; Bruce 1971:176; Bultmann 1976:238; Furnish 1984:xii; Lambrecht 1999:220; Windisch [1924] 1970:412).

The reader is referred to the discussion of the structure of 2 Cor 10—13 in chapter 14.1.

15.2 Discourse analysis: 2 Corinthians 13,1—4

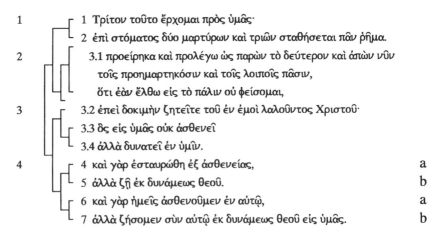

1   1 Τρίτον τοῦτο ἔρχομαι πρὸς ὑμᾶς·

       2 ἐπὶ στόματος δύο μαρτύρων καὶ τριῶν σταθήσεται πᾶν ῥῆμα.

2   3.1 προείρηκα καὶ προλέγω ὡς παρὼν τὸ δεύτερον καὶ ἀπὼν νῦν τοῖς προημαρτηκόσιν καὶ τοῖς λοιποῖς πᾶσιν, ὅτι ἐὰν ἔλθω εἰς τὸ πάλιν οὐ φείσομαι,

3   3.2 ἐπεὶ δοκιμὴν ζητεῖτε τοῦ ἐν ἐμοὶ λαλοῦντος Χριστοῦ·

       3.3 ὃς εἰς ὑμᾶς οὐκ ἀσθενεῖ

       3.4 ἀλλὰ δυνατεῖ ἐν ὑμῖν.

4   4 καὶ γὰρ ἐσταυρώθη ἐξ ἀσθενείας,   a

       5 ἀλλὰ ζῇ ἐκ δυνάμεως θεοῦ.   b

       6 καὶ γὰρ ἡμεῖς ἀσθενοῦμεν ἐν αὐτῷ,   a

       7 ἀλλὰ ζήσομεν σὺν αὐτῷ ἐκ δυνάμεως θεοῦ εἰς ὑμᾶς.   b

15.2.1 A few notes on the structure of 2 Corinthians 13,1—4

In colons 1—2 the numerical aspect of Paul's visit is emphasised: Τρίτον ... δύο ... τριῶν. This aspect is continued in colon 3 with reference to the previous visit (... τὸ δεύτερον); the prefix προ-, which is repeated three times: προείρηκα ... προλέγω ... προημαρτηκόσιν; the reference to the coming visit.

By inserting the phrase ἐὰν ἔλθω εἰς τὸ πάλιν within the statement ὅτι ... οὐ φείσομαι, the words οὐ φείσομαι are displaced from their normal position and receive special emphasis. These words are made the focal point not only of colon 3, but also of the whole passage (cf Loubser 1980:275).

Colon 2 relates to colon 1, due to the numerical aspect emphasised in both pericopes. Colon 2 contains an allusion to Scripture (Deut 19,15), adding more weight to Paul's argument.

Colon 3 relates to colons 1—2 due to the emphasis on the numerical aspect: προείρηκα ... προλέγω ... δεύτερον ... προημαρτηκόσιν ... πάλιν. After stressing the importance of his coming (third) visit, Paul adds his warning which stands in the centre of this whole pericope, ... οὐ φείσομαι.

In comma 3.2 the reason (ἐπεί) for Paul's stern warning is given. The relationship between Christ and the apostles, focused upon in 3.2 due to the Corinthians' demanding of proof that Christ is speaking through him, is explicated in colons 4—7. Weakness and power, important motifs in the exposition of colons 4—7, occur for the first time in this pericope in 3.3 and 3.4. Note the chiastic construction:

εἰς ὑμᾶς οὐκ ἀσθενεῖ ἀλλὰ δυνατεῖ ἐν ὑμῖν.

The fact that a close relationship exists between colons 4 and 5, and 6 and 7 is evident from the parallel construction (colons 4—5 and 6—7 are structured identically). Colons 4 and 5 deal with weakness and strength in the life of Christ. This exposition serves as the ground for the relationship between these elements in the life of the apostle and his associates.

It may be pointed out again that a very close (motivative [cf καὶ γάρ colons 4 and 6]) relationship exists between colons 4—7 and colon 3 (with 3.2 serving as a hinge between 3.1, and 3.3 and 3.4):[1] The relationship

---

[1] Structural markers and actants occurring in these colons prove this close relationship: The relationship between Christ and the apostle is the leading motif in 3.2 (in which the motivation for Paul's statement in 3.1 is given). This relationship is expounded in 6 and 7. This relationship is focused upon with regard to weakness and strength, motifs occurring for the first time in this pericope in 3.3—4 and which are explicated in 4—7. (Cf also Loubser 1980:274.)

between Christ and the apostle (and his associates — 3.2) in terms of weakness and strength (cf 3.3 & 3.4) is explicated in colons 4—7 in a stylistically well-structured way. This exposition profoundly determines the nature of the proof (δοκιμήν) demanded by the Corinthians. The argumentation in this entire pericope is specifically related to the Corinthians (cf πρὸς ὑμᾶς [13,1], ἐν ὑμῖν [13,3], εἰς ὑμᾶς [13,4]).

15.3 An exegetical overview

In 2 Cor 12,14 Paul has already mentioned his keenness to visit the Corinthians for a third time. By repeating it in 13,1 he must believe that it will somehow support the warning he is about to give. Paul seems to want his readers to associate this third visit with the traditional rule of evidence that requires three, or at least two witnesses to establish the facts in a case (cf Deut 19,15) (Furnish 1984:574—5).

It is unlikely that Paul intends to hold a formal hearing in Corinth, as some interpreters suggest.[2] Paul quotes this rule of evidence immediately after emphasising that he is about to come for *the third time*. It seems that he is thinking of his impending visit as potentially the third and decisive witness against wrongdoers in the Corinthian church. The first two "witnesses" could be his first two visits. Furnish (1984:595), however, points out that in view of verse 2, and because it is difficult to understand how the first ("founding") visit could have constituted a witness against them, it may be that Paul is thinking of the first two witnesses as, respectively, his second, "sorrowful visit" (2,1) and the present letter.[3] Klauck's interpretation (1986:100) seems, however, to be the most unforced way of interpreting this verse within this context. The two or three witnesses here means in a free allegorical way (cf 1 Cor 9,9—10) Paul's three visits and two admonitions at different occasions (referred to in verse

---

[2] Furnish points out that according to these interpreters the apostle intends to hold a formal hearing in Corinth, and he quotes the rule about evidence to assure his readers that he will follow due process in evaluating whatever charges of misconduct may be brought against any member of the congregation (so, e g Schlatter, Allo, Filson, Hughes, Delkor). For exact references to these interpreters, cf Furnish (1984:575).

[3] Cf Bultmann 1976:243: "... προείρηκα — offenbar bei dem zweiten Besuch, wie παρὼν τὸ δεύτερον gleich erläutert; so προλέγω — jetzt von dem bevorstehenden dritten Besuch in diesem Brief als ἀπών. Diese beiden Aussagen sind also die beiden Zeugen ...".

2). Strictly speaking, the requirements of Deut 19,15 are not met since the same witness testifies on different occasions.[4]

It has been pointed out that in Palestinian Judaism the Deuteronomic rule was widely used to support the requirement that persons suspected of wrongdoing should be carefully forewarned about the possibility of punitive action against them. In this context, Paul's quotation of the rule makes good sense; he will have given the requisite *two or three* warnings, so he will not hesitate to exercise discipline when he comes to Corinth. This is precisely what Paul says in verse 2 (cf Furnish (1984:575).

With reference to the visit mentioned in 2 Cor 2,1, Paul mentions in verse 2 that he has already extended a warning during his second stay, and that he will not spare those who sinned earlier or any of the others. This he repeats in the present letter. The Corinthians have, therefore, been warned twice. (During the visit, referred to in 2 Cor 2,1 he could not carry out his warning.)[5]

As stated in the notes pertaining to the structure of this passage, verses 3—4 supply the motivation for Paul's stern warning in verse 2. In verses 3 and 4 one also learns how Paul related his concern about misconduct among the Christians of Corinth (12,20—13,2) to the broader and *fundamental concern of this letter* (cf Furnish 1984:576). That concern, evident throughout 2 Cor 10—13, but especially in 11,1—12,13, is with the *challenge to his apostleship* represented by the appearance in Corinth of certain persons who have sought, with some success, to take over the leadership of the congregation. Those intruders not only have assailed Paul's apostolic credentials and conduct (e g 10,10; 11,6.7—11) but have also made extravagant claims about themselves (e g 10,7b.12; 11,12.21b—23). Against this background the Corinthians have demanded proof from Paul that Christ really speaks through him. From 2 Cor 10,1.10 it seems that in the eyes of the Corinthians Paul lacked spiritual boldness and power during his previous visits. Now, says Paul, he is prepared to give them proof of Christ's power working through him — although it will not be the kind of proof they wanted. It will come on his next visit when he refuses to "... spare those who sinned earlier or any of the others ..." (2 Cor 13,2).

---

[4] "Aber solche Freiheiten sind in der Allegorese möglich" (Klauck 1986:100).

[5] "Beim Zwischenbesuch hatte er sich nicht durchsetzen können; aber beim dritten Besuch wird er von seiner apostolischen Vollmacht zur Bestrafung Gebrauch machen, wie er schon 12,20 f. angedeutet hatte" (Lang 1986:356).

Bultmann (1976:244—5) comments that it is not impossible that Paul's statement ὃς εἰς ὑμᾶς οὐκ ἀσθενεῖ ἀλλὰ δυνατεῖ ἐν ὑμῖν was caused by the Corinthians' assertion: Χριστὸς δυνατεῖ ἐν ἡμῖν, ἀσθενεῖ δὲ ἐν σοί. However, then Paul attaches to ἐν ὑμῖν a meaning which differs from that of the ἐν ἡμιν that the Corinthians had.[6]

These phrases (3.3—4) seem, however, to be interpreted in the most unforced way within this context if they are taken to indicate that Paul is pointing away from himself (and his supposed weakness) to Christ, "... who is not weak in dealing with you, but is powerful among you". Paul is thinking of the work of Christ in the church. His own weakness was the stage upon which the power of God in Christ was at work. The power of Christ became visible in miracles (2 Cor 12,12; Rom 15,19; Gal 3,5), in Paul's preaching (1 Cor 2,4), and in the conversion of sinners, who were washed, sanctified, and justified (1 Cor 6,11). Christ had overcome the powers of evil, which were no longer in a position to separate from God those who were in him (Rom 8,35—39) (cf Barrett 1973:335).

It is of the power of Christ, δυνατεῖ ἐν ὑμῖν, that Paul will be an agent when, on his arrival in Corinth, he boldly disciplines the errant members of the congregation.

As was pointed out in the notes on the structure of this pericope, a very close motivative relationship exists between verse 4 (colons 4—7) and verse 3 (3.2—4).[7] The relationship between Christ and the apostle (a proof of which is demanded by the Corinthians [3.2]) is explicated in colons 4—7. This exposition profoundly illuminates the *nature of the power of God* operative in the apostle. The reason for the δύναμις of Christ becoming active in the life of the apostle living in ἀσθένεια is to be found in the fact that also with Christ himself ἀσθένεια and δύναμις are connected to each other. 2 Cor 13,4 affirms that in Christ the profound relation of ἀσθένεια and δύναμις has been revealed (cf Bultmann 1976:245—6).

The parallel which Paul draws between Christ's crucifixion "*in weakness*" and his own weakness shows that he understands his life to involve a continuing participation in Jesus' death (cf Tannehill 1967:98—9). Paul is not merely asserting here that his own experience is

---

[6] "Denn wenn diese dabei die Einwohnung des Christus in den einzelnen Pneumatikern meinten, so versteht Paulus: unter euch, der Gemeinde, und zwar eben als kritische Macht" (Bultmann 1976:244).

[7] Cf Lambrecht (1985:263): "... the whole of v.4 'proves' v.3".

similar to that of Christ. Paul's thought goes deeper than that. The prepositional phrases ἐν αὐτῷ and σὺν αὐτῷ[8] in 13,4 indicate that *Paul's weakness and life through God's power* are not independent of Christ but are manifestations of his participation in Christ. "Out of Christ's death and life come Paul's weakness and strength" (Lambrecht 1999:224—5).[9]

The christological affirmation in colons 4 and 5 underlines the importance of both crucifixion and resurrection. It must be borne in mind that while Christ lives (and rules) by the power of God who raised him from the dead,[10] he also lives and rules as the Crucified (Furnish 1984:576—7).[11] The Resurrected remains the Crucified, the Crucified is

---

[8] Under the influence of the following σὺν αὐτῷ, several witnesses replace ἐν αὐτῷ (in the phrase καὶ γὰρ ἡμεῖς ἀσθενοῦμεν ἐν αὐτῷ) with σὺν αὐτῷ (codex Sinaiticus, codex Alexandrinus, codices F and G, a few Greek manuscripts, Old Latin witness r, the Syriac Peshitta, the Bohairic version). In other witnesses an inverse assimilation has occurred, the phrase σὺν αὐτῷ being replaced by ἐν αὐτῷ (papyrus 46 [apparently], codex Claromontanus [original scribe], minuscule manuscripts 33, 326, a few Greek manuscripts, Old Latin witness g [despite certain negligible variations], five or more witnesses of Pelagius). The text adopted (ἐν αὐτῷ) has overwhelming external support (codex Vaticanus, codex Claromontanus, codex Ψ, uncial manuscript 0243, the Majority text, Old Latin witness a, the Vulgate, Syriac Harclensis, Sahidic version as well as the Ambrosiaster) (cf Metzger 1994:518).

[9] Lambrecht (1999:226) points to the interesting chiastic movement within 13,1—4: from Paul (vv 1—2) to Christ (v 3); and from Christ (v 4ab) back to Paul (v 4cd).

[10] God's power as the "agency of Christ's resurrection" (Furnish 1984:571) is an important motif in the main Pauline letters: Rom 6,4 (where δόξα is used as a synonym for δύναμις); 1 Cor 6,14, cf also Phil 3,10.

[11] Although Barrett (1973:335—6) gives the preposition ἐκ (in the phrases ἐξ ἀσθενείας and ἐκ δυνάμεως) its causal sense, he remarks that the translation is nevertheless inadequate. "Paul does not mean simply that Christ was crucified because he was weak — that is, not strong enough to escape so unpleasant a fate — or that he now lives because God was strong enough to overcome death and raise him up. The crucifixion was the supreme expression of part of the truth about him ... It was of his grace, of his primary characteristic, that he became poor [viii.9], and the weakness shown in his crucifixion, being a mark of his grace, is not an unfortunate lapse from strength but one aspect of the action God intended to his Son ... Similarly, though it is true it is also inadequate to say that the resurrection was a signal manifestation of divine power. Since the resurrection Christ is alive, and at work in power. Power is as characteristic of him as weakness, wealth as characteristic as poverty [viii.9]. This is one basic form of New Testament christology — Christ is both weak and strong."

Bultmann (1976:245) doubts whether a causal interpretation of ἐξ ἀσθενείας can be justified. With reference to Phil 2,7—8 he comments that the crucifixion was the climax of the ἀσθένεια. "Es bedeutet nur 'als Schwacher', und das ἐκ wird nur um der rhetorischen Entsprechung zu ἐκ δυνάμεως θεοῦ willen gewählt sein."

Furnish (1984:571) remarks that Paul seems to view Christ's death as a demonstration of that weakness in and through which God's power is operative for salvation (e g 1 Cor 1,17—31, especially vv 25 and 27).

the Resurrected (Bultmann 1976:245). Paul's apparent weakness (cf 2 Cor 10,1.10; 11,21a ...) must be understood as the weakness of one who has been crucified with Christ (ἐν αὐτῷ; cf Rom 6,6; Gal 6,14 ...) and who carries around the "death of Jesus" in his own body (2 Cor 4,10—12). Paul and his associates carry around in their body the death of Jesus, *so that the life of Jesus may also be revealed in our body* (2 Cor 4,10, cf also 4,11). Paul, therefore, not only carries the "death of Jesus" in his body, it is also true that Christ now lives in him (Gal 2,20), so that when Paul comes he will be able to exhibit, in addition, that resurrection life and thus *the power of God* (Furnish 1984:577).

It is noteworthy that a temporal disjunction is evident in Paul's description of weakness and power in this passage: In colons 4—5 Christ's crucifixion is stated in the aorist and his life by the power of God in the present tense. In colons 6—7 the apostle's weakness is portrayed in the present tense and his life with Christ through the power of God in the future tense. Weakness has a temporary nature, while power reveals an eschatological openness (Loubser 1980:281).

In these verses elements from early christological confessions as well as leading motifs from 2 Cor 12,9—10 (upon which the present passage comments), are integrated. The way of Christ comprises two phases: the death on the cross and the resurrection. The death on the cross concerns Christ's earthly existence. The lasting power and vitality of the exalted Christ is the consequence of his resurrection through the power of God.

The exalted Lord is powerfully active in the Corinthian congregation (v 3c [comma 3.4]), for example in miracles (12,12), in preaching (1 Cor 2,4), in the conversions, in the rich treasure of charismatic gifts. This is the result of Paul's preaching, inspired by Christ. Yet it remains, that both elements, *power and weakness, belong inseparably to the Christ event*. The Resurrected carries the wounds of the Crucified. This remains valid for the present Christian existence in which divine power is experienced in the midst of sufferings. In the example of Paul's life this becomes especially clear. His life is subjected to suffering and service for the sake of the congregation (4,12). It has been pointed out several times how this image of Paul's ministry was raised against him. Against this objection, Paul always gives the answer: This must be so, for this alone corresponds to the sincerity of the cross of Christ and this is demanded by his great commission.[12] Complete partaking of the life of the Exalted is reserved for the end time.[13] This is one reason why weakness dominates in the present. This difference between the present and the coming ages may not be overlooked — a tendency to which the Corinthians were inclined. The present dimension may, however, also not be overlooked. In the present passage the words εἰς ὑμᾶς point in this direction. In his dealings with the congregation Paul may have the confidence that miraculous divine power may come to his aid; the resurrected Christ acts and speaks through him already in the present. In this sense the future tense may refer to an act of punishment during Paul's forthcoming visit to Corinth (cf Klauck 1986:101). At this occasion it will become clear that Christ, not only as the "Crucified in weakness", but also as the "Resurrected in power" will become actively present through his apostle.

Life with Christ certainly belongs primarily to the future. Christ himself has been raised from the dead as the first fruits of those who sleep (1 Cor 15,20), and for the rest of mankind resurrection remains a future event. In some measure, however, it has been anticipated (2 Cor 4,10—12; also Rom 6,4—5; Col 3,1) and here Paul says it will be anticipated εἰς ὑμᾶς (cf Barrett 1973:337). God will grant him such a measure of resurrection life as will suffice to deal with the situation in Corinth. In his weakness, God's power will be perfectly revealed (12,9).

2 Cor 10—13 is full of Paul's famous "theology of suffering". Yet, in 13,1—4 the focus is on strength:

> "Verse 4 explains: for Christ, power without any more weakness; for Paul, future visible strength notwithstanding persistent hardships and suffering ... 2 Cor 13,4 as a whole clarifies Paul's firm intention announced at the end of v. 2: at his third visit to Corinth he will be strong! The reader pauses and suddenly realizes that Paul strikingly presents his strength as anticipative resurrection power" (Lambrecht 1985:269).

---

[12] "Der zweite Pol des Christusweges steht in seiner Anwendung auf Paulus bezeichnenderweise im Futur: Wir werden mit ihm Leben, wobei 'mit ihm' auf die vollendete Christusgemeinschaft nach dem Tode [Phil 1[23]] oder bei der Parusie [1 Thess 4[14]] hindeutet" (Klauck 1986:101).

[13] Siber (1971:168—77) has pointed out that all σύν-expressions in Pauline literature referring to the resurrection or resurrection life of Jesus, must be understood futuristically. 2 Cor 13,4 represents the only exception to this rule.

Chapter 16

Romans 1,4

16.1 Location within the macrocontext of Romans

Rom 1,1—7 constitutes the letter opening to Paul's letter to the Romans, dealing with the author and his message (Rom 1,1—6), the addressees (verse 7a) and expressing a salutation (verse 7b) (Du Toit 1984,9—16; Pelser 1985:50).[1] This pericope (Rom 1,1—7) may be regarded as the

---

[1] The views of a few commentators may be mentioned:
Cranfield (1975:45): "Superscription, address and salutation (1.1—7)"
Kertelge (1983:13):

Der Briefkopf (1,1—7)

1. Der Absender: Paulus (1,1—6)
a) Sein Beruf (1,1)
b) Sein Evangelium (1,2—4)
c) Sein Dienst unter den Heiden (1,5—6)
2. Die Adressaten: die Römer (1,7a)
3. Segenswunsch (1,7b)

Michel (1978:7) headlines Rom 1,1—7: "Zuschrift und Gruß".

The following commentators consider Rom 1,1—7 as a sub-pericope within Rom 1,1—17:

Käsemann (1974:V):
    A)   1,1—17: Briefeingang
    I.   1,1—7 : Das Präskript
    II.   1,8—15: Das Prooemium
    III. 1,16—17: Thema
Schlier (1979:IX):
    A   Der Briefeingang (1,1—17) ...
    I.   Das Präskript (1,1—7) ...
    II.   Das Proömium (1,8—17) ...
Wilckens (1978:IX):
    A   1,1—17 Briefeingang ...
    1.   1,1—7 Briefkopf (Präskript) ...
    2.   1,8—17 Dank, Bitte. Hinführung zum Briefthema (Proömium) ...

introduction to the letter and Rom 1,8—17 as a transitional pericope (concluded by the mentioning of the theme/programmatic thesis of the letter), leading to the letter body. Typical features of the genre of a letter in antiquity are found in this passage: the reference to the author and the addressees, and a salutation.[2]

The words πρῶτον μέν in Rom 1,8 signal the start of a new pericope. In Rom 1,8—12 the element of thanksgiving is introduced and in 1,13—17 the reader finds the introduction to the main argument: Paul's intention to visit the congregation and in verses 16 and 17 the gospel in a nutshell.

Zeller (1984:299):
  DER BRIEFEINGANG 1,1—17 ...
    Das Präskript 1,1—7 ...
    Das Proömium 1,8—17 ...
Dunn (1988:vii):
  I. INTRODUCTION (1,1—17)
  A. Introductory Statement and Greetings (1,1—7)
  B. Personal Explanations (1,8—15)
  C. Summary Statement of the Letter's Theme (1,16—17)
Haacker (1999:vii):
  I. Präskript und Einleitung 1,1—17
    1. Präskript 1,1—7
    2. Einleitung 1,8—17

[2] For more information on the elements which constituted a letter in antiquity, cf Klauck 1998:35—54. Pauline transitions to the letter body is discussed by Roberts (1986a:29—35, 1986b:93—9 [a bibliography is also supplied]; 1986c:187—201; 1988:81—97 [esp 85—7]).

16.2 Discourse analysis: Romans 1,1—7[3]

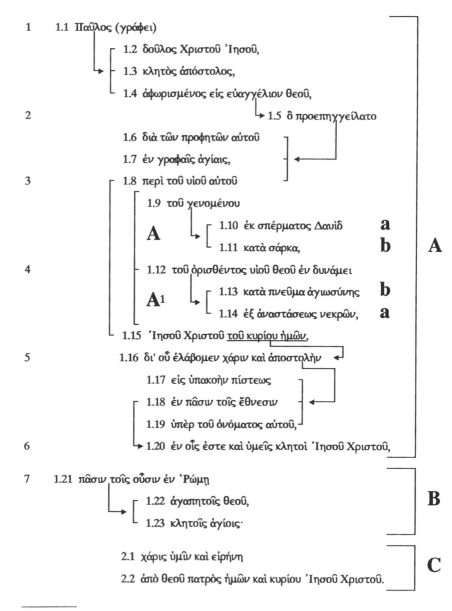

1   1.1 Παῦλος (γράφει)

        1.2 δοῦλος Χριστοῦ 'Ιησοῦ,

        1.3 κλητὸς ἀπόστολος,

        1.4 ἀφωρισμένος εἰς εὐαγγέλιον θεοῦ,

2   1.5 ὃ προεπηγγείλατο

        1.6 διὰ τῶν προφητῶν αὐτοῦ

        1.7 ἐν γραφαῖς ἁγίαις,

3   1.8 περὶ τοῦ υἱοῦ αὐτοῦ

        1.9 τοῦ γενομένου

        A   1.10 ἐκ σπέρματος Δαυὶδ   **a**

                1.11 κατὰ σάρκα,   **b**   **A**

4   1.12 τοῦ ὁρισθέντος υἱοῦ θεοῦ ἐν δυνάμει

        A¹   1.13 κατὰ πνεῦμα ἁγιωσύνης   **b**

                1.14 ἐξ ἀναστάσεως νεκρῶν,   **a**

        1.15 'Ιησοῦ Χριστοῦ <u>τοῦ κυρίου ἡμῶν</u>,

5   1.16 δι' οὗ ἐλάβομεν χάριν καὶ ἀποστολὴν

        1.17 εἰς ὑπακοὴν πίστεως

        1.18 ἐν πᾶσιν τοῖς ἔθνεσιν

        1.19 ὑπὲρ τοῦ ὀνόματος αὐτοῦ,

6   1.20 ἐν οἷς ἐστε καὶ ὑμεῖς κλητοὶ 'Ιησοῦ Χριστοῦ,

7   1.21 πᾶσιν τοῖς οὖσιν ἐν 'Ρώμῃ

        1.22 ἀγαπητοῖς θεοῦ,   **B**

        1.23 κλητοῖς ἁγίοις·

        2.1 χάρις ὑμῖν καὶ εἰρήνη

        2.2 ἀπὸ θεοῦ πατρὸς ἡμῶν καὶ κυρίου 'Ιησοῦ Χριστοῦ.   **C**

---

[3] This pericope is constituted by only two colons. In the portraying of the structure of this pericope, special attention has been given to the relations of the different constituent units (constituent analysis).

Headings of the pericope and sub-pericope

Pericope heading: Paul, a servant of Christ Jesus and apostle, set apart for the gospel of God regarding his Son, addresses all in Rome who are loved by God and called to be saints, and sends them greetings.

Sub-pericope A: Sender and his message
Sub-pericope B: Addressees
Sub-pericope C: Salutation

16.2.1 A few observations suggested by the discourse analysis

It has been pointed out in the discourse analysis that the author and his message as well as the receivers of the letter are mentioned in colon 1. In colon 2 a salutation is given. Paul qualifies himself in three ways:

(i)   δοῦλος Χριστοῦ 'Ιησοῦ
(ii)   κλητὸς ἀπόστολος
(iii) ἀφωρισμένος εἰς εὐαγγέλιον θεοῦ

The fact that Paul comments in commata 1.5—15 on this εὐαγγέλιον θεοῦ has far-reaching consequences for the interpretation of this pericope.[4] Commata 1.5—7 emphasise the origin of the gospel in God.[5]

The fact that the gospel is determined as to its contents by Jesus Christ is underlined by the ring construction περὶ τοῦ υἱοῦ αὐτοῦ (1.8) ... 'Ιησοῦ Χριστοῦ τοῦ κυρίου ἡμῶν (1.15). The commata describing Jesus Christ (1.9—14) constitute the main part of this colon.[6] The importance of this passage is underlined by its parallelistic (A,A[1]) and chiastic (a-b-b-a) construction. This pericope sharply focuses on Jesus Christ, our Lord, as the centre of the gospel for which Paul has been set apart.

---

[4] "Indem Paulus das Evangelium vorstellt, stellt er sich selbst vor ... Es ist klar, daß er sich auch bei einem Grußwort nicht anders als von Christus her an seine Leser wenden kann" (Kertelge 1983:23).

[5] As Kertelge (1983:22) comments: "Das *Vorausverkündete* des Evangeliums verweist also weniger auf bestimmte alttestamentliche Voraussagen, sondern auf den aller Geschichte vorausliegenden Anfang und Ursprung des Evangeliums in Gott."

[6] Louw (1979b:34) writes of "... Jesus Christ ... the center of the information conveyed by colon 1".

16.3 An exegetical overview

In this passage the interpreter encounters an unusually large number of problems, listed by Cranfield (1975:61) as follows:

(i)   Does ὁρίζειν here mean "appoint"/"constitute", or "declare"/"show to be"?

(ii)   Does ἐν δυνάμει qualify ὁρισθέντος or υἱοῦ θεοῦ?

(iii)   What is the significance of κατὰ πνεῦμα ἁγιωσύνης?

(iv)   What sense does ἐξ have?

(v)   How is νεκρῶν to be explained?

As to the first question, we should probably choose the meaning "appoint".[7] This does not mean, however, that this passage must be interpreted in an adoptianistic way.[8] It is significant that Paul describes the contents of "... the gospel ... regarding his Son ... Jesus Christ our Lord" (Rom 1,2—4) in the language of an already existing confessional formula.[9]

In the antithetical parallelism of Rom 1,3—4, the emphasis falls on the second part (A) (Michel 1978:73). In a certain sense the phrase ἐν δυνάμει disrupts the parallelism of this expression — it has no equivalent in the first part of the formula. Paul emphasises that through the resurrection from the dead Jesus Christ has become the Son of God "in power".

---

[7] Cranfield mentions that no clear example, either earlier than, or contemporary with the New Testament of the use of ὁρίζειν in the sense "declare" or "show to be" has been adduced. Many important German commentators translate ὁρίζειν here with "einsetzen" (Cf Kertelge [1983:21]; Michel [1978:63]; Schlier [1979:17] and Wilckens [1978:55]). Newman and Nida (1973:10) state that the verb ὁρίζειν literally means "to set limits [or boundaries]" and to "define", "decide", or "determine", and they point out that it is often used in the New Testament in connection with God's will and decision (Lk 22,22; Acts 2,23; 10,42; 17,26.31; Heb 4,7).

[8] As is the case with Käsemann (1974:9). He refers to v 3 (marked in the discourse analysis with an A) and then states: "Die Antithese der beiden Zeilen und die Verwendung des Terminus 'einsetzen' machen vielmehr deutlich, daß Jesus die Würde des Gottessohnes erst bei seiner Erhöhung und Inthronisation erhielt ... wie in Apg 2,36; 13,33 tritt hier eine adoptianistische Christologie der frühen Christenheit zutage ... ."

Wilckens (1978:65) correctly affirms: "Die Aussage des zweiten Gliedes der Formel V 4a versteht Paulus zweifellos nicht in dem Sinne, daß Christus erst als Auferstandener zum Sohn Gottes geworden ist, sondern daß Gott ihn als seinem Sohn seit seiner Auferstehung die Machtstellung des himmlischen Herrschers übertragen hat ... ."

[9] Cf Cranfield (1975:57 especially note 5); Kertelge (1983:22 especially note 6); Michel (1978:72—4); Schlier (1979:24); Wilckens (1978:63—5).

Most commentators agree that ἐν δυνάμει must be seen as qualifying υἱοῦ θεοῦ. Cranfield (1975:62) states the following in favour of this interpretation:

(i) ἐν δυνάμει is used elsewhere in the New Testament (Mk 9,1; 1 Cor 15,43; 1 Thess 1,5) in the sense of "invested with power".

(ii) The sense which results from taking ἐν δυνάμει with υἱοῦ θεοῦ accords well, while the sense which is yielded by taking it with ὁρισθέντος seems to accord ill, not only with Paul's teaching in other places but also with the presence of τοῦ υἱοῦ αὐτοῦ at the beginning of verse 3.

Other commentators such as Käsemann, Kertelge, Michel, Schlier and Wilckens also support this interpretation. (For further literature, cf Schlier 1979:24, note 28.)[10]

Cranfield (1975:62) sees the meaning of the phrase τοῦ ὁρισθέντος υἱοῦ θεοῦ ἐν δυνάμει as, "... who was appointed Son-of-God-in-power" — in contrast to his being Son of God in apparent weakness and poverty for the duration of his earthly existence. Elements of this interpretation may underlie the meaning of this phrase. In the context of the prescript of Romans, Paul may, however, especially be thinking of the power with which Christ works through the proclamation of the gospel (cf Rom 1,16; 1 Cor 1,18.24; 2,4; 2 Cor 13,3—4) (Wilckens 1978:65).

One of the greatest problems in the interpretation of Rom 1,3—4 relates to the meaning of πνεῦμα ἁγιωσύνης. Although ἁγιωσύνη occurs twice in the sense of sanctification and holiness in a paranetic context in the Pauline letters (2 Cor 7,1; 1 Thess 3,13), it is never used by Paul in

---

[10] Schlier (1979:24—5) argues that when, according to Paul, the gospel proclaims Jesus Christ as Son of God "... kann dieser nicht erst durch die Auferstehung der Toten zum Sohn Gottes werden, wohl aber zum Sohn Gottes 'in Macht'. Er ist ja für Paulus auch sonst der durch die Macht Gottes von den Toten Erweckte [1 Kor 6,14], gibt sich als der Auferstandene in seiner δύναμις als δύναμις zu erfahren [1 Kor 5,4; 2 Kor 12,9; Phil 3,10], und zwar durch den Geist und sein Wirken [15,13; 1 Kor 2,4.5] und kraft des Evangeliums [1,16; 1 Kor 1,18; 1 Thess 1,5 u.a.], des Wortes seiner Macht. Er ist nun selbst θεοῦ δύναμις [1 Kor 1,24]. In seiner Parusie wird sich seine Macht endgültig offenbaren [2 Thess 1,7]. 'Der Sohn Gottes in Macht' ist Jesus Christus als der Kyrios." Schlier (1979:25) interprets Romans 3,4 as meaning that Jesus Christ does not become the "Son of God", but "through the resurrection from the dead" becomes "the Son of God in power", "... die differenzierende Interpretation des Apostels einer ihm vorgegebenen Credo-Formel ...".

relation to πνεῦμα (instead, he speaks of πνεῦμα ἅγιον). How must this un-Pauline expression be understood?

Excursus: Interpretation of the phrase πνεῦμα ἀγιωσύνης

Cranfield (1975:64) comments that he is inclined to think that the most probable explanation is that which (taking κατά as meaning "according to") understands the phrase to refer to the Holy Spirit, who, as given by the exalted Christ, is the manifestation of his power and majesty, and so the guarantee of his having been appointed Son of God in might.

Ulrich Wilckens (1978:65) affirms that commata 1.8—11 περὶ τοῦ υἱοῦ ... κατὰ σάρκα must be interpreted in the sense that the eternal Son of God became man — "als Davidide, d.h. als der verheißene Messias. Die Menschwerdung des Christus *in ihrer heilsgeschichtlichen Bedeutung ist es, die Paulus im ersten Glied der Formel ausgesprochen hört".*

With regard to the meaning of commata 1.12—14 τοῦ ὁρισθέντος υἱοῦ θεοῦ ἐν δυνάμει ... ἐξ ἀναστάσεως νεκρῶν he proceeds assuming the instrumental interpretation of ἐν δυνάμει, "... Der Sohn Gottes ist durch Gottes Macht, nämlich entsprechend der [Totenauferweckenden] Kraft des Geist Gottes, auferweckt und in die himmlische Herrschaftsfunktion des Erhöhten eingesetzt worden".

Michel (1978:73—5) writes: "Die Unterscheidung 'nach dem Fleisch' — 'nach dem Geist' ist nicht *als paulinischer Zusatz aufzufassen. Gemeint ist einerseitz die irdische Abstammung, die Erhöhung zur Rechten Gottes [nach Ps 110,1]) anderseits ... Es geht Paulus hier ... um das Verständnis Jesu 'vom Menschen her' und 'von Gott her'." According to Michel* πνεῦμα ἀγιωσύνης *must be seen as a Hebraistic expression in the light of passages such as Is 63,10; Ps 50,13 and especially 4QTLevi 18,11. Schlier (1979:26—7) also emphasises that this expression points to a (Hellenistic) Jewish Christian origin: "In der LXX ist* ἀγιωσύνη *bemerkenswerterweise die Heiligkeit Jahwes, die mit seiner Königsherrschaft gegeben ist. Sie ist Übersetzung von* הוד *[Hoheit; Ps 144,5],* קדֹש *[Heiligkeit; Pss 29,5; 96,12] und* עז *[Macht, Herrlichkeit; Ps 95,6] ...* Ἁγιωσύνη *ist Jahwes heilige Hoheit und Macht als Wesenzug seiner* δόξα, *seiner* כבד. *Dieser Zusammenhang von* ἀγιωσύνη *und* δόξα *wird bestätigt durch eine Stelle in TestLev 18,11. Dort wird gesagt, daß der messianische 'neue Priester' 'den Heiligen zu essen geben wird vom Holz des Lebens, und der Geist der Heiligkeit* (πνεῦμα ἀγιωσύνης) *wird auf ihnen ruhen'. Hier haben wir den*

Begriff πνεῦμα ἁγιωσύνης *und auch sein Zusammenhang mit der* δόξα *wird angedeutet. "*

Attention must also be drawn to a few important articles that appeared on this subject: Bernardin Schneider (1967:359) mentions that it is generally accepted that Rom 1,3—4 has a pre-Pauline origin: "In composing them Paul may well have advisedly borrowed from an early baptismal profession of faith or credal formulary in use or known at Rome in order thus to open this highly doctrinal epistle with a sort of 'captatio benevolentiae'. "

*A positive feature of Schneider's article is that the writer takes into account the structure of this passage: "*ἐκ σπέρματος Δαυὶδ *seems to parallel* ἐξ ἀναστάσεως νεκρῶν ... κατὰ σάρκα *is balanced by the* κατὰ πνεῦμα ἁγιωσύνης *of v 4" (p 361).*

As to the meaning of the phrase πνεῦμα ἁγιωσύνης *Schneider gives (with reference to the work of Kuss in this regard) a summary of the most important intepretations:*

(i)   πνεῦμα ἁγιωσύνης *may refer to the divine nature of Christ.*

(ii)   πνεῦμα ἁγιωσύνης *refers to the spiritual part of Christ's human nature, "... endowed with extraordinary, supernatural holiness ..." (p 369).*

(iii) πνεῦμα ἁγιωσύνης *refers to the Holy Spirit.*

Schneider quotes Fr Stanley with approval: "We believe that the phrase κατὰ πνεῦμα ἁγιωσύνης *expresses something which, in Paul's view, is intrinsic to the glorified Christ — and that, not in the order of essences or natures, but in the existential order [i e the order of activity]" (D M Stanley. Christ's resurrection in Pauline soteriology; quoted by Schneider 1967:386).*

In an article entitled "The Jesus that Paul preached", S Lewis Johnson (1971:131) criticises the interpretation that πνεῦμα ἁγιωσύνης *refers to the Holy Spirit: "A difficulty with this interpretation is the strange antithesis of the human nature of the Lord with the Holy Spirit ... ." As a solution to this problem Johnson proposes: "One may take the phrase, 'according to the spirit of holiness', to characterize Christ spiritually, just as 'according to the flesh', characterizes him physically. It expresses the spirit of holiness which dominated all his thoughts and actions" (p 132). Johnson paraphrases this passage as follows: "He who was Son of David according to his physical being was appointed God's powerful Son according to his spiritual conservation following the resurrection. "*

Johnson has an eye for the structure of this passage, as well as for the fact that the interpretation of πνεῦμα ἀγιωσύνης *as the Holy Spirit is problematic in this context. However, his own interpretation is just as unconvincing.*

The article of E Linnemann (1971), "Tradition und Interpretation in Röm. 1,3f", discusses the views of R Bultmann, E Schweizer, F Hahn and P Stuhlmacher, followed by Linnemann's own interpretation and a reply by Schweizer. This article reflects on the way in which Paul integrates the adoptianistic view of his "Vorlage" with his own christology. While this article conveys valuable information about the way in which the present text was formed, it has limited value for its interpretation.

In an interesting article, "Zur vorpaulinischen Bekenntnisformel im Eingang des Römerbriefes", H W Bartsch (1967) argues that the confessional formula in Rom 1,3—4 points out that both the early church and Paul were more deeply rooted in the Old Testament and Judaism in the time of Jesus than has been recognised. Bartsch is sceptical of the assertion that Paul appeals in Rom 1,3—4 to a formula that was known in Rome "... um damit 'eine gemeinsame Basis zu gewinnen' " (1967:339). He proceeds: "Ist ... der Römerbrief in dem Bemühen geschrieben, die Judenchristen und Heidenchristen dort zu einer Gemeinde zusammenzuführen, und wendet er sich vor allen an die Heidenchristen, so darf für die Zitierung eines Bekenntnisses, das wesentlich auf dem Hintergrund der apokalyptischen Erwartung des Judentums zu verstehen ist und darum judenchristlich sein dürfte, eine direkte polemische Bedeutung anzunehmen sein." Paul wants to convey to the Christians who have a pagan background that when they became Christians, they adopted the Jewish hope clothed in the Christian confession.

J D G Dunn (1973) discusses the meaning of Rom 1,3—4 in an extensive article, "Jesus — Flesh and Spirit" with the purpose of shedding more light on the relationship between the early Christian view of Christ and the Spirit. According to Dunn (1973:48) σάρξ *represents a "range of meanings" rather than separate points on a spectrum of meanings. He affirms that* σάρξ *often carries a negative connotation which is not always evident at a glance: "... it must be judged highly probable that for Paul* σάρξ *in Rom. i.3 carries its normal note of depreciation" (p 49).*

Dunn is of the opinion that Paul's soteriology in terms of σάρξ *and* πνεῦμα *must have influenced his christological use of these terms: "*κατὰ σάρκα, κατὰ πνεῦμα in Rom. i.3f denote not successive and mutually exclusive spheres of power, but modes of existence and relationship which overlap and coincide in the earthly Jesus" (p 54).

On the meaning of πνεῦμα ἁγιωσύνης Dunn states: "πνεῦμα ἁγιωσύνης is unquestionably to be taken as a Semitic form for 'Holy Spirit' " (p 58). He proceeds: "The 'deity' of the earthly Jesus is a function of the Spirit, is, in fact, no more and no less than the Holy Spirit." This close relationship between Jesus and the Spirit is also portrayed by Dunn in the following way: "... if the Spirit gave Jesus his power, Jesus gave the Spirit his personality" (p 59).

Dunn argues that concerning this matter Paul shared the general conviction of the early church. He points out the following passages in the New Testament:

1 Tim 3,16:	ὃς ἐφανερώθη ἐν σαρκί,
	ἐδικαιώθη ἐν πνεύματι ...
1 Pet 3,18:	θανατωθεὶς μὲν σαρκὶ
	ζωοποιηθεὶς δὲ πνεύματι·

Both σαρκί and πνεύματι must be seen as datives of reference. "In which case", Dunn proceeds, "it looks rather as though we are back in the same sort of christological thought which finds more formalized expression in Rom. i.3f and 1 Tim. iii.16. Jesus was put to death as flesh: it was because he was flesh that death was possible, indeed necessary for him. But he was brought to life as Spirit: it was because he possessed the Spirit, because the Spirit wrought in him and on him, that ζωοποίησις followed death" (p 65).

James Dunn has drawn attention to a very important issue, by stating that we can never be as certain of an earlier form of a saying or pericope as of the form that has been delivered to us. "This being so, the present form and meaning of the saying must serve as control for and test of the more speculative hypotheses aimed at uncovering the earlier form and its significance ... " (p 42).

Dunn's discussion of the meaning of σάρξ in this article, however, does not take sufficient account of the principle that a word has different possibilities of meaning in different contexts. The components of meaning that a word has in one context must not necessarily be transferred to another. It is, therefore, not the case that the meaning of σάρξ has a negative undertone in all contexts.

Dunn's view that πνεῦμα ἁγιωσύνης is a pre-Pauline Semitism for the
Holy Spirit, used by Paul in this context, must be taken seriously.
It is clear that the majority of exegetes (e g Cranfield, Dunn, Michel,
Schlier, Wilckens ...) are of the opinion that πνεῦμα ἁγιωσύνης refers to
the Holy Spirit. The unusual form is caused by Hebraistic influence due to
its pre-Pauline (Hellenistic) Jewish Christian origin.

Schneider and Johnson have, however, pointed in another direction. In
support of the Today's English Version ("... as to his divine holiness, he
was shown with great power to be the Son of God by being raised from
death"), Newman and Nida (1973:10) affirm that the phrase κατὰ πνεῦμα
ἁγιωσύνης stands in formal contrast to "... 'as to his humanity', which
definitely refers to one aspect of Jesus' person". Secondly, Newman and
Nida argue that there is no other example in the Pauline letters of this
phrase being used to refer to the Holy Spirit, and though some scholars
maintain that Paul adopted it as a set formula from the Palestinian
Christians, there is not clear evidence in the New Testament or in other
early Christian literature that it was used for the Holy Spirit.

This interpretation is also defended by Louw (1979b:35):

> "The term ἁγιωσύνη in Greek means 'unique', having divine
> overtones, while πνεῦμα in this combination carries the
> meaning of 'personality, inner being'. The middle section of
> the enlargements upon υἱοῦ ... conveys the culmination of his
> glory — his resurrection designating him powerfully ... to be
> the Son of God."

In the light of the antithetical parallelistic structure of this passage (cf
discourse analysis) this last interpretation seems to be the more probable.

The phrase ἐξ ἀναστάσεως νεκρῶν may be understood in either a
temporal or a causal sense.[11] The style of this phrase — the absence of an
article and of ἐκ before νεκρῶν — points to its archaic character (cf Schlier
1979:24, note 24). As the last phrase of verse 4 (Ἰησοῦ Χριστοῦ τοῦ κυρίου
ἡμῶν) indicates, ἐξ ἀναστάσεως νεκρῶν refers undoubtedly to the resurrec-

---

[11] The second interpretation seems the more probable. (So e g Michel 1978:63.74;
Wilckens 1978:65; while Cranfield 1975:62; Käsemann 1974:9; Kertelge 1983:21—3 and
Schlier 1977:23—7 prefer the first interpretation.)

tion of Christ (cf Phil 3,10).[12] *Its position at the end underlines the importance of this phrase.*[13]
Paul concludes the christological definition of the gospel which he has been appointed to proclaim, by adding to the Son of God title (which describes Christ's relation to God) the confession Ἰησοῦ Χριστοῦ τοῦ κυρίου ἡμῶν *(which describes the relationship between Christ and all believers).*[14] *Behind this statement lies the call of acclamation:* κύριος Ἰησοῦς *(Rom 10,9—10; Phil 2,11; 1 Cor 12,3) with which believers answer the proclamation of the gospel and submit themselves to the Lordship of the exalted Son of God (cf Wilckens 1978:66). The personal pronoun in the genitive combined with* κύριος *underlines the sense of personal commitment and allegiance (Cranfield 1975:65).*

16.4 Conclusion

In this pericope ἐν δυνάμει refers to the power of the resurrected Jesus Christ — the power with which the Son of God has been invested through his *resurrection* from the dead.[15] Δύναμις in this pericope has a distinct christological slant.

The *christological* remarks, emphasised in this pericope, function as a description of the *gospel* for which Paul has been set apart. Jesus Christ, the risen Lord is the basis of Paul's message and authority.

Here, in the prescript of his letter, Paul has prepared the way for his programmatic statement in Rom 1,16 that the *gospel is the power of God.*

---

[12] "Doch steht hier die Auferweckung Christi als Beginn der endzeitlichen Totenauferweckung im Blick [vgl. 1 Kor 15,20; Apg 26,23]" (Wilckens 1978:65).

[13] "Es ist der Auferstandene als Repräsentant der durch die Totenauferweckung angebrochenen vollendeten Heilswirklichkeit Gottes, durch den Paulus seinen Apostolat empfangen hat zur Verkündigung dieser Heilswirklichkeit" (Wilckens 1978:65).

[14] As has been pointed out in the discourse analysis, the phrase, Ἰησοῦ Χριστοῦ τοῦ κυρίου ἡμῶν stands in apposition to περὶ τοῦ υἱοῦ αὐτοῦ. The ring composition emphasises the importance of the christological section in this pericope.

[15] The divine overtones of the context in which δύναμις is used in Rom 1,4 are emphasised by the phrase κατὰ πνεῦμα ἁγιωσύνης.

Chapter 17

Romans 1,16

17.1 Location within the broader context[1]

Our study of δύναμις has brought us to a very important passage of Paul's letter to the Romans. In Rom 1,16—17 Paul states a programmatic thesis of his message (Haacker 1999:36),[2] "the Gospel in a nutshell" (Pelser 1985:50).[3] Rom 1,16 forms part of the pericope 1,8—17.[4] The *formula valetudinis* of the Greek letter appears as a regular element in Paul's correspondence, primarily as a thanksgiving section. Whereas the thanksgiving in the Greek letter mostly concerns the addressee's physical welfare, Paul thanks God in Rom 1,8 for his readers' spiritual well-being (Du Toit 1985:10). In an allusion to the *proskunema* of the Graeco-Roman letter, Paul mentions in

---

[1] See also the discussion under 16.1.

[2] Zeller (1985:7) speaks of the *thesis* of the argument at stake. It is customary to describe Rom 1,16—17 as the *theme* of the letter, cf for example Cranfield (1975:87), Käsemann (1974:18); Kertelge (1983:35). Wilckens (1978:90) portrays verses 16—17 as "... die Überschrift zu dem gesamten folgenden Gedankengang des Briefkorpus [1,18—11,36] ...". Dunn (1988:36) describes Rom 1,16—17 as the summary statement of the letter's theme.

Haacker (1999:36) cautions however against the use of the category of a "theme", as it presupposes that Romans is a dogmatic document: "... nur eine *Abhandlung* hat ein 'Thema'!" He emphasises the multi-dimensional character of the letter and prefers to describe verses 16—17 as "... eine programmatische These des Paulus".

[3] Schlier (1979:42.46) comments that in verses 16—17 Paul reaches the end and climax of his introductory notes. "So ist Paulus in den VV 16—17 von persönlichen Erwägungen zur Sache gelangt und legt ... der römischen Gemeinde dar, was das Evangelium nach seiner Überzeugung ist ..." (1979:46).

[4] According to Kertelge (1983:13), Michel (1978:7), Wilckens (1978:IX), Schlier (1979:IX). Cranfield (1975:87), however, considers Rom 1,16—17 as a separate main division, whereas Käsemann (1974:V) regards 1,16—17 as a separate section, distinguished from 1,1—7 and 8—15 under the main heading "Briefeingang" (1,1—17).

Rom 1,10 his prayer to God for the congregation. The remembrance motif appears in 1,9.

Another characteristic of the ancient Greek letter, the *parousia*,[5] also appears in Rom 1,8—17. Paul's letters function as a kind of presence of the apostle. This "letter"-presence is, however, recognised as defective. The apostle's incomplete letter-*parousia* is supplemented by an actual visit to his readers, which he announces. It is significant that Paul frames the main section of his communication to the believers in Rome, whom he has not previously visited, with assurances of his intention to do so (Rom 1,10—12; 15,22—24).

The *philophrónesis*, a characteristic of the Greek letter pointed out by Koskenniemi (1956), is also present in this pericope. Paul's letters are full of proof of his affection for his readers. This becomes apparent in his custom of addressing his readers as "brothers" and his assurance that he thanks God for this particular congregation (Rom 1,8—10; cf also 1 Cor 1,4—9; Phil 1,3—6). These elements have a very important communicative function in that they create ties of friendship and sympathy between readers and author.

Rom 1,16—17 has a pivotal function as conclusion of the pericope, Rom 1,8—17, and as transition to the letter body of Romans.[6] Roberts (1986c:197) describes the transitional function of these verses (which he considers to be a credal statement) as follows: "… the credal statement has the function of determining the essential core of the argument to be made by the letter".[7]

Rom 1,16—17 relates both to the christological formula (1,3—4) and to the rest of Rom. In the formulation of verses 16—17 Paul unfolds the christological formula in terms of his message of justification, which is then

---

[5] For a more detailed discussion of the *parousia* as well as the *philophrónesis* (discussed in the next paragraph) see Du Toit (1985:4.20—21).

[6] W. Wuellner (referred to by Haacker 1999:36 n 50) portrays verses 16—17 as *Transitus* at the end of the *Exordium* before the beginning of the *Confirmatio* (1,18—15,13).

[7] See also Roberts (1988:85—7).

further developed in the following passages of this letter (cf Hahn 1980:212).[8]

17.2 Discourse analysis: Romans 1,8—17[9]

8   1.1 Πρῶτον μὲν εὐχαριστῶ τῷ θεῷ μου
         διὰ 'Ιησοῦ Χριστοῦ περὶ πάντων ὑμῶν,
         1.2 ὅτι ἡ πίστις ὑμῶν καταγγέλλεται ἐν ὅλῳ τῷ κόσμῳ.

9   2.1 μάρτυς γάρ μού ἐστιν ὁ θεός,
                    ↳ 2.2 ᾧ λατρεύω ⎡ 2.3 ἐν τῷ πνεύματί μου
                                                  ⎣ 2.4 ἐν τῷ εὐαγγελίῳ
                                                           τοῦ υἱοῦ αὐτοῦ,

         2.5 ὡς ἀδιαλείπτως μνείαν ὑμῶν ποιοῦμαι   A
10   πάντοτε ἐπὶ τῶν προσευχῶν μου,
         2.6 δεόμενος εἴ πως ἤδη ποτὲ εὐοδωθήσομαι
         ἐν τῷ θελήματι τοῦ θεοῦ ἐλθεῖν πρὸς ὑμᾶς.

11   3.1 ἐπιποθῶ γὰρ ἰδεῖν ὑμᾶς,
         3.2 ἵνα τι μεταδῶ χάρισμα ὑμῖν πνευματικὸν εἰς τὸ στηριχθῆναι ὑμᾶς,

12   3.3 τοῦτο δέ ἐστιν συμπαρακληθῆναι ἐν ὑμῖν
         διὰ τῆς ἐν ἀλλήλοις πίστεως ὑμῶν τε καὶ ἐμοῦ.

---

[8] The relationship between Rom 1,2—4 and 1,16—17 is very important. In his explication of Pauline theology, Goppelt (1985:389—90) starts with Rom 1,2—4 as well as 1,16—17 as key passages for the understanding of the way in which the Christ tradition was accepted and carried further by Paul. "Er [Paulus:PJG] kennzeichnet das Evangelium zuerst als die verheißene Botschaft von *Jesus Christus* [Röm 1,2—4], verweist zugleich auf ihre Vermittlung durch die *Verkündigung des Apostels* [Röm 1,1.5—15; 15,14—33] und entfaltet sie dann soteriologisch [Röm 1,16f. als Thema des Briefes]."

With reference to Rom 1,17, Eichholz (1985:38) points out that "... Evangelium und Christologie ... untrennbar miteinander verflochten sind". Rom 1,3—4 show: "Das Evangelium ist in seiner Mitte das *Christusgeschehen selbst.*" This gospel is translated in Rom 1,16—17 into the language of the theology of justification: "Rechtfertigungstheologie ist deshalb bei Paulus eine *Interpretation der Christologie.*"

[9] Cf Du Toit (Eksegese-Handleiding:5); Louw (1979a:2).

13   4.1 οὐ θέλω δὲ ὑμᾶς ἀγνοεῖν, ἀδελφοί,

      ↳ ὅτι   ⌐ 4.2 πολλάκις προεθέμην ἐλθεῖν
                  πρὸς ὑμᾶς,
            ⌐ 4.3 καὶ ἐκωλύθην ἄχρι τοῦ δεῦρο,

4.4 ἵνα τινὰ καρπὸν σχῶ καὶ ἐν ὑμῖν καθὼς καὶ ἐν τοῖς λοιποῖς ἔθνεσιν.

14   5.1 ὀφειλέτης εἰμί

      ↳ ⌐ 5.2 Ἕλλησίν τε καὶ βαρβάροις,
        ⌐ 5.3 σοφοῖς τε καὶ ἀνοήτοις·

15   6.1 οὕτως τὸ κατ' ἐμὲ πρόθυμον
     καὶ ὑμῖν τοῖς ἐν 'Ρώμῃ εὐαγγελίσασθαι.

16   7.1 Οὐ γὰρ ἐπαισχύνομαι τὸ εὐαγγέλιον,

                     ↳ 7.2 δύναμις γὰρ θεοῦ ἐστιν   **B**
                       ↳ 7.3 εἰς σωτηρίαν
            7.4 παντὶ τῷ πιστεύοντι,

                 ↳ ⌐ 7.5 'Ιουδαίῳ τε πρῶτον
                  ⌐ 7.6 καὶ Ἕλληνι·

17   8 δικαιοσύνη γὰρ θεοῦ ἐν αὐτῷ ἀποκαλύπτεται ἐκ πίστεως εἰς πίστιν,
     9 καθὼς γέγραπται, 'Ο δὲ δίκαιος ἐκ πίστεως ζήσεται.

Headings of the pericope and sub-pericopes

Pericope heading: Paul and the believers in Rome: Paul prays for them and expresses his great desire to visit them with the gospel of righteousness — the power of God for the salvation of everyone who believes.

Sub-pericope A: Paul thanks God and prays for the believers in Rome. He expresses his desire to visit them.

Sub-pericope B: Paul's great desire to visit them with the gospel of righteousness — the power of God for the salvation of everyone who believes.

17.2.1 A few notes pertaining to the structure of this pericope

The identifying of certain structural markers and actants can be useful in underlining the main themes of pericopes and sub-pericopes.

The verb in the first person singular and the corresponding personal pronouns, as well as the second person plural occur throughout the whole pericope. Paul and the Christians in Rome are, therefore, the dominating actants in Rom 1,1—17 (from v 18 onwards this function is fulfilled by God and the heathen).

Occurring at the beginning, as well as at the end of this pericope:
πίστις (comma 1.2)
πίστεως (comma 3.3)
τῷ πιστεύοντι (comma 7.4)
ἐκ πίστεως εἰς πίστιν (colon 8)
πίστεως (colon 9)

τῷ εὐαγγελίῳ (comma 2.4)
εὐαγγελίσασθαι (comma 6.1)
εὐαγγέλιον (comma 7.1)
αὐτῷ (referring to εὐαγγέλιον) (colon 8)

It is clear that πίστις and εὐαγγέλιον are important motifs in this passage.

Words referring to Paul's eagerness to visit the believers in Rome are prominent in colons 2—4:
εὐοδωθήσομαι ... ἐλθεῖν (2.6)
ἐπιποθῶ ... ἰδεῖν (3.1)
πολλάκις προεθέμην ἐλθεῖν (4.2)

Words of prayer and thanksgiving occur in colons 1—2:
εὐχαριστῶ (1.1)
προσευχῶν (2.5)
δεόμενος (2.6)

In verse 13 (colon 4) a traditional introductory formula occurs (cf Du Toit 1985:10): οὐ θέλω δὲ ὑμᾶς ἀγνοεῖν, ἀδελφοί ... (cf also 2 Cor 1,8; Phil 1,12). The question may arise whether Rom 1,8—12 and 13—17 are not perhaps two separate pericopes.[10] In this study Rom 1,8—17 is regarded as one pericope with 1,8—12 and 1,13—17 as two sub-pericopes:

— The attention has already been drawn to the structural markers and actants that occur both at the beginning and the end of this pericope.

— In colons 3 and 4 Paul's desire to visit the Romans is mentioned (cf ἐπιποθῶ ... ἰδεῖν ὑμᾶς and προεθέμην ἐλθεῖν πρὸς ὑμᾶς).

---

[10] Pelser (1985:50) and Du Toit (1984:9) regard Rom 1,8—12 and 13—17 as two separate pericopes. This view is, however, not held by the following commentators: Cranfield (1975:XI); Käsemann (1974:V) [in a certain sense]; Michel (1978:7); Schlier (1979:IX); Wilckens (1978:IX).

A division into two pericopes between colons 3 and 4, therefore, does not seem to be justified.

17.3 Textual criticism: Romans 1,16—17

Rom 1,16: τοῦ Χριστοῦ is inserted by the corrector of codex Claromontanus, codex Ψ and the Majority text.

The witnesses for the reading printed in the text (Nestle-Aland twenty seventh edition) are: papyrus 26, codex Sinaiticus, codex Alexandrinus, codex Vaticanus, codex Ephraemi, codex Claromontanus (the original scribe), codex G, as well as the minuscules 33, 81, 1506, 1739, 1881 and a few other Greek manuscripts, a part of the Old Latin and Vulgate versions, all the Syriac witnesses as well as all the Coptic versions available for this passage.

The number of witnesses in favour of the insertion is notably small. In evaluating the witnesses, the characteristic freedom of the Western text, of which codex Claromontanus is the principal representative (Metzger 1968:51) must be taken into account.

Some of our best manuscripts, representative of different text families, are witnesses for the reading printed in the text. External evidence is, therefore, decisive.

The words εἰς σωτηρίαν are omitted by the uncial codex G. Viewed in the light of the very slender external evidence for this omission (only one manuscript) it may be concluded that it was probably not original.

The omission of πρῶτον by the uncials codex Vaticanus and codex G, the Sahidic version and Marcion is, according to Metzger (1994:447), perhaps due to Marcion to whom the privilege of the Jews was unacceptable.

Rom 1,17: The original scribe of the uncial codex Ephraemi (dated in the fifth century) adds the word μου so that the quotation from Hab 2,4 reads: ὁ δὲ δίκαιος μου ἐκ πίστεως ζήσεται. The Septuagint reads here: ὁ δε δίκαιος ἐκ πίστεως μου ζήσεται.

This addition can not be accepted due to very slender external evidence — only the original scribe of one manuscript.

17.4 More detailed exegesis: Romans 1,16—17

The *gospel* is a very important motif in this pericope (cf 17.2.1) and stands in the centre of verse 16.[11] This gospel is δύναμις θεοῦ.[12] It must immediately be mentioned that Paul makes this statement in response to his remark οὐ γὰρ ἐπαισχύνομαι τὸ εὐαγγέλιον. It is true that the confessional element stands in the foreground here.[13] Yet, the theme explicit in 1 Cor 1,18 plays an implicit role in this passage too. The gospel is essentially ὁ λόγος τοῦ σταυροῦ and as such in the eyes of the Greeks folly (μωρία, cf 1 Cor 1,18.21.23) and in the eyes of the Jews a stumbling block. From the perspective of man, the gospel is weak — from God's perspective, however, it is the power for salvation (Kertelge 1983:33).[14] With the concept of "shame" Paul touches on the issue of *values* in society, from which it is very difficult for individuals to withdraw themselves. Those who do not respect these values run the risk of being despised and persecuted, which in the end may lead to the denial of those beliefs which caused this conflict (cf Mk 8,38 par.; Lk 9,26; Mt 10,32—33 par.; Lk 12,8—9; 2 Tim 1,8.12; Herm Sim 8,6,4; 9,21,3). In this context Paul might have thought about the conflict with Hellenistic culture in the world capital, Rome, or with Jewish traditions that confronted him in Jerusalem (cf 1 Cor 1,22—24) (Haacker 1999:37).

The gospel[15] is an entity that takes grip of him,[16] because it is the power *of God* (cf εὐαγγέλιον θεοῦ [Rom 1,2]). The apostolic gospel is not only proclaimed ἐν δυνάμει (πνεύματος) (cf Rom 15,19; 1 Cor 4,20; 1

---

[11] "Die verschiedenen Teilaussagen in V.16f sammeln sich in dem Stichwort 'Evangelium' " (Kertelge 1983:32).

[12] Käsemann (1974:19) remarks: "Evangelium ist mehr als bloß die kirchlich aktualisierte Botschaft, nämlich die dem Menschen nicht verfügbare, auch der Kirche und ihren Dienern selbständig gegenüberstehende Heilskundgabe Gottes an die Welt, welche sich kraft des Geistes in der Verkündigung stets neu verwirklicht. So eben kann es als δύναμις θεοῦ bezeichnet werden."

[13] Glombitza (1960:80) speaks of the "... Charakter eines feierlichen Bekenntnisses in dieser Aussage ...". Cf also Wilckens (1978:82): " 'Sich nicht schämen' ist gesteigertes Äquivalent zu ὁμολογεῖν."

[14] Cf also Eichholz (1985:222): "... in der Ansage des Themas des Römerbriefs heißt es vom Evangelium, daß es Gottes Macht ist [wie Paulus in 1. Kor 1,18 den λόγος τοῦ σταυροῦ Gottes δύναμις sein läßt!]".

[15] τὸ εὐαγγέλιον is often used absolutely by Paul: 1 Cor 4,15; 9,23; 15,1; Gal 2,6.14; Phil 1,7; 2,22; 1 Thess 2,4.

[16] "... eine Größe, die ihn selbst in Pflicht nimmt ..." (Wilckens 1978:82).

Thess 1,5), but it *is* the power of God which makes God's eschatological salvation accessible to those who believe (cf 1 Cor 1,18; 2,4) (Schlier 1973:133).[17] Paul's statement in Rom 1,16 that the gospel is the power of God is closely related to his statements concerning the proclamation of the gospel in the power of the Holy Spirit (Rom 15,19; 1 Thess 1,5 [cf also the discussion of 1 Cor 2,4—5]).[18] The relationship between Rom 1,3—4 and 16—17 makes it clear that the gospel is essentially the Christ event in soteriological perspective. While verses 3 and 4 describe the contents of the gospel as message about Jesus, verses 16 and 17 explain the *effect* of this message on those who accept it in faith (Haacker 1999:36). Through the Spirit the eschatological salvation (and life) becomes a reality (cf Hahn 1974b:141). In Romans this is illustrated in 8,1—39.[19]

The concept of δύναμις (power) has become a *theological* concept in the Pauline letters. With this concept he has in mind a divine force that operates with marked effect on people, transforming them — as evident particularly in conversion (1 Cor 2,4—5; 1 Thess 1,5) and resurrection (Rom 1,4; 1 Cor 6,14; 15,43; 2 Cor 13,4; Phil 3,10) — and providing a source of energy to sustain that qualitatively different life. This power was not just a matter of blind trust, but had a specific experiential dimension as indicated also by the plural δυνάμεις ("miracles") — a visible alteration in a current condition that could not be attributed to human causation (cf Rom 15,19; 1 Cor 12,10.28—29; 2 Cor 12,12; Gal 3,5) (Dunn 1988:39).[20]

In the gospel God's power of salvation is given (cf Prete 1975:299—328). The gospel is δύναμις ... θεοῦ ... εἰς σωτηρίαν. The concept σωτηρία was common in New Testament times and had a high emotional value. The predicaments and fears of late antiquity, in which context was spoken of saviours and salvation, could have been of political

---

[17] Cf also Wilckens (1978:83): "Das Evangelium ist selbst δύναμις θεοῦ, sofern es λόγος τοῦ σταυροῦ ist [1Kor 1,18], d.h. Proklamation des Gekreuzigten als 'Gottes Kraft und Gottes Weisheit' [1Kor 1,24], die den Glaubenden Heil schafft [1Kor 1,18.21], so daß durch das Evangelium, das der Apostel verkündigt, die Glaubenden, sofern sie daran festhalten, am endzeitlichen Heil teilhaben [1Kor 15,2 vgl. Röm 10,9f]."

[18] In his commentary on Rom 1,16 Käsemann (1974:19) also points to the role of the Spirit.

[19] Summarised by Zeller (1985:9) as "... Leben im Geist als Gesetzeserfüllung und Hoffnung auf vollendetes Heil — trotz Leiden".

[20] Of the Old Testament passages which speak of the effectiveness of God's word and which Paul might have had in mind, Dunn mentions Ps 107,20, particularly in view of its use in the ancient form of the kerygma preserved in Acts 10,36—38.

and social, physical or psychic nature. When the early Christian message used this concept, it promised an answer to the sufferings which were part of human existence in those times.[21] Within the context of Paul's theology σωτηρία refers to the salvation of humanity fallen in sin (cf Kertelge 1971:86—7) and refers to the eschatological salvation, revealed finally in its most profound sense at the *parousia* of Jesus Christ (cf 5,9; 13,11; 1 Cor 3,15; 5,5; Phil 1,19).[22] In accordance with the apocalyptic tradition, salvation includes deliverance from God's judgement (cf 1,18—3,20; 5,9). Positively salvation may be portrayed as "life" (cf v 17b), partaking in God's glory. This σωτηρία is also a present reality.[23] Paul, therefore, states in Rom 1,16 that the gospel is God's effective power active in the world to bring about deliverance from his wrath and re-instalment in that glory of God which was lost through sin (cf Cranfield 1975:89).

Σωτηρία also has a critical dimension. The gospel is presented not as salvation for everybody, but for those who believe. At the same time the universality of God's work of salvation in the gospel is stressed: παντὶ τῷ πιστεύοντι, Ἰουδαίῳ τε πρῶτον καὶ Ἕλληνι.

While the Qumran community expected salvation only for themselves, the gospel brought at this point a decisive break with the concept of salvation of early Judaism: a break expressed by the words παντὶ τῷ

---

[21] "... und tritt damit in Konkurrenz zu anderen 'Heilswegen' ..." (Haacker 1999:38).

[22] " 'Heil' bezeichnet die eschatologische Wirkung des Evangeliums für den Menschen" (Zeller 1985:42).

[23] "... und zwar sofern sie als in Jesus Christus geschehene sich im Evangelium vollzieht [vgl. 8,24; 11,11.14; 1 Kor 1,18.21; 2 Kor 2,15; 6,2 u.a.]" (Schlier 1979:43).

Kertelge (1971:151) points out that Paul's statement concerning justification cannot be divided into a first preliminary and a second final act of justification, "... sondern daß die Rechtfertigung für Paulus eine Ganzheit darstellt, *wie auch der Begriff der σωτηρία nicht in Anfangs- und Endheil auseinanderfällt* und ebenso der Begriff der ζωή nicht zerlegt werden darf. Paulus kennt nur eine Rechtfertigung ... die auf Grund der Heilstat Jesu Christi jetzt schon gegenwärtig ist ..." (emphasis: PJG).

Cranfield (1975:88—9) observes that in Paul's letters σώζειν and σωτηρία are used only in connection with man's relationship with God. They have a primarily eschatological connotation. It is the restoration of the δόξα which sinful men lack. While salvation is characteristically referred to by means of verbs in *the future* tense, Paul can use a *past* tense in this connection (in 8,24 we have the statement ἐσώθημεν which, however, is qualified by τῇ ἐλπίδι), since the decisive act of God, by which the believers' final salvation has been secured, has already been accomplished, and also a *present* tense as in 1 Cor 1,18 and 2 Cor 2,15, to describe the believers' present waiting, hoping and struggling which have salvation as their goal.

πιστεύοντι.[24] The gospel not only puts aside the social difference between Greek and Barbarian (1,14), but for the Jew the even more radical distinction between Jew and Greek (διαστολὴ Ἰουδαίου τε καὶ Ἕλληνος [10,12]).[25]

Paul's message calls for an appropriate response: faith — "... faith in the message, and so faith in Jesus Christ who is its content and in God who has acted in him and whose power the message is" (Cranfield 1975:87). Faith must, however, not be seen as a precondition man has to fulfil in order to obtain salvation.[26] It belongs to the very essence of faith, as Paul understands it, that it is opposed to all human deserving, all human establishing of claims on God (cf Cranfield 1975:90). Yet, in faith a most important decision is taken. Faith is expression of the liberty God restored to man — the liberty to obey him.[27] While the gospel announces the saving action of God, this saving action of God becomes a reality in the existence of man through faith. In faith man experiences salvation as a new relation to God. Faith is, indeed, the way in which man partakes in the eschatological salvific activity of God in the present (cf Kertelge 1983:34).

---

[24] Wilckens (1978:85) correctly comments: "Daß Gottes heilschaffende Gerechtigkeit den Sünder 'ohne das Gesetz' allein aufgrund des Glaubens an Christus zum Gerechten macht [3,21f], das ist der Charakter des Evangeliums, der dieses von jüdischer Gottesverkündigung trennt und so christlichen Glauben von jüdischem unterscheidet."

[25] Strack and Billerbeck (1926:29) remark in this regard: "... das jüdische Schrifttum [hat] die gesamte Menschheit in die beiden Teile: 'Israel' u. 'Völker der Welt' geteilt". With this Jewish devision correlates Paul's Ἰουδαίῳ τε ... καὶ Ἕλληνι.

Just a few words on the interpretation of πρῶτον in the phrase Ἰουδαίῳ τε πρῶτον καὶ Ἕλληνι: Käsemann (1974:21) writes: "Paulus hat um der Kontinuität des Heilsplans Willen dem Judentum eine Prävalenz eingeräumt." Cranfield (1975:91) mentions that the paradoxical insistence on the fact that there is no διαστολή as well as on the continuing validity of the Ἰουδαίῳ ... πρῶτον ... belongs to the substance of the epistle. This issue is treated in depth in chapters nine to eleven.

[26] "Er ist nicht eine Bedingung an die Gottes Kraft gebunden ist, sondern Antwort, Folge und Wirkung ..." (Michel [referring to Schlatter] 1978:88).

[27] "Darin, daß das Evangelium bei den Menschen Glauben hervorruft, erweist es sich als *Heilsgeschehen*, eben als das machtvolle Wirken Gottes zur Rettung der ihrer Sünde verhafteten Menschheit" (Kertelge 1983:33).

The close relation between Rom 1,16 and 17²⁸ must be taken into account in interpreting δύναμις in verse 16. In which sense is the gospel δύναμις θεοῦ? Verse 17 gives the reason why the gospel *is the power of God for the salvation of everyone who believes*: δικαιοσύνη γὰρ θεοῦ ἐν αὐτῷ ἀποκαλύπτεται ἐκ πίστεως εἰς πίστιν ...

17.4.1 Gospel (εὐαγγέλιον) — power of God (δύναμις θεοῦ) — righteousness of God (δικαιοσύνη θεοῦ)

The issue of the relationship between the power of God and the righteousness of God was especially brought into the scholarly discussion by Ernst Käsemann (1961:367—78 [=1986:160—72]). Käsemann criticises Bultmann's mainly forensic interpretation of δικαιοσύνη θεοῦ (cf Bultmann 1968:273) and affirms that δικαιοσύνη θεοῦ occurs in *(inter alia)* Rom 1,17 personified as power ("Macht"). Käsemann stresses that δικαιοσύνη θεοῦ is not only a gift, but also a power — justification means that Christ gains control over our lives (1986:166; cf also Gräbe 1990:57—9). This view of Käsemann was criticised by *(inter alia)* Eduard Lohse (1973:225) who observed that Paul did not relate the word δύναμις to the δικαιοσύνη θεοῦ but to the *gospel* (τὸ εὐαγγέλιον) (cf Haacker 1999:40). Δικαιοσύνη θεοῦ may correctly be described as a summary of Paul's message,²⁹ presented from a soteriological perspective. It is a leading theological-soteriological motif in Pauline theology most intimately related to Jesus' cross and resurrection. In the *gospel* the *righteousness of God* has been revealed.³⁰

---

²⁸ Owing to the importance of the correct understanding of the relationship between Rom 1,16 and 17 a few commentators may be quoted in this regard:

Cranfield (1975:91): "δικαιοσύνη γὰρ θεοῦ ἐν αὐτῷ ἀποκαλύπτεται ἐκ πίστεως εἰς πίστιν is introduced as explanation and confirmation [γάρ] of v 16b: the gospel is God's δύναμις εἰς σωτηρίαν παντὶ τῷ πιστεύοντι because in it δικαιοσύνη θεοῦ is being revealed ἐκ πίστεως εἰς πίστιν."

Schlier (1979:44): "Doch in welchem Sinn ist das Evangelium eine δύναμις θεοῦ? Das bedenkt der Apostel noch im V 17 mit einem Begründungssatz. Im Evangelium wird die δικαιοσύνη θεοῦ, 'die Gerechtigkeit Gottes', geoffenbart."

Ulrich Wilckens (1978:86) describes the relationship between Rom 1,16 and 17 as follows: "V 17 begründet [γάρ], warum das Evangelium Kraft Gottes zum Heil für jeden, der glaubt, ist [V 16b]."

²⁹ "... eine kerygmatische 'Kurzformel' "; cf Kertelge (1980a:790).

³⁰ A discussion of the scholarly debate on the concept of justification by Paul lies beyond the scope of this monograph. For a recent overview of this issue, the reader is referred to Söding (1997:291—5).

The "righteousness of Jahwe" (צדקת יהוה) in the Old Testament is related to his conduct within the covenant with his people (Kertelge 1980a:790). It seems probable that Paul also uses the expression δικαιοσύνη θεοῦ in the context of the covenant relation (cf Louw & Nida 1988a:452).[31] Louw and Nida (1988a:452) correctly discuss the meaning of δικαιοσύνη within the semantic subdomain "Establish or Confirm a Relation". They translate Rom 1,17: "... how God puts people right with himself is revealed in it [the gospel] as a matter of faith from beginning to end". The new reality of those who have been justified is not a mere formal and static condition. It is essentially a *relational* reality. Within the context of Pauline theology this new reality which came into being when God established a new relationship between himself and believing humanity has profound consequences: From God's perspective it may be described as "Lordship" and from the believer's viewpoint as "obedience" (cf Kertelge 1971:127).

This salvific activity of God through which he puts people right with himself occurs independently of the law in the ἀπολύτρωσις ἡ ἐν Χριστῷ which is the realisation of the χάρις τοῦ θεοῦ (cf Schlier 1973:134—6). It has been made possible by the vicarious atoning death of Jesus (Rom 3,25—26). It is the grounding in Christ's atoning death which distinguishes the Pauline concept of justification from all Jewish outlines of this concept (Zeller 1985:49). Righteousness is a gracious gift from God (cf Lohse 1973:227), "... for if righteousness could be gained through the law, Christ died for nothing!" (Gal 2,21).

In order to explain and emphasise the δύναμις of the gospel (cf Rom 1,16) Paul presents an explicit theological exposition of the history of salvation as an event of *justification* (cf Kertelge 1971:286).[32] The gospel which has as its contents the δικαιοσύνη θεοῦ has a *powerful effect*. The

---

[31] "Gott teilt seine sündenvergebende und den Bund erneuernde Gerechtigkeit den Menschen mit" (Kertelge 1980a:791).

[32] It is noteworthy, that in giving the motivation for the fact that the gospel is God's power unto salvation Paul could have pointed to Christ reigning in God's power as he has done in Rom 1,4. "Aber er blickt auf die Voraussetzung für die Rettung beim Menschen, die Gerechtigkeit. Niemand kann sie aufbringen, wie 1,18—3,20 ausführen werden; deshalb sind alle verloren. Und doch gibt es im Evangelium Gerechtigkeit, und zwar die von Gott geschenkte" (Zeller 1985:43).

justification of sinners therefore not only has a forensic meaning, but also an "effective" dimension (cf Kertelge 1971:123).[33]

17.5 Conclusion

Rom 1,16—17 focuses on the gospel, the gospel which centres on the Christ event: his crucifixion and resurrection (cf Eichholz 1985:38). The gospel is portrayed as the *concrete power of God* for the *salvation* of everyone who believes. To underline and explain his statement concerning the gospel as the power of God, Paul gives a rich theological exposition of God's act of salvation as an act of justification.

Δύναμις θεοῦ in the context of Pauline soteriology (as expressed in Rom 1,16—17) is therefore very closely related to his message concerning the δικαιοσύνη θεοῦ. It may be said that the *mode of action of the gospel* is portrayed as δύναμις θεοῦ. As to its *contents* this gospel may be described as δικαιοσύνη θεοῦ. Or — formulated in another way — the *effect* of the gospel *on this world* is described in terms of power (δύναμις).

What is at stake is God's saving action of humanity caught in its sin. Rom 1,18—3,20 clearly points out that people cannot save themselves. It is in this context that Paul's statement that the gospel is δύναμις θεοῦ ... εἰς σωτηρίαν must be interpreted, a statement motivated and explained by verse 17: δικαιοσύνη γὰρ θεοῦ ἐν αὐτῷ ἀποκαλύπτεται ἐκ πίστεως εἰς πίστιν ... .

---

[33] This "effective" dimension of δικαιοσύνη θεοῦ is emphasised by Stuhlmacher (1965:83—4) when he considers δικαιοσύνη θεοῦ in Rom 1,17 as "... Gottes eigene, im Evangelium durch die Welt ziehende Schöpfermacht ... welche Glauben-stiftend die neue Welt Gottes heraufführt".

Hübner (1987:2698—9) criticises Stuhlmacher as over emphasising the thesis of his book (1965), namely that justification means divine creative activity ("göttliches Schöpfungshandeln"). It is, however, clear from the preceding discussion that the various concepts Paul uses overlap in a certain sense. The gospel which is explained in terms of δικαιοσύνη θεοῦ is δύναμις θεοῦ. δύναμις *is* therefore indirectly related to δικαιοσύνη θεοῦ (cf Hübner 1987:2702). When one bears in mind that δύναμις has a distinctive pneumatological undertone in Paul's preaching (cf chapter 24), one's criticism of Stuhlmacher may be softened.

Chapter 18

Romans 1,20

18.1 Location within the macrocontext of Romans

The broader context in which Rom 1,20 occurs may be schematised as follows:

1,18—4,25 ALL ARE GUILTY BEFORE GOD, BUT HE WHO
BELIEVES, IS JUSTIFIED THROUGH GRACE.

1,18—3,20 The wrath of God is revealed over all sin.
3,21—4,25 He who believes is justified through grace
(Cf Du Toit 1984,9; Kertelge 1983,13).

Rom 1,18—32 constitutes the first pericope of the section 1,18—3,20 and is also the first pericope of the letter body of Romans. The words ἀποκαλύπτεται γάρ ... (1,18), clearly introduce a new pericope, while διό in 2,1 also indicates the beginning of another pericope. Rom 1,18—32 focuses on the guilt of the heathen, while in 2,1—3,8 the guilt of the Jews is described (cf Du Toit 1984:35; Louw 1979b:144; Zeller 1984:9).

18.2 Discourse analysis: Romans 1,18—21a[1]

The wrath of God has been revealed against the sinfulness of humankind, who have perceived his qualities, but have not glorified him as God.

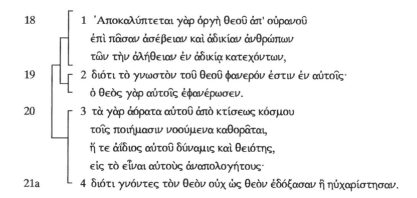

18   1 'Αποκαλύπτεται γὰρ ὀργὴ θεοῦ ἀπ' οὐρανοῦ
     ἐπὶ πᾶσαν ἀσέβειαν καὶ ἀδικίαν ἀνθρώπων
     τῶν τὴν ἀλήθειαν ἐν ἀδικίᾳ κατεχόντων,
19   2 διότι τὸ γνωστὸν τοῦ θεοῦ φανερόν ἐστιν ἐν αὐτοῖς·
     ὁ θεὸς γὰρ αὐτοῖς ἐφανέρωσεν.
20   3 τὰ γὰρ ἀόρατα αὐτοῦ ἀπὸ κτίσεως κόσμου
     τοῖς ποιήμασιν νοούμενα καθορᾶται,
     ἥ τε ἀίδιος αὐτοῦ δύναμις καὶ θειότης,
     εἰς τὸ εἶναι αὐτοὺς ἀναπολογήτους·
21a   4 διότι γνόντες τὸν θεὸν οὐχ ὡς θεὸν ἐδόξασαν ἢ ηὐχαρίστησαν.

18.2.1 A few notes pertaining to the structure of Romans 1,18—21a[2]

In this sub-pericope the following motifs are related to one another:

— The anger of God (resulting in judgement) ὀργὴ θεοῦ (cf Louw 1979b:42).

— People's sin. Cf: ἀσέβειαν (v 18), ἀδικίαν ἀνθρώπων (v 18), ἀδικίᾳ (τὴν ἀλήθειαν ἐν ἀδικίᾳ κατεχόντων) (v 18).[3]

— The fact that (the nature of) God could be known (because God has made it known). (Cf τὸ γνωστὸν τοῦ θεοῦ φανερόν ἐστιν [v 19], ὁ θεὸς ... ἐφανέρωσεν [v 19]; τὰ γὰρ ἀόρατα αὐτοῦ ... νοούμενα καθορᾶται [v 20]; γνόντες τὸν θεόν [v 21]).

— Humankind is without excuse: αὐτοὺς ἀναπολογήτους (v 20).

---

[1] Rom 1,18—21a constitutes the first sub-pericope of the pericope Rom 1,18—32. This sub-pericope is closely related to the next (1,21b—23). These two sub-pericopes represent the first main section of the pericope (1,18—32). Rom 1,18—23 may be headlined: The sin of the heathen: "De-deification" of God (Du Toit Eksegese-Handleiding:8).

[2] Note the parallel structure of the opening phrases of verses 17 and 18:
     Rom 1,17: δικαιοσύνη γὰρ θεοῦ ἐν αὐτῷ ἀποκαλύπτεται ...
     Rom 1,18: 'Αποκαλύπτεται γὰρ ὀργὴ θεοῦ ἀπ' οὐρανοῦ ...

[3] The sin of humankind is also portrayed by the phrase: οὐχ ὡς θεὸν ἐδόξασαν ἢ ηὐχαρίστησαν (v 21).

The mutual relationships within which these motifs function are of great importance: In verse 19 διότι introduces a colon giving the reason why God sends his anger down as judgement upon people's sins. Verse 21 (also introduced by διότι) gives the reason why humankind is without excuse. God's invisible qualities, which can be perceived in the things he has made, involve his eternal power and divinity (v 20).[4] Verses 20—21 continue the argument of verses 18—19. The argument of this sub-pericope can be reformulated logically as: Ever since the world was made people could have known God, and could have worshipped him. Instead, they sinned against him. Therefore God is angry and will punish them as they have no excuse (Louw 1979b:42—3).

18.3 Exegetical perspectives

With the righteousness of God, as revealed in the gospel, the wrath of God provoked by all the godlessness and wickedness of humankind who suppress the truth by their wickedness (v 18) is also being revealed.[5] The depth of human guilt is portrayed by Paul in two respects:

— People have denied God, their Creator, the thanksgiving which they as creatures owe their Creator (Rom 1,18—32).
— Humankind have — in the concrete form of the history of Israel — rejected the gift of covenant and law and have, therefore, rejected God himself as God of the covenant (Rom 2,1—3,20) (cf Kertelge 1987:87).

It has been common knowledge for quite a long time now that behind Paul's argumentation in this pericope (commencing with Rom 1,18), lies a significant Jewish tradition (Wilckens 1978:96 especially note 140).[6] Although it can not be said with certainty that Paul was acquainted with a

---

[4] The phrase ἥ τε ἀΐδιος αὐτοῦ δύναμις καὶ θειότης stands in apposition to τὰ γὰρ ἀόρατα αὐτοῦ.

[5] "Damit kennzeichnet Paulus die Schuld der Menschen, die das Gericht Gottes auf sich herabzieht, aus dem keine Macht rettet als nur die im Evangelium geoffenbarte, in Jesus Christus in Kraft gesetzte Gerechtigkeit Gottes" (Kertelge 1987:87).

[6] Cf Kertelge (1983:243 note 9): "Man wird Paulus daher auf dem Hintergrund einer hellenistisch beeinflußten jüdisch-apokalyptischen Lehrtradition zu verstehen haben."

document like the Wisdom of Solomon, the similarity of the motifs and even the vocabulary is significant.[7]

Similar judgements upon the godlessness of the heathen in their worship of idols can also be found in other literature of Hellenistic Judaism, for example in the Sibylline Oracles (Wilckens 1978:97 notes 143—5). The same connection of motifs also occurs in apocalyptic literature (cf 2 Bar 54,17—19).[8]

It is important to notice that although the above-mentioned witnesses from "diaspora" Judaism have been influenced by Hellenistic-philosophical ideas, the context of these sayings has an essentially different scope. The knowledge of God obtained from the harmony and beauty of the "cosmos" was taught and celebrated in educated circles, especially since the Middle Stoa. It was thought that intelligent people could correspond in their conduct to the λόγος and in this way become "wise".

The scope of the Jewish reception of natural theology is, however, totally different. Already in the Wisdom of Solomon, in which Hellenistic influence is very prominent, the non-Jewish world is accused of rejecting the true knowledge of God which can be obtained from the works of creation. Although the natural knowledge of God is asserted as an open possibility for all mankind since creation, it has been reached only by Israel's devoted ones.[9]

With a view to the present study, the Wisdom of Solomon 13,1—9 is especially important, for not only does the line of argument in this passage resemble that of Rom 1,18—23, but the word δύναμις figures prominently in both passages.[10] (Cf 13,4 εἰ δὲ δύναμιν καὶ ἐνέργειαν ἐκπλαγέντες, νοησάτωσαν ἀπ' αὐτῶν πόσῳ ὁ κατασκευάσας αὐτὰ δυνατώτερός ἐστιν·)

---

[7] A more detailed discussion of Wisdom 13,1—9 will be presented further down.

[8] In the Dutch translation by De Goeij (1981:103): "17 Maar gij die nu boosdoeners zijt keert terug tot de vergankelijkheid, want gij zult streng gestraft worden, omdat gij ooit de kennis van de Allerhoogste verworpen hebt. 18 Want zijn werken hebben u niets geleerd en ook die kunstige inrichting van zijn schepping, die altijd bestaat, heeft u niet overtuigd. 19 Zo is Adam slechts voor zichzelf verantwoordelijk geweest en zijn wij ieder voor zich een Adam geworden."

[9] "Eine Erkenntnis der Ordnungen des Kosmos ist außerhalb des israelitischen Gottesglaubens schlicht unmöglich … Paulus steht mit seiner Gerichtsrede über 'alle Gottlosigkeit und Ungerechtigkeit [!] der Menschen' [1,18] deutlich in dieser apokalyptischen Tradition" (Wilckens 1978:100).

[10] Δύναμις in the context of God's power is also mentioned in Wisdom of Solomon 12,17 (δυνάμεως τελειότητι).

New Testament scholars do not all agree concerning the date of origin of this document. Proposed dates range from the second century BCE to the second century CE, although the majority of commentators favour the first century BCE (Reese 1970:161).[11]

The literary genre employed by the author of the Wisdom of Solomon is the "logos protreptikos" or exhortatory discourse (Winston 1979:18). The style and method of reasoning of 13,1—9 are so typically philosophical that the text could only have been composed by a person who was acquainted with the speculation that is characteristic of Hellenistic theosophy (Reese 1970:51). The author of this document followed certain well-known biblical patterns, but also borrowed freely from Hellenistic and more especially from Jewish-Hellenistic themes (Winston 1979:249).[12]

Reese (1970:55) affirms that Aristotle was the first to employ as technical philosophical terms the words δύναμις καὶ ἐνέργεια "power and activity", used to describe the marvels of nature in the Wisdom of Solomon 13,4. They appear frequently in Hellenistic religious and astronomical writings (cf Reese 1970:55 note 106). The wide varieties of "powers" present in the cosmos prompted theories about the nature and activities of the gods.

In the light of what has been said above, the Hellenistic influence on Rom 1,18—23 is clear. Paul uses the Platonic category of invisibility to characterise the essence of God. It can, however, paradoxically be seen in the creatures who witness of their Creator.[13]

---

[11] A noteworthy exception is David Winston (1979:23) who maintains that the reign of Gaius "Caligula" (CE 37—41) provides the likeliest setting for this document.

[12] Reese (1970:161—2) mentions the educated Hellenistic Jew had to steer between two erroneous courses: a) the dualism of Platonistic philosophies which looked upon matter as evil and upon immortality as an intrinsic quality of the soul to be achieved by escape from the body; (b) the pantheism of contemporary philosophy, especially Stoicism, which identified humankind and its destiny with the universe in some fashion.

[13] The participle νοούμενα relates to the preceding τοῖς ποιήμασιν. "So dient diese Wendung als erklärende Näherbestimmung zu dem Oxymoron τὰ ἀόρατα ... καθορᾶται, und νοούμενα zeigt darin ein Stück 'geistiger Verarbeitung des Gesehenen' an" (Kertelge 1987:88).

Zeller (1985:55—6) affirms that the conclusion "... vom Werk auf den Meister verbindet sich mit einer späten Abwandlung des biblischen Gedankens, daß die 'Herrlichkeit Gottes' [vgl. V. 23] Himmel und Erde erfüllt [vgl. Ps 19,2ff; Sir 42,16]". Revelation occurs also in creation. God's eternal power and divine nature (cf Pl Leg III 69le: ... θείᾳ ... δυνάμει; Cic NatD 1 18,44: "vis et natura deodorum" [cf Wilckens 1978:106 note 179]) are revealed, "... mithin sein Abstand vom Geschaffenen, was gerade seine Verwechslung mit Irdischem ausschließen sollte" (Zeller 1985:56).

While making use of the ideas from Hellenistic philosophy, that the order in the cosmos refers to a founding and maintaining source (cf Kertelge 1987:87), Paul is in line with the Jewish mediation of this idea in which this "Source" of all Being is identified with the Creator from the Old Testament.[14]

Paul doesn't speak of the *possibility*, but of the fact of the natural knowledge of God by the heathen (φανερόν ἐστιν, v 19; γνόντες τὸν θεόν, v 21). However, he focuses on the wrath of God against the sin of humankind. The sin of the heathen, however, does not lie in the fact that they did not recognise God — as in Wisdom of Solomon 13 — but in the fact that although they had obtained knowledge of God, they did not *honour* him as God (Kertelge 1987:88).

18.4 Conclusion

In Rom 1,20 δύναμις (qualified by ἀΐδιος) is used together with θειότης as a further qualification of *God's invisible qualities* which can be perceived from the works of creation.

The Hellenistically orientated Jewish-Apocalyptic background to Paul's use of δύναμις in this pericope is of considerable importance.

---

[14] "Mehr noch: die hellenistische philosophische Anschauung vom gründenden Prinzip des Seins wird eingeschmolzen in die Schöpfungstheologie des Alten Testaments" (Kertelge 1987:87).

Chapter 19

Romans 15,13

19.1 Location within the macrocontext of Romans

The pericope Rom 15,1—13, must be interpreted against the background of Rom 12,1—15,13. This section of Paul's letter to the Rom deals with Christian conduct (Du Toit 1984:14; Kertelge 1983:16), or — as Käsemann (1974:vi) poignantly formulates: "Gottesgerechtigkeit im christlichen Alltag." Dunn (1988:x) defines Rom 12,1—15,13 as "The Outworking of the Gospel for the Redifined People of God in Everyday Terms" and Moo (1996:vi) characterises this section of Romans as "The Transforming Power of the Gospel".[1]

Rom 12,1—15,13 may be divided as follows:

12,1—2   Introduction
12,3—13,14 Aspects of the Christian life
14,1—15,13 The weak and the strong (Du Toit 1984:14).

Rom 15,1—13 completes the trilogy (Rom 14,1—12; 14,13—23; 15,1—13) discussing the relationship between "the weak" and "the strong" among Christians.[2]

For a motivation of the demarcation of the pericope Rom 15,1—13, compare 19.2.1.

---

[1] Cranfield (1979:592) headlines Rom 12,1—15,13: "The obedience to which those who are righteous by faith are called." Cf also Zeller (1985:300) who summarises the essence of Rom 12,1—15,13 as: "Verwirklichung des Christseins in Gemeinde und Welt."

[2] According to Louw (1979b:134). Cf also Kertelge (1983:16). Michel (1978:441) expresses the same thought: "Wir dürfen Röm 15,1—13 als dritten Abschnitt in der apostolischen Mahnrede über das Verhältnis der 'Starken' zu den 'Schwachen' ansehen."

Although distinguishing four pericopes (by dividing Rom 15,1—13 into two pericopes), Käsemann (1974:vi) and Wilckens (1982:100.104) are also in accord.

19.2 Discourse analysis: Romans 15,1—13

1
a
2

1 Ὀφείλομεν δὲ ἡμεῖς οἱ δυνατοὶ τὰ ἀσθενήματα
τῶν ἀδυνάτων βαστάζειν,
καὶ μὴ ἑαυτοῖς ἀρέσκειν.
2 ἕκαστος ἡμῶν τῷ πλησίον ἀρεσκέτω
εἰς τὸ ἀγαθὸν πρὸς οἰκοδομήν·

3

3 καὶ γὰρ ὁ Χριστὸς οὐχ ἑαυτῷ ἤρεσεν·

4 ἀλλὰ καθὼς γέγραπται,
4.1 Οἱ ὀνειδισμοὶ τῶν ὀνειδιζόντων σε ἐπέπεσαν ἐπ' ἐμέ.

4
b

5 ὅσα γὰρ προεγράφη,
εἰς τὴν ἡμετέραν διδασκαλίαν ἐγράφη,
ἵνα διὰ τῆς ὑπομονῆς καὶ διὰ τῆς παρακλήσεως τῶν γραφῶν
τὴν ἐλπίδα ἔχωμεν.

5
c
6

6 ὁ δὲ θεὸς τῆς ὑπομονῆς καὶ τῆς παρακλήσεως δῴη ὑμῖν
τὸ αὐτὸ φρονεῖν ἐν ἀλλήλοις κατὰ Χριστὸν Ἰησοῦν,
ἵνα ὁμοθυμαδὸν ἐν ἑνὶ στόματι δοξάζητε τὸν θεὸν καὶ πατέρα
τοῦ κυρίου ἡμῶν Ἰησοῦ Χριστοῦ.

A

7
a
8

7 Διὸ προσλαμβάνεσθε ἀλλήλους,
καθὼς καὶ ὁ Χριστὸς προσελάβετο ὑμᾶς,
εἰς δόξαν τοῦ θεοῦ.
8 λέγω γὰρ Χριστὸν διάκονον γεγενῆσθαι περιτομῆς
ὑπὲρ ἀληθείας θεοῦ,
εἰς τὸ βεβαιῶσαι τὰς ἐπαγγελίας τῶν πατέρων,

9

τὰ δὲ ἔθνη ὑπὲρ ἐλέους δοξάσαι τὸν θεόν·

9 καθὼς γέγραπται,
9.1 Διὰ τοῦτο ἐξομολογήσομαί σοι ἐν ἔθνεσιν,
9.2 καὶ τῷ ὀνόματί σου ψαλῶ.

10

10 καὶ πάλιν λέγει,
10.1 εὐφράνθητε, ἔθνη, μετὰ τοῦ λαοῦ αὐτοῦ.

11
b

11 καὶ πάλιν,
11.1 Αἰνεῖτε, πάντα τὰ ἔθνη, τὸν κύριον,
11.2 καὶ ἐπαινεσάτωσαν αὐτὸν πάντες οἱ λαοί.

B

12

12 καὶ πάλιν Ἡσαΐας λέγει,
12.1 Ἔσται ἡ ῥίζα τοῦ Ἰεσσαί,
12.2 καὶ ὁ ἀνιστάμενος ἄρχειν ἐθνῶν·
12.3 ἐπ' αὐτῷ ἔθνη ἐλπιοῦσιν.

13
c

13 ὁ δὲ θεὸς τῆς ἐλπίδος πληρώσαι ὑμᾶς
πάσης χαρᾶς καὶ εἰρήνης ἐν τῷ πιστεύειν,
εἰς τὸ περισσεύειν ὑμᾶς ἐν τῇ ἐλπίδι
ἐν δυνάμει πνεύματος ἁγίου.

Headings of the pericope and sub-pericopes

Pericope heading: Help and accept one another, following the example of Christ. May God be praised and cause your hope to continue to grow (cf Louw 1979b:147).

Sub-pericope A: Help the weak to carry their burdens, following the example of Christ who did not please himself — an example testified to in the Scriptures in order to give us hope. May God in this way be praised.

Sub-pericope B: Accept one another, following the example of Christ who became a servant of the Jews so that the Gentiles may praise God as the Scriptures testify. May God give that your hope will continue to grow.

19.2.1 A few notes pertaining to the structure of Romans 15,1—13 with special reference to actants and structural markers

'Οφείλομεν δέ ... in Rom 15,1 introduces a new pericope. Many New Testament scholars consider Rom 15,1—6 and 15,7—13 as two separate pericopes.[3] The inner structure of Rom 15,1—13 shows, however, that this passage is to be considered as one pericope.[4]

Louw (1979b:135—6) has pointed out that colons 1—3 contain an admonition as well as the reason for it. Colons 4—5 motivate the reason from Scripture. Colon 6 is a prayer stating that God is the source of

---

[3] According to Dodd (1932:x). However, Dodd joins 15,1—6 to chapter 14 and considers 15,7—13 as a separate pericope.

Cf also Käsemann (1974:vi):
15,1—6: "Das Vorbild Christi",
15,7—13: "Die Annahme auch der Heiden als Merkmal der Christusherrschaft".

Schlier (1979:X):
15,1—6: "Christi Vorbild für die Starken",
15,7—13: "Die Annahme der Juden und Heiden durch Christus".

Wilckens (1982:100.104):
15,1—6: "Das Vorbild Christi",
15,7—13: "Heilsgeschichtliche Motivation".

Zeller (1985:300):
14,1—15,7: "Toleranz und Rücksicht zwischen Starken und Schwachen",
15,7—13: "Christus nahm die Heiden an, damit sie Gott loben".

[4] Cf Louw (1979a:37; 1979b:134—7); Michel (1978:441—2).

patience and encouragement. Colons 7—13 have the same structural pattern, repeating the central theme in colon 7 with the example set by Christ (colon 8) as motivation. Colons 9—12 contain quotations from Scripture (resembling colons 4—5). Colon 13, which contains a final prayer, resembles colon 6.

Both Rom 15,1—6 and 7—13 have, therefore, the following pattern:

a — admonition with reason

b — motivation of reason from Scripture

c — prayer[5]

Internal cohesion binding this pericope together as a coherent whole is, therefore, evident from the symmetry in structure of pericopes A and B, as well as from the following structural markers occurring throughout this pericope (cf also discourse analysis [19.2]).

Words referring to the inner relationship within the congregation occur in both sub-pericopes of Rom 15,1—13 (i e 15,1—6.7—13) and give expression to the central theme of this section (Louw 1979b:136). The following words and phrases serve as structural markers in this regard and serve to bind these two sub-pericopes (Rom 15,1—6.7—13) together into one pericope:

ἕκαστος ... τῷ πλησίον (v 2);

ὁμοθυμαδὸν ἐν ἑνὶ στόματι (v 6);

ἀλλήλους (v 7).

The repeated reference to Christ throughout this pericope points to the Christ-centredness of Rom 15,1—13: ὁ Χριστός (v 3), ἐμέ (v 3); Χριστὸν Ἰησοῦν (v 5); κυρίου ...Ἰησοῦ Χριστοῦ (v 6); ὁ Χριστός (v 7); Χριστόν (v 8).

In the same way the following words illustrate the "theo"-logical dimension of this pericope: σε (v 3); ὁ δὲ θεός (v 5); θεὸν καὶ πατέρα (v 6); θεοῦ (v 7); θεοῦ (v 8); θεόν (v 9), σοι (v 9), τῷ ὀνοματί σου (v 9); αὐτοῦ (v 10); τὸν κύριον (v 11), αὐτόν (v 11); ὁ ... θεός (v 13).

It is also interesting to note that the motif of "hope" occurs throughout this pericope: τὴν ἐλπίδα (v 4); ἐλπιοῦσιν (v 12); τῆς ἐλπίδος (v 13), τῇ ἐλπίδι (v 13).

---

[5] Cf also Käsemann (1980:368.371—2); Michel (1978:44—5); Wilckens (1982:100.104).

The attention may also be drawn to verbs indicating a quotation from the Scriptures: γέγραπται (v 3); (προεγράφη ... ἐγράφη [v 4]); γέγραπται (v 9); λέγει (v 10); λέγει (v 12).

The parallel structure of verses 5 and 13 is indeed very obvious. The following may be mentioned in this regard:

1 The optative construction: δῴη (v 5);
                                     πληρώσαι (v 13).

2 θεός + Genitive of source: ὁ δὲ θεὸς τῆς ὑπομονῆς ... (v 5);
                                     ὁ δὲ θεὸς τῆς ἐλπίδος ... (v 13).

The way in which the scope of verse 13 extends beyond that of verse 5 will be discussed in the exegetical overview. However, it is important to note even now that although δῴη (v 5) and πληρῶσαι (v 13) are used parallel to each other, the meaning of πληρῶσαι extends beyond that of δῴη.

Certain structural markers and themes occur only within the separate sub-pericopes or clusters (groups of colons) (ἀρέσκειν occurs e g only within cluster a [vv 1—3a]). Sub-pericope A (vv 1—6) is introduced by Ὀφείλομεν δέ. Διό introduces the concluding paragraph of this section (Cranfield 1979:739).

While the "strong" and the "weak" are contrasted in sub-pericope A (cf οἱ δυνατοί ... τῶν ἀδυνάτων [v 1]), the contrast in sub-pericope B is between the Jews (indicated by περιτομῆς [v 8]; λαοῦ αὐτοῦ [v 10]), and the Gentiles/gentile people (cf ἔθνη [v 11], πάντες οἱ λαοί [v 11]; ἐθνῶν [v 12], ἔθνη [v 12]).

19.3 An exegetical overview

19.3.1 Verses 1—3a (colons 1—3)

Verses 1—3a (colons 1—3) may be grouped together. These first three verses of chapter 15 summarise Paul's exhortation to the strong (Cranfield 1979:729). Under the gospel the strong have an inescapable obligation (ὀφείλομεν) to help carry the infirmities of their brothers who are having to live without that inner freedom which they themselves enjoy. Their response to this obligation will be a test of the reality of their faith, for what is required of them is utterly opposed to the tendency of fallen human nature (cf Cranfield 1979:730).

It may be taken as certain that Paul is still thinking especially of the problem with which he has been concerned in chapter 14. The possibility that he is already beginning to widen the scope of his exhortation in 15,1 should, however, not be excluded (cf Cranfield 1979:731).[6]

It has already been mentioned that ἀρέσκειν occurs only in this part of the pericope. Paul normally uses ἀρέσκειν in relation to God. To please God is the highest goal of man's life (cf 8,8; Gal 1,10; 1 Thess 2,4.15; 4,1). He who only pleases himself neglects that which pleases God, namely love to the neighbour (cf 13,8—10). Only through love the church can be built. Verse 3a (colon 3) adds a reason for the behaviour prescribed in verses 1—2: the example of Christ.[7]

19.3.2 Verses 3b—4 (colons 4—5)

The quotation from the Old Testament in this passage can only be understood against the background of the great importance that Paul attaches to the view that Jesus Christ is the true meaning and substance of the law and the prophets (cf e g 1,2; 3,21; 9,30—10,8). In view of the whole early church's interest in assuring itself that the scandal of the passion was actually an essential element of God's eternal plan, the appeal to the Old Testament is thoroughly understandable (Cranfield 1979:732—3).

The prayer of Ps 69, quoted in verse 3, has played a very important roll in the establishment of the tradition of Christ's passion (cf Mk 15,23.36—41; John 2,17; 15,25; 19,29; Heb 11,26) (Wilckens 1982:101), and is quoted here as the voice of the suffering Christ, bearing men's hostility toward God (Cranfield 1979:733).

Verse 4 (colon 5) comments on colon 4 stating a double purpose: What was written intends to instruct us and give us hope.[8] The second purpose is in itself the result of the first (Louw 1979b:135).[9] Hope (from the biblical

---

[6] Käsemann (1980:368) is quite convinced of his stand: "Läßt er sich anders als in c.14 nicht mehr konkret auf die Streitigkeiten in Rom ein ... so bereitet er [Paulus] damit schon den Abschluß des Ganzen vor."

[7] "Für die Nächstenliebe als unbedingte Pflicht gibt es keine 'natürliche', anthropologische Begründung ... Damit klingt das Motiv aus dem Hymnus in Phil 2,6—8 an, das wie dort eine passionstheologische Spitze hat ..." (Wilckens 1982:101).

[8] The phrase τῶν γραφῶν may grammatically be taken with τῆς παρακλήσεως alone or with both ὑπομονῆς and παρακλήσεως.

[9] "Worum es geht ist die Konsequenz aus Christi Leiden: daß wir durch die Geduld und durch den Trost den die Schriften uns zu geben vermögen, die Hoffnung behalten" (Wilckens 1982:102).

point of view: confidence in something which one knows is going to take place, though it has not yet taken place [Newman & Nida 1973:93]) will be enhanced by patience and encouragement.

At first sight it may seem rather surprising that Paul introduces the theme of *hope* in this passage. Cranfield (1979:735) points out, however, that in view of the importance of *hope* in Rom (cf 4,18; 5,2.4—5; 8,17—30; 12,12; 15,12—13; 13,11—14) it is not really surprising. The introduction of this motif here, must be understood as an anticipation of verses 7—13.[10]

19.3.3 Verses 5—6 (colon 6)

This cluster, containing a prayer wish (with the optative [δῷη] as a distinguishing feature) forms the conclusion of the first part of this pericope.[11] The style of this passage reminds us of the liturgical use of this letter.[12] The genitive constructions state that God is the source of patience and encouragement. Paul prays that God may enable them to be of one accord (Louw 1979b:135).[13] Cranfield (1979:737—8) mentions in this regard that this may or may not include identity of conviction on the matters at issue between the weak and the strong, but must certainly mean a common sincere determination to seek to obey the Lord Jesus Christ (cf also Käsemann 1980:370—1). The purpose *cum* result (ἵνα) of having the same point of view is that God (defined as the Father of Jesus Christ) may be glorified. The manner in which δοξάζειν should take place is stated by two synonymous phrases: with one mind, with one voice! This group of colons actually repeats the content of a and b in the form of a prayer, the fulfilment of which will be to the glory of God (Louw 1979b:136).[14]

---

[10] Cf Käsemann (1980:370); Wilckens (1982:102).

[11] Cf Käsemann (1980:37): "Der Gebetswunsch in 5f. hat wie oft die Funktion, eine Argumentation abzuschließen."

[12] "Feierliche Gottesprädikationen, wie sie im Psalter vorgebildet sind, haben hier ihren guten Platz" (Käsemann 1980:370).

[13] τὸ αὐτὸ φρονεῖν "... können Christen untereinander nur nach dem *einen* Maßstab: Christus Jesus ..." (Wilckens 1982:102).

[14] Käsemann (1980:370) goes even further when he defines the content of this prayerful wish: "Inhalt des Wunsches ist, was in 12,16a befohlen wurde."

19.3.4 Verses 7—9a (colons 7—8)

Διό introduces the concluding section of this pericope. It can even be said that the conclusion which the Christians of Rome must draw from what has been said in 14,1—15,6 is summarised in the command which follows (Cranfield 1979:739). Paul now addresses the whole congregation. What was addressed to the "strong" in 14,1 now applies to all Christians in Rome: Concrete mutual acceptance is the basis for all Christian community life (cf Wilckens 1982:105).

In this group of colons we witness a remarkable shift of emphasis since the opposition "Jew-Gentile" becomes focal while the "weak-strong" duality takes second place (cf discussion under 19.2.1). The natural inference to be drawn from this would seem to be that the division between the weak and the strong with which Paul has been concerned in this pericope was also, to a large extent at any rate, a division between Jewish and Gentile Christians (Cranfield 1979:740—1). It is quite possible that those Christians termed as "weak in faith" (clinging to all kinds of regulations concerning food and specific days) were mainly Jewish Christians (Louw 1979b:136).

It is important to keep the correlation with the preceding trail of thought as well as the broadening scope in mind. Käsemann draws our attention to the change in style in this sub-pericope: The paraenesis in verse 7 turns into doxology (v 6 points already in this direction).[15] This passage illustrates how the theme of Romans (the Pauline doctrine of justification) serves as motivation and ground for the exhortation found in this passage. The most profound dimension of Christ's acceptance of us can be seen in the fact that God had mercy upon the Gentiles.[16]

In verse 7 (colon 7) the central theme of this pericope is repeated, with the example set by Christ (colon 8) as motivation (Louw 1979b:136).[17] In

---

[15] Käsemann (1980:372) observes: "Schließlich ist wenigstens in 9—12 nicht die Einheit der Gemeinde, sondern die Annahme der Heiden als eschatologisches Wunder ... proklamiert."

[16] "Wo quer durch alles Irdische die Gottlosen zu Gotteskindern werden, kann nichts die Glieder der Gemeinde mehr unüberbrückbar trennen ... sind die Differenzen zwischen Starken und Schwachen nur Kinderspiel, müssen alle Verschiedenheiten zur Erbauung des Ganzen führen. Sogar die Paränese des Apostels beweist noch, daß seine Ekklesiologie von der Rechtfertigungslehre her gestaltet ist ..." (Käsemann 1980:372).

[17] Käsemann (1980:372) states: "Nicht ohne Grund ist 7 darum als 'Summe' ... betrachtet worden."

verse 7 (colon 7) two aspects which were already stated are repeated: the example of Christ, and the glorification of God.[18]

Γάρ in verse 8 shows that this verse is to be understood as an explication of the christological motivation set forth in verse 7. Paul declares emphatically: Christ has become (γεγενῆσθαι) a servant of the Jews. The perfect infinitive emphasises this event as an existing state of affairs. Paul preferably uses διάκονος when referring to the function of a missionary (Wilckens 1982:105; cf 11,13 as well as specifically 1 Cor 3,5; 2 Cor 3,6—7.9; 6,4). Further is — in differentiation to δοῦλος — a commissioned and legitimated official in view.

The example set by Christ is related to his ministering to the Jews, while a dual purpose is added: to show that God is faithful and to establish his promises made to the Jewish patriarchs as well as to enable the Gentiles to praise God for his mercy (Louw 1979b:137). In this explication the syntactic structure of this verse has been understood in the following way:

λέγω γὰρ Χριστὸν διάκονον γεγενῆσθαι περιτομῆς

⌐> ὑπὲρ ἀληθείας θεοῦ,

    εἰς τὸ

⌐> ⌐βεβαιῶσαι τὰς ἐπαγγελίας τῶν πατέρων,

    ⌐ τὰ δὲ ἔθνη ὑπὲρ ἐλέους δοξάσαι τὸν θεόν.[19]

In contrast to this mode of interpretation, Wilckens prefers to make verse 9a subordinate to λέγω in verse 8a so that verse 9a stands against verse 8 in its totality.[20]

A final decision between these two options is very difficult and has to be left open.[21] Käsemann (1980:372) holds the opinion that the reason for this stylistic "unevenness" may be found in the dual intention of the apostle who wants to emphasise the grace which has become available to all, and at

---

[18] The phrase εἰς δόξαν τοῦ θεοῦ must be linked with προσλαμβάνεσθε ἀλλήλους. (For a detailed discussion of this problem cf Cranfield [1979:739—40].)

[19] According to Louw (1979b:137). Käsemann (1980:372) mentions that virtually all exegetes prefer this probability of interpretation.

[20] "Die Schwierigkeit des Subjektwechsels läßt sich durch die Annahme beheben, daß Paulus in V 9a unausgesprochen läßt, daß Christus zugleich auch zum Diener für die Unbeschnittenen geworden ist ... In der Tat überstürzen sich die Gedanken des Paulus gerade im Römerbrief häufig; und hier ist es nicht einmal schwer, in V 9a διάκονον δὲ ἀκροβυστίας ὑπερ ἐλέους ὥστε o.ä. zu ergänzen" (Wilckens 1982:106).

[21] A detailed discussion of this problem is provided by Cranfield (1979:742—4). With Cornly, Cranfield emphasises the elliptical nature of what Paul has said here.

the same time wishes to point out the advantage of the Jews (as he has done already many times in this letter).

19.3.5 Verses 9b—12 (colons 9—12)

By quoting from Scripture, Paul motivates what he has just said (especially in v 9a).[22] Although a good rabbinic combination of words from the Torah, Nebiim and Ketubim could have been used by Jewish Christians for missionary preaching, these quotations most probably originated from Paul himself, constantly drawing wider circles (Käsemann 1980:373).

Of the four quotations given (Ps 17,50; Deut 32,43; Ps 116,1; Is 11,10) only the fourth is introduced by naming the source. All four deal with God's mercy towards the Gentiles, though the fourth also relates to the promises made to the patriarchs (Louw 1979b:137). With the key word ἔθνη Paul emphasises that those who are in Jewish eyes without God are called to praise him. This is made possible by Christ's universal Lordship (cf Käsemann 1980:374).[23]

19.3.6 Verse 13 (colon 13)

In verse 13 we find the conclusion of Paul's exhortations in Rom 14 and 15,1—13 (Schlier 1979:425). He concludes the exhortations with a final prayer wish. "Joy", "peace", "faith", "hope", "power of the Holy Spirit" — these are all major theological concepts in Paul's message (Kertelge 1983:225). Rhetorically, this verse plays a very important role.[24]

The prayer wish in verse 13 parallels the prayer wish of verses 5—6. Barth has pointed out that the fulfilment of the prayer wish in verse 13 would carry with it the success of all the exhortations of this section and, indeed, of all Paul's exhortations from 12,1 onward.[25]

---

[22] Cranfield (1979:744—5) affirms that these quotations from Scripture are intended as support, not just for verse 9a, but for Paul's solemn declaration (vv 8—9a) as a whole, in view of the close connection between verses 8 and 9a.

[23] These words express the Pauline message of justification by faith "... die mit der Offenbarung der Gottesgerechtigkeit in der Christusherrschaft zusammenfällt ... Mit seiner Lehre vollstreckt der Apostel in eschatologischer Funktion den göttlichen, in der Schrift proklamierten Willen" (Käsemann 1980:374).

[24] The strategic position of this verse is also strongly emphasised by John Paul Heil. He is of the opinion that Paul's prayer in Rom 15,13 climaxes the entire letter's theological demonstration. "It brings the main body of the letter [Rom 1,18—15,13] to a hope-filled climax" (Heil 1987:3; cf also 96.98).

[25] Noted by Cranfield (1979:748).

Verse 13 may be summarised as follows: It is a prayer to God who is the source of hope to afford joy and peace by means of faith and with the result of (spiritual) growth in the area of hope through the power of the Holy Spirit (Louw 1979b:137).

Verse 13 is closely related to the preceding group of colons in this pericope and well-known motives recur in this verse.[26] John Paul Heil (1987:96) observes that the climax to the series of Scriptural quotes (Rom 15,12) most explicitly illustrates how Christ has fulfilled and confirmed "... the promises made known to the patriarchs" (15,8), so that they are now a valid basis of hope for Christians. Having become a servant of the Jews (15,8) Christ has fulfilled the promise of a "root of Jesse", a Jewish Messiah, who would also rule the Gentiles. Christ has thus "confirmed" this promise as a valid basis of hope, so that its promise that the Gentiles "will hope in him" may now be fulfilled by the Roman Christians "accepting" one another in love (15,7). Paul urges the Romans to the mutual exercise of Christian love (15,1—12) precisely so that they may have and maintain hope (15,4).

The Old Testament context is very important for the understanding of "hope" in verses 12 and 13. There is an important relationship between the Pauline concept of hope and the Old Testament confession of faith and trust.[27] Paul prays that the God of hope — God as the one who enables and gives hope — may fulfil the addressees with joy and peace (cf 14,17), the fruit of the Spirit (cf Gal 5,22).[28]

Περισσεύειν takes up the idea of abundance already suggested by πληρῶσαι, while ἐν τῇ ἐλπίδι picks up the τῆς ἐλπίδος by which God has

---

[26] Schlier (1979:425—6) also points to the fact that the prayer of verse 13 is, just like verses 5—6, "... plerophorisch, und zwar so, daß unter anderem bereits genannte Motive wieder auftauchen und in ihrem inneren Zusammenhang deutlich werden".

[27] Cf Nebe (1983:173): "So behält Gott also das Heft auch in der Hand, wenn soteriologisch Jesus Christus als direktes Objekt unserer Synonyme [ἐλπίς and its synonyms:PJG] in der Perspektive der eschatologischen Zukunft hervortritt. Deshalb wird schließlich die Bezeichnung 'Gott der Hoffnung' [Röm 15,13] sinnvoll. Sie korrespondiert dem 'Gott alles in allem' [1 Kor 15,28] ... So kann schließlich gefolgert werden, daß es dem Paulus bei der 'Hoffnung' christlich gesehen um Gottes universale Zukunft in Jesus Christus zum Heil geht, die die Macht des Bösen endgültig beseitigen und Gottes Herrsein völlig durchsetzen wird."

[28] Schlier (1979:426) comments on *joy and peace*: "Sie tragen die Hoffnung in sich und werden von der Hoffnung getragen [vgl. Röm 12,12]. Sie durchdringen sich [vgl. 1 Thess 2,19]. Der Gott der Hoffnung ist auch der Gott des Friedens [vgl. Röm 15,33; 16,20; 2 Kor 13,11; Phil 4,7.9; 1 Thess 5,23; 2 Thess 3,16]."

just been described. The double mentioning of hope in this verse is very important. The epistle to the Romans has very clearly shown that hope is an essential characteristic of the believer (Cranfield 1979:748). In view of the present infinitive τὸ περισσεύειν one may agree with Newman and Nida (1973:277—8) that the best translation of the phrase is: "... so that your hope will continue to grow" (Today's English Version). The goal and fruit of the gifts provided in faith by the God of hope is the fullness, the overflowing of hope, corresponding the abundance of grace in Rom 5,15 (cf Schlier 1979:426).

The final phrase, ἐν δυνάμει πνεύματος ἁγίου, indicates the fact that the existence of this hope is no human possibility but the creation of the Spirit of God.[29]

The attention may be drawn to Rom 8 in which Paul has shown that it is because the life promised to those who are righteous by faith is a life characterised by the indwelling of the Holy Spirit, that it is also a life characterised by hope (cf Cranfield 1979:748). Käsemann (1980:374) interprets the phrase ἐν δυνάμει πνεύματος ἁγίου as the "... Doxologie inspirierende und christliche Lebensführung bestimmende Macht".[30] Just as the horizon of this sub-pericope (vv 7—13) is broader than that of the previous sub-pericope (vv 1—6), the prayer wish in verse 13 reaches out beyond that of verses 5—6. The conclusion to this section of apostolic exhortations creates the transition to the last part of the letter (cf Käsemann 1980:375).

---

[29] Cf Heil (1987:96): "... this superabundance of hope takes place through the power of the Holy Spirit, whose essential role for hope we have already seen (5,5; 8,23—27)".

    Schlier (1979:426) formulates: "Solches Überströmen der Hoffnung geschehe ἐν δυνάμει πνεύματος ἁγίου. Das ἐν ist wohl instrumental zu verstehen. Nur der Heilige Geist gibt ihnen in seiner Macht ihr unglaubliches Hoffen. Durch ihn erfüllt Gott im Glauben und seiner Freude und seinem Frieden mit überschwenglicher Hoffnung."

[30] Δύναμις τοῦ πνεύματος ἁγίου is, according to Schlier (1979:426 note 10) "... das πνεῦμα ἅγιον hinsichtlich seiner vielfältigen Auswirkungen [vgl. Röm 15,19; 1 Kor 2,4]. So steht auch δύναμις manchmal für πνεῦμα, z.B. 1 Kor 5,4; 6,14; 15,43; 2 Kor 6,7; 12,9; 13,4; 2 Thess 1,11, oder neben πνεῦμα, z.B. 1 Thess 1,5". The close relationship between δύναμις and πνεῦμα will be discussed in section C (chapter 24). Schlier's view that δύναμις occurs often for πνεῦμα cannot, however, be accepted.

19.4 Conclusion

The fact that Rom 15,13 constitutes the conclusion of the section of this letter dealing with Christian living (12,1—15,13 [Morris 1988:34])[31] has profound consequences for the interpretation of this passage.

Rom 15,5 and 13 point to people's complete dependence on God. Verse 13 is a prayer to God who is the source of hope to afford joy and peace by means of faith and with the result of growth in the area of hope through the power of the Holy Spirit. Hope, joy and peace within the life of faith are no human possiblities, but gifts of God. It is noteworthy that while God is the source of hope, the continued *growth of hope* in the believer's mind takes place by the *power of the Holy Spirit.* (In Gal 5,22 joy and peace are also mentioned as fruit of the Spirit.) The fact that the prayer wish of Rom 15,13 concludes the section of Romans dealing with Christian behaviour (cf also Kertelge 1983:16) underlines the importance of hope, joy and peace as essential virtues of the Christian life.

---

[31] Cf also Schlier (1979:x): "Apostolische Paraklese [12,1—15,13]."

Chapter 20

Romans 15,19

20.1 Romans 15,14—21 within the macrocontext
of Paul's letter to the Romans

With this pericope we have reached the conclusion of Paul's letter to the
Romans. The conclusion of Rom (Rom 15,14—16,27) may be divided as
follows:

15,14—33   Paul's ministry and travel plans
16,1—23   Greetings
16,25—27   Concluding doxology (Moo 1996:885.912.936; cf also
           Louw 1979b:148; Du Toit 1984:14)

Rom 15,14—21 is the first of two pericopes (15,14—21; 15,22—33)
dealing with Paul's apostleship.[1] Once more he provides a justification for
writing this letter.[2]

For a motivation of the demarcation of Rom 15,14—21 as a coherent
unit, compare 20.2.1.

---

[1] Practically all commentators agree in this regard (cf Käsemann 1974:vi; Schlier
1979:x; Wilckens 1982:116). Cf also note 2.

[2] Cf Kertelge (1983:16); Michel (1978:8); Zeller (1985:236).

20.2 Discourse analysis: Romans 15,14—21

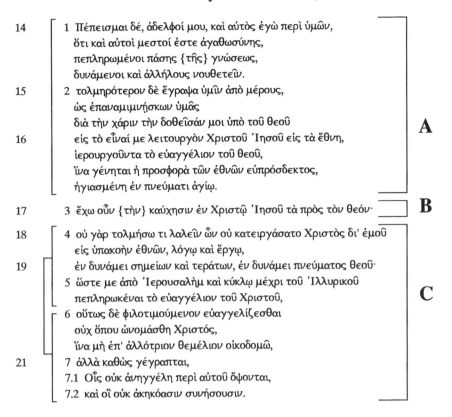

14   1 Πέπεισμαι δέ, ἀδελφοί μου, καὶ αὐτὸς ἐγὼ περὶ ὑμῶν,
ὅτι καὶ αὐτοὶ μεστοί ἐστε ἀγαθωσύνης,
πεπληρωμένοι πάσης {τῆς} γνώσεως,
δυνάμενοι καὶ ἀλλήλους νουθετεῖν.

15   2 τολμηρότερον δὲ ἔγραψα ὑμῖν ἀπὸ μέρους,
ὡς ἐπαναμιμνῄσκων ὑμᾶς
διὰ τὴν χάριν τὴν δοθεῖσάν μοι ὑπὸ τοῦ θεοῦ

16   εἰς τὸ εἶναί με λειτουργὸν Χριστοῦ Ἰησοῦ εἰς τὰ ἔθνη,
ἱερουργοῦντα τὸ εὐαγγέλιον τοῦ θεοῦ,
ἵνα γένηται ἡ προσφορὰ τῶν ἐθνῶν εὐπρόσδεκτος,
ἡγιασμένη ἐν πνεύματι ἁγίῳ.

A

17   3 ἔχω οὖν {τὴν} καύχησιν ἐν Χριστῷ Ἰησοῦ τὰ πρὸς τὸν θεόν·   **B**

18   4 οὐ γὰρ τολμήσω τι λαλεῖν ὧν οὐ κατειργάσατο Χριστὸς δι' ἐμοῦ
εἰς ὑπακοὴν ἐθνῶν, λόγῳ καὶ ἔργῳ,

19   ἐν δυνάμει σημείων καὶ τεράτων, ἐν δυνάμει πνεύματος θεοῦ·
5 ὥστε με ἀπὸ Ἰερουσαλὴμ καὶ κύκλῳ μέχρι τοῦ Ἰλλυρικοῦ
πεπληρωκέναι τὸ εὐαγγέλιον τοῦ Χριστοῦ,

C

   6 οὕτως δὲ φιλοτιμούμενον εὐαγγελίζεσθαι
οὐχ ὅπου ὠνομάσθη Χριστός,
ἵνα μὴ ἐπ' ἀλλότριον θεμέλιον οἰκοδομῶ,

21   7 ἀλλὰ καθὼς γέγραπται,
7.1 Οἷς οὐκ ἀνηγγέλη περὶ αὐτοῦ ὄψονται,
7.2 καὶ οἳ οὐκ ἀκηκόασιν συνήσουσιν.

Headings of the pericope and sub-pericopes

Pericope heading: Justification for writing this letter and discussion of Paul's apostleship.

Sub-pericope A: Paul has written to the Romans so boldly, because God has bestowed on him the privilege of being a servant of Christ Jesus, of serving the Gentiles like a priest in the preaching of the gospel.

Sub-pericope B: In union with Christ Jesus Paul is proud of being a minister of God.

Sub-pericope C: A detailed explanation of the way in which Christ worked through Paul in order to lead the Gentiles to obey God, and the effect of his ministry.

20.2.1 A few notes pertaining to the structure of Romans 15,14—21 with special reference to actants and structural markers

The present pericope commences with πέπεισμαι δέ in 15,14, while a new pericope is introduced by διό in verse 22. Διό refers not only to the immediately preceding colon, but to the preceding pericope as a whole.[3]

The second person plural (referring to the Romans) occurs only in *cluster A* (vv 14—16, colons 1—2):

— ὑμῶν ... αὐτοί (v 14),
— ἐστε (v 14),
— ὑμᾶς (v 15).

Note the emphatic way in which the relationship between Paul and the Romans is described: καὶ αὐτὸς ἐγὼ ... καὶ αὐτοί (v 14).

There is an abundance of dative constructions in *cluster C* (vv 18—21, colons 4—7): λόγῳ καὶ ἔργῳ (v 18); ἐν δυνάμει ... ἐν δυνάμει (v 19).

The repetition of ἐν δυνάμει emphasises what is said here and closely connects the phrase ἐν δυνάμει σημείων καὶ τεράτων with ἐν δυνάμει πνεύματος θεοῦ. Note also: ἐν πνεύματι ἁγίῳ (v 16); ἐν δυνάμει πνεύματος θεοῦ (v 19).

Ἔθνη occurs abundantly throughout this whole passage: ἔθνη (v 16), ἐθνῶν (v 16); ἐθνῶν (v 18); (οἷς [v 21]), (οἵ [v 21]).

Also occurring throughout this pericope are the following actants:
— God: θεοῦ (v 15); θεοῦ (v 16); θεόν (v 17); θεοῦ (v 19).
— Jesus Christ: Χριστοῦ Ἰησοῦ (v 16); Χριστῷ Ἰησοῦ (v 17); Χριστός (v 18); Χριστοῦ (v 19); Χριστός (v 20); αὐτοῦ (v 21).

The (preaching of the) gospel is also an important theme in this pericope: εὐαγγέλιον (v 16); εὐαγγέλιον (v 19); εὐαγγελίζεσθαι (v 20).

Note: τὸ εὐαγγέλιον τοῦ θεοῦ (v 16);
        τὸ εὐαγγέλιον τοῦ Χριστοῦ (v 19).

The way in which the above-mentioned actants and themes function within this pericope, will be discussed in the exegetical overview.

---

[3] Käsemann (1980:382) connects διό with vv 20—21. Wilckens (1982:123) differs from him in this regard: " 'Daher' [διὸ] bezieht sich nicht auf das in VV 20f, sondern auf das in VV 17—19a Gesagte."

The total structure of this pericope may be summarised as:

Cluster A: Paul justifies his position as an apostle
Cluster B: short restatement of A
Cluster C: detailed explanation of A (Louw 1979b:139)
(B is considered a separate sub-pericope as it functions as a hinge between A and C. B is both a short restatement of A, as well as an anticipation of C.)

With this summary we have already reached the subject matter of 20.4.

20.3 Textual criticism: Romans 15,19

Αὐτοῦ is added between δυνάμει and σημείων by the following witnesses: papyrus 46, the original scribe of codex Claromontanus, codex F, codex G, an Old Latin witness and Speculum (Pseudo-Augustine). This addition cannot be accepted[4] due to the very slender external evidence: Codex Claromontanus, belonging to the Western tradition, codices F and G, from the Byzantine textual tradition, and only one Old Latin witness and an ecclesiastical witness from the fifth century.

However, the second Chester Beatty Biblical papyrus (p46) dates from around the year 200 and is in general closer to the Alexandrian than to the Western type of text (Metzger 1968:37—8).

τε is added after σημείων by only one witness: p[46].

The phrase ἐν δυνάμει πνεύματος θεοῦ presents the most important textual problem of this passage. θεοῦ is omitted in codex Vaticanus and by Vigilius. Codex Alexandrinus, the original scribe as well as the second corrector of codex Claromontanus, codices F and G as well as the minuscule manuscripts 33, 81, 104, 365, 630, 1739, 1881, a few other Greek manuscripts, a part of the Old Latin and Vulgate witnesses, the margin of the Syriac Harclean version as well as the Coptic version read ἁγίου instead of θεοῦ. The phrase as cited above (from Nestle-Aland[27]) is affirmed by the following witnesses: papyrus 46, codex Alexandrinus, the first corrector of codex Claromontanus, codex Ψ, the Majority text, Old Latin witness b, all the Syriac witnesses (codex Ephraemi [unreadable]).

---

[4] Schlier (1979:432 note 20) is of the opinion, however, that the reading ἐν δυνάμει αὐτοῦ "... vielleicht wegen der Seltenheit des Ausdrucks ursprünglich ist ...".

Metzger (1994:473) has pointed out that it can be argued on the one hand, that the presence of ἁγίου in some witnesses and θεοῦ in others is suspicious because each can be explained as a scribal addition to complete what in B and Vigilius seems to be an unfinished expression. On the other hand, despite the generally excellent text preserved by B, a majority of the committee preparing the "United Bible Societies' Greek New Testament" (fourth revised edition) was unwilling to adopt a reading based on such slender Greek evidence. As a compromise it was, therefore, decided to follow the testimony of the earliest witness (p⁴⁶), but in deference to transcriptional considerations to enclose θεοῦ within square brackets. For the purpose of this study θεοῦ is regarded as part of the original text.[5]

20.4 An exegetical overview of Romans 15,14—21

In this pericope Paul returns to the subject with which he was concerned in the second pericope of his letter to the Romans (Rom 1,8—17).[6] In the conclusion of Rom we find something of a "... specifically Pauline strategy of missions" (cf Käsemann 1980:376).[7] Paul emphasises his confidence in the Christian maturity of the believers in Rome so as to prevent possible misinterpretation of the boldness which he is conscious of having shown in part of his letter. His words of explanation in verse 15 lead quite naturally to some statements in verses 16—21 about his ministry as apostle of the Gentiles (Cranfield 1979:749; cf summary of the structure given in 20.2.1).

---

[5] Wilckens (1982:119 note 579) also contends that θεοῦ was perhaps original. Cranfield (1979:758 note 5), Käsemann (1974:376), Schlier (1979:432 note 21) and Michel (1978:459 note 21) consider the reading of codex Vaticanus, however, as correct.

[6] "Unverkennbar greift dieser Briefteil auf das Anliegen des Proömiums in 1,8—15 zurück ..." (Käsemann 1980:376). Cf Cranfield (1979:749); Louw (1979b:138); also Kertelge (1983:227—8): "... ähnlich wie im Briefeingang 1,8—17 tritt am Schluß des umfangreichen Briefes die Absicht des Apostels deutlicher zutage".

[7] It must, however, be noted that this letter is "... weder einfach ein Lehrtraktat noch nach Sprache, Argumentation und theologischem Niveau zentral ein Missionsdokument, obgleich er unter der Prämisse wie der Zielsetzung der Weltmission geschrieben wurde ..." (Käsemann 1980:376).

20.4.1 Clusters A (vv 14—16, colons 1—2) and B (v 17, colon 3)

In addressing the particular exhortation of 12,1—15,13 to a church he had not himself founded, and which he had not yet visited, Paul took a liberty, but in view of his commission as apostle to the Gentiles, he did not need to apologise for this. It seems, however, that Paul probably thought that a word of explanation would be appropriate.[8] In verse 14 we have an example of Christian courtesy, not flattery, though there is an element of hyperbole in the use of the words μεστοί, πεπληρωμένοι πάσης (cf Cranfield 1979:752—3). The words καὶ αὐτὸς ἐγώ emphasise Paul's personal commitment to the conviction expressed, while the corresponding καὶ αὐτοί underlines Paul's acknowledgement of the Roman Christians' adulthood as Christians: you yourselves ... .

Nevertheless, Paul wrote to them boldly because God had called him to be his special messenger (v 15). Newman and Nida (1973:279) point out that emphasis is placed on τολμηρότερον due to its position in the sentence ("but quite boldly I wrote to you"). The words ἀπὸ μέρους may either mean "about certain subjects" or "in parts of this letter".[9] The purpose of Paul's writing is to remind the Romans of truths they already know (Cranfield 1979:754).[10]

διὰ τὴν χάριν τὴν δοθεῖσάν μοι ὑπὸ τοῦ θεοῦ εἰς τὸ εἶναί με λειτουργὸν Χριστοῦ Ἰησοῦ εἰς τὰ ἔθνη indicates the basis of Paul's authority to address the Christians in Rome in the way explained at the beginning of this pericope (Cranfield 1979:754).

The result of the privileged position God has put him in entails his being a servant of Jesus Christ for the Gentiles and functioning like a priest to spread the Good News in order that the Gentiles may be presented to God as an offering (cf Louw 1979b:139). Λειτουργός, both in the LXX and as used by Paul, is not a formalised cultic concept, but has the more general

---

[8] This view of Cranfield (1979:752) is to be preferred to Käsemann's explanation of this passage as an "... unverhohlene captatio benevolentiae" (1980:376).

[9] Newman and Nida (1973:279) give a summary of the decisions made in this regard by the main English versions of the New Testament.

[10] Käsemann (1980:377—8) argues: "... ἐπαναμιμνήσκειν bezeichnet fast technisch die in Judentum wie Griechentum übliche Wiederholung von Lehrtradition ...". Paul is preparing the way for his visit to Rome, as well as his further missionary plans. "Er will und muß Rechenschaft über seine Verkündigung geben und möchte andererseits Anstoß vermeiden ... ."

meaning of a servant who acts in obedience to his master (cf Wilckens 1982:118). The context here shows clearly that Paul portrays his apostolic service, the preaching of the gospel, as a priestly offering. With reference to 4 Mac 7,8 (δημιουργοῦντας τὸν νόμον) Cranfield (1979:756) argues that although the possibility clearly exists, the thought of specifically priestly activity does not seem to be necessarily present in the use of the verb. Within this context the verb may mean, "serve with a holy service".

As was already the case in Rom 12,1—2, cultic terminology and motives are being translated into eschatological terms. The genitive in the phrase ἡ προσφορὰ τῶν ἐθνῶν is epexegetical (Käsemann 1980:378). The purpose behind God's giving his gracious commission to Paul to be Christ's λειτουργός with regard to the Gentiles by means of his service of the gospel was that the sacrifice consisting of the Gentiles might be acceptable to God, sanctified by the Holy Spirit. ἡγιασμένη ἐν πνεύματι ἁγίῳ amplifies the meaning of εὐπρόσδεκτος (Cranfield 1979:756—7).[11]

The main elements of the semantic content of verse 15 are contained in the purpose of Paul's calling: God has called him to be his messenger. The main line of argument in verses 14—16 (cluster A) can be summarised as: You are mature Christians; nevertheless, I had to write to you boldly because God called me to do so. The implication of the subject matter in verses 14—16 is that Paul is defending or justifying his position as an apostle. His actions must be ascribed to the χάρις given to him by God (Louw 1979b:139).

Verse 17 (colon 3) is merely a restatement to the same effect: Paul is proud of what he can do for God, because Christ is the authority. In union with Christ Jesus (because he is joined with Christ Jesus), Paul can be proud of his work for God (Louw 1979b:139).[12]

---

[11] Newman and Nida (1973:280) translate the phrase ἡγιασμένη ἐν πνεύματι ἁγίῳ as: "Dedicated to him by the Holy Spirit ...".

[12] Newman and Nida (1973:280) note that here we have an unusual expression in Greek, but that it is generally understood in the sense of "... I can be proud of my service for God". Cranfield (1979:757) argues that the article τήν has the effect of a demonstrative adjective referring to what has been said in verse 16. Paul is asserting that the glorying which he has allowed himself in verse 16 is a legitimate glorying, since it is a glorying in Christ concerned with what truly pertains to God. For the expression τὰ πρὸς τὸν θεόν, Cranfield points to Heb 2,17; 5,1. Cf also Blass & Debrunner (1961:87—8).

Zeller (1985:238) renders this phrase: "... in den Dingen, die Gott angehen".

20.4.2 Verses 18—21 (cluster C, colons 4—7)

20.4.2.1 Verses 18—19a (colon 4)

This passage explains the reason why the glorying contained in verse 16 truly is, as verse 17 has claimed it to be, a glorying ἐν Χριστῷ Ἰησοῦ τὰ πρὸς τὸν θεόν (Cranfield 1979:757).[13] What we have here are the characteristics of Paul's apostleship in a nutshell (cf Nielsen 1980:151). What Paul has done as the λειτουργός of Christ Jesus has not only been a subordinate service subsidiary to Christ's own priestly work, it has been something which Christ has actually himself effected, working through his minister (Cranfield 1979:758).

Christ works through the apostle in order to lead the Gentiles to obey God. The expression of means in the phrase λόγῳ καὶ ἔργῳ must be understood with the verb "to lead" (Newman & Nida 1973:280). The two following phrases characterise Paul's ministry as both powerfully confirmed and attested by accompanying miracles and also accomplished as a whole in the power of the Holy Spirit. Here the focus is on "... die von Wundern begleitete Predigt, von der auch Hebr 2,4 spricht" (Käsemann 1980:379). Nielsen (1980:151 note 18, with reference to Jervell and Friedrich) correctly opposes the view of Schmithals and Betz that it is not miracles which are at stake here, but the miracle of the preaching of the gospel itself.

It is notable how unrestrained Paul can speak of the extraordinary signs and wonders which accompany his ministry and contribute to the effectiveness of the "message of the cross" (cf Zeller 1985:239) when he is not involved in the polemics of 2 Cor 10—13 (cf also 1 Cor 2,4; Gal 3,5; 1 Thess 1,5). Paul emphasises that it is Christ who works through him and brings the Gentiles to the "obedience of faith" (Rom 1,5) through his preaching, and also through the Spirit's signs and miracles, which legitimise his message (Zeller 1985:238).

Dunn (1988:868) points to the overtones and allusions that would be clear to Paul's readers: his ministry as continuous with and manifesting the

---

[13] "Denn wie sollte er in seiner Verkündigung irgend etwas zu sagen wagen, was nicht Christus selbst durch ihn bewirkte, so daß es allein Christi Werk ist, wenn die Heiden zum Glaubensgehorsam kommen" (Wilckens 1982:118—9). Wilckens mentions also the following parallel passages: Rom 1,5; 6,16; 16,19; 2 Cor 10,5; 1 Pet 1,2.14.22 as well as ὑπακούειν Rom 6,17; 10,16; 2 Thess 1,8; Heb 5,9; Acts 6,7.

same power/finger of God as every Jew knew to have characterised the
Exodus (e g 7,3; 8,19); Christ's ministry through Paul in the power of the
Spirit as the eschatological equivalent of the epochal ministry of Moses (cf
Mt 12,28/Lk 11,20). As Moses had established the first assembly of God in
the old epoch, so Christ through Paul was now establishing the redefined
people of God for the end time.

Σημεῖα καὶ τέρατα is a set phrase which occurs frequently in biblical
literature and it is not possible to establish any significant difference
between the two words (Newman & Nida 1973:281). In his article
"Zeichen und Wunder: Die prophetische Legitimation und ihre
Geschichte", F Stolz (1972:125—44) studied the meaning and function of
σημεῖα καὶ τέρατα as well as the Hebrew counter-expression in the
writings of the Jahwist, the Deuteronomist, the priestly writing as well as
the New Testament (especially Paul and Luke). He reached the conclusion
that this expression indicates the immediate experience of the divine
presence (Stolz 1972:144). Within the New Testament the tradition is
continued by Paul, the author of the letter to the Hebrews and Luke.[14]
Käsemann (1980:380) recognises a relationship between this passage and a
Christian variation of the θεῖος ἀνήρ concept. A connection with the Old
Testament Jewish tradition pointed out by Stolz (1972) seems, however, to
be more probable.

The phrase ἐν δυνάμει πνεύματος is best understood neither as saying
again in a different way what has just been said in the preceding phrase, nor
yet as limited in its reference to Paul's ministry by "word" (in spite of the
very close association between this and πνεῦμα indicated by 1 Cor 2,4), but
as indicating that Paul's ministry as a whole is accomplished and put into
operation by the Spirit (cf Cranfield 1979:759 note 2).

Stolz (1972:143 note 74) points out that σημεῖα καὶ τέρατα is
sometimes supplemented by δυνάμεις (in Rom 15,19 the expressions
δύναμις, πνεῦμα, σημεῖα and τέρατα are related to one another; in 2 Cor
12,12 as well as Heb 2,4 σημεῖα, τέρατα and δύναμις are completely

---

[14] "Diese Gemeinden erlebten in ihren Gottesdiensten unmittelbar die Macht des
Erhöhten, die sich in den Wirkungen des Geistes erwies, und diese Erscheinungen konnte
man als Verbürgung der Herrschaft Christi als 'Zeichen und Wunder' bezeichnen" (Stolz
1972:143).

In Jn 4,48, however, this expression is used in a negative way. The people demand
σημεῖα καὶ τέρατα, but Jesus refuses to give way to the people's demand for legitimation
(Stolz 1972:142).

parallel expressions). The normal expression for the experience of a miracle was probably δύναμις, which was then interpreted in the light of Old Testament imagery through σημεῖα καὶ τέρατα.

In the light of Rom 15,18—19 it is clear that God's δύναμις — which has already raised Christ from the dead and which will raise us also — is a visible reality in Paul's apostolic activity.[15] With the dative constructions (so obvious in this passage) Paul describes the way in which Christ has worked through him with the purpose of leading the Gentiles to obey God.[16] The repetition of ἐν δυνάμει emphasises the importance of what Paul is saying.[17] The emphasis of this passage, therefore, is on Paul's description of the way in which Christ works through him[18] (interpreted pneumatologically) in order to lead the Gentiles to obedience to God.

20.4.2.2 Verse 19b (colon 5)

With ὥστε Paul wants to indicate that the progress of the gospel described in verse 19b is the result of the work of Christ through him referred to in

---

[15] Michel (1978:459) correctly affirms, "... δύναμις ist die Selbstoffenbarung Gottes, die sowohl das Zeichen ermöglicht als auch das Wort bestätigt".

[16] How must the dative in ἐν δυνάμει σημείων καὶ τεράτων, ἐν δυνάμει πνεύματος θεοῦ be interpreted?

The Greek dative also represents the instrumental case (Louw 1966:83), ἡ χρηστικὴ πτῶσις (Robertson 1919:525). Many contextual variations of the use of this case can be distinguished (cf Louw 1966:73). Chamberlain ([1941] 1979:36) points out that the instrumental case may be used with expressions of time, expressing the associative idea, expressing the idea of manner, it may be used to express cause, motive or occasion, while the most common usage is to express means.

The instrumental (dative) ἐν δυνάμει ... is used in this context to express means (cf Newman & Nida 1973:281) (as to the preposition ἐν, it may be noted that in Greek prepositions are used to increase the precision of the statement [Louw 1966:82]). Cf also Blass, Debrunner & Rehkopf (1976:160—1); Goodwin (1894:251); Radermacher (1912:105—6).

Louw and Nida (1988a:798 note 2) affirm that the category of "Means" involves a relation between two events while the category of "Instrument" includes objects which are employed in some activity or event. It is, however, sometimes difficult to distinguish between these two categories. What appears to be instrument on a superficial level, may be a matter of means when interpreted on a deeper level.

[17] Michel (1978:459) comments on these two prepositional phrases: "Beide beginnen betont mit ἐν δυνάμει und bezeichnen damit die göttliche Vollmacht des apostolischen Wirkens."

[18] Cf Kertelge (1983:228—9): "... [ ] der Apostel [stellt] sich selbst und sein ganzes Wirken unter den einen entscheidenden Maßstab: das Wirken Christi in der Gegenwart ... Nicht Paulus und sein Auftreten sind entscheidend, sondern Christus, der im Evangelium zur Sprache kommt".

verses 18 and 19a (Cranfield 1979:760). κύκλῳ may be taken with Ἰερουσαλήμ and means "from Jerusalem and its vicinity". It is more probable, however, that it means "from Jerusalem [and its territories] around to Illyricum". (Illyricum [also known as Dalmatia] was a Roman province northwest of Macedonia, situated on the Adriatic coast opposite Italy [Newman & Nida 1973:281]).

It has been pointed out (cf e g Cranfield 1979:760—1; Käsemann 1980:380—1; Wilckens 1982:119—20) that in view of Gal 1 and 2 (as well as Acts) reference to a significant preaching mission conducted by Paul in Jerusalem would seem to be ruled out. A preaching mission in Jerusalem would not naturally be visualised as part of the Gentile mission, with which this context is concerned. Cranfield (1979:760—1, with reference to Bruce) affirms that "... the most probable explanation would seem to be that Paul refers to Jerusalem as being the 'starting-point' and metropolis of the Christian movement as a whole".[19]

It is impossible to decide, on the basis of the Greek, whether Paul is saying that he actually went into the territory of Illyricum or just went as far as its southern and eastern boundaries. In view of what is known elsewhere about Paul's ministry, it is possible that he does not state that he actually went into Illyricum, but rather that he reached as far as that territory (cf Newman & Nida 1973:281).

As far as the meaning of πεπληρωκέναι is concerned, Stuhlmacher (1967b:430 note 15) is of the opinion that πεπληρωκέναι means the salvation historical, eschatological completion of Paul's task of spreading the gospel. J Knox (1964:9—10) mentions that πληροῦν may mean to complete what is incomplete; to amplify what has been partly done. He argues that Paul is saying simply that the gospel has now been preached to every nation or in every province of Greece and Asia Minor, and of course, in Syria and Palestine. He does not mean that he has done all the preaching or even that he has preached in all the places — indeed he says in the very next sentence that he has not. But where others had not proclaimed the gospel, he has made it a point to do so; and now he has in this sense,

---

[19] It may be agreed with Wilckens (1982:119) that this description of Paul, "... ist zwar nicht im Sinne einer Beschreibung der geschichtlichen Bewegung seiner Mission gemeint ...". Dunn (1988:868—9) also points out that what we have here is in no sense a detailed itinerary, but simply a grand design. It is a sweeping vision of missionary strategy in a single stroke of the brush.

"completed" the preaching in that whole north-eastern segment of the Mediterranean world he has described.

The Today's English Version reads "... I have proclaimed fully the Good News about Christ". This statement must certainly be viewed against the background of the comments of John Knox stated above.

20.4.2.3 Verses 20—21 (colons 6—7)

Verse 20 justifies the particular localities of Paul's preaching, backed by Scripture in verse 21 (Louw 1979b:139). It may also be said that verse 20a qualifies the claim made in verse 19b: Paul's statement that he has completed the gospel in the area mentioned is not to be taken in an absolute sense, but in relation to what he understands to be his own particular function in the service of the gospel, namely, that of a pioneer preacher (cf Cranfield 1979:763).[20]

Building is a figure of speech originating from missionary language. The ground for Paul's statement is surely not the avoidance of possible rivalry, but within the context of verses 17—21, Paul's understanding of himself as missionary to the heathen. His task was the spreading of the gospel, with the result that the places where the gospel had already been preached, could not be the goal of his mission. The same care which Paul had taken in Rom 1,11—13 can also be seen in the conclusion of his letter, where Paul speaks again of his forthcoming visit to Rome.[21] The quotation from Scripture shows that in this passage the emphasis is on Paul as the apostle to the Gentiles.

---

[20] "Er will [ἵνα] nicht auf 'fremden' — das heißt: von anderen Missionaren bereits gelegtem ... Fundament aufbauen, sondern, dem Schriftwort Jes 52,15 entsprechend, nur dort verkündigen, wo Botschaft und Kunde ... noch nicht gehört und angenommen worden sind" (Wilckens 1982:121).

[21] Cf Wilckens (1982:121): "... [ ] er [formuliert] ... hier den ἵνα-Satz bewußt scharf [ἐπ' ἀλλότριον θεμέλιον], damit ein für allemal klargestellt ist, daß Paulus sich in Rom selbstverständlich seiner *Gast*rolle bewußt ist ... Er kommt in einer *besonderen* Gastrolle nach Rom, nämlich als der 'Diener Jesu Christi für die Heidenvölker' [V 16], der, nachdem er die Ausbreitung des Evangeliums im Osten vollendet hat, demnächst mit der im Westen beginnen wird und dafür die Starthilfe der römischen Gemeinde in Anspruch nehmen möchte".

20.5 Conclusion

The importance of Paul's letter to the Romans lies not only in the statement
it contains of Paul's message or "gospel" but it is also significant because
of the light it throws on his own personal situation at the time and his
understanding of it. Paul reveals himself in Rom 15,14—21, (as so often
elsewhere) as being primarily concerned with the gospel. Furthermore he
interprets his calling as an apostle primarily as a call to proclaim the gospel
(cf Knox 1964:1—2).[22]

The theological, christological and pneumatological substrata of this
pericope are very important and can be seen in the abundant reference to
God, Jesus Christ and the Holy Spirit in this passage (cf discussion under
20.2.1). This pericope contains an important explanation of the relationship
between Christ and the Holy Spirit. It is Christ who works through the
apostle in order to lead the Gentiles to obey God, yet it is mentioned that
Paul's ministry as a whole is made possible by the Spirit. Paul's ministry
— by means of words and deeds, as well as the accompanying miracles —
is most intimately connected with the power of the Holy Spirit. The crucial
role of the Holy Spirit in dedicating the offering (of the Gentiles) to God is
mentioned in verse 16, a passage in which cultic terminology and motives
are being translated into eschatological terms.

Paul's usage of δύναμις in this pericope points to the crucial role of the
power of the Holy Spirit (most intimately connected with the power of
accompanying *miracles*) in Paul's mission of spreading the gospel. In the
centre of his apostolic service there is *God*, who has put him in the
privileged position of a servant of *Christ*, who works through him and the
Holy Spirit, who empowers him. The result of this apostolic service is
expressed in verse 19b: ὥστε με ἀπὸ Ἰερουσαλὴμ καὶ κύκλῳ μέχρι τοῦ
Ἰλλυρικοῦ πεπληρωκέναι τὸ εὐαγγέλιον τοῦ Χριστοῦ ... . The impact of
the gospel as Christ's work (cf Wilckens 1982:122) is interpreted
pneumatologically by Paul (... ἐν δυνάμει σημείων καὶ τεράτων, ἐν δυνάμει
πνεύματος θεοῦ [Rom 15,19]).

---

[22] "... unser Text gibt in der Tat einige Aufschlüsse darüber, wie Paulus sein
Apostolat verstand. Es ist für ihn u.a. die priesterliche, amtlich-öffentliche,
eschatologische 'Liturgie' des Evangeliums, durch die er die Völker in aller Welt im
Heiligen Geist Gott als wohlgefälliges Opfer darbringt. In ihrer Einheit von Sendung und
Evangelium ist diese 'Liturgie' Ausweis und Auswirkung der Gnade Gottes" (Schlier
1968:259).

Chapter 21

Overview of the remaining Corpus Paulinum

21.1 1 Thessalonians 1,5

1 Thess 1,3—6 contains the earliest reference to Christian conversion in the
New Testament (cf Fee 1994:41) and is part of the "thanksgiving" section
of this letter.[1] The thanksgiving following the prescript is attested in Greek
epistolography and was developed as a special feature of Paul's epistolary
style (cf Bruce 1982:11).

Although the ὅτι in verse 5 may be interpreted in an epexegetical sense,
it seems better to take it in a causal sense.[2] The results achieved by the
gospel preaching assured Paul of his readers' election. Paul appeals to their
own conversion as a means of encouragement in the midst of present
suffering. His reminder is twofold: i. of the nature of his proclamation of
the gospel — that it was accompanied by the power of the Holy Spirit (v
5), and ii. of their own experience of receiving the gospel — that it was
accompanied by joy, inspired by the Holy Spirit, despite the sufferings they
also experienced (v 6) (Fee 1994:42—3).

According to Paul his preaching of the gospel (τὸ εὐαγγέλιον) was οὐκ
... ἐν λόγῳ μόνον ἀλλὰ καὶ ἐν δυνάμει καὶ ἐν πνεύματι ἁγίῳ καὶ (ἐν)
πληροφορίᾳ πολλῇ ("not simply with words, but also with power, with the
Holy Spirit and with deep conviction" NIV). The gospel was preached —
of course — the spoken word remains the fundamental way in which it was
communicated (cf Rom 10,14). The act of preaching the gospel was,

---

[1] Cf Holtz (1986:41): "Der Eingangsdank für die Erwählung der Gemeinde
[1,2—10]."

[2] The epexegetical sense would require that the election motif in verse 4 be
understood as meaning "the manner of your election". Wanamaker (1990:78) correctly
points out that this seems unlikely, because it was probably not the manner of the
Thessalonians' election that caused Paul to give thanks, but the fact of their election.

however, more than the mere communication of human words. The same basic thought encountered in 1 Cor 2,4 is echoed here (although, due to the difference in situation, it was interpreted in a more polemic and apologetic way in 1 Cor 2,4). Paul affirms that his message (the gospel) was proclaimed under the manifestation of the power of the Spirit. "Power and the Holy Spirit" prove that the gospel message is indeed true.[3] The same function is attributed to the power of signs and miracles and the power of the Spirit, confirming the work of Christ through the apostle (Rom 15,19). Within this context the "things that mark an apostle — signs, wonders and miracles" (2 Cor 12,12) need to be mentioned (Holtz 1986:47).

Paul's apostolic work was indeed accompanied by manifestations of power. An interpretation of power ($\delta\acute{v}\nu\alpha\mu\iota\varsigma$) in 1 Thess 1,5 which only refers to the "weight of his thoughts" or the "power of his message over hearts" *excluding* the miraculous dimension, therefore does not do justice to the portrayal op Paul's ministry.[4] Also in 1 Thess 1,5 the concept of power points to his Spirit-empowered preaching, most probably accompanied by miraculous signs and wonders (cf also Gal 3,5), which led to the Thessalonians' own reception of the Spirit in conversion (cf Fee 1994:45; Wanamaker 1990:79).

21.2 Philippians 3,10

21.2.1 *The context: 3,7—11*

Phil 3,7—11 is a coherent unity, closely linked with both the preceding as well as following pericopes.[5] In this pericope Paul's personal testimony continues, but now focuses on the fundamental change in orientation that occurred when he encountered Christ. After he has mentioned the merits and achievements of his former way of life (vv 4b—6), he now emphasises

---

[3] Cf Horn (1992:123): "Die Trias ... [δ]$\acute{v}\nu\alpha\mu\iota\varsigma$, $\pi\nu\epsilon\tilde{v}\mu\alpha$ $\overset{\circ}{\alpha}\gamma\iota\sigma\nu$ und $\pi\lambda\eta\rho\sigma\phi\sigma\rho\acute{\iota}\alpha$ sind das Mittel, das der Predigt des Evangeliums Wirksamkeit verlieh."

[4] As proposed by von Dobschütz ([1909] 1974:70—1): "Bei $\delta\acute{v}\nu\alpha\mu\iota\varsigma$ denkt Paulus hier nicht an äußere Wunder als Machterweise [vgl. Röm 15$_{18f}$ II Kor 12$_{12}$ u. ö.] ... sondern an die Macht seiner Predigt über die Herzen."

[5] The $\dot{\alpha}\lambda\lambda\acute{\alpha}$ at the beginning of verse 7 is missing in most of the better early evidence. By inserting this $\dot{\alpha}\lambda\lambda\acute{\alpha}$, the scribes have however correctly read the context, which implies a decisive contrast. For a detailed discussion of this text critical problem, cf Fee 1995:311 n 1.

the rejection of his old way of thinking in favour of the much greater advantage of knowing Christ. In the light of the far greater gain of knowing Christ and entering into intimate fellowship with him, the apparent assets of his former life turned out to be a worthless investment, which he has now written off (Bockmuehl 1997:203).

The motif of "considering", ἡγέομαι, plays an important role in this pericope (and also distinguishes it from both the preceding as following pericopes): ἥγημαι (v 8), ἡγοῦμαι (v 8: 2x). Contrast is very prominent: cf gain — loss (κέρδος ... ζημία, v 7; ζημία ... κερδαίνω, v 8); own righteousness — righteousness through faith in Christ/righteousness of God by faith (v 9); power of his resurrection — fellowship of sharing in his sufferings/in growing conformity with his death[6] — attaining to the resurrection from the dead (vv 10—11).

The reason for this radical change in Paul's present values (cf O'Brien 1991:381), is to be found in Christ, who is the central theme of this passage, cf "because of [διά][7] *Christ*" (v 7), "the surpassing greatness *of knowing* [τῆς γνώσεως] Christ Jesus my Lord ... that I may gain Christ" (v 8), "be found in *him* ... righteousness through faith in Christ" (v 9), "*know* Christ ... power of his resurrection ... sharing in his sufferings, in growing conformity with his death" (v 10).[8]

Verses 10—11 constitute the final purpose clause of a very long sentence, commencing in verse 8. Although the grammar is uncertain, it is best understood as modifying verses 8c—9. It concludes the sentence by returning to the theme of "knowing Christ" (v 8b), which is then explained[9] by referring both to the power of his resurrection and the fellowship of sharing in his sufferings. The chiastic structure of verses 10 and 11 is noteworthy:

A   power of his resurrection
    B   participation in his sufferings
    B'   being conformed to his death
A'   attaining to the resurrection, which is from the dead
       (Fee 1995:313.329)

---

[6] Cf the NEB, cited by Zerwick and Grosvenor 1979:599.

[7] For a discussion of the meaning of διά here, cf Fee 1995:315 n 8.

[8] Cf Dodd (1999:184): "The christocentric focus of Paul's example is reiterated again in 3.10 with the fourfold him/his as the centre of Paul's passion... ."

[9] The καί is interpreted epexegetically.

Verse 9 explains what it means to be "found in him" *positionally* (i e not having the own righteousness that comes from the law, but the righteousness of God which is through faith in Christ) — and serves primarily as the *ground* for verses 10—11: The aim of everything is "to know Christ" *relationally*: both the present power of his resurrection (A) and the fellowship of his sufferings (B), in growing conformity to his death (B'), so as to realise the future dimension of the former ("attaining the resurrection from the dead," [A']).

Fee points out that, though the content differs considerably, both the linguistic echoes and the general "form" of the narrative seem intentionally designed to recall the Christ narrative in 2,6—11. As Paul appealed to the Philippians to do, he himself exemplifies Christ's mind set, embracing suffering and death. As he (Christ) was raised and exalted to the highest place, so Paul and the Philippian believers (because they are now "conformed to Christ" in his death, will also be "conformed" to his glory [Fee 1995:314—5]).

The purpose of the radical change of values in Paul's life is "to know Christ". "Knowing Christ" implies an intimate relationship, concretely the experience of the power of his resurrection and the participation in his sufferings. These two appositional phrases (intimately linked together) represent two aspects of knowing Christ — not two different modes to be separated (cf 2 Cor 4,7—11; 12,9—10) (cf Bockmuehl 1997:214).

Paul never uses the resurrection of Christ as a sign of *his* power, but rather of God's: It was God's power that raised Christ from the dead (Rom 1,4; 8,11; 1 Cor 6,14; 2 Cor 13,4; Col 2,12; cf Acts 2,24; Eph 1,20).[10] Although the resurrection is only implicit in Phil 2,9, Christ's exaltation is clearly identified as God's work. Paul therefore desires to experience personally the power of God that was shown in Christ's resurrection (Bockmuehl 1997:214—5).[11] Paul has come to know — and continues to desire to know — God's power, manifested in the resurrection of Christ in his present mortal body. Within these present "jars of clay" we have a "treasure ... to show that this all-surpassing power is God's and not from

---

[10] Bockmuehl (1997:214) points out that this is in keeping with standard Jewish views about resurrection as being by the power of God, cf already Ezk 37,12; 2 Mac 7,9.14; 4 Q521 ii 2.12. The second benediction of the *Amidah* affirms: "... you revive the dead, mighty to save".

[11] For a detailed discussion of different interpretations of this phrase, cf Fitzmyer 1970:418—20.

us" (2 Cor 4,7); we "... are always being given over to death for Jesus' sake, so that his life might be revealed in our mortal body" (2 Cor 4,11).

"Power" in Paul's writings is intimately linked to the Spirit. The present personal narrative begins with the assertion in verse 3 that must be understood to be presuppositional throughout this passage: In contrast to the Judaizers, Paul and the Philippians live by the power of the (eschatological) Spirit of God (Fee 1995:330—1).

21.2.2 Conclusion

This passage is indeed "... quintessential Paul, and a quintessential expression of the NT view of Christian life" (Fee 1995:336). "Knowing Christ" means to experience the divine power of his resurrection now through the Spirit, as God's empowering presence for present "participation in his sufferings." All of Christian life bears the divine imprint of the cross as believers live out the gospel in the present age, while awaiting the hope of resurrection (Fee 1995:337).

The glimpses of his personal history Paul gives us in the present pericope, as well as in 1,21 and 2,5—11 emphasise how totally Christ-focused he is.[12] Christian life is not a matter of "salvation" and "ethics", but is ultimately a matter of *knowing Christ* (cf Fee 1995:337).

21.3 The power of God in Ephesians

21.3.1 Ephesians 1,19

This verse forms part of the section of the letter containing Paul's thanksgiving and prayer for the believers (1,15—23). The prayer in verses 18—19 is a petition for a threefold enlightenment. Beginning each clause with τίς and τί he asks for hope God's calling brings, knowledge of the wealth of glory laid up in his inheritance in the saints, and knowledge of the immensity of his power. Believers should be experiencing these three different aspects of the salvation.

---

[12] In his study on personal example as a literary strategy in Paul's letters, Dodd (1999:237—8) concludes that Paul's literary style reflects his leadership style of modelling and embodying the teaching he propagated. This is further underlined by epistolary theory of the time which urged the creation of a letter as an alter ego, a surrogate for one's personal presence with one's readers.

In verse 19 the writer desires believers to know the greatness of God's power and — as Lincoln correctly affirms — "... attempts to exhaust the resources of the Greek language by piling up four synonyms for power in order to convey an impression of something of the divine might" (Lincoln 1990:60). Note the three terms which are in a double genitive construction at the end of verse 19. It has been suggested, that if there is any distinction of nuance, δύναμις denotes ability to accomplish something, ἐνέργεια inherent strength or power, κράτος the power to overcome what stands in its way and ἰσχύς the exercise of power.[13] With the heaping up of these expressions the purpose of the writer is however not to point to their distinctiveness, but they are used synonymously to emphasise the greatness of God's power. The present passage shows great similarity to the prayer in Col 1,11: ἐν πάσῃ δυνάμει δυναμούμενοι κατὰ τὸ κράτος τῆς δόξης αὐτοῦ ("being strengthened with all power according to his glorious might"). The accumulation of terms in Ephesians, however, outweighs that in Colossians. This immense power of God is exercised εἰς ἡμᾶς τοὺς πιστεύοντας ("towards us who believe"). εἰς in this verse is used synonymously with ἐν in 3,20 (κατὰ τὴν δύναμιν τὴν ἐνεργουμένην ἐν ἡμῖν, "according to his power that is at work within us"). Verse 20 affirms that the life-giving power of the new age was the power which raised Christ from the dead. It is the revelatory power at work in Paul's gospel (3,7: κατὰ τὴν ἐνέργειαν τῆς δυνάμεως αὐτοῦ)[14]. It is the power available for the people of God in the continuing communication of God's grace. The prayer in verse 18 is that believers should know and appropriate this divine power (Lincoln 1990:61).

21.3.2 Ephesians 3,16

In Eph 3,14—21 we encounter a further prayer for the completeness of the readers' experience of God (with a doxology) (Lincoln 1990:196).

The intercessory prayer-report in this passage constitutes one long sentence: Verses 14—15 introduce the prayer, verses 16—19 relate its content. The contents consists of three main requests, each introduced by ἵνα. The first main request begins with ἵνα δῷ ὑμῖν, "that he may grant you ...". This is followed by two parallel infinitive clauses and a participial

---

[13] Lincoln 1990:60 (referring to Schlier and Barth).
[14] Note the way in which δύναμις is connected to ἐνέργεια in verse 7 and ἐνεργέω in verse 20.

clause. The first infinitive clause (δυνάμει κραταιωθῆναι διὰ τοῦ πνεύματος αὐτοῦ εἰς τὸν ἔσω ἄνθρωπον) explains that what the readers are to be granted is "... to be strengthened with power through his Spirit in the inner person". Although Paul explicitly links the Spirit here to the concept of power, the power of the Spirit is probably also in view in verse 20, as well as in 1,19. As is the case in Rom 15,13, this passage clearly states that within the Corpus Paulinum the "power of the Spirit" is not only for more visible and extraordinary manifestations of God's presence, but also fulfills a very important function in the empowering necessary to be his people in the world, so as to be true reflections of his glory.

This strengthening through the Spirit in the inner man — the dwelling of Christ in their hearts through faith[15] — has important ethical consequences, leading to the fruit of the Spirit in their lives and the same love for one another that Christ has for them.[16]

Eph 1,19 describes the power available to believers as the same power with which God *raised Christ from the dead*. Paul's *apostolic ministry* is said to be energised by such power (3,7) and in 6,10 the writer exhorts his readers to be strong in their battle against evil.

In the present verse there is a direct prayer for their strengthening, reminiscent of Col 1,11. The tautologous style ("to be strengthened with power") is similar to that found in the Qumran writings (e g 1 QH 7,17. 19; 12,35; 1 QM 10,5). This power is to be mediated to believers by the Spirit, described in 1,13—14 as the one by whom believers are sealed, the guarantee of the full salvation of the age to come and as the means by which God is present in the church (2,22). In Paul's writings the Spirit (seen as the power of the age to come) and power were closely associated, cf 1 Thess 1,5; 1 Cor 2,4; 15,43.44; 2 Cor 6,6.7; Rom 1,4; 15,13. This association is continued in Ephesians.

The strengthening of the Spirit is to take place in the "inner person": the base of operation at the centre of a person's being where the Spirit does his work of renewal and strengthening. Its equivalent in the parallel clause

---

[15] Fee (1994:696) points out that this is what it means for them to be strengthened by the Spirit in the inner person, namely, that Christ himself dwells in their hearts — all of this transpires by faith.

[16] Fee (1994:697) affirms that the basic concern of Christian ethics is at stake here, namely the issue of "... Christ being formed in us" so that we reflect the character of God, as it is disclosed to us in his Son.

(v 17a) is the heart and in 4,23 it is the spirit of the mind which is said to be renewed (cf 1 Pet 3,4: ὁ κρυπτὸς τῆς καρδίας ἄνθρωπος, "the hidden person of the heart").[17]

---

[17] Lincoln (1990:197.204—7). For a discussion of the different views on the interpretation of the phrase ἔσω ἄνθρωπον, as well as its religio-historical background, see p 205.

Chapter 22

Perspectives from the broader New Testament context

22.1 God's power in Luke[1]

22.1.1 Introduction

Δύναμις occurs in the following *sections of Luke's Gospel*: the infancy prologue (1,35); right at the beginning of Jesus' ministry in Galilee (4,14), his preaching in Capernaum (4,36), the healing (and forgiveness) of a paralyzed man (5,17); the section dealing with the disciples and people coming to hear and be healed (6,19), the healing of the woman with the flow of blood (8,46); the empowerment and sending of the twelve (9,1); the return of the seventy-two (10,19—20), the section towards the close of the Gospel, dealing with the coming of the Son of Man (21,27), Jesus before Pilate and Herod (22,69) as well as the final section, dealing with the empowerment of he disciples to become trustworthy witnesses (24,49).[2]

The dimension of power, therefore occurs (i) at the beginning of Luke's narrative about Jesus (already at the inception and right at the beginning of his ministry), (ii) in connection with his healing ministry and ministry of exorcism, (iii) relating to the empowerment of his disciples, (iv) at the conclusion of the Gospel in an eschatological context and (v) in connection with his instruction to the disciples to wait in Jerusalem for the "power from on high".

22.1.2 The dimension of power in the Jesus narrative

The importance of the dimension of power (interpreted in terms of the Holy Spirit) in the Jesus narrative is evident from the fact that it appears on the

---

[1] In this brief overview of the power of God in the broader New Testament context the Gospel of Luke has been selected to serve as an *example from the synoptic tradition*, as the concept of δύναμις occurs most in this Gospel.

[2] "Befähigung der Jünger zu glaubwürdigen Zeugen" (Kremer 1988:20; cf also Nolland 1986:vii—xii).

scene even before the birth of Jesus. The role of the Spirit in Jesus' origin is linked to an Old Testament statement of God's activity (Is 32,15).[3] The role of the Spirit in this verse (as well as in Acts 1,8) alludes to the eschatological coming of the Spirit, causing the wilderness to become a fruitful field. Although Luke often links the Spirit (πνεῦμα) and power (δύναμις) closely,[4] he never identifies them quite as in Lk 1,35 (cf the *parallelismus membrorum*):

Πνεῦμα ἅγιον ἐπελεύσεται ἐπὶ σέ,
καὶ δύναμις ὑψίστου ἐπισκιάσει σοι

It is noteworthy that the beginning of Jesus' ministry in Galilee is described with the phrase ἐν τῇ δυνάμει τοῦ πνεύματος ("in the power of the Holy Spirit", 4,14). Luke's statement that Jesus returned to Galilee in the power of the Spirit[5] serves as a general description, illuminating the whole of Luke's account of Jesus' ministry. Jesus' *whole redemptive ministry* (both of preaching and of working liberating miracles) is empowered by the Spirit (Turner 1996:211).[6]

Jesus' whole ministry is grounded in his baptism (3,21—22). Since this event he is "full of the Spirit" (πλήρης πνεύματος ἁγίου, 4,1). With δύναμις in verse 14 Luke emphasises the *pneumatic* (charismatic) activity of Jesus. On the one hand his teaching (διδάσκειν, 4,15) has authority (ἐν ἐξουσίᾳ, v 32); on the other hand the pneumatological miracles (δυνάμεις, cf Mk 6,2), the healings and especially the exorcisms prove that his ministry is "with authority and power" (ἐν ἐξουσίᾳ καὶ δυνάμει, 4,36; cf Schürmann 1969:222).[7]

---

[3] Nolland (1986:54) points out that ἐπέρχεσθαι ἐπί, "to come upon", is Septuagintal idiom, but is used in connection with the Spirit only at Is 32,15 (A ℵ) where the MT has עָרָה ("will be poured out"). Acts 1,8 has ἐπελθόντος τοῦ ἁγίου πνεύματος ἐφ᾽ ὑμᾶς, "when the Holy Spirit comes upon you". As Luke nowhere else refers to the coming of the Spirit in these terms, he is probably drawing attention to the Greek text of Is 32,15 in both cases.

[4] Cf e g Lk 4,14; Acts 1,8; 10,38 (cf also 1,17: "spirit and power of Elijah").

[5] Lk 4,14—15 is a redaction of the summary in Mk 1,14—15, Luke adding the phrase ἐν τῇ δυνάμει τοῦ πνεύματος (cf Turner 1996:210).

[6] In the light of verses 14b and 23 Schürmann (1964:248) emphasises that the phrase ἐν τῇ δυνάμει τοῦ πνεύματος refers to the δυνάμεις in Jesus' ministry.

[7] J B Shelton (1991:75) points out, that although the two meanings sometimes overlap (e g Lk 4,36; 9,1; 10,19; 21,27) Luke usually maintains the traditional distinction between δύναμις as effective power and ἐξουσία as official authority.

"Power" (δύναμις) in 5,17, 6,19 and 8,46 refers to *Jesus' healing power*. The reference of power in 5,17 links back to 4,14 and prepares for the references to tangible power proceeding from Jesus in 6,19 and 8,46. Luke is continuing to clarify what it means that Jesus — through the descent of the Spirit — has become the repository of the power of God (3,22; 4,1; 14,18—19; 6,19; 8,46; cf Nolland 1986:234). 8,46 portrays God's transcendent power to be present in a way that goes beyond Jesus' own action. Jesus not only opened the way to the transcendency of God, but the divine power of God became active through him in a way that even transcended his own activity (Schürmann 1969:492). Spiritual power is seen in a quasi-substantial manner, but is never isolated from religious categories of a relational and ethical kind (Nolland 1986:420).

This divine pneumatic power is not only an essential element of Jesus' ministry, but is also of vital importance to the ministry of the disciples. Nolland aptly gives the pericope 9,1—6 the title: "Sharing in Jesus' Ministry".[8] Luke adds "power and" to Mark's "authority", which may be an anticipation of postressurrection empowering (cf Acts 1,8; Nolland 1986:426). The Twelve are empowered by Jesus' own power. The dimension of power is so important that it is mentioned not only at the beginning of *Jesus' ministry* (4,14), but also at the beginning of that of his disciples.[9]

Lk 10,17—20 reports how the seventy-two were excited as they explored the reality of the power and authority entrusted to them by Jesus. Although Jesus acknowledges and interprets this experience, he bids them to focus rather on the place secured for them in heaven (cf Nolland 1986:566). The statement about the authority to trample on snakes and scorpions and to overcome all the power of the enemy, follows directly from Jesus' exclamation about the fall of Satan (v 18). Allusions to Deut 8,15 and Ps 91,13 are probable in this text. Similarities with Rev 9,3—4 (within the context of Jesus' remark about Satan in v 18) point to the

---

[8] Cf also Schürmann (1969:498): "Jesu Wirksamkeit im Wirken der Jünger."

[9] Cf Schürmann (1969:499): "Deutlich beginnt mit der Aussendung der Zwölf 9,1—6 etwas Neues."

probability that the text is here using imagery of the end-time conflict between good and evil.[10]

In Lk 21,27 and 22,69 the notion of power (δύναμις) is connected with Jesus' sayings about the "Son of Man". In 21,25—28 the *eschatological* discourse of Jesus in Luke's Gospel takes on another dimension. The first part of the discourse was a prophetic utterance with overtones of prophecy fulfilled. In this passage Jesus utters prophetic utterances about the future, with overtones of prophecy yet to be fulfilled. He returns to the topic of the coming of the Son of Man (cf 17,22—37; Fitzmyer 1985:1348). The coming of the Son of Man is described in the language of Dan 7,13—14 as well as in terms of Old Testament theophany accounts: with power and glory (cf Ex 16,7; Kremer 1988:206).[11]

Lk 22,69 states Jesus' answer to Pilate, that "... from now on, the Son of Man will be seated at the right hand of the mighty God [τῆς δυνάμεως τοῦ θεοῦ]". Δύναμις is an indirect way of *referring to God*. In Mk 14,62 δύναμις is used in a personified way to refer to *God himself* (τῆς δυνάμεως), whereas in Lk 22,69 δύναμις is coupled with a direct mention of God.[12]

It is noteworthy that motifs that appeared in the infancy narratives (esp chap 1) are echoed in 24,49: "I send", as the angel Gabriel had been sent in 1,26; anticipation of "the promise" — the infancy events themselves had been in fulfilment of the covenant promise (1,54—55.70.72—73); a revelation of the father/son relationship, as in 1,32 and 35; action focused in the holy city, Jerusalem; endowment with power — cf 1,35[13] (also 1,17). As was the case with Lk 1, we are standing here again on a *major threshold*.[14]

---

[10] Nolland (1986:566—7) warns, however, against interpreting this language in a way that is too triumphal and that leaves no place for the Christian call to suffering (cf the paradoxical juxtaposition in Lk 21,16—17 and v 18). In the present journey section of the Gospel the coming fate of Jesus in Jerusalem is stressed. Cf also Bovon (1996:57): "Die Ereignisse der Endzeit setzen also ein."

[11] It is noteworthy that in Dan 7,14 (LXX) the son of man was given ἐξουσία and glory (δόξα); cf Johnson 1991:328.

[12] Cf Nolland 1988:1110; for the Old Testament and early Jewish background to this phrase, cf Fitzgerald 1988:1467.

[13]   δύναμις ὑψίστου (1,35)
        ὕψους δύναμιν (24,49).

[14] Nolland (1986:1220) also points to the echoing of the beginning at the end in 24,50—53.

Within the present context (Lk 24,44—49), the Spirit is anticipated specifically as *empowerment for the witnessing task* that lies ahead. This prospect of empowerment has its counterpart in the *power of the Spirit* that undergirded *Jesus' own ministry* (cf 4,14; 5,17; Nolland 1986:1220).

In relation to Jesus' experience of the power of God (the Spirit) and his ministry of exorcism (and healing), *Dunn* emphasises three aspects:

i. Jesus was conscious that he cast out demons by the *power of God*. The visible evidence of the power of God flowing through him became manifest in the ability to overcome other superhuman power, evil power, to restore and make whole.

ii. The exercise of this power was evidence that the longed-for kingdom of God had already come upon his hearers — the *eschatological* kingdom was *already* present. Jesus' exorcisms acted as a sign of the binding of the powers of evil which was sought after at the end of the age. The final battle had already begun and Satan was already being routed (cf Lk 10,18). Power in the ministry of Jesus has a distinctive eschatological meaning: Jesus' powerful acts were as epochal as the miracles of the Exodus and likewise heralded a *new age*.

iii. *"The eschatological kingdom was present for Jesus only because the eschatological Spirit was present in and through him ... ."* Jesus saw in his experience to cast out demons a manifestation of God — acting through him in a decisively new and final way (Dunn 1975:47—9).

The empowering of the disciples at the time of Pentecost was *prefigured in the "power" given in 9,1.* The disciples already participated in the ministry of Jesus in an anticipatory manner (cf 9,1—6; 10,1—20). In future they will carry his ministry forward when he sits exalted at the right hand of God. Although the giving of the Spirit needs to wait for Jesus' exaltation, the anticipation of this promise of power is prominent already in the time of his ministry: Jesus was conceived through the power of the Spirit (cf 1,35); he was empowered by the Spirit for ministry (4,14; 5,17). In turn Jesus gave power to his disciples, who were sent out to speak and act in his name (cf 9,1—6; 10,1—20; Nolland 1986:1220—1).

22.2 The power of the Spirit in Acts

22.2.1 "Power" as part of the early message about Jesus (10,38)

Peter's speech to Cornelius in Caesarea (10,34—43) is unique among the speeches in Acts as it contains the only extended summary of the ministry of Jesus. At the heart of Peter's speech lies pre-Lukan material. The use of the Old Testament in this passage also points to a very early period (Stanton 1974:80.81.84—5).[15]

The message that "... God anointed Jesus of Nazareth with the Holy Spirit and power", which enabled him to "... go around doing good and healing all who were under the power of the devil" belongs to the heart of the early Christian *kerygma*.[16] In affirming that "... God anointed Jesus with the Spirit", the wording of Is 61,1 is used to interpret what happened to Jesus at the Jordan (Lk 4,18; Marshall 1980:192). Luke describes Jesus' acts of beneficence in terms of healing, of the overthrow of the devil and of the presence of God himself. Jesus' work constitutes God's decisive attack upon the power of evil (cf Mk 3,23—27 and parallels; Barrett 1994:524—5). In Acts (as was the case in Luke's Gospel) the *Spirit* and *power* are very closely related to each other. The Spirit is in the first place the source of miraculous power.[17] The activity of Jesus, performing miracles, signs and wonders[18] was the proof that God was with him, because only God is able to do such things as these. Jesus' ministry represents God's involvement with his people.

22.2.2 Power to be Jesus' witnesses

Acts 1,8

This verse receives special emphasis as the last words of Jesus before his departure and are closely parallel to his last recorded words in the Gospel

---

[15] Cf also Dunn (1996:143): "This rehearsal of Jesus' ministry is unique in the sermons of Acts and bears several marks of very old tradition." Already Dodd (1936:37) had pointed out that these speeches of Peter represent the *kerygma* of the Church at Jerusalem at an early period.

[16] Hawthorne (1991:132) points to the analogy of the anointing of Old Testament kings in order that they might be enabled to fulfill their divine mission.

[17] Shelton (1991:75) points out that of the twenty-five times Luke uses the word δύναμις in Luke-Acts, eighteen specifically refer to miracles, especially healings.

[18] "mirakulöse Wunderkraft" (Jervell 1998:311).

(Lk 24,46—49), spoken just before he left the disciples. For their worldwide task the disciples are promised the power of the Spirit (Lk 24,49). This promise was primarily fulfilled at Pentecost and secondarily on many other occasions (Marshall 1980:61).

Acts 1,8 provides the outline for the Lukan account: the beginnings in Jerusalem (Acts 1—5), the first stirrings resulting in expansion into Judea and into apostate Samaria (Acts 6—12), and finally to the "ends of the earth" (Acts 13—28). A world-wide mission is envisaged, with perhaps an echo of Is 49,6 (cf Lk 2,32; Acts 13,47; 26,23). Paul's success in bringing the gospel to Rome was therefore the most significant step on the way to that goal, but not the goal in itself (Dunn 1996:10—1).

The present verse (Acts 1,8) looks forward to Acts 2 and receives a measure of interpretation from that chapter when the apostles (represented by Peter) act as witnesses, after they have received power through the gift of the Spirit. The connection with the preceding verse 6 is important. A certain measure of contrast may be intended: not the kingdom for Israel, but the power of the Holy Spirit for the church.[19] In these verses the fundamentally important question is raised of the relation between the gift of the Spirit and the end. The Spirit is an anticipation of the end-time in the present (Barrett 1994:78). The disciples are not to know the times and the dates of God's history of salvation. They will however receive *power for their task of witnessing* through which salvation will be brought to all peoples (Lk 24,47; Pesch 1986:69).

The power ($\delta\acute{u}\nu\alpha\mu\iota\varsigma$) promised in Acts 1,8 is the power the apostles needed to fulfil their mission — to speak, to bear oral testimony, and to perform miracles, the power to act with authority in general (Barrett 1994:79; cf also Turner 1996:402). For Luke a very close relation exists between the oral witness and accompanying miracles.[20] Miracles are part and parcel of the entire mission of witness. By the divine power the gospel is preached, the church is established, opposing powers — whether human

---

[19] Dunn (1996:11) points out that the answer provided by 1,8 (and the whole of the following narrative) to the question of 1,6 is that the question itself is not closed: "The gospel goes on, the proclamation of the kingdom continues. The hope and mission of Israel has not yet been completely fulfilled [cf 28.20]."

[20] Cf Jervell (1998:115): "Der Geist drückt sich als $\delta\acute{u}\nu\alpha\mu\iota\varsigma$ aus, als die mirakulöse Kraft in Wunder und Wort, weswegen bei Lukas die Verkündigung stets von Wundern begleitet ist… ."

or demonic — are conquered and signs of healings are performed (Lampe 1965:171).[22]

The promise of the Spirit, already mentioned in verse 5, is reiterated in verse 8, where the meaning of the experience of the Spirit is clarified:

"The Spirit is the power of God within creation and human life. The impact of the Spirit is therefore characteristically one of transformation, of enabling what would be impossible in human strength alone ... [F]or Luke the mission of the church could not hope to be effective without this empowering from God [the Spirit of God] which transcends human ability and transforms human inability" (Dunn 1996:11—2).

Acts 4,33

The apostles, especially called to be witnesses of the resurrection of Jesus (cf 1,22; 3,15; 4,2), continued their witness δυνάμει μεγάλῃ ("with great power") despite the Jewish prohibition to their preaching (Marshall 1980:108). This "great power" refers to their *boldness* (4,31) as well as the *miracles* (cf 2,43; 5,12) they performed in the name of Jesus through the power of the Spirit which they had received (cf Lk 24,48—49; Acts 1,8; Pesch 1986:182—3).

Luke relates δύναμις in this verse to χάρις (cf δυνάμει μεγάλῃ / χάρις τε μεγάλη). God's favour rests upon them all — "all" (πάντας) referring within the context of verse 33 to the apostles in the first place, but within the context of verses 32 and 34 to all the Christians (cf Barrett 1994:254).[23]

Excursus: Social impact of the presence of the power of God

In the theological post-script to his essay on "Sociology and Theology", Barton underlines the theological importance of social-scientific interpretation of Luke-Acts, because it helps to fill out our picture of the impact of the Spirit of God in and through Jesus, the Son of God in the first place, and subsequently, the Spirit-inspired

---

[22] Cf also the discussion of miracles in Acts in Witherington (1998:220—4).

[23] Dunn (1996:59) interprets "grace"/χάρις here as "the outreach of God's generous power".

apostles and the communities of believers brought into being by their testimony. This impact was such as to affect people in body and soul, individually and corporately — "a world turned upside down" (Acts 17,6) (Barton 1998:472).[24]

After the disciples had been reassured of the power and presence of the Spirit among them, Luke emphasised the unanimity of mind and purpose of the first believers. Verse 34 mentions that there were no needy persons among them. "Needy" may be an allusion to Deut 15,4, indicating that the new congregation of the Nazarene fulfilled Israel's hope for a people blessed by the Lord (Dunn 1996:59).[25] The presence of the power of God in their midst had concrete *sociological consequences*.

The history of the effect of these events can be traced in a passage such as Did 4,8: "Thou shalt not turn away the needy, but shalt share everything with thy brother, and shalt not say that it is thine own, for if you are sharers in the imperishable, how much more in the things that perish?" (Lake [1912] 1977a:317; cf Pesch 1986:188).

Acts 6,8

Whereas it was stated in 4,33 that the apostles testified with *great* power and *much* grace was with them all, Stephen is portrayed in 6,8 as "... full of God's grace and power" (πλήρης χάριτος καὶ δυνάμεως). "Grace" (χάρις), worked by the Spirit of God, is a general term — the favour of God expressed in an abundance of gifts. "Power" (δύναμις) is, as affirmed by 1,8, the result of the work of the Holy Spirit and corresponds to "faith" (πίστις) in verse 5. Luke associates both these terms with miracles which are immediately mentioned: "Stephen did great wonders and miraculous signs." Instead of the δυνάμει μεγάλη ... χάρις τε μεγάλη of 4,33, we find here the τέρατα καὶ σημεῖα μεγάλα. As the Twelve had done (cf 2,43; 4,30; 5,12), Stephen also worked miraculous signs and wonders (Barrett 1994:322; cf also Marshall 1980:129).

---

[24] Some work has already been done in this regard, cf Neyrey 1991.

[25] Jervell (1998:192) mentions that the unity of the congregation is brought about by the power of the Spirit. With reference to the events described in 5,3—10 he points out: "... wer in ökonomische, also Gemeinschaftssachen, lügt, sündigt gegen den Heiligen Geist ...".

22.2.3 Miracles

Power (δύναμις) that effects miracles

3,12. After the healing of the crippled beggar, the question about the power to do these miracles arises twice. Because the people do not recognise that God is personally at work they marvel at what they have seen and gaze at Peter and John as if they were themselves responsible for what had happened (3,12). Luke emphasises that the powers the apostles possessed, they had as a gift from God (Barrett 1994:192). The people should not stare at the apostles, because they did not perform this miracle by their own power and piety (δύναμις and εὐσέβεια) (cf Jervell 1998:164).[26]

4,7. The Sanhedrin asked Peter and John: "By what power [ἐν ποίᾳ δυνάμει] or what name did you do this?" Δύναμις is the more general term, denoting supernatural force which is capable of overthrowing disease. Ὄνομα links this force with a particular person, whose name is invoked in order to set the required power in motion. Peter, "filled with the Holy Spirit", gives the answer to this question in verse 10 (cf also 3,6): "It is by the name of Jesus Christ of Nazareth ..." (cf Barrett 1994:226). Something of the ancient idea of the power vested in a name is reflected here. The name represents the person and carries his authority (Dunn 1996:41).

Δυνάμεις — miracles

In 2,22, 8,13 and 19,11 δυνάμεις means "miracles". 2,22 states that through the δυνάμεις, God showed that Jesus was (or was to be, if ἀποδεικνύναι hear means to designate) his special agent: God performed the signs through Jesus for their benefit (εἰς ὑμᾶς) (cf Barrett 1994:141).

Δυνάμεις in 8,13 refers to the miracles performed by Philip and 19,11 to the miracles performed by Paul.

Δύναμις in Acts 10,8

In chapter 8 (cf vv 4—25) it is described how it came about that Philip took the place previously occupied by Simon. Simon's

---

[26] Dunn (1996:44) points to the assumption reflected here that piety could be a factor in bringing about healing. Luke makes a particular point of denying any thought of piety as a kind of manipulation of divine power.

statement about himself is reflected in verse 9 — quite vague and unspecific: "someone great". Popular opinion probably accepted what Simon claimed for himself: ἡ δύναμις τοῦ θεοῦ ἡ καλουμένη μεγάλη.[27]

Δύναμις can be used to mean God: cf Lk 22,69 where τῆς δυνάμεως τοῦ θεοῦ is parallel to the τῆς δυνάμεως of Mk 14,62. The equation between "power" and "God" is supported by the use of גבורה for God and of חיל which stands for God in Samaritanism.[28]

The text can also be taken as its stands and does not mean that Simon claimed to be the supreme God. Various inscriptions support a *distinction* between the supreme Being and a "great power" (μεγάλη δύναμις): A description from Lydia, dealing with the religion of Men, states Εἷς θεὸς ἐν οὐρανοῖς, μέγας Μὴν Οὐράνιος, μεγάλη δύναμις τοῦ ἀθανάτου θεοῦ. (It seems to distinguish between Men and the immortal God.)

Another inscription from Samaria runs: Εἷς θεός, ὁ πάντων δεσπότης, μεγάλη κόρη ἡ ἀνείκητος. In Philo speculation regarding *powers* of God had reached an advanced stage. He normally distinguished the δυνάμεις from the God whose powers they were, but could however also speak of God himself as ἡ ἀνωτάτω καὶ μεγίστη δύναμις (*Moses* 1,111).

Simon might have inculcated the belief that of all the powers of God he was the great one (Barrett 1994:406—8).

22.2.4 Conclusion

Δύναμις in Acts portrays the power of the Holy Spirit enabling the disciples of Jesus to fulfil their world-wide mission (also mentioning the fact that Jesus himself was anointed with the Holy Spirit and with power). The power of the Holy Spirit enabled them to *speak the word of God boldly*, as well as to *perform miracles, wonders and signs*.[29] The source of the power by which the apostles were able to carry out their astounding work of

---

[27] For a discussion of the relevant text critical problems in this passage, cf Barrett 1994:407.

[28] Barret 1994:407 (who quotes here from Black).

[29] Cf Menzies' informative diagram, illustrating the relation between the Spirit, δύναμις, prophetic speech and exorcisms and miracles of healing (Menzies 1991:115).

communication of the gospel and healing was a paramount question (cf the way the high priestly group interrogated the apostles, 4,1—7). Peter, filled with the Spirit, declares that it is "... by the name of Jesus Christ of Nazareth" that the crippled beggar was healed. The ensuing prayer of the believers indicates how important the bold preaching of the word, as well as the accompanying healings and miraculous signs and wonders were to them (cf 4,29—30). Concrete healings and discernible actions, such as the shaking of the place where they were assembled (4,31) demonstrated to them the continuing presence and power of the Spirit among them (Kee 1990:36—7).

22.3 The power of God in Revelation

"Power" is an important category in apocalyptic literature.[30] The theocentric use of δύναμις is important for interpreting this motif in the Book of Revelation.[31] After the author has portrayed the risen Christ with his people on earth (1,9—3,22), John is taken up to heaven (4,1). It is in this vision of God's sovereignty in heaven that the concept of power (δύναμις) first occurs. With this vision John helps his readers to view their own situation within the broader context of God's universal purpose of overcoming all opposition to his rule and establishing his kingdom in the world (Bauckham 1993:31).

Rev 4 draws on Old Testament visions of God (cf Ezek 1; Is 6; Ezek 28,13). Verse 11b has a very close parallel in Nebuchadnezzar's concluding hymn of praise in Dan 4,37 in the Septuagint and Dan 4,35 in Theodotion.[32] Chapter 4 is the first of several hymnic passages in the Book

---

[30] In the preface to *The Book of Revelation. Justice and Judgment* Elisabeth Schüssler Fiorenza (1985) expresses her gratitude to Ernst Käsemann for teaching her to understand apocalyptic *in terms of power*.

[31] Δύναμις is directly related to God in the following verses: 4,11; 7,12; 11,17; 12,10; 15,8; 19,1.

[32] For the Old Testament-Jewish background of the liturgical praise language, cf Beale 1999:335—6.364—5.

D H Milling (quoted by Beale) concludes in his unpublished Cambridge PhD dissertation (1972:181—2.215) that 1 Chron 29,11—12 stands behind the combination of δύναμις ("power"), πλοῦτος ("wealth"), ἰσχύς ("might"), and δόξα ("glory") and that the use of σοφία ("wisdom") is drawn from Dan 2,20 (in Dan 2,23 [Theod], "wisdom" is coupled with "power").

Beale mentions that the combination of the terms for "might", "honour", and "glory" is also found in Job 37,22—23 and 40,10.

of Revelation. Worship plays a central role in this book: The worship of God is set in the context of acknowledgement of him in particular deeds. "The paeans of praises are related to God's actions in history" (Rowland 1993:72).

It is within the context of the hymnic expressions of worship that the motif of power (δύναμις) functions in Revelation:

4,11   The elders honour God as Creator

5,12   The Lamb is worthy to receive the same worship of God, because of his redemptive work, which is hailed as the basis for the opening of the seals. He is the one who is to bring God's rule into effect on earth (cf Bauckham 1993:32).

7,12   God and the Lamb's sovereignty is proclaimed within the context of those who "... have washed their robes and made them white in the blood of the lamb" (7,14).

11,17 God is thanked for the demonstration of power and sovereignty in the face of the rage of the nations.

12,10 Salvation belongs to God and this is exemplified in the casting out of Satan from heaven.

19,1   The justice of God's judgements is praised, particularly with regard to the judgement of the harlot by a vast throng (cf Rowland 1993:72).

God (as well as the Lamb who was slain, 5,12) alone is to be worshipped as the source of all power and authority. Bauckham (1993:31—9) correctly points out that the vision of the one who sits on the throne (Rev 4) mixes cultic and political imagery. Cultic imagery is present as the throne room is the heavenly sanctuary (cf 11,19; 15,5—8), prototype of the earthly temple. In the worship of God and the Lamb by the whole creation (5,13) the eschatological goal of God's purpose for the creation is anticipated.

Political imagery is, however, also present in this passage, since the throne-room is the place from which God exercises his rule over the world. The twenty-four elders is a political, rather than cultic term. They are the angelic beings who compose the divine council (cf Is 24,23; Dan 7,9; 2 En 4,1; 4 QTLevi 3,8). They acknowledge that as created beings (4,11), they completely derive their authority from God. *God alone is to be worshipped as the source of all power and authority.*

It is noteworthy that the Roman Empire, like most political powers in the ancient world propagated its power also in religious terms (cf Bauckham

1993:34). It absolutised its power and claimed for itself the ultimate divine sovereignty over the world. There is therefore a conflict of sovereignties. It is noteworthy that this conflict of sovereignties is often portrayed in Revelation by references to worship. Rome's usurpation of divine rule (note 13,2 where it is stated that the dragon gave the beast[33] its power [δύναμιν])[34] is indicated by the universal worship of the beast (13,4.8.12), whereas the coming of God's kingdom is indicated by universal worship of God (15,3—4;[35] cf 19,5—6).

The line between those who worship the beast and those who worship God is drawn in the conflict of sovereignties. Through chapters 7—19 every stage of God's victory is accompanied by worship in heaven. Within this context the affirmation that the ultimate eschatological power (δύναμις) belongs to God alone, is reinterpreted in a way which directly affected the lives of the believers.[36]

In his critique of Roman power it is evident to John that if Christians are faithful witnesses to God, they have to suffer the inevitable clash between Rome's divine pretensions and their witness to the one and only God. The critique of Rome in Revelation follows from the vision of God's rule, power and justice in chapter 4.

> "For John and those who shared his prophetic insight, it was the Christian vision of the incomparable God, exalted above worldly power, which relativised Roman power and exposed Rome's pretensions to divinity as a dangerous delusion" (Bauckham 1993:39).

---

[33] Representing the military and political power of the Roman emperors.

[34] Cf also 17,13.

[35] After the hymnic expression of worship in verses 3 and 4, it is stated in verse 5 that the temple was opened in heaven ... and was filled with the smoke from the glory of God and from his power (ἐκ τῆς δυνάμεως αὐτοῦ)... (v 8).

[36] Cf also the author's pastoral concern reflected in 2,7.17.26—29; 3,5—6.12—13.21—22: the challenge to repent or stand firm (Rowland 1982:440).

Section C:

Theological Scope of the Concept of God's Power in the Pauline Letters

Chapter 23

Theological-Christological emphasis

23.1 Introduction

As stated in the introduction to this monograph, it is not the author's purpose to draw up a conclusive scheme into which all passages containing δύναμις neatly fit. The nature of Pauline theology simply does not allow this. It is typical of Pauline theology that the different themes are so intertwined that although they can be distinguished from one another, they cannot be separated. As will be pointed out below this is very much the case with Pauline theology and christology.

It may seem self-evident that the systematic section of a study of power in Pauline theology ought to commence with a discussion of God's *creative power*. In Paul's use of δύναμις it seems, however, that the creative dimension of God's power is not focused upon. This aspect does, however, play a role in the following cases: In Rom 1,20 the creative power of God is touched upon. As pointed out in the exegetical section δύναμις (qualified by ἀΐδιος) is used together with θειότης as a further qualification of God's invisible qualities which can be perceived from the works of creation. Δύναμις used in the context of the resurrection certainly also has the dimension of creative power (this will be discussed further in 24.2.2).

23.1.1 The "place" of the concept of God's power in Paul's message

Before proceeding with the discussion of the specific dimensions of power in Paul's letters, a few words may be said on the fundamental place of "power" in Paul's message. It needs to be emphasised that δύναμις describes the effect of Paul's divine message *on this world*. At the same time this power is associated with God, Christ and the Holy Spirit, because it is *God's power* in this world. Where Paul's message of the cross intersects this world, the message of "power" in Paul's letters finds its place.[1] This applies to the soteriological and ethical dimensions, as well as the pneumatological dimension of the concept of power. The Spirit is indeed *God's empowering presence* (Fee 1994) *in this world*. This also holds true for Paul's reflections on his own sufferings as an apostle: The many sufferings he had to endure in his service for Christ forced him to reflect on the power of God in the light of the realities of this world. Interpreted from the perspective of the cross and resurrection of Jesus the concept of power in his ministry obtains a very profound meaning. The concept of power belongs to the heart of Paul's message. It is his deepest conviction that the gospel has a decisive effect on people's lives. In the midst of the broken earthly existence (cf Gräbe 1994), experienced by Paul himself, he reflects on the divine power of the message he proclaims.[2]

23.2 Soteriological dimension

Key passages in which the power of God (δύναμις θεοῦ) occurs in the main Pauline letters focus on the soteriological dimension of Paul's use of δύναμις. The importance of Rom 1,16—17 and 1 Cor 1,18 is evident from the fact that in Rom 1,16—17 the programmatic thesis of this letter is stated. It has been pointed out above that 1 Cor 1,18 also has an important function within this letter as a whole (cf 7.4.2.1).

Paul's soteriology is in the first place *theocentrical*.[3] By means of the cross the God of Jesus Christ has come close to man and has brought man's fate to its decisive turning-point. In 1 Cor 1,18 and 24 as well as Rom 1,16 the power of God (δύναμις θεοῦ) is connected with Christ. Within a *soteriological* context Paul interprets the power of God *christologically*.

In relating the power of God to Christ, the *cross* is emphasised particularly, especially in 1 Cor 1,18 and 24. The gospel which centres in the (crucified) Christ as the power of God for salvation is viewed from two perspectives in Rom 1,16—17, and 1 Cor 1,18 and 24 respectively: in

---

[1] As Hotze (1997:342) pointed out, this is true for Paul's paradoxical passages in general: " 'Ort' der paulinischen Paradoxien ist also der *Schnittpunkt von irdischer Existenz und göttlicher Offenbarung, Zeit und Eschaton ... Gott und Welt*."

[2] Hotze (1997:343) points out that the paradoxical passages in Paul's letters "... sind gleichsam eine 'Feuerprobe' seines Evangeliums in der Begegnung mit der Welt".

[3] Cf Kertelge (1976:135): "Für die paulinische Kreuzestheologie ist die Gottesfrage 'ihr heimlicher Horizont und Ziel'."

Romans from the viewpoint of the rejection of justification through works of the law as a basis for salvation and in 1 Corinthians by the rejection of worldly wisdom as grounds for salvation. It is evident from 1 Cor 1,23—24 that Paul speaks of power and wisdom only within the framework of the theology of the cross. In both Romans and 1 Corinthians, Paul focuses on God's saving action in such a way as to exclude all boasting on the side of man. The polemical dimension of Paul's affirmations is evident. The crucified Christ becomes the expression of the incompatibility of the "way of the law" and "the way of faith".[4]

The power of God in both 1 Cor 1,18 and 24, as well as in Rom 1,16—17 is a power for salvation. Not the words of wisdom so highly esteemed in Corinth, but the message of the cross is God's power for salvation. The gospel is *not only a theoretical doctrine*, but *God's effective power of salvation* for those who believe.[5] Σωτηρία has to do with the salvation of man who has fallen under sin.[6] Sin is the deadly poison that has lead to death. In the discussion of 1 Cor 15,56 it has been pointed out that despite the fact that this group of words (law-sin-death) does not occur frequently in 1 Cor to describe the Corinthian behavioural aberrations, it is beyond question that Paul considered their action sinful and in need of divine forgiveness. The full explication of 1 Cor 15,55—57 emerges later in Paul's letter to the Romans.

To explain the salvific power of the gospel Paul describes it in Rom 1,17 as the righteousness of God (δικαιοσύνη θεοῦ) — how God puts people in the right relation with himself is revealed in the gospel as a matter of faith from beginning to end. In the light of Rom 3,25—26 it is clear that Paul grounds the righteousness of God in Christ's vicarious atoning death (cf Kertelge 1976:123—4). The salvific activity of God described by δικαιοσύνη θεοῦ occurs independently of the law as an act of sheer grace. It is a gift from God made possible by Christ's loving sacrificial death (Gal 2,21).

---

[4] Cf Käsemann (1967:16): "Für Paulus enthält Jesu Tod unwidersprechlich jenen Konflikt in sich, der seine Theologie zentral durch das unversöhnliche Gegeneinander von Gesetz und Evangelium charakterisiert."

[5] It has been pointed out in the exegetical section that the way in which the gospel is effective, its "Wirkungsweise", is described in Rom 1,16 by δύναμις, while its content is elaborated upon in terms of δικαιοσύνη θεοῦ.

[6] Cf Kertelge (1971:86—7). Friedrich (1980:862) affirms: "Gottes eschatologische Schöpfermacht ist imstande, durch das Evangelium Menschen aus ihrem Verderben zu erretten Röm 1,16; 1 Kor 1,18; 2,4f."

"The word of the cross" (1 Cor 1,18) is not merely a variation of the traditional early Christian statement concerning the atoning death of Christ, but in a specific sense its radicalization. The mystery of the cross of Jesus, which cannot be fully understood by man is accepted as God's self-revelation. In this way every effort to dissolve God's revelation in human wisdom is rejected (cf Kertelge 1976:125).

Paul's theology of the cross is a theology of salvation. And although Paul does not apply the principle of resurrection as a special theme in his theology of the cross, it is evident from the totality of his proclamation, that the death and resurrection of Jesus are most intimately connected to each other. Only because of his encounter with the risen Lord could Paul accept and proclaim the salvific significance of Jesus' death. Paul attaches importance to proclaiming Jesus not only as the Crucified *and* Risen, but especially as the *crucified Risen*. In his proclamation the assurance of Jesus' resurrection and its salvific significance is presupposed.[7]

While the gospel announces the saving power of God, this saving action of God becomes a reality in the existence of man through *faith* (Rom 1,16). Faith is the way in which man partakes in God's salvific actions in the present (Kertelge 1971:33). It is important to note that in 1 Cor 2,5 Paul grounds the Corinthians' faith on God's power (δύναμις) which he has related in the preceding verse to the Spirit. This *pneumatological* dimension of the power of God within a soteriological context (with specific reference to *faith*) must not be lost sight of.

23.2.1 Theology of the cross — message of justification, from Corinth to Rome

In 1 Cor the power of God is related to the *message of the cross*, while it is related in Romans to the gospel, described as the *righteousness of God*. Despite the mentioning of δικαιοσύνη in 1 Cor 1,30, the message of justification does not function in 1 Corinthians as in Romans and Galatians. Although the issue of a development in Paul's theology cannot be discussed here, much can be said for the thesis that Paul's message of justification was developed in the course of his missionary activity in the controversies regarding the value of the law and in conflict with his opponents in

---

[7] Cf Käsemann (1967:20): "Kreuz und Auferweckung werden ... auf engste verbunden, unterschiedbar, aber nicht voneinander zu scheiden."

different congregations (Söding 1997:157—8).[8] It is therefore not the case that the theology of the cross in Corinthians has to be interpreted in the light of a developed message of justification, but just the other way round: The message of justification is to be seen in the light of his theology of the cross. The crucial presupposition for the development of the message of justification is the interpretation of the gospel as *word of the cross*, as is done in 1 Corinthians (Söding 1997:157—8.180). It is important to note that in both letters this message of salvation — the word of the cross, developed in Romans as the message about the righteousness of God — is described as *God's power.*[9]

23.3 Ethical dimension

It is noteworthy that in 1 Cor 1,18—2,5 in which power (δύναμις) is used essentially soteriologically, a distinct *ethical* theme can also be observed. In which sense is "... the word of the cross the ... to us who are being saved the power of God" (1 Cor 1,18)? The crucified Christ (cf also 1 Cor 1,24) is the power of God in the sense that he has become for us "... righteousness and sanctification and redemption" (δικαιοσύνη τε καὶ ἁγιασμὸς καὶ ἀπολύτρωσις — 1 Cor 1,30).

The three closely associated concepts "righteousness", "sanctification" and "redemption" represent the whole process of salvation (cf 7.4.3).[10] In Pauline theology, soteriology and ethics are most closely related to one another. He views holiness as the proof of the reality of justification.[11] Ἀπολύτρωσις is used by Paul concerning the very essence of the gospel. It

---

[8] For a detailed discussion of the issue of a development in Paul's thought, cf Söding (1997:31—56).

[9] Although a certain development may be detected in the way Paul formulates his message throughout his missionary career, the firm conviction of the gospel as God's power remained unchanged (cf 1 Thess 1,5; Phil 3,10 and even the deutero-Pauline Eph 1,19; 3,16).

[10] Schelkle (1981:170) correctly affirms: "Nach Gehalt und Wesen wird das 'Heil' in Christus (Röm 1,16) weiter beschrieben als 'Gerechtigkeit, Heiligung und Erlösung' (1 Kor 1,20 [sic]) ... ".

[11] Cf Kertelge 1976:282: "In diesem Sinne läßt sich schließlich sogar sagen, daß es Paulus über die Rechtfertigung hinaus um die Heiligung geht, nicht als einen zweiten Akt nach der Rechtfertigung, *sondern als Erweis der Kraft des von ihm verkündeten Heilswerkes* ..." (emphasis: PJG).

refers to the redemption God offers through the death of his Son. It is God's merciful turning to man in need of salvation. As *abstractum pro concreto* ἀπολύτρωσις refers to Jesus Christ and the salvation brought by him for those who believe (cf Kertelge 1980b:332). In 1 Cor 1,30 Paul connects "sanctification" and "redemption" to "righteousness" (δικαιοσύνη). In this way he interpreted the tradition he received concerning the cross of Jesus in the sense of his message of justification.[12]

Justification is for Paul the result of Jesus' death and has as consequence the reign of God on earth (cf Käsemann 1967:23). Justification in Pauline theology also has ethical implications. This is also a dimension and consequence of the gospel (explained by the "righteousness of God" (δικαιοσύνη θεοῦ) as God's power. An implication of justification in Paul's message is that Christ takes control of believers' lives. The new relationship which God has established between himself and believing humanity is not a mere forensic issue but has a powerful effect. It is a relationship in which God's Lordship correlates with believing humanity's obedience.

Since a passage such as 2 Cor 12,9—10 not only applies to Paul's apostolic ministry, but also to his daily existence as a believer, it certainly has ethical consequences. An ethical dimension is also present in the notion of being strengthened by the Spirit in the "inner person", cf 24.2.3.

---

[12] Cf Käsemann (1967:20.23): "Er hat diese Rechtfertigungslehre vom Kreuze aus gewonnen, und sie ist umgekehrt seine Interpretation des Todes Jesu."

Chapter 24

Pneumatological emphasis

24.1 Introduction

In this chapter the attention will be drawn firstly to passages where "power" (δύναμις) is directly related to the Spirit (πνεῦμα), especially in connection with the preposition ἐν followed by the instrumental-associative dative, e g:

Rom 15,13: "by the power of the Holy Spirit" (ἐν δυνάμει πνεύματος ἁγίου)

Rom 15,19: "by the power of signs and wonders, by the power of the Holy Spirit" (ἐν δυνάμει σημείων καὶ τεράτων, ἐν δυνάμει πνεύματος)

cf also 1 Cor 2,4—5: "in demonstration of the Spirit and of power" (ἐν ἀποδείξει πνεύματος καὶ δυνάμεως ... ἐν δυνάμει θεοῦ); 1 Thess 1,5: "in power and in the Holy Spirit ..." (ἐν δυνάμει καὶ ἐν πνεύματι ἁγίῳ ...)

The second section of this chapter will be devoted to passages where the concept of power is not explicitly connected to the Spirit, but where the context makes it clear that this is indeed the case.

24.2 "Power" explicitly connected with the Spirit

24.2.1 The power of the Holy Spirit to enkindle hope

Rom 15,13 forms the conclusion of Paul's exhortations in Rom 14 and 15,1—13. It brings the main body of the letter (Rom 1,18—15,13) to a hope-filled climax (cf Heil 1987:3). The twofold reference to hope in this verse (as well as in the previous verse) is noteworthy. The epistle to the Romans has clearly shown that hope is an essential characteristic of the believer. In the prayer wish of Rom 15,13 Paul prays that the Romans' hope may continue to grow *by the power of the Holy Spirit.* Paul has shown in Rom 8 that because the life promised to those who are righteous by faith is a life characterised by the indwelling of the Holy Spirit, it is also a life characterised by hope. The phrase "by the power of the Holy Spirit" (ἐν δυνάμει πνεύματος ἁγίου) indicates that the realisation of this hope in man is no human possibility, but the creation of the Spirit of God.

The early church saw the presence of the Holy Spirit among them as a pledge that a climax had been reached in God's design and that a future consummation was to be looked for.[1] The Spirit's presence in God's people is a deposit, guaranteeing what is to come (ἀρραβών — 2 Cor 1,22; 5,5; Eph 1,14). Those who are in Christ have the "first fruits of the Spirit" (τὴν ἀπαρχὴν τοῦ πνεύματος — Rom 8,23) (Engelbrecht 1969:68—70; Hamilton 1957:19—21; Kuss 1959:574). By putting his Spirit in the hearts of the believers, God sets his seal of ownership upon them (ὁ καὶ σφραγισάμενος ἡμᾶς ... [2 Cor 1,22; cf also Eph 1,13; 4,30]). All these metaphors convey the conviction that the presence of the Spirit now is a guarantee of the fulfilment of God's purposes in the end.[2]

---

[1] Schweizer (1959:420) refers to the πνεῦμα as "Zeichen des Kommenden". He correctly proceeds: "Seit dem Ereignis der Auferstehung Jesu ist die Auferstehung am Ende der Zeiten nicht mehr unbestimmte Hoffnung; die Wirklichkeit des gegenwärtigen Geistes bürgt für die Wirklichkeit des Kommenden."

In his essay on the Holy Spirit, Barrett (1970:1—9) commences with the concept of eschatology and points to the importance of this concept for the whole Bible, especially for the New Testament (and also first-century Judaism). He places his discussions of the Holy Spirit within this context by putting the question, "... what is the context of the hoped for end?" He proceeds (1970:4 ff): "Part of the answer to this question is, the Holy Spirit. This hope is contained in the Old Testament, for example in Ezek. xxxvii, where the vision of the valley of the dry bones leads up to the promise, 'I will put my spirit in you, and ye shall live'; in Joel ii,28—32, the passage quoted in the account in Acts ii of the day of the Pentecost; and in Is. xi,2 'The spirit of the Lord shall rest upon him'. The same hope was taken up and developed in Judaism, for example in the belief that God would renew the gift of prophecy. It is present also in the New Testament ... Paul makes this point particularly clear. He describes the Spirit as first fruits [Rom. viii,23]. Those who have received the Spirit have received a partial fulfilment of God's promise, but they are thereby encouraged to look forward to the fullness which still lies ahead. The same point is made in II Cor. i,22; v,5 ... ."

[2] Moule (1978:34) mentions that the Dead Sea Sectarians (contrary to other types of Judaism at that time) also saw the presence of the Holy Spirit among them as pointing to a climax that had been reached in God's plan and that a future consummation was to be expected.

Although the new era has dawned with Christ's coming[3] and the power
of the Spirit is already a reality in the present, the old dispensation has not
yet been destroyed. Our reflection on the Holy Spirit in the context of
Pauline theology brings us to the heart of the tension between the "already"
and the "not yet".[4]

It is the present experience of the *Spirit* which gives Christians the *sure
hope*[5] that their salvation and sonship will be perfected in glory in the end
through the same Spirit (Rom 8,23—24; cf Gal 3,3 with Phil 1,6), for it is
the same Spirit who even here and now is busy transforming Christians into
the very image of the Lord "with ever-increasing glory" (2 Cor 3,18). The
Spirit himself is the presently enjoyed part of the whole which is yet to be
realised (Dunn 1970—71:37). In this period between the ages the hope of
glory is kept alive in the people of God by the ministry of the Spirit (Bruce
1977:284; cf also Benjamin 1976:47; Meyer 1979:11).[6]

24.2.2 The Holy Spirit empowering Paul's apostolic ministry

In *Rom 15,19* and its immediate context the reader finds the characteristics
of Paul's apostolate in a nutshell (Nielsen 1980:151). What Paul has done
as the servant (λειτουργός) of Christ Jesus, has been something which

---

[3] Cf Schweizer (1978:148): "*Was die Propheten für die Endzeit erwartet haben, ist ja
nach dem Glauben der neutestamentlichen Gemeinde in Jesus schon erfüllt.*"

[4] Cf Versteeg (1971:392): "*Ondánks het delen in het heil in het heden blijft er een
perspektief open naar de toekomst. Positief is het ook zo te zeggen: Juist op grond ván het
delen in het heil in het heden blijft er een perspektief open naar de toekomst.*"

Also Kuss (1959:574) emphasises the tension between the "already" and the "not yet"
in Pauline pneumatology: "*Das Pneuma ist so die 'Sphäre' in welcher sich das Leben derer
vollzieht, die auf Grund von Glauben ihre ganze Hoffnung auf das Heilsgut setzen; denn
mag das Heil auch da sein — und es ist eben so da, daß das Pneuma da ist — so bleibt es
doch in seiner Vollendung wieder erst zu erwarten. Die Existenz der Glaubenden wird
durch Geist, Glaube und Hoffnung bestimmt: 'Denn wir erwarten durch Geist auf Grund
von Glauben die Hoffnung [das Hoffnungsgut] der Gerechtigkeit' [Gal 5,5] ... Der Besitz
des Geistes ist das Heil, und er ist die Garantie des kommenden Vollendungsheiles, der
eschatologischen Erfüllung.*"

[5] Louw and Nida (1988a:296) describe the meaning of ἐλπίζω; ἐλπίς ... as follows:
"... to look forward with confidence to that which is good and beneficial ...".

[6] Cf also Wendland (1952:458—9): "Ist aber das Pneuma Vergegenwärtigung des
Eschaton, so schenkt es auch die Gewißheit der Auferstehung und des ewigen Lebens
[Röm. 8, 10f; 8,2; 2. Kor. 3,4ff] ... Die Hoffnung trägt pneumatischen Charakter wie
umgekehrt das Pneuma den Charakter der Erwartung: durch den Geist erwarten wir das
Hoffnungsgut der Gerechtigkeit [Gal. 5,5]. Diese Hoffnung aber ist Gewißheit, nicht ein
vages menschliches Träumen und Ersehnen ... ."

Christ has actually himself effected, working through his minister. Paul's ministry, or more accurately, this working of Christ through him in word and deed in order to lead the Gentiles to obey God is further qualified in verse 19: "... by the power of signs and wonders, by the power of the Holy Spirit" (ἐν δυνάμει σημείων καὶ τεράτων, ἐν δυνάμει πνεύματος). The emphasis has now shifted to the Holy Spirit. Paul's ministry is characterised as powerfully confirmed and attested by accompanying miracles, as accomplished as a whole in the power of the Holy Spirit. As pointed out in the exegetical section, it may be agreed with Käsemann (1980:379) that the focus is here on the apostolic preaching, which is accompanied by miracles (cf also Heb 2,4).

1 Cor 2,1—5 is an illustration (taken from Paul's apostolic ministry) of the thesis that God repudiated the wisdom of the world in the events on the cross (cf Klauck 1984:26). The contrast between worldly wisdom and Godly wisdom/power is the central idea of this pericope. The expression "in demonstration of the Spirit and of power" (ἐν ἀποδείξει πνεύματος καὶ δυνάμεως) underlines the contradiction of worldly and Godly wisdom. Paul points away from himself and his own abilities to the *Spirit as the only power in which his ministry is performed*, with the specific purpose "... that your faith might not rest in the wisdom of men but in the power of God" (v 5). The confirmation of the truth of Paul's message is neither the result of nor demanded by logical premises, but brought about by God himself, through the Spirit.[7] Paul understood his apostolic activity as a manifestation of God's Spirit. The Spirit gives him confidence in his missionary preaching and he ascribes the success of his preaching to the power of the Spirit (cf Schnackenburg 1978:186).

---

[7] Under the heading, "πνεῦμα als Kraft der πίστις", Schweizer (1959:422—3) affirms: "Die Wunderkraft πνεῦμα bestimmt Inhalt und Form der Verkündigung ... Was aber ist der Inhalt dieser pneumatischen Belehrung? ... Das Heilshandeln Gottes am Kreuz". According to 1 Cor 1,24 the σοφία θεοῦ, which is revealed through the πνεῦμα according to 1 Cor 2,7—10, is nothing else than the Χριστός ἐσταυρωμένος (1,23; 2,2). The Spirit is the power, "... die den Menschen 'diesen Aeon' entnimmt und in jenen Aeon versetzt."

Also Knoch (1975:86) mentions that Paul is convinced, "... daß sein Dienst als Apostel nicht den rein menschlichen Versuch darstellt, 'durch wortgewandte Überredungskunst' Menschen von der Wahrheit des Evangeliums zu überzeugen, sondern 'einen Erweis von [göttlichem] Geist und [göttlicher] Kraft' [1 Kor 2,4] bildet. Darum kann er auch behaupten, daß der Glaube seiner Gemeinden 'sich nicht auf menschliche Weisheit stützt, sondern auf die Kraft Gottes' [1 Kor 2,5]."

The power of the Holy Spirit in Paul's apostolic ministry can only be understood in the light of the fact that Pauline pneumatology is inseparable from his theology and christology. The work of the Holy Spirit is based upon God's act of salvation through Jesus Christ.[8]

In Pauline theology the Spirit of God is conceived of as the effective agent of the power of God (Easly 1984:312; cf also Barrett 1970:8). The power the believer has through his relationship with the living God becomes *a reality in the present through the Holy Spirit* (Hahn 1979:430). The Spirit is that power of inner life (cf Gloël 1888:181), elevated far above all the merely ritual and outward elements of religion and causes faith in God and worship of God to become *existentially real* (Dunn 1975:201). "Der Heilige Geist ist im neutestamentlichen Denken die Kategorie der Gegenwart"[9] (Wendland 1952:466; cf also Niederwinner 1972:15: "... im Geist ist das Eschaton gegenwärtig"[10]).

The Spirit opens up new dimensions[11] which are closed to the mind of natural man. In this way he reveals a wisdom of a completely different nature. This knowledge is of vital importance for believers, as it concerns the reality of God's power of salvation (cf Hahn 1979:431 note 47). The message of the cross bears the signs of humility. But in its weak external form which cannot compete with the "plausible words of wisdom" ($\pi\varepsilon\iota\theta o\hat{\imath}$

---

[8] Cf Schlier (1974:119): "Geist Gottes ist Gott selbst in ... seiner Heilsgeheimnis offenbarenden Macht ... Er ist dies als die Jesus Christus in seiner Wahrheit vergegenwärtigende Kraft. In ihm ist der Geist ... in die Welt ... eingebrochen."

Wendland (1952:464—5) also points to this close relation between God, Christ and the power of the Spirit in Paul's ministry: "*Christus* wirkt durch Paulus ἐν δυνάμει πνεύματος [Rom 15,19]; [vgl. 1. Kor. 2,4]; Gal. 3,5 ... Im Geist ist der erhöhte Christus als Kraftspender gegenwärtig; diese Kraft ist *Gottes* Kraft ... Sie wirkt auf dem Weg der neuen Gottesoffenbarung, d.h. durch das Evangelium vom Kreuz [1. Kor. 1,18.24], wie denn der Auferstandene und Erhöhte der Gekreuzigte ist und bleibt" (emphasis:PJG).

[9] "The Holy Spirit is in New Testament thought the category of the present."

[10] "In the Spirit the eschaton is a present reality."

[11] To those who in faith and obedience accept what the Spirit says through the gospel, the Holy Spirit opens up a new dimension, "... die Heils- und Herrschaftsdimension Christi ... Er öffnet uns Gottes Gerechtigkeit und d.i. seine Gnade, und gewährt uns seinen unbegreiflichen, unsagbaren und unmachbaren Frieden, der als Gabe des Geistes unser Herz und Denken in Hut nimmt ..." (Schlier 1974:124.126).

Knoch (1975:97) correctly concludes: "Der Geist Gottes ist ... das eigentliche Lebensprinzip der christlichen Existenz als Grundentwurf und Norm des Lebens und Handelns wie auch als Antrieb und gestaltende Kraft. Gerade dies gezeigt und dargestellt zu haben, ist das Verdienst der Lehre des Paulus vom Wirken des Heiligen Geistes im Christen."

σοφίας λόγοι) its internal power becomes visible. This is what is meant by the phrase "in demonstration of the Spirit and of power" (ἐν ἀποδείξει πνεύματος καὶ δυνάμεως). Of crucial importance is the intimate connection between the "message about the cross" and the Spirit which generates faith and reveals the mystery of God (cf Hahn 1979:431 note 47).

The Spirit fills and moves the preacher of the gospel, it supports his activity in an extraordinary way. Rom 15,19 (cf also 1 Thess 1,5; 2 Cor 12,12) makes it clear that the ministry of Christ through Paul which led the gentiles to obey God was conducted not only with words, but also "... by the power of signs and miracles, through the power of the Spirit". The specific charismatic activity of the Spirit brings the truth of the gospel of salvation through faith alone and without the works of the law, closer to real life (cf Kuss 1959:551). As Rand (1980:209) correctly observes, there was a power at work accompanying the preacher and having an effect which was additional to the preaching and which was different from the persuasiveness of the preacher and the force of logic in his words and arguments.[12]

24.2.3 The power of the Holy Spirit in the inner person

In his prayer for the Ephesians (3,16—17) Paul prays that God may grant the Ephesians to be strengthened with power through his Spirit in the inner person and that Christ may dwell in their hearts through faith. In the light of Paul's interpretation of "power" in terms of the Spirit in this verse, it may be concluded that the power of the Spirit is also in view in verse 20 as well as 1,19. The power of the Spirit in the *Corpus Paulinum* is not only for visible and extraordinary manifestations of God's presence, but also for the empowering necessary to be his people in the world, bringing forth the fruit of the Spirit in their lives and so reflecting the character of God as it is disclosed to us in his Son.[13]

---

[12] Cf Kuss (1959:552): "Auch in Korinth bestanden nach 1 Kor 2,4 'das Wort' und 'die Verkündigung' des Apostels ... 'nicht in überredenden Weisheitsworten, sondern im Erweis von Geist und Kraft' ... auch für 1 Kor 2,4 [sind] außerordentliche Erscheinungen, Wunder nicht auszuschließen ... wenngleich die gesamte geisterfüllte Missionstätigkeit in allen ihren Äußerungen gemeint sein wird."

[13] Cf Fee 1994:695—7. Also Stuhlmacher (1992:355) emphasises in his discussion of Paul's understanding of the Spirit: "Der Hl. Geist ist ... die *Kraft und Norm des neuen Wandels* ...".

24.3 The power of God closely related to the Spirit

24.3.1 The pneumatological substratum of God's power in Paul's ministry

2 Cor 4,7

In the exegetical section it has been pointed out that Paul's statement in 2 Cor 4,7 should be interpreted in the light of the broader context, including the previous pericope, 2 Cor 3,4—4,6. The antithetical structure is a very prominent characteristic of both 2 Cor 3,4—4,6 and 4,7—5,10. In the discussion of the latter pericope a whole series of contrasting concepts has been listed. Two categories may be discerned, namely the category of what can be *seen* and the category of the *unseen*. To the category of what can be seen may be ascribed: The outward man, the present sufferings, transitoriness, the earthly vessel, the veiled face, the letter that kills and finally Jesus' sufferings in death. To the category of the unseen belong: the inward man, salvation in the midst of sufferings, the eternal and lasting, the valuable treasure, the heart and the Spirit as well as the life of Jesus (cf Klauck 1986:48).

It is precisely from the tension between these two categories that Paul's statement concerning the *all-surpassing power* gains its full meaning. The fact that this *treasure* (belonging to the second, eschatological category) is contained in *jars of clay* (a concept belonging to the first this-worldly category) has a specific purpose: "... to show that the all-surpassing power belongs to God and not to us" (ἵνα ἡ ὑπερβολὴ τῆς δυνάμεως ᾖ τοῦ θεοῦ καὶ μὴ ἐξ ἡμῶν).

Although the Spirit is not often mentioned explicitly in 2 Cor 4,7—5,10,[14] Paul's affirmation in 2 Cor 5,5 is of crucial importance as far as the interpretation of this pericope is concerned: "Now it is God who has prepared us for this very purpose" (for the life which shall engulf our mortality [v 4]), "... by giving us the Spirit as a deposit, guaranteeing what is to come". It is the Spirit who guarantees that what belongs to the eschatological sphere will not be overwhelmed by this world or by the sufferings the apostles have to endure in it. Paul's affirmation concerning the *all-surpassing power* that *is from God*, therefore, has an important *pneumatological substratum*.

---

[14] In 2 Cor 3,4—4,6 the Spirit is, however, often mentioned explicitly: 3,6 (2x); 3,8; 3,17 (2x); 3,18.

2 Cor 6,7

In stressing the hardships accompanying the apostolic ministry Paul makes it very clear that his ministry is solely dependent on the power of God. Among the hardships Paul enumerates, the reader suddenly encounters a short list of virtues (related to "through great endurance" [ἐν ὑπομονῇ πολλῇ] in v 4). Of these eight expressions (connected with ἐν) the last, ἐν δυνάμει θεοῦ, provides an apt summary. The Pauline apostolate is commended as an agency through which God's power is made manifest and in which the Holy Spirit is at work. Apart from the explicit reference to the Holy Spirit (ἐν πνεύματι ἀγίῳ), ἐν γνώσει ("by knowledge") points to a gift of the Holy Spirit and the phrases ἐν μακροθυμίᾳ, ἐν χρηστότητι and ἐν ἀγάπῃ ἀνυποκρίτῳ ("by forbearance", "by kindness" and "by genuine love") refer to the fruit of the Holy Spirit present in Paul's ministry (cf 1 Cor 12,8; Gal 5,22).

The way in which *God's power* is realised in *Paul's apostolic ministry* is therefore explained *pneumatologically.*

24.3.2 The pneumatological dimension of God's resurrection power

Rom 8,11, 1 Cor 6,14 and 15,43 make it very clear that God is the author of the resurrection — of both the resurrection of Christ and the eschatological resurrection of the believer.

Two very important aspects of God's act of resurrection are emphasised by Paul:

1 It happens with *power.*

2 The *Spirit* plays a crucial role in this event.[15]

In the context of the resurrection, *God's life-giving and creative power* is closely related to the Spirit.

Paul bases the reality of God's resurrection of those who are "in Christ" on the reality of Jesus' resurrection. From the *reality* of Jesus' resurrection Paul deduces the eschatological *reality* of the resurrection of those who are in Christ Jesus (Wilckens 1980:134).

The Spirit (πνεῦμα) and power (δύναμις) are closely related to each other in the context of the resurrection. In Rom 8,11 Paul states: "... he

---

[15] Although God is the subject of the resurrection "... deze levendmaking staat tegelijk in onlosmakelijk verband met de Geest ..." (Versteeg 1971:374—5; cf also Engelbrecht 1969:67).

who raised Christ Jesus from the dead will give life to your mortal bodies *through the Spirit who dwells in you*",[16] while 1 Cor 6,14 reads: "And God ... will also raise us *by his power*".[17]

In the pericope to which 1 Cor 15,43 belongs, the eschatological new creation is contrasted with the imperfection of the present world. "Power" (δύναμις) together with "immortality" (in the sense of imperishable — ἀφθαρσία) and "glory" (δόξα) belongs to this eschatological new creation. As pointed out in the exegetical section, the antithesis "sown in weakness, raised in power", receives special emphasis due to its position at the end of colon group A. It is noteworthy that in the colon following immediately on Paul's affirmation ἐγείρεται ἐν δυνάμει ("raised in power"), the Spirit emerges as the crucial factor pertaining to the eschatological creation.[18]

24.3.3 The kingdom of God anticipated in the present through the power of the Holy Spirit

The role of the Holy Spirit in the interpretation of power in 1 Cor 4,20 has been pointed out in the exegetical section. The power with which the kingdom of God works, is the power of the Holy Spirit (cf Rom 14,17), by which God's purpose is put into effect and the future is anticipated in the present. Paul indeed combines the already of the eschatological events with the expression of power (δύναμις) (Nielsen 1980:156).

---

[16] ... ὁ ἐγείρας Χριστὸν ἐκ νεκρῶν ζωοποιήσει καὶ τὰ θνητὰ σώματα ὑμῶν διὰ τοῦ ἐνοικοῦντος αὐτοῦ πνεύματος ἐν ὑμῖν.
The Spirit is here obviously regarded as the true resurrecting force. For us he is the pledge that we shall be made like the resurrected Christ. Wilckens (1980:134) poignantly remarks: "Der Geist als πνεῦμα ζωοποιοῦν ... verbindet uns in unserer irdischen Gegenwart mit dem Auferstandenen, so daß seine Kraft in uns allen Kräften der σάρξ ἁμαρτίας überlegen ist."

[17] ὁ δὲ θεὸς ... καὶ ἡμᾶς ἐξεγερεῖ διὰ τῆς δυνάμεως αὐτοῦ.

[18] Cf Wolff 1982:201: "... das Pneuma wirkt in der Gegenwart auf die kommende Herrlichkeit hin, die sich wiederum ganz dem Pneuma verdankt".
J P Versteeg (1971:389—90) also underlines the fact that in 1 Corinthians Paul emphatically mentions the eschatological character of the Spirit: "De pregnante uitdrukking daarvan wordt gegeven in de woorden van vers 45, dat de laatste Adam [een] levendmakende Geest geworden is. De Geest is voor Paulus verbonden aan de opgestane Christus als de laatste Adam. Uit deze verbondenheid van de Geest aan de láátste Adam, blijkt onmiskenbaar het eschatologisch karakter van de Geest." The relationship between the resurrected Christ and the Spirit in a passage such as this must be seen as an eschatological oneness: "Het is een eenheid betrokken op het eschaton. In de opstanding van Christus is het eschaton gerealiseerd en door de Geest wordt het eschaton gerealiseerd" (1971:381).

Schnackenburg (1961:202—3) correctly points out that the kingdom of God (βασιλεία τοῦ θεοῦ) in 1 Cor 4,20 may not be interpreted in a sense referring to the future. Although the apostolic existence and experience point to the fact that the full revelation of the kingdom of God is not yet a present reality, the kingdom of God already reveals itself in the power of the Spirit of God (cf 2,1—5). The fact that the kingdom of God already becomes visible in the present through powerful demonstrations (in the activity of God's Spirit) is a conviction Paul shared with the whole early church.

The relationship existing between the Spirit and the kingdom of God, is an important one: The Spirit not only guarantees its full inheritance; he is himself the beginning and first part of that inheritance: "... the kingdom of God is not a matter of eating and drinking, but of righteousness, peace and joy in the Holy Spirit" (Rom 14,17). οὐ γὰρ ἐν λόγῳ ἡ βασιλεία τοῦ θεοῦ ἀλλ' ἐν δυνάμει — "the kingdom of God does not consist in talk, but in the power of the Holy Spirit" (1 Cor 4,20).

24.4 Conclusion

Paul's pneumatology — especially as it emerges through this study of power (δύναμις) — is deeply rooted in the Old Testament message about the רוח יהוה (cf chapter 2, especially 2.4). Themes such as the empowerment of a servant of God for a specific task, the Spirit and the *eschaton*, the Spirit and God's recreative power and the Spirit referring to God in his relation to mankind, communicating with and revealing himself to his creatures are also central themes in Pauline pneumatology.

The study of the power of the Spirit reveals *two main emphases*: an *eschatological* emphasis and a dimension of the *present*. The experience of the Spirit kindles in the Christian a sure and confident hope, as the Spirit is a guarantee of the fulfilment of God's purposes in the *eschaton*. Both the resurrection of Christ and the eschatological resurrection of the believer are closely related to the power of the Spirit.

The Spirit, however, not only relates to the *eschaton*, but is also the category of the *present*. The relationship with the living God has a powerful effect on the believers' life *in the present* through the Holy Spirit. God's kingdom is anticipated in the present by the power of the Holy Spirit.

Power in *Paul's ministry* is also characterised by these two dimensions, the eschatological and the present. He not only knows the Spirit's powerful confirmation of his preaching by accompanying miracles, but also the power of God through the Spirit in the midst of terrible hardships. His ministry as a whole is accomplished in the power of the Spirit because it is the Spirit who opens up new dimensions which are closed to the mind of natural humankind (cf Gräbe 1992:226—35).

Chapter 25

Paul's ministry within the christological perspective on weakness and power

25.1 The catalogues of hardships as horizon for the understanding of power in Paul's ministry

It is noteworthy that in three of the pericopes in which Paul reflects on power he also mentions the hardships which beset his ministry: 2 Cor 4,7—5,10; 6,3—10; 11,16—12,10.

"Peristasis" catalogues were a traditional means of demonstrating virtue in Hellenistic times (cf the extensive study of Fitzgerald [1988] and also Ebner [1991]). Since the "peristasis" catalogue was an established device for distinguishing true philosophers from false ones, it provided Paul with a tool in his task of establishing himself as a true apostle. His use of these catalogues shows that he is familiar with the traditions about the sage and the means used to depict him. Paul's own use of "peristasis" catalogues is, however, highly creative. It is also influenced by Old Testament traditions about the afflicted righteous man and suffering prophet (cf Kleinknecht 1988). The most important aspect of Paul's "peristasis"-catalogues is, however, the fact that they are transformed by his fixation on the *cross of Christ*. These catalogues present the convergence of several traditions and reflect Paul's own personal experiences of *suffering and divine power*. They take us to the centre of his understanding of God as well as his own self-understanding, yet anchor him in the culture and conventions of his time (Fitzgerald 1988:206—7; cf also Klauck 1996:77—113; Hotze 1997:56—9.70).

Within the context of the catalogues of hardships Paul emphasises a very important (critical) aspect of his understanding of power (δύναμις). All power and all confidence entirely belong to God and may in no way be ascribed to human achievement. The catalogues of hardships are aimed at the same crucial insight as the message about justification and the "word of the cross", namely to exclude all human self-confidence and boasting. While the message about justification and the message about the cross focus on the "iustitia aliena" and "sapientia aliena" (Rom 1,16—17; 1 Cor 1,18—2,5), the emphasis falls in the context of Paul's sufferings on the "vis aliena", the "virtus aliena", the "vita aliena" (cf Schrage 1974:152). This may further be illustrated by a look at the pericopes in which "power" (δύναμις) is used in the context of the catalogues of hardships.

The main point Paul wants to make in *2 Cor 4,7* is that the frailty of the apostles is a demonstration of the essential point *that this all-surpassing power is God's and is not from us*. The catalogue of hardships in 4,8 and 9 has been formulated in a series of antitheses, and (as has been pointed out in the exegetical part) this serves to illustrate not just the weakness of apostles but the way in which that weakness discloses the incomparable power of God. Paul emphasises in 2 Cor 4,7 that power comes from God alone and may only be expected from him. The power and life which are bestowed on those who suffer are nothing else than the "life of Jesus" (2 Cor 4,10) (cf Schrage 1974:152—3).

It has been pointed out in the notes on the structure of *2 Cor 6,3—10* that the phrases ἐν πνεύματι ἁγίῳ, ἐν ἀγάπῃ ἀνυποκρίτῳ and ἐν λόγῳ ἀληθείας receive special emphasis and that both the climax and summary are expressed by ἐν δυνάμει θεοῦ. The hardships mentioned in verses 4—5 are contrasted with the "powers" in verses 6—7 which enable Paul to stand fast and conquer in the midst of suffering. The accentuation of the hardships accompanying the apostolic ministry in this pericope has an important function. By stressing the hardships, Paul points away from the apostles and their own competence to God and his power. The apostles are tools in the hand of God who are aware of the fact that they are being borne by the power and Spirit of God in the midst of the hardships and distress accompanying their ministry. 2 Cor 6,3—10 is a characterization from an eschatological point of view of power in Paul's apostolic ministry parallel to 2 Cor 4,7 (Bultmann 1976:171).

2 Cor 11,16—12,10 is of crucial importance to our present study. The catalogue of hardships fulfils a very important function in Paul's development of the leading motifs in this pericope: boasting, weakness and power. The larger catalogue of hardships (11,23—28) leads to the conclusion: Εἰ καυχᾶσθαι δεῖ, τὰ τῆς ἀσθενείας μου καυχήσομαι (2 Cor 11,30). The smaller catalogue (2 Cor 12,9b—10) leads to the same conclusion (expressed by the ἵνα-phrase: *so that Christ's power may rest on me*), interpreted now in the light of the Lord's answer in 12,9.[1] "Power" (δύναμις) and "weakness" (ἀσθένεια) are closely related. The key to the understanding of this relationship, which seems paradoxical at first glance, is to be found in the motif "grace" (χάρις). Χάρις is a central concept in Pauline theology that most clearly expresses his understanding of the salvation event as an act of wholly unmerited generosity on God's part. For Paul grace means power, a power at work in and through the believer's life, the experience of God's Spirit (cf Dunn 1975:202—3).[2] Grace does not manifest itself only in particular compartments of the believer's life. There is a dimension to the believer's existence which determines all (Rom 5,2; 1 Cor 10,26), there is an energizing of his existence of whose God is the source (cf 2 Cor 12,9). "Grace gives the believer's life both its source, its power and its direction" (Dunn 1975:205).

25.2 The christological perspective within the context of the "eschatological tension"[3]

In chapter 24 the reality of the power of the Holy Spirit (including the charismatic dimension) in Paul's apostolic ministry has been emphasised. This is an integral aspect of power in his ministry, but needs to be

---

[1] In his article, "Too weak not to lead: The form and function of 2 Cor 11.23b—33", Andrews emphasises that Paul willingly submits to hardships and in this way lowers himself socially. By being weak as a populist who accommodates the people, he claims leadership of the Corinthian Christians. Andrews is of the opinion that the catalogue of chapter 11 differs greatly from other catalogues in Paul (1 Cor 4,9—13; 2 Cor 4,7—12; 6,3—10). While some type of battle against or endurance of the hardships is evident in these previous lists, no such embattlement or endurance is found in 2 Cor 11,23b—33 (Andrews 1995:273 n 43).

Lambrecht (1997:289) however correctly points out that Andrews neglects the implicit but unmistakable presence in this catalogue of Paul's endurance and especially in verses 27—29 his positive stand. He also fails to view 11,23b—33 within the broader context comprising also 12,9—10. Also in this context Paul is convinced that in the midst of his weakness and while suffering afflictions and tribulations, God's extraordinary power and the life of Jesus are made visible in him (cf 4,7—11) (Lambrecht 1997:290).

[2] The pneumatological dimension of 2 Cor 12,7—9 must not be neglected or forgotten. Schnackenburg (1978:185) correctly affirms that Paul's call to the Lord "… war doch gewiß ein Gebet im Heiligen Geist, dem Geist der Sohnschaft".

[3] Cf Dunn's (1998:482—7) discussion of the concept of "sharing Christ's sufferings" within the context of the eschatological tension in Paul's theology.

complemented by the christological view he holds on power.[4] This christological perspective serves as necessary criticism of a possible "enthusiastic" misunderstanding of power.

In 2 Cor 4,7—12, 11,16—12,10 and 13,1—4 Paul clearly portrays the weaknesses (hardships) he experienced in every day life. The weakness of the Christian and especially the apostles is, however, not viewed negatively, but positively as the area in which God's power is paradoxically at work (Siber 1971:174).

Paul interprets weakness and power in his ministry in a fundamentally *christological* sense. The understanding of the crucifixion as the event in which Christ proved radically "weak" is the basis of Paul's discussion. In the case of the crucifixion and resurrection, weakness and power constitute an indivisible unity. By raising Christ, God's power was effected and manifested in the face of that ultimate "weakness" which the crucifixion meant. The apostolic ministry undertaken on Christ's behalf involves participation in this weakness and power of Calvary and Easter. It is against this background that Paul, in 2 Cor 12,9, can boast of that "weakness" which, by aligning him with Christ's death, causes him to experience the

---

[4] Paul's opponents in Corinth considered a proclamation of Christ, produced by the Spirit and filled with power, as essential. Paul accepts this underlying conception of an apostle (cf 2 Cor 12,12), but interprets the resulting image of an apostle in a very different manner. "Christ himself must be proclaimed as crucified, and only in the second place as risen in the life of the one who proclaims [cf 13,3f], or better, Christ wants to show his power of life to those who receive the gospel, primarily through the weakness of the herald" (Schnackenburg 1970:298).

power of the resurrection.[5] Suffering with Christ is *the* way in which taking part in Christ in the present manifests itself (Siber 1971:174).[6] Paul's own weakness, which was clearly manifest, was the stage upon which the power of God in Christ was at work. This power of Christ became visible in miracles, in Paul's preaching and in the conversion of sinners. In his ministry through power in weakness Paul is a representation of the crucified and resurrected Lord. His apostolic ministry is wholly grounded in and accompanied by God's grace (χάρις). Through grace the power of Christ which triumphs in weakness is revealed in the life of the apostle (cf Stöger 1985:149).

Paul speaks of dying with Christ as a past event and as a continuing aspect of Christian existence (Tannehill 1967:127; Dunn 1998:484—5).[7] Through dying with Christ, the Christian has been released from the old world and has entered the new. If this were all Paul wished to say about God's eschatological act, he could only speak of dying with Christ as something which has already happened to the Christians. But the old world has not yet accepted God's judgement of and claim to it, and the Christian

---

[5] Cf 2 Cor 4,7—12: The idea of "weakness", frailty, vulnerability, mortality we find in ἐν ὀστρακίνοις σκεύεσιν (4,7) seems to be taken up in the expressions ἐν τῷ σώματι ἡμῶν (4,10) and ἐν τῇ θνητῇ σαρκὶ ἡμῶν (4,11). At the same time the ἵνα-clauses in these verses possess something of a conclusion, pointing to the purpose and consequence of what has been said. The purpose-clause of 4,11b, like the one it parallels in 4,10b, refers to the manifestation of the *resurrection life of Jesus (and thus of the all-surpassing power of God [4,7b])* in and through the weakness, suffering, and death of Jesus borne by the apostle.

Tannehill (1967:84) also correctly comments: "The 'life of Jesus' of which Paul speaks in vs. 10 corresponds to the 'power of God' of vs. 7. Just as the power of God manifests itself in the experiences of physical deliverance summed up in vss. 8—9, so this 'life of Jesus' manifests itself 'in our body', that is, in these same experiences of physical deliverance. Thus the 'life of Jesus' is another way of referring to this divine power. This is supported by the fact that in vs. 12 Paul speaks of this life as 'at work' in the Corinthians. That Paul understands the 'life of Jesus' as divine power is not surprising when we realise that he is referring to the resurrection life of Jesus, for Paul frequently connects δύναμις and Jesus' resurrection. [Tannehill refers here to Rom 1,4; 1 Cor 6,14; 2 Cor 13,4; Phil 3,10 and also 1 Cor 15,43.] Two passages, Phil.3$_{10}$ and II Cor. 13$_4$, are especially important, for in both Paul speaks of sharing in Jesus' resurrection power, just as in II Cor. 4$_{10—11}$. Thus the 'life of Jesus' is to be understood as the power of Jesus' resurrection life, which is God's redeeming power in the specific form in which it comes to the person whose life is shaped by Jesus' death and resurrection."

[6] Cf also Abraham (1983:64): "Suffering for Paul is at once the identification with the crucified Lord ... ."

[7] The interpretation of weakness and power in terms of dying and rising with Christ is not confined to the apostle, but it is preeminently exemplified in him.

is still bound to this old world through his present body. This means that the Christian is still exposed to the powers of the old aeon. Therefore, the new existence, which is based upon the past death with Christ takes on the form of a continuing dying with Christ. However, he makes clear that the dying with Christ which takes place in suffering is also a dying to the old world, the world of trust in self. The Christian's continuing participation in Christ's death through suffering points him beyond the present to the life which God will grant in future (Tannehill 1967:129). On the other hand it must be pointed out that the eschatological resurrection from the dead or glorification is not merely expected from the future, but has already commenced with the resurrection of Jesus (cf Siber 1971:188). Already in the present the Christian may live from the power of Jesus' resurrection.[8] 2 Cor 4,7—11 deals with the paradoxical fact that at the present moment, notwithstanding appearances to the contrary, the life of Jesus — and thus the all-surpassing power of God — breaks through and manifests itself.

In 2 Cor 4,13—14, however, a different nuance is present: Paul is proclaiming *now* because he believes in the *future* resurrection. It is the future which underscores the present. Hope to live a resurrection life later, with Christ and fellow believers, supports the apostle in his present suffering ministry. This eschatological motivation is emphasised by the fact that this motif plays such an important role towards the end of this pericope (2 Cor 4,7—5,10).

From 2 Cor 13,3—4 it is also evident that complete partaking of the life of the exalted is reserved for the end time. Paul may, however, in his dealings with the congregation trust on the reality of God's miraculous power already in the present time (cf Klauck 1986:101).[9]

According to Paul, the theology of the cross is not an issue of interpreting the cross. On the contrary, from the perspective of the cross he interprets the world, the congregation and men (cf Luz 1974:122). In the same way Paul views the power and weakness of his apostolic ministry in the light of the cross and resurrection of Jesus. In his own life he proclaims

---

[8] Cf Siber (1971:188—9): "Im unmittelbaren oder weitern Kontext der Aussagen über das künftige Teilgewinnen an der Auferweckung Jesu finden sich darum Aussagen über die gegenwärtige Manifestation der Auferstehung oder Herrlichkeit Jesu ins Leben der Christen hinein."

[9] It has been pointed out in the exegetical section that a temporal disjunction exists in Paul's description of weakness and power in 2 Cor 13,1—4. Weakness has a temporary nature, while power reveals an eschatological openness.

the cross of Christ. As apostle of the crucified and resurrected Christ, Paul, in his sufferings becomes the primary and living commentary on his theology of the cross (cf 2 Cor 4,7—15; 12,7—10; 13,3—4) (Stuhlmacher 1976:515).

Dying with Christ in Pauline theology is connected with the exclusion of trust in self or exalting oneself, so as to trust in God alone. The Lord's answer to Paul's pleading in 2 Cor 12,9 is a key passage in this regard. The statement that "power is made perfect in weakness" constitutes the *Magna Charta* of Christian existence. The power of Christ wants to make its dwelling in Paul's broken existence. The word of the Lord quoted by Paul in 2 Cor 12,9 is a special formulation of the gospel itself: salvation, one's only true sufficiency is by God's grace and in God's power (Furnish 1984:550—1). *The power of Christ is, therefore, interpreted in terms of grace.* Both Paul's pastoral ministry as well as his missionary activity were rooted in the *character and meaning of the gospel* to which he was committed, the gospel which is built upon the death and resurrection of Christ (cf Furnish 1981:103).

In the light of the christological perspective described above, it is now possible to turn to a few ways of interpreting power in Paul's apostolic ministry. Jacob Jervell (1976:185—98) mentions that the interpretation of δύναμις in Paul's ministry remains problematic in modern scholarship. The question is asked how it is possible that Paul can appeal to miracles he has performed — how does this fit into his understanding of suffering and his theology of the cross? The suffering and weak apostle couldn't possibly have been a charismatic miracle worker.

New Testament scholars have tried to solve this dilemma by asserting that Paul understood the Spirit (πνεῦμα), grace (χάρισμα) and power (δύναμις) in a sense diametrically opposed to his opponents. He did not speak of the same phenomena as they did. Charisma and suffering (or weakness) could, for instance, be identical entities in Paul's view. Another line of thought followed by some scholars may be formulated as follows: The charismatic-divine power could never have been pointed out overtly, but was always hidden under sufferings — and, therefore, only "visible" to the eyes of faith (cf Jervell 1976:190—1). H D Betz, for example, denies a miraculous dimension in Paul's ministry in the light of passages such as Rom 15,18—19; 1 Cor 2,4; 2 Cor 12,12 and Gal 3,5.[10]

---

[10] He states (1972:71): "Ein klares Zeugnis dafür, daß Paulus Wunder getan hat, liegt daher nicht vor."

Paul, however, made it very clear that the weakness of the believer was not something which prevented the power of God from being effective. It was *not* experiences of power leaving behind bodily weakness which Paul saw as the mark of grace, but experiences of power *in the midst of* weakness. Human weakness was not a denial of divine power, but in the light of the crucifixion of Christ a necessary presupposition for the experience of divine power in the present overlap of the ages (cf Dunn 1998:483—4). The solution to the problems relating to the understanding of power in Paul's ministry cannot, therefore, be found in the denial of the charismatic miraculous aspect of his ministry. This is an integral part of his ministry. In Paul's writings weakness (ἀσθένεια) is not identical with power (δύναμις), "... sondern 'Ort' der Kraftoffenbarung"[11] (cf Jervell 1976:197 note 63). *Paul does not say that power reveals itself as weakness,*[12] but *in weakness.*[13] The view that God's power reveals itself only in the form of weakness, does not stand the test (cf also Nielsen 1980:145; Hübner 1987:2726—9).

The profound meaning of power in Paul's apostolic ministry will only be grasped when the consequences of the catalogues of hardships as horizon for the understanding of δύναμις in his ministry are borne in mind, when it is realised that the cross and the resurrection of Jesus Christ are the foundation of Paul's understanding of power, when it is acknowledged that the reality of power in Paul's ministry is in the final analysis a reality constituted by the Holy Spirit. Just as Paul's gospel points man away from himself and his own competence and achievements, the study of δύναμις in Paul's ministry has repeatedly shown the theocentricity of his view in this regard: God's power in the midst of man's (the apostle's) powerlessness, sickness and weakness.

The power of God does not only make the apostolic preaching effective, but also renews from an anthropological point of view, in a second eschatological act of creation day after day the inner person (2 Cor 4,7.16), protects him from despair (2 Cor 4,7—9), assures him now

---

[11] "... the 'place' where God's power is manifested".

[12] Cf Güttgemanns" (1966:168.169): "Die Schwachheit des Apostels ist die δύναμις des gekreuzigten Kyrios ... Paulus [sieht] die jetzt an ihm sichtbare Schwachheit als die Epiphanie Jesu göttlicher Kraft [an] ... ."

[13] Cf Thrall 1994:331: "[T]o say that power is found within a situation of weakness is not to say that power *is* weakness ... ." Cf also Lambrecht 1996:325.338; Hafemann 1990:66—88.

already of his hope of future resurrection with Jesus (2 Cor 4,7.14) and gives him the Spirit of faith as a guarantee of eternal life (2 Cor 4,10—14; 5,4—5; cf Rom 8,23) (Heckel 1993:316).

Suffering and death is not viewed any longer — as in the Old Testament laments — as a sign of being forsaken by God, but is viewed against the christological background (2 Cor 4,9—11). It is understood as analogy to the passion of Jesus, as being weak in him, as suffering with him and is recognised as the sharing of his sufferings (2 Cor 13,4; Rom 8,17; Phil 3,10—11). The power of God does not exclude suffering, but leads in Christ through his death to the certainty of the resurrection. With the Lord's answer to Paul in 2 Cor 12,9 — and his reaction in 9b — Paul moves beyond questions regarding the meaning of his "thorn in the flesh" through the realisation that it is weakness which leads to the experience of the divine power of Christ.[14] It must however be emphasised that it is not "weakness" as such which is for Paul the sign of God's approval of his apostolic ministry, but the power of Christ at work *in the midst* of weakness. Paul is content with weaknesses (v 10a) for the sake of the *power of Christ*. Christ is not the ground of his sufferings, but the source of his power. This paradox between weakness and power in his apostolic ministry is solved in 2 Cor 13,4 from the perspective of its christological foundation. The fact that Paul attributes weakness to his own person, and power exclusively to Christ is characteristic of the way in which he understands his apostolic authority. The more he moves into the background, the more space is available for God's power (Heckel 1993:324).

"Paulus stellt den schwachen, kranken Charismatiker so dar, daß dieser zu einem lebendigen Zeichen der alleinwirkenden göttlichen Gnade wird. Der wahre Charismatiker ist nur der schwache ... der keine eigene Lebensmöglichkeit besitzt und dessen Wirken nur von fremder Kraft getrieben werden kann. Er bleibt auf die Schöpfermacht Gottes angewiesen" (Jervell 1976:197—8).[15]

---

[14] Heckel (1993:317) points out that weakness becomes "... Verheißungsträger, Wirkungsfeld und Ansatzpunkt für die göttliche Kraft Christi".

[15] "Paul portrays the weak, ill charismatic in such a way, that he becomes a living sign solely of God's grace. The true charismatic is only one that is weak ... who has no possibilities of living by himself and whose ministry can only be driven by a power outside himself. He remains dependent on God's creative power" (translated freely:PJG).

Chapter 26

Conclusion

26.1 The broader New Testament context

The concept of "God's power" functions prominently at important intersections of different New Testament traditions. In the synoptic tradition the power of God (closely related to the Spirit) occurs already in the infancy prologue of Luke's Gospel (1,35), right at the beginning of Jesus' ministry in Galilee (4,14) and throughout his preaching, healing and exorcising ministry. The concept of power is not only mentioned at the beginning of *Jesus'* ministry, but also at the very beginning of that of his *disciples* (Lk 10,19—20) and in the final section of Luke's Gospel, dealing with the empowerment of the disciples to become trustworthy witnesses (24,49).[1]

Acts 10,38 confirms that the message that "… God anointed Jesus of Nazareth with the *Holy Spirit and power*" which enabled him to "… go around doing good and healing all who were under the power of the devil" belongs to the heart of the early Christian kerygma.

In his last words — spoken in the inner circle of his disciples before his ascension — the resurrected Jesus promises them the power of the Spirit for their world wide task. The power (δύναμις) promised in Acts 1,8 is the power to act with authority in general — to speak and to perform miracles. A very close relation exists in the Lukan narrative between the oral witness and accompanying miracles.

The concept of "power" plays an important role in apocalyptic literature. In the Book of Revelation δύναμις is directly related to God in 4,11; 7,12; 11,17; 12,10; 15,8 and 19,1. This theocentric use of δύναμις is important for interpreting this motif in Revelation. God (as well as the

---

[1] Cf also Lk 21,27 where the concept of power occurs within an eschatological concept, dealing with the coming of the Son of Man.

Lamb who was slain, 5,12) *alone* is to be worshipped as the source of all power and authority. This view of God's rule, power and justice implies a solemn criticism of Roman power, which claimed for itself the ultimate divine sovereignty over the world.

26.2 The Pauline perspective

How does Paul's understanding of power fit within this broader New Testament context? The use of "power" in Revelation is a good example of the contextuality of all theology — of the way in which a concept, firmly rooted in the early Christian tradition, is reinterpreted in the light of specific political and socio-historical circumstances. The essential dimensions of "power" in Luke and Acts, namely the power enabling ministry, both with regard to effective witness and accompanying signs and miracles are not foreign to Paul and are affirmed by him. In the light of Paul's many *tribulations and sufferings* for the sake of the gospel, the *concept of power in his letters is however deepened* in a way that goes beyond the rest of the New Testament.

Paul understands the gospel as God's power, manifested through the resurrection of Christ and now evidenced through the presence of the Spirit. This includes miracles in the assembly (Gal 3,5), to which Paul appeals in a matter-of-fact way as proof that salvation in Christ is based on faith and not on observance of the law. This power of God also includes the effective proclamation of Christ accompanied by the Spirit's manifest power in bringing about conversions (1 Thess 1,5—6; 1 Cor 2,4—5), despite the obvious weakness of the messenger himself (1 Cor 2,1—3; 2 Cor 12,7—10).

The gospel is God's power, and yet Paul emphasises the closest correlation between the power (of the Spirit) and present weaknesses. As a passage such as 2 Cor 12,9 indicates, the Spirit is seen as the source of empowering in the midst of affliction and weaknesses. "Knowing Christ" means to know *both* the power of his resurrection *and* the fellowship of sharing in his sufferings (Phil 3,9—10). Though the content of Phil 3,7—11 differs considerably, both the linguistic echoes and the general "form" of the narrative seem intentionally designed to recall the Christ narrative in 2,6—11. As he appealed to the Philippians to do, Paul himself exemplifies Christ's mind set, embracing suffering and death (Fee 1995:314—5).

Paul interprets the concept of God's power in the light of the *primary metaphor of Christ's crucifixion (in weakness) and his resurrection (in power)*. Present suffering is a mark of discipleship, but the same power that raised the crucified One from the dead is also already at work in our mortal bodies. In 2 Cor 4,10—11 Paul affirms that the apostles are "... always carrying in the body the death of Jesus, so that the life of Jesus may also be manifested in [their] bodies. For while [they] live [they] are always being given up to death for Jesus' sake, so that the life of Jesus may be manifested in [their] mortal flesh". Rom 8,17 affirms that the Christians are God's children and fellow heirs with Christ "... provided [they] suffer with him in order that [they] may also be glorified with him". In Rom 6,3—4 burial with Christ by baptism into death is mentioned, and in 6,6 being crucified with him. In 2 Cor 5,14 Paul points out that all have died, since one has died for all. He therefore sees his suffering in connection with the death of Christ. To be united with Christ implies the necessity to suffer as Christ did. Through his trials Paul really participates in the suffering of Christ. He expresses the hope to "... know him and the power of his resurrection"; he hopes to share in his sufferings, "... becoming like him in his death, that if possible [he] may attain the resurrection from the dead" (Phil 3,10—11)[2]. It is clear that Paul's profound christological conviction offers him the ultimate explanation for his suffering — and the power to overcome.

Paul's account of his near-death experience in 2 Cor 1,8—10 is to be taken seriously as the record of a critical episode in his life. The way in which he came to terms with it, and was therefore able to find positive value in suffering is an important key to the interpretation of 2 Cor 4—5, Rom 6,1—11 and Phil 3,10 (Harvey 1996:112—21). Paul does not regard suffering as evil in itself, irrational or challenging to faith — his experience of suffering brings the sufferer closer to Christ, causes an inward renewal and spills over into benefit for others.[3]

When reflecting on Paul's understanding of power, the *Spirit* may never be ignored. The reality of the Spirit means the presence of divine power, power to overflow with hope (Rom 15,13). This power is

---

[2] Quotations from the RSV.
[3] Harvey (1996:129) points out that this understanding of suffering is without precedent in any Jewish or pagan sources known to us, and is hard to parallel in the revered writings of any other major religion.

sometimes attested by signs and wonders — at other times however by joy
in great affliction (cf 1 Thess 1,6). The tensions present in the Pauline
understanding of power are put into proper perspective in the light of his
message about the Spirit. The Spirit is both the *fulfilment* of the
eschatological promises of God and the *down payment* on our certain *future*
— the evidence of the one, the guarantee of the other (Fee 1994:824—6,
here 826).

In his understanding of *God's power* in the light of *Christ*'s crucifixion
and resurrection — and yet in the final analyses as a *pneuma*tological
concept — the basically Trinitarian thrust of Paul's theology becomes
evident.

Bibliography

Abbot, E & Mansfield E D 1971. *A Primer of Greek Grammar: Accidence and Syntax.* London: Rivingtons.

Abraham, M V 1983. Diakonia in the Early Letters of Paul. *Indian Journal of Theology* 32, 61—7.

Aland, Kurt, Hg. 1996. *Synopsis Quattuor Evangeliorum.* 15. revidierte Auflage. Stuttgart: Deutsche Bibelgesellschaft.

Albertz, R & Westermann, C 1976. s v רוח ... Geist. *THAT.*

Allen, L C 1976. *The Books of Joel, Obadiah, Jonah and Micah.* Grand Rapids: Wm B Eerdmans. (NICOT.)

Althaus, P 1970. *Der Brief an die Römer.* Göttingen: Vandenhoeck & Ruprecht. (NTD.)

Andrews, S B 1995. Too Weak Not to Lead. The Form and Function of 2 Cor 11.23b—33. *NTS* 41, 263—76.

Barnett, P W 1984. Opposition in Corinth. *JSNT* 22, 3—17.

Barré, M L 1975. Paul as "Eschatologic Person": A New Look at 2 Cor 11:29. *CBQ* 37, 500—26.

Barrett, C K 1962. *A Commentary on the Epistle to the Romans.* London: Adam & Charles Black. (BNTC.)

--- 1968. *A Commentary on the First Epistle to the Corinthians.* London: Adam & Charles Black. (BNTC.)

--- 1970. The Holy Spirit. *ABR* 18, 1—9.

--- 1973. *A Commentary on the Second Epistle to the Corinthians.* London: Adam & Charles Black. (BNTC.)

--- 1982. *Essays on Paul.* London: SPCK.

--- 1994. *The Acts of the Apostles.* Edinburgh: T&T Clark. (CECNT.)

Barton, S C 1998. Sociology and Theology. In Marshall, I Howard and David Peterson (eds), *Witness to the Gospel. The Theology of Acts,* 459—72. Grand Rapids: Eerdmans.

Bartsch, H W 1967. Zur vorpaulinischen Bekenntnisformel im Eingang des Römerbriefes. *ThZ* 23, 329—39.

Bauckham, R 1993. *The Theology of the Book of Revelation.* Cambridge: Cambridge University Press. (New Testament Theology.)

Bauer, Walter; Aland, Kurt und Aland, Barbara 1988. *Griechisch-deutsches Wörterbuch zu den Schriften des Neuen Testaments und der frühchristlichen Literatur.* 6., völlig neu bearbeitete Auflage. Berlin; New York: Walter de Gruyter.

Baumann, R 1968. *Mitte und Norm des Christlichen: Eine Auslegung von 1 Korinther 1,1—3,4.* (NTA.)

Beale, G 1999. *The Book of Revelation. A Commentary on the Greek Text.* Grand Rapids: Eerdmans; Carlisle: Paternoster. (NIGTC.)

Benjamin, H S 1976. Pneuma in John and Paul: A Comparative Study of the Term with particular Reference to the Holy Spirit. *Biblical Theology Bulletin* 6, 27—48.

Berger, K 1984. s v Geist/Heiliger Geist/Geistesgaben: Neues Testament. *TRE.*

Betz, H D 1969. Eine Christus-Aretalogie bei Paulus (2 Kor 12,7—10). *ZThK* 66, 288—305.

--- 1972. Der Apostel Paulus und die sokratische Tradition: Eine exegetische Untersuchung zu seiner "Apologie" 2 Korinther 10—13. Tübingen: J C B Mohr (Paul Siebeck). (BHTh 45.)

Bieringer, R (ed) 1996. *The Corinthian Correspondence.* Leuven: University Press. (BEThL CXXV.)

Bieringer, R & Lambrecht, J (eds) 1994. *Studies on 2 Corinthians.* Leuven: University Press. (BEThL CXII.)

Bishop, E F F 1971. Pots of Earthenware. *EvQ* 43, 3—5.

Black, D A 1984. *Paul, Apostle of Weakness. Astheneia and its Cognates in the Pauline Literature.* New York-Bern-Frankfurt/M: P Lang. (American University Studies, Series 7: Theology and Religion 3.)

Blass, F 1961. *Grammatik des neutestamentlichen Griechisch,* bearb von A Debrunner. II. Aufl.

Blass, F & Debrunner, A 1975. *Grammatik des neutestamentlichen Griechisch,* bearb von Friedrich Rehkopf. 14., völlig neubearb u erw Aufl. Göttingen: Vandenhoeck & Ruprecht.

Blunt, A 1911. *The Apologies of Justin Martyr.* Cambridge: Cambridge University Press. (CPT.)

Bockmuehl, M 1997. *A Commentary on the Epistle to the Philippians.* London: A&C Black. (BNTC.)

Bornkamm, G [1969] 1987. *Paulus.* 6. Aufl. Stuttgart: W Kohlhammer. (Urban-Taschenbücher 119.)

Botha, S P 1988. Diskoersanalise van 1 Korintiërs. *Theologia Viaterum* 16, 54—68.

Bottorff, J F 1973. The Relation of Justification and Ethics in the Pauline Epistles. *SJTh* 26, 421—30.

Bovon, F 1996. *Das Evangelium nach Lukas.* Zürich: Benziger/Neukirchen-Vluyn: Neukirchener. (EKK III.)

Brandenburger, E 1988. Pistis und Soteria. Zum Verstehenshorizont von "Glaube" im Urchistentum. *ZThK* 85, 165—98.

Bratcher, R G 1982. *A Translator's Guide to Paul's First Letter to the Corinthians.* London: United Bible Societies. (Helps for Translators Series.)

--- 1983. *A Translator's Guide to Paul's Second Letter to the Corinthians.* London: United Bible Societies. (Helps for Translators Series.)

Braun, H 1966a & b. *Qumran und das Neue Testament,* 2 Bände. Tübingen: J C B Mohr (Paul Siebeck).

Bruce, F F 1971. *1 and 2 Corinthians.* London: Oliphants. NCeB.

--- [1971] 1980. *1 and 2 Corinthians.* Softback. Grand Rapids: Wm B Eerdmans; London: Marshall, Morgan & Scott.

--- 1977. Christ and Spirit in Paul. *BJRL* 59, 259—85.

--- 1982. *1 & 2 Thessalonians.* Waco, Texas: Word Books, Publisher. (Word Biblical Commentary 45.)

Bultmann, R 1968. *Theologie des Neuen Testaments.* 6. durchgesehene Aufl. Tübingen: J C B Mohr (Paul Siebeck).

--- 1976. *Der zweite Brief an die Korinther.* Hrsg von Erich Dinkler. Göttingen: Vandenhoeck & Ruprecht. (KEK.)

Byatt, A 1989. The Holy Spirit — A Further Examination. *ET* 100, 215—6.

Cambier, J 1962. Le Critère paulinien de l'apostolat en 2 Cor. 12.6s. *Biblica* 43, 481—518.

Chamberlain, W D [1941] 1979. *An Exegetical Grammar of the Greek New Testament.* Paperback. Grand Rapids: Baker Book House.

Chance, J B 1982. Paul's Apology to the Corinthians. *Perspectives in Religious Studies* 9, 145—55.

Collange, J F 1972. *Énigmes de la dieuxième épître de Paul aux Corinthians: Études exégétique de 2 Cor. 2:14—7:4.* Cambridge: University Press. (SNTSMS 18.)

Combrink, H J B 1969. Die verhouding pneuma-dunamis. *Neotestamentica* 3, 45—51.

Conzelmann, H 1981. *Der erste Brief an die Korinther.* 2. Aufl. Göttingen: Vandenhoeck & Ruprecht. (KEK.)

Cranfield, C E B 1965. Minister and Congregation in the Light of II Corinthians 4:5—7. *Interp.* 19,163—7.

--- 1975—79. *A Critical and Exegetical Commentary on the Epistle to the Romans,* 2 vols. Edinburgh: T & T Clark. (ICC.)

Dahl, N A 1967. Paul and the Church at Corinth According to 1 Corinthians 1—4, in Farmer, W R, Moule, C F D & Niebuhr, R R (eds), *History and Interpretation: Studies Presented to John Knox,* 313—35. Cambridge: Cambridge University Press.

De Goeij, M 1981. *Jozef en Asenath; Apokalyps van Baruch.* Kampen: Kok. (De Pseudepigrafen 2.)

De Villiers, J L 1970. Die aard van die bediening volgens die Korinthiërbriewe. *NGTT* 11, 173—80.

Diels, H 1966. *Die Fragmente der Vorsokratiker: Griechisch und Deutsch,* hrsg von W Kranz, Erster Band. 12. Aufl. Dublin/Zürich: Weidman.

Dieterich, A [1923] 1966. *Eine Mithrasliturgie,* hrsg von O Weinreich. Nachdruck. Darmstadt: Wissenschaftliche Buchgesellschaft.

Dodd, B 1999. *Paul's Paradigmatic "I". Personal Example as Literary Strategy.* Sheffield: Sheffield Academic Press. (JSNT.S 177.)

Dodd, C H 1932. *The Epistle of Paul to the Romans.* London: Hodder & Stoughton. (MNTC.)

--- 1936. *The Apostolic Preaching and Its Developments.* London: Hodder & Stoughton.

Duggan, M W 1980. The Spirit in the Body in First Corinthians. *BiTod* 18, 388—93.

Dunn, J D G 1970. 2 Corinthians III.17 — "The Lord is the Spirit". *JThS* 21, 309—20.

--- 1970—71. Spirit and Kingdom. *ET* 82, 36—40.

--- 1973. Jesus — Flesh and Spirit: An Exposition of Romans i.3—4. *JThS* 24, 40—68.

--- 1975. *Jesus and the Spirit. A Study of the Religious and Charismatic Experience of Jesus and the First Christians as Reflected in the New Testament.* London: SCM. (NTLi.)

--- 1988. *Romans.* Two Vols. Dallas, Texas: Word Books. (Word Biblical Commentary Volume 38.)

--- 1996. *The Acts of the Apostles.* Peterborough: Epworth. (Epworth Commentaries.)

--- 1998. *The Theology of Paul the Apostle.* Wm. B. Eerdmans: Grand Rapids.

Du Plessis, P J 1969. The Concept of Pneuma in the Theology of Paul. *Neotestamentica* 3, 9—20.

Dupont, D J 1952. ΣΥΝ ΧΡΙΣΤΩΙ: *L'Union avec le Christ suivant Saint Paul.* Bruges: Abbaye de Saint-André.

Du Toit, A B 1969. Die formule εν πνευματι by Paulus. *Neotestamentica* 3, 52—60.

Du Toit, A B 1979. Dikaiosyne in Röm 6: Beobachtungen zur ethischen Dimension der paulinischen Gerechtigkeitsauffassung. *ZThK* 76, 261—91.

--- 1984. *Room van Romeine*. Wellington: Bybelkor.

--- (ed) 1985. *The Pauline Letters: Introduction and Theology*, tr by D Roy Briggs. Pretoria: N G Kerkboekhandel Transvaal. (Guide to the New Testament V.)

--- [s a]. Eksegese-Handleiding: Rom 1, 6, 8. Universiteit van Pretoria. Fakulteit Teologie. Departement Nuwe Testament. Typescript.

Easly, K H 1984. The Pauline Usage of *Pneumati* as a Reference to the Spirit of God. *JETS* 27, 299—313.

Ebner, M 1991. *Leidenslisten und Apostelbrief. Untersuchungen zu Form, Motivik und Funktion der Peristasenkataloge bei Paulus*. Würzburg: Echter. (FzB 66.)

Eichholz, G 1961. Paulus in Umgang mit jungen Kirchen, in Hermelink, J & Margull, H J (Hrsg), *Basileia: Walter Freytag zum 60. Geburtstag*, 49—59. Darmstadt: Wissenschaftliche Buchgesellschaft.

--- 1985. *Die Theologie des Paulus im Umriss*. 5. Aufl. Neukirchen-Vluyn: Neukirchener Verlag.

Engelbrecht, J J 1969. Pneuma en eskatologie by Paulus. *Neutestamentica* 3, 61—75.

Fascher, E 1959. s v Dynamis. *RAC*.

--- 1980. *Der erste Brief des Paulus an die Korinther. Erster Teil: Einführung und Auslegung der Kapitel 1—7*. 2. Aufl. Berlin: Evangelische Verlagsanstalt. (ThHK.)

Fee, G D 1987. *The First Epistle to the Corinthians*. Grand Rapids: William B Eerdmans. (NIC.)

--- 1994. *God's Empowering Presence. The Holy Spirit in the Letters of Paul*. Peabody, Massachusetts: Hendrickson.

--- 1995. *Paul's Letter to the Philippians*. Grand Rapids: Eerdmans. (NICNT.)

Fiorenza, E S 1985. *The Book of Revelation. Justice and Judgment*. Philadelphia: Fortress.

Fitzgerald, J T 1988. *Cracks in an Earthen Vessel: An Examination of the Catalogues of Hardships in the Corinthian Correspondence*. Atlanta: Scholars Press. (S B L Dissertation Series 99.)

Fitzmyer, J A 1970. "To Know Him and the Power of his Resurrection" (Phil 3.10). In *Mélanges Bibliques en Hommage Au R.P. Béda Rigaux*, 411—25. Gembloux: J. Duculot.

--- 1985. *The Gospel According to Luke*. New York: Doubleday. (AncB 28.)

Forbes, C 1986. Comparison, Self-Praise and Irony: Paul's Boasting and the Conventions of Hellenistic Rhetoric. *NTS* 32, 1—30.

Forster, A H 1950. The Meaning of Power for St. Paul. *AThR* 32, 177—85.

Fridrichsen, A 1928. Zum Stil des paulinischen Peristasenkatalogs, 2 Cor. 11,23ff. *Symbolae Osloenses* 7, 25—9.

Friedrich, G 1963a. *Amt und Lebensführung. Eine Auslegung von 2. Kor. 6,1—10*. Neukirchen-Vluyn: Neukirchener Verlag des Erziehungsvereins. (BSt39.)

--- 1963b. Die Gegner des Paulus im 2. Korintherbrief, in Betz, O, Hengel, M & Schmidt, P (Hrsg), *Abraham unser Vater: Juden und Christen im Gespräch über die Bibel. Festschrift für Otto Michel zum 60. Geburtstag*, 181—215. Leiden: E J Brill.

--- 1971. Die Bedeutung der Auferweckung Jesu nach Aussagen des Neuen Testaments. *TZ* 27,1.

--- 1980. s v δύναμις ... Kraft. *Exegetisches Wörterbuch zum Neuen Testament*.

Furnish, V P 1968. *Theology and Ethics in Paul.* Nashville: Abingdon Press.

--- 1981. Theology and Ministry in the Pauline letters, in Shelp, E E & Sunderland, R (eds), *A Biblical Basis for Ministry.* Philadelphia: Westminster.

--- 1984. *II Corinthians.* New York: Doubleday. (AncB 32A.)

Georgi, D 1964. *Die Gegner des Paulus im 2. Korintherbrief.* Neukirchen-Vluyn: Neukirchener Verlag.

Gilchrist, J M 1988. Paul and the Corinthians — The Sequence of Letters and Visits. *JSNT* 34, 47—69.

Gillman, J 1988. A Thematic Comparison of 1 Cor 15:50—57 and 2 Cor 5:1—5. *JBL* 107, 439—54.

Gloël, J 1888. *Der Heilige Geist in der Heilsverkündigung des Paulus: Eine biblisch-theologische Untersuchung.* Halle a.S.: Verlag von Max Niemeyer.

Glombitza, O 1960. Von der Scham des Gläubigen: Erwägungen zu Rom. 1 14—17. *NT* 4, 74—80.

Goodwin, W W 1894. *A Greek Grammar.* Basingstoke: Macmillan.

Goppelt, L 1985. *Theologie des Neuen Testaments*, hrsg von Jürgen Roloff. 3. Aufl. Göttingen: Vandenhoeck & Ruprecht. (Uni-Taschenbücher 850.)

Gräbe, P J 1990. Die verhouding tussen indikatief en imperatief in die Pauliniese etiek: Enkele aksente uit die diskussie sedert 1924. *Scriptura* 32, 54—66.

--- 1992. Δύναμις (in the Sense of Power) as a Pneumatological Concept in the Main Pauline Letters. *BZ* 36, 226—35.

--- 1994. The All-Surpassing Power of God through the Holy Spirit in the Midst of our Broken Earthly Existence: Perspectives on Paul's Use of δύναμις in 2 Corinthians. *Neotestamentica* 28, 147—56.

The Greek New Testament 1994. Fourth Revised Edition, in Cooperation with the Institute for New Testament Textual Research, Münster, Westphalia. Stuttgart: Deutsche Bibelgesellschaft/United Bible Societies.

Greenwood, D 1972. The Lord is the Spirit: Some Considerations of 2 Cor 3:17. *CBQ* 34, 467—72.

Gruber, M M 1998. *Herrlichkeit in Schwachheit. Eine Auslegung der Apologie des Zweiten Korintherbriefs 2 Kor 2,14—6,13.* Würzburg: Echter. (FzB 89.)

Grundmann, W 1932. *Der Begriff der Kraft der neutestamentlichen Gedankenwelt.* Stuttgart: W Kohlhammer. (BWANT.)

--- 1935. s v δύναμαι ktl. *ThWNT.*

--- 1964. s v δύναμαι ktl. *ThDNT.*

Guardini, R 1959. *Wunder und Zeichen.* Würzburg: Werkbund-Verlag.

Güttgemanns, E 1966. *Der leidende Apostel und sein Herr.* Göttingen: Vandenhoeck & Ruprecht. (FRLANT 90.)

Haacker, K 1999. *Der Brief des Paulus an die Römer.* Leipzig: Evangelische Verlagsanstalt. (ThHK 6.)

Hafemann, S 1990. "Self-Commendation" and Apostolic Legitimacy in 2 Corinthians: A Pauline Dialectic. *NTS* 36, 66—88.

Hahn, F 1974a. Der Apostolat im Urchristentum: Seine Eigenart und seine Voraussetzungen. *KuD* 20, 54—77.

--- 1974b. Das biblische Verständnis des Heiligen Geistes: Soteriologische Funktion und "Personalität" des Heiligen Geistes, in Heitmann & Mühlen, 131—47.

--- 1979. Charisma und Amt: Die Diskussion über das kirchliche Amt im Lichte der neutestamentlichen Charismenlehre. *ZThK* 76, 419—49.

Hahn, F 1980. Bekenntnisformeln im Neuen Testament, in Brantschen, J & Selvatico, P (Hrsg), *Unterwegs zur Einheit: Festschrft für Heinrich Stirnimann, 200—14.* Freiburg: Herder.

Hamilton, N Q 1957. *The Holy Spirit and Eschatology in Paul.* Edinburgh: Oliver and Boyd. (SJTh.OP 6.)

Hanson, A T 1987. *The Paradox of the Cross in the Thought of St. Paul.* Sheffield: JSOT Press. (JSNT. S 17.)

Harrisville, R A 1987. *1 Corinthians.* Minneapolis: Augsburg Publishing House. (Augsburg Commentary on the New Testament.)

Harvey, A E 1996. *Renewal Through Suffering: A Study of 2 Corinthians.* Edinburgh: T & T Clark. (Studies of the New Testament and its World.)

Hatch, E & Redpath, H A 1954. *A Concordance to the Septuagint and the other Greek versions of the Old Testament,* Vol 1. Graz-Austria: Akademische Druck- u Verlagsanstalt.

Hawthorne, G F 1991. *The Presence and the Power. The Significance of the Holy Spirit in the Life and Ministry of Jesus.* Dallas: Word Publishing.

Heckel, U 1993. *Kraft in Schwachheit. Untersuchungen zu 2. Kor 10—13.* Tübingen: J C B Mohr (Paul Siebeck). (WUNT 2. Reihe 56.)

--- 1993a. Der Dorn im Fleisch. Die Krankheit des Paulus in 2 Kor 12,7 und Gal 4,13f. *ZNW* 84, 65—92.

Heil, J P 1987. *Romans — Paul's letter of Hope.* Rome: Biblical Institute Press. (AnBib 112.)

Heininger, B 1996. *Paulus als Visionär. Eine religionsgeschichtliche Studie.* Freiburg; Basel; Wien; Barcelona; Rom; New York: Herder. (HBS 9.)

Heitmann, C & Mühlen, H (Hrsg) 1974. *Erfahrung und Theologie des Heiligen Geistes.* Hamburg: Agentur des Rauhen Hauses; München: Kösel-Verlag.

Hermann, I 1961. *Kyrios und Pneuma: Studien zur Christologie der paulinischen Hauptbriefe.* München: Kösel-Verlag.

Heron, A I C 1983. *The Holy Spirit in the Bible, the History of Christian Thought and Recent Theology.* Philadelphia: The Westminster Press.

Holmberg, B 1978. *Paul and Power. The Structure of Authority in the Primitive Church as Reflected in the Pauline Epistles.* Lund: C W K Gleerup. (CB New Testament Series 11.)

Holtz, T 1986. *Der erste Brief an die Thessalonicher.* Zürich: Benziger; Neukirchen-Vluyn: Neukirchener. (KEK XIII.)

Horn, F G 1992. *Das Angeld des Geistes. Studien zur paulinischen Pneumatologie.* Göttingen: Vandenhoeck & Ruprecht. (FRLANT 154.)

Hotze, G 1997. *Paradoxien bei Paulus. Untersuchungen zu einer elementaren Denkform in seiner Theologie.* Münster: Aschendorff. (NTA NF 33.)

Hübner, H 1987. Paulusforschung seit 1945. Ein kritischer Literaturbericht, in Haase, W & Temporini, H, *Aufstieg und Niedergang der römischen Welt.* Teil II: Principat. Band 25.4. Berlin: Walter de Gruyter.

--- 1993. *Biblische Theologie des Neuen Testaments, Band 2. Die Theologie des Paulus und ihre neutestamentliche Wirkungsgeschichte.* Göttingen: Vandenhoeck & Ruprecht.

Hughes, P E 1962. *Paul's Second Epistle to the Corinthians*. Grand Rapids, Michigan: W M B Eerdmans. (NIC.)

Jervell, J 1976. Der schwache Charismatiker, in Friedrich, J, Pöhlmann, W & Stuhlmacher, P, *Rechtfertigung: Festschrift für Ernst Käsemann zum 70. Geburtstag*. Tübingen: J C B Mohr (Paul Siebeck).

--- 1977. Das Volk des Geistes, in Jervell, J & Meeks, W A, *God's Christ and His People: Studies in Honour of Nils Alstrup Dahl*, 87—106. Oslo: Universitetsforlaget.

--- 1998. *Die Apostelgeschichte*. Göttingen: Vandenhoeck & Ruprecht. (KEK.)

Johnson, L T 1991. *The Gospel of Luke*. Collegeville: The Liturgical Press. (Sacra Pagina 3.)

Johnson, S L 1971. The Jesus that Paul Preached. *Bibliotheca Sacra* 128, 120—34.

Käsemann, E 1956. *Die Legitimität des Apostels. Eine Untersuchung zu II Korinther 10—13*. Darmstadt: Wissenschaftliche Buchgesellschaft.

--- 1967. Die Heilsbedeutung des Todes Jesu nach Paulus, in Conzelmann, H, Flesseman-Van Leer, E, Haenchen, E, Käsemann, E & Lohse, E, *Zur Bedeutung des Todes Jesu: Exegetische Beiträge*. Gütersloh: Gütersloher Verlagshaus Gerd Mohn. (STAEKU.)

--- 1969. *Paulinische Perspektiven*. Tübingen: J C B Mohr (Paul Siebeck).

--- 1974. *An die Römer*. 2. Aufl. Tübingen: J C B Mohr (Paul Siebeck). (HNT8a.)

--- 1980. *An die Römer*. 4. Aufl. Tübingen: J C B Mohr (Paul Siebeck). (HNT8a.)

--- 1986. Gottesgerechtigkeit bei Paulus, in Käsemann, E, *Exegetische Versuche und Besinnungen: Auswahl*. Göttingen: Vandenhoeck & Ruprecht.

Kee, H C 1990. *Good News to the Ends of the Earth. The Theology of Acts*. London: S C M; Philadelphia: Trinity.

Kehl, M 1979. Kirche — Sakrament des Geistes, in Kasper, W (Hrsg), *Gegenwart des Geistes: Aspekte der Pneumatologie*. Freiburg: Herder. (Q D 85.)

Kent, H A (Jr) 1981. The Glory of Christian Ministry: An Analysis of 2 Corinthians 2:14—4:18. *Grace Theological Journal* 2, 171—89.

Kern, W 1977. Die Kirche — Gottes Kraft in menschlicher Schwäche. *GuL* 321—6.

Kertelge, K 1971. *"Rechtfertigung" bei Paulus: Studien zur Struktur und zum Bedeutungsgehalt des paulinischen Rechtfertigungsbegriffs*. Münster: Aschendorff. (NTA NS 3.)

--- 1976. Das Verständnis des Todes Jesu bei Paulus, in Kertelge, K (Hrsg), *Der Tod Jesu. Deutungen im Neuen Testament*, 114—36. Freiburg, Basel, Wien: Herder. (Q D 74.)

--- 1980a. s v δικαιοσύνη. *Exegetisches Wörterbuch zum Neuen Testament*.

--- 1980b. s v ἀπολύτρωσις. *Exegetisches Wörterbach zum Neuen Testament*.

--- 1983. *Der Brief an die Römer*. 2. Aufl. Düsseldorf: Patmos. (Geistliche Schriftlesung 6.)

--- 1987. "Natürliche Theologie" und Rechtfertigung aus dem Glauben bei Paulus, in Baier, W, Horn, S O, Pfnür, V, Schönborn, C, Weimer, L & Wiedenhofer, S (Hrsg), *Weisheit Gottes — Weisheit der Welt*. Band 1, 83—95. Erzabtei St. Ollien: Eos Verlag. Festschrift für Joseph Kardinal Ratzinger zum 60. Geburtstag.

Kießling, E 1966. *Wörterbuch der griechischen Papyrusurkunden*, 4. Band 3. Lieferung. Marburg: Selbstverlag des Verfassers.

Klauck, H J 1984. *1. Korintherbrief*. Würzburg: Echter Verlag. (NEB.) (Third Edition 1992.)

Klauck, H J 1986. 2. *Korintherbrief.* Würzburg: Echter Verlag. (NEB.) (Third Edition: 1994.)

— 1995. *Die religiöse Umwelt des Urchristentums I. Stadt und Hausreligion, Mysterienkulte, Volksglaube.* Stuttgart; Berlin; Köln: W Kohlhammer. (Kohlhammer Studienbücher Theologie Band 9,1.)

— 1996. *Die religiöse Umwelt des Urchristentums II. Herrscher und Kaiserkult, Philosophie, Gnosis.* Stuttgart; Berlin; Köln: W Kohlhammer. (Kohlhammer Studienbücher Theologie Band 9,2.)

— 1998. *Die antike Briefliteratur und das Neue Testament. Ein Lehr- und Arbeitsbuch.* Paderborn; München; Wien; Zürich: Ferdinand Schöningh. (U T B 2022.)

Kleinknecht, K T 1988. *Der leidende Gerechtfertigte. Die alttestament-jüdische Tradition vom "leidenden Gerechten" und ihre Rezeption bei Paulus.* 2. durchgesehene und um ein Nachwort erweiterte Auflage. Tübingen: J C B Mohr (Paul Siebeck). (WUNT 2. Reihe 13.)

Knoch, O 1975. *Der Geist Gottes und der neue Mensch: Der Heilige Geist als Grundkraft und Norm des christlichen Lebens in Kirche und Welt nach dem Zeugnis des Apostels Paulus.* Stuttgart: Verlag Katholisches Bibelwerk. (Geist und Leben.)

Knox, J 1964. Romans 15$_{14-33}$ and Paul's Conception of his Apostolic Mission. *JBL* 83, 1—11.

Koenig, J 1978. From Mystery to Ministry: Paul as Interpreter of Charismatic Gifts. *USQR* 33, 167—74.

Koskenniemi, H 1956. *Studien zur Idee und Phräseologie des griechischen Briefes bis 400 n. Chr.* Helsinki: Akateeminen, Kirjakauppa.

Kosmala, H 1959. *Hebräer-Essener-Christen. Studien zur Vorgeschichte der frühchristlichen Verkündigung.* Leiden: E J Brill. (StPB.)

Kramer, W 1966. *Christ, Lord, Son of God,* tr by B Hardy. London: SCM. (SBT 50.)

Kremer, J 1970. Die Auferstehung Jesu, Grund und Vorbild unserer Auferstehung. *Concilium* 6, 707—12.

— 1988. *Lukasevangelium.* Würzburg: Echter Verlag. (NEB.NT 3.)

Kuss, O 1959. Der Geist, in Kuss, O, *Der Römerbrief,* Zweite Lieferung, 540—95. Regensburg: Friedrich Pustet.

Lake, K (ed and trans) 1912. *The Apostolic Fathers in Two Volumes.* Cambridge, Massachusetts: Harvard University Press; London: William Heinemann. (Loeb Classical Library.)

Lambrecht, J 1985. Philological and Exegetical Notes on 2 Cor 13,4. *Bijdr.* 46, 261—9.

— 1986. The Nekrōsis of Jesus: Ministry and Suffering in 2 Cor 4, 7—15. *BEThL* 73, 120—43.

— 1994. The Eschatological Outlook in 2 Corinthians 4,7—15, in Bieringer & Lambrecht 1994:335—49.

— 1996. Dangerous Boasting. Paul's Self-Commendation in 2 Cor 10—13, in Bieringer 1996:325—46.

— 1997. Strength in Weakness. A Reply to Scott B Andrews' Exegesis of 2 Cor 11.23b—33. *NTS* 43, 285—90.

— 1999. *Second Corinthians.* Collegeville, Minnesota: The Liturgical Press. (Sacra Pagina 8.)

Lampe, G W H 1965. Miracles in the Acts of the Apostles. In Moule, C F D (ed), *Miracles. Cambridge Studies in Their Philosophy and History,* 165—78. London: A R Mowbray.

Lang, F 1986. *Die Briefe an die Korinther*. Göttingen: Vandenhoeck & Ruprecht. (NTD.)

Lang, F G 1973. *2. Korinther 5,1—10 in der neueren Forschung*. Tübingen: J C B Mohr (Paul Siebeck). (BGBE 16.)

Lategan, B C 1985. 1 & 2 Corinthians, in Du Toit 1985:53—88.

Lemmer, H R 1988. Pneumatology and Eschatology in Ephesians — The Role of the Eschatological Spirit in the Church. Doctor of Theology Thesis, Unversity of South Africa, Pretoria.

Liddell, H G & Scott, R 1968. *A Greek-English Lexicon*, revised by Sir Henry Stuart Jones. Oxford: Clarendon.

Lietzmann, H 1969. *An die Korinther I/II*, ergänzt von W G Kümmel. Tübingen: J C B Mohr (Paul Siebeck). (HNT.)

Lim, T H 1987. "Not in Persuasive Words of Wisdom, but in the Demonstration of the Spirit and Power". *NT* 29, 137—49.

Lincoln, A T 1990. *Ephesians*. Dallas: Word Books, Publisher. (Word Biblical Commentary.)

Linnemann, E 1971. Tradition und Interpretation in Röm 1,3f. *EvTh* 31, 264—75.

Lohse, E 1973. *Die Einheit des Neuen Testaments: Exegetische Studien zur Theologie des Neuen Testaments*. Göttingen: Vandenhoeck & Ruprecht.

Loubser, J A 1980. II Korintiërs 10—13: Struktuuranalise met die oog op 'n semantiese verkenning van die teks. DTh Verhandeling, Universiteit van Stellenbosch.

Louw, J P 1966. Linguistic Theory and the Greek Case System. *Acta Classica* 7, 73—88.

--- 1976. *Semantiek van Nuwe Testamentiese Grieks*. Pretoria: Author.

--- 1979a & b. *A Semantic Discourse Analysis of Romans*, 2 vols. Pretoria: Author.

--- 1982. *Semantics of New Testament Greek*. Philadelphia: Fortress. (Society of Biblical Literature Semeia Studies.)

Louw, J P & Nida, E A 1988 a & b. *Greek-English Lexicon of the New Testament based on Semantic Domains*, 2 vols. New York: United Bible Societies.

Luz, U 1974. Theologia Crucis als Mitte der Theologie im Neuen Testament. *EvTh* 34, 116—41.

--- 1980. s v βασιλεία. *Exegetisches Wörterbuch zum Neuen Testament*.

Ma, W 1999. *Until the Spirit Comes. The Spirit of God in the Book of Isaiah*. Sheffield: Sheffield Academic Press. (JSOT Supplement Series 271.)

Mangan, C 1980. Christ the Power and Wisdom of God: The Semitic Background to 1 Cor 2:4. *Proceedings of the Irish Biblical Association* 4, 21—34.

Marshall, I H 1980. *The Acts of the Apostles*. Leicester: Inter-Varsity Press. (TNTC.)

Marshall-Green, M 1988. 1 Corinthians 1:18—31. *RExp* 85, 683—6.

McCant, J W 1988. Paul's Thorn of rejected Apostleship. *NTS* 34, 550—72.

McCasland, S V 1957. Signs and Wonders. *JBL* 76, 149—52.

McClelland, S E 1980. Paul's Defence of His Apostleship in 2 Corinthians 10—13 and its Relation to the Collection for the Church at Jerusalem. Doctor of Philosophy Thesis, University of Edinburgh.

Mealand, D L 1976. "As having nothing and yet possessing everything" 2 Kor 6_{10c}. *ZNW* 67, 277—9.

Menzies, R P 1991. *Empowered for Witness. The Spirit in Luke-Acts*. Sheffield: Sheffield Academic Press. (JPT Monograph Series 6.)

Metzger, B M 1968. *The Text of the New Testament*. 2nd ed. Oxford: Claredon Press.

--- 1994. *A Textual Commentary on the Greek New Testament*. 2nd ed. Stuttgart: Deutsche Bibelgesellschaft; New York: United Bible Societies.

Meyer, H A W 1890. *Critical and Exegetical Handbook to the Epistles to the Corinthians*, tr by D Bannermann and W P Dickson. New York: Funk & Wagnalls.

Meyer, P W 1979. The Holy Spirit in the Pauline Letters: A Contextual Exploration. *Interp.* 33, 3—18.

Michel, O 1940. Zum Sprachgebrauch von ἐπαισχύνομαι in Röm 1, 16 (οὐ γὰρ ἐπαισχύνομαι τὸ εὐαγγέλιον), in, Volz, P, Herrmann, J, Bauernfeind, O (Hrsg), *Glaube und Ethos: Festschrift für Professor D Wehrung*, 36—53. Stuttgart: Kohlhammer.

--- 1978. *Der Brief an die Römer*. 5. Aufl. Göttingen: Vandenhoeck & Ruprecht. (KEK 6; 14. Aufl.)

Moo, D J 1996. *The Epistle to the Romans*. Grand Rapids: Wm B Eerdmans. (NICNT.)

Morgenthaler, R 1973. *Statistik des neutestamentlichen Wortschatzes*. 2. Aufl. Zürich: Gotthelf-Verlag.

Morris, L 1988. *The Epistle to the Romans*. Grand Rapids: Wm B Eerdmans; Leicester: Inter-Varsity Press.

Moule, C F D 1978. *The Holy Spirit*. London: Mowbrays. (Mowbrays Library of Theology.)

Müller, K 1966. 1 Kor 1, 18—25. Die eschatologisch-kritische Funktion der Verkündigung des Kreuzes. *BZ* NS 10, 246—72.

Murphy-O'Connor, J 1979. *1 Corinthians*. Dublin: Veritas Publications. (New Testament Message 10.)

--- 1988. Faith and Resurrection in 2 Cor 4:13—14. *RB* 95, 543—50.

Nebe, G 1983. *"Hoffnung" bei Paulus: Elpis und ihre Synonyme in Zusammenhang der Eschatologie*. Göttingen: Vandenhoeck & Ruprecht.

Nestle-Aland 1993. *Novum Testamentum Graece*. 27. revidierte Auflage. Stuttgart: Deutsche Bibelgesellschaft.

Newman, B M 1971. *A Concise Greek-English Dictionary of the New Testament*. London: United Bible Societies.

--- & Nida, E A 1973. *A Translator's Handbook on Paul's Letter to the Romans*. Stuttgart: United Bible Societies.

Neyrey, J H 1991. *The Social World of Luke-Acts. Models for Interpretation*. Peabody: Hendrickson.

Niederwinner, K 1972. Die Gegenwart des Heiligen Geistes nach dem Zeugnis des Neuen Testaments, in Niederwinner, K, Sudbrack, J & Schmidt, W, *Unterscheidung der Geister: Skizzen zu einer neu zu lernenden Theologie des Heiligen Geistes*, 9—34. Kassel: Johannes Stauda Verlag.

Nielsen, H K 1980. Paulus' Verwendung des Begriffes Δύναμις: Eine Replik zur Kreuzestheologie, in Pedersen, S (Hrsg), *Die paulinische Literatur und Theologie: Skandinavische Beiträge*, 137—58. Arhus: Forlaget Aros; Göttingen: Vandenhoeck & Ruprecht.

Nillsson, M P 1941. *Geschichte der griechischen Religion. Erster Band: Bis zur griechischen Weltherrschaft*. München: C H Beck'sche Verlagsbuchhandlung. (Handbuch der Altertumswissenschaft. Fünfte Abteilung; zweiter Teil; erster Band.)

--- 1950. *Geschichte der griechischen Religion. Zweiter Band: Die hellenistische und römische Zeit*. München: C H Beck'sche Verlagsbuchhandlung. (Handbuch der Altertumswissenschaft; fünfte Abteilung, zweiter Teil, zweiter Band.)

Nolland, J 1986. Grace as Power. *NT* 28, 26—31.

Nolland, J 1993. *Luke.* Dallas: Word. (Word Biblical Commentary Vol 35.)

O'Brien, P T 1991. *The Epistle to the Philippians. A Commentary on the Greek Text.* Grand Rapids: Eerdmans. (NIGTC.)

O'Collins, G G 1971. Power Made Perfect in Weakness: 2 Cor 12:9—10. *CBQ* 33, 528—37.

Ortkemper, F-J 1967. *Das Kreuz in der Verkündigung des Apostels Paulus: Dargestellt an den Texten der paulinischen Hauptbriefe.* Stuttgart: Verlag Katholisches Bibelwerk. (SBS 24.)

Patte, D 1983. *Paul's Faith and the Power of the Gospel. A Structural Introduction to the Pauline Letters.* Philadelphia: Fortress.

--- 1987. A Structural Exegesis of 2 Corinthians 2:14—7:4 with special Attention on 2:14—3:6 and 6:11—7:4. *Society of Biblical Literature. Seminar Papers* 26, 23—49.

Pelser, G M M 1985. Romans, in Du Toit, 39—52.

Penna, R 1967. La δύναμις Θεοῦ: Riflessioni in margine a 1 Cor. 1,18—25. *RivBib* 15, 281—94.

Pesch, R 1986. *Die Apostelgeschichte.* Zürich: Benziger; Neukirchen-Vluyn: Neukirchener. (EKK V/1.)

Peterson, E 1951. 1 Kor 1,28f und die Thematik des jüdischen Busstages. *Biblica* 32, 97—103.

Plank, K A 1983. Paul and the Irony of Affliction: A Literary and Rhetorical Analysis of 1 Corinthians 4:9—13. Doctor of Philosophy Dissertation. Vanderbilt University, Nashville, Tennessee.

Plato, 1926. *Laws.* Loeb Classical Library.

Plummer, A 1915. *A Critical and Exegetical Commentary on the Second Epistle of St Paul to the Corinthians.* Edinburgh: T & T Clark. (ICC.)

Polhill, J B 1983. The Wisdom of God and Factionalism: 1 Corinthians 1—4. *RExp* 80, 325—37.

Pop, F J 1962. *Die tweede brief van Paulus aan de Corinthiërs.* Nijkerk: Callenbach.

Preisigke, F 1920. *Vom göttlichen Fluidum nach ägyptischer Anschauung.* Berlin und Leipzig: Vereinigung wissenschaftlicher Verleger, Walter de Gruyter. (Papyrusinstitut Heidelberg, Schrift 1.)

--- 1922. *Die Gotteskraft der frühchristlichen Zeit.* Berlin & Leipzig: Vereinigung wissenschaftlicher Verleger, Walter de Gruyter. (Papyrusinstitut Heidelberg, Schrift 6.)

Prete, B 1975. La formula δύναμις θεοῦ in Rom. 1,16: E sue motivazioni. *RivBib* 23, 299—328.

Prinsloo, W S 1985. *The Theology of the Book of Joel.* Berlin: Walter de Gruyter. (BZAW 163.)

Prümm, K 1961a. Dynamis in griechisch-hellenistischer Religion und Philosophie als Vergleichsbild zu göttlicher Dynamis im Offenbarungsraum. *ZKTh* 83, 393—430.

--- 1961b. Das Dynamische als Grund-Aspekt der Heilsordnung in der Sicht des Apostels Paulus. *Gr* 42, 643—700.

Radermacher, L 1912. *Neutestamentliche Grammatik.* Tübingen: J C B Mohr (Paul Siebeck). (HNT 1.)

Ramsay, W M 1915. *The Bearing of Recent Discovery on the Trustworthiness of the New Testament.* London: Hodder and Stoughton.

Rand, C 1980. The Holy Spirit Transforms Us into a New Creation in Christ and Thereby Incorporates Us into the Christian Community. *One in Christ* 16, 206—13.

Reese, J M 1970. *Hellenistic Influence on the Book of Wisdom and its Consequences.* Rome: Biblical Institute Press. (AnBib 41.)

Rissi, M 1969. *Studien zum zweiten Korintherbrief: Der alte Bund — der Prediger — der Tod.* Zürich: Zwingli Verlag. (AThANT 56.)

Roberts, A & Donaldson, J (eds). MDCCCLXVII. *Ante-Nicene Christian Library Vol. II. Ante-Nicene.* Edinburgh: T and T Clark.

Roberts, J H 1981. Righteousness in Romans with Special Reference to Romans 3:19—31. *Neotestamentica* 15, 12—22.

--- 1986a. The Eschatological Transitions to the Pauline Letter Body. *Neotestamentica* 20, 29—35.

--- 1986b. Pauline Transitions to the Letter Body. *BEThL* 73, 93—9.

--- 1986c. Transitional Techniques to the Letter Body in the Corpus Paulinum, in Petzer, J H & Hartin, P J (eds), *A South African Perspective on the New Testament: Essays by South African New Testament Scholars presented to Bruce Manning Metzger during his visit to South Africa in 1985*, 187—201. Leiden: Brill.

--- 1988. Belydenisuitsprake as Pauliniese Briefoorgange. *HTS* 44, 81—97.

Robertson, A T 1919. *A Grammar of the Greek New Testament in the Light of Historical Research.* 2nd ed. New York: Hodder and Stoughton.

Rowland, C 1982. *The Open Heaven. A Study of Apocalyptic Judaism and Early Christianity.* London: SPCK.

--- 1993. *Revelation.* London: Epworth Press. (Epworth Commentaries.)

Saake, H 1972. Pneumatologia Paulina: Zur Katholizität der Problematik des Charisma. *Catholica* 26, 212—23.

--- 1973. Paulus als Ekstatiker, pneumatologische Beobachtungen zu 2 Kor. 12:1—10. *NT*, 153—60.

Satake, A 1968. Apostolat und Gnade bei Paulus. *NTS* 15, 96—107.

Savage, T B 1996. *Power Through Weakness. Paul's Understanding of the Christian Ministry in 2 Corinthians.* Cambridge: Cambridge University Press. (SNTS.MS 86.)

Schelkle, K H 1981. *Paulus: Leben — Briefe — Theologie.* Darmstadt: Wissenschaftliche Buchgesellschaft. (Erträge der Forschung 152.)

Schierse, F J 1968. Oster- und Parusiefrömmigkeit im Neuen Testament, in Schlier, H, Severus, E V, Sudbrack, J, Pereira, A (Hrsg), *Strukturen christlicher Existenz*, 33—57. Würzburg: Echter.

Schlatter, A 1962. *Paulus der Bote Jesu: Eine Deutung seiner Briefe an die Korinther.* 3. Aufl. Stuttgart: Calwer.

Schlier, H 1958. *Mächte und Gewalten im Neuen Testament.* Freiburg: Herder (Q D 3.)

--- 1968. Die "Liturgie" des apostolischen Evangeliums (Röm 15,14—21), in Semmelroth, O (Hrsg), *Martyria Leitourgia Diakonia: Festschrift für Hermann Volk.* Mainz: Matthias-Grünewald.

--- 1973. Εὐαγγέλιον im Römerbrief, in Feld, H & Nolte, J (Hrsg), *Wort Gottes in der Zeit: Festschrift Karl Hermann Schelkle zum 65. Geburtstag*, 127—42. Düsseldorf: Patmos.

Schlier, H 1974. Herkunft, Ankunft und Wirkung des Heiligen Geistes im Neuen Testament, in Heitman & Mühlen 1971:118—30.

--- 1979. *Der Römerbrief.* 2. Aufl. Freiburg: Herder. (HThK 6.)

Schmidt, W H 1984. s v Geist/Heiliger Geist/Geistesgaben I: Altes Testament. *TRE.*

Schmithals, W 1956. *Die Gnosis in Korinth: Eine Untersuchung zu den Korintherbriefen.* Göttingen: Vandenhoeck & Ruprecht. (FRLANT NS 48.)

--- 1961. *Das kirchliche Apostelamt: Eine historische Untersuchung.* Göttingen: Vandenhoeck & Ruprecht. (FRLANT NS 61.)

Schmitz, O 1927. Der Begriff ΔύNAMIΣ bei Paulus: Ein Beitrag zum Wesen urchristlicher Begriffsbildung, in *Festgabe für Adolf Deissmann zum 60. Geburtstag 7. November 1926,* 139—67. Tübingen: J C B Mohr (Paul Siebeck).

Schnackenburg, R 1961. *Gottes Herrschaft und Reich.* 2. Aufl. Freiburg: Herder.

--- 1970. Apostles Before and During Paul's Time, in Gasque, W W & Martin, R P (eds), *Apostolic History and the Gospel: Biblical and Historical Essays Presented to F F Bruce on His 60th Birthday,* 287—303. Exeter: Paternoster.

--- 1978. *Maßstab des Glaubens: Fragen heutiger Christen im Licht des Neuen Testaments.* Freiburg: Herder.

Schneider, B 1967. "Kata Pneuma Hagiosynes" (Romans 1,4). *Biblica* 48, 359—87.

Schneider, D 1987. *Der Geist des Gekreuzigten. Zur paulinischen Theologie des Heiligen Geistes.* Neukirchen-Vluyn: Aussaat.

Scholtissek, K 1992. *Die Vollmacht Jesu. Traditions- und redaktionsgeschichtliche Analysen zu einem Leitmotiv markinischer Christologie.* Münster: Aschendorff. (NTA NF 25.)

--- 1993. *Vollmacht im Alten Testament und Judentum. Begriffs- und motivgeschichtliche Studien zu einem bibeltheologischen Thema.* Paderborn; München; Wien; Zürich: Ferdinand Schöningh. (Paderborner Theologische Studien, Band 24.)

Schrage, W 1974. Leid, Kreuz und Eschaton: Die Peristasenkataloge als Merkmale paulinischer theologia crucis und Eschatologie. *EvTh* 34, 141—75.

--- 1991. *Der erste Brief an die Korinther.* Three Vols. Zürich: Benziger; Neukirchen-Vluyn: Neukirchener. (EKK VII.)

Schröter, J 1996. Der Apostolat des Paulus als Zugang zu seiner Theologie. Eine Auslegung von 2 Kor 4,7—12, in Bieringer 1996:679—92.

Schürmann, H 1964. Der "Bericht vom Anfang": Ein Rekonstruktionsversuch auf Grund vom Lk. 4, 14—16. *SE* II, 242—58.

--- 1969. *Das Lukasevangelium, Drei Teile.* Freiburg: Herder. (HThK.)

--- 1983. *Gottes Reich — Jesu Geschick: Jesu ureigener Tod im Licht seiner Basileia-Verkündigung.* Freiburg: Herder.

Schweizer, E 1959. s v πνεῦμα, πνευματικός. *ThWNT.*

--- 1978. *Heiliger Geist.* Stuttgart: Kreuz Verlag. (Bibliothek Themen der Theologie: Ergänzungsband.)

Shelton, J B 1991. *Mighty in Word and Deed. The Role of the Holy Spirit in Luke-Acts.* Peabody: Hendrickson.

Siber, P 1971. *Mit Christus leben: Eine Studie zur paulinischen Auferstehungshoffnung.* Zürich: Theologischer Verlag. (AThANT 61.)

Skarsaune, O 1988. Justin der Märtyrer. In *TRE 17,* 471—8. Berlin: Walter de Gruyter.

Smith, M 1971. Prolegomena to a Discussion of Aretalogies, Divine Men, the Gospel and Jesus. *JBL* 90, 174—99.

Smith, W H 1983. The Function of 2 Corinthians 3:7—4 in its Epistolary Context. PhD Thesis, Southern Baptist Theological Seminary.

Söding, T 1997. Der Erste Thessalonicherbrief und die frühe paulinische Evangeliumsverkündigung. Zur Frage einer Entwicklung der paulinischen Theologie. In Söding, T (ed), *Das Wort vom Kreuz*, 31—56. Tübingen: J C B Mohr (Paul Siebeck). (WUNT 93.)

--- 1997. Kreuzestheologie und Rechtfertigungslehre. Zur Verbindung von Christologie und Soteriologie im Ersten Korintherbrief und im Galaterbrief. In Söding, T (ed), *Das Wort vom Kreuz. Studien zur paulinischen Theologie*, 153—82. Tübingen: J C B Mohr (Paul Siebeck). (WUNT 93.)

--- 1997. s v Rechtfertigung. *Neues Bibel-Lexikon.*

--- 1997. Zur Chronologie der paulinischen Briefe. Ein Diskussionsvorschlag. In Söding, T (ed), *Das Wort vom Kreuz*, 3—30. Tübingen: J C B Mohr (Paul Siebeck). (WUNT 93.)

Stalder, K 1962. *Das Werk des Geistes in der Heiligung bei Paulus.* Zürich: EVZ-Verlag.

Stanton, G 1974. *Jesus of Nazareth in New Testament Preaching.* Cambridge: Cambridge University Press. (SNTS Monograph Series 27.)

Stöger, A 1985. Amt und Amtsführung nach 2 Kor 10,1—13,10. *Bibel und Liturgie* 58, 145—52.

Stolz, F 1972. Zeichen und Wunder. Die prophetische Legitimation und ihre Geschichte. *ZThK* 69, 125—44.

Strack, H L & Billerbeck, P 1926. *Kommentar zum Neuen Testament aus Talmud und Midrasch.* Dritter Band. München: C H Beck'sche Verlagsbuchhandlung.

Stuhlmacher, P 1965. *Gerechtigkeit Gottes bei Paulus.* Göttingen: Vandenhoeck & Ruprecht. (FRLANT 87.)

--- 1966. Glauben und Verstehen bei Paulus. *EvTh* 26, 337—48.

--- 1967a. Erwägungen zum ontologischen Charakter der καινή κτίσις bei Paulus. *EvTh* 27, 1—35.

--- 1967b. Erwägungen zum Problem von Gegenwart und Zukunft in der paulinischen Eschatologie. *ZThK* 64, 423—50.

--- 1976. Achtzehn Thesen zur paulinischen Kreuzestheologie, in Friedrich, J, Pöhlmann, W & Stuhlmacher, P (Hrsg), *Rechtfertigung: Festschrift für Ernst Käsemann zum 70. Geburtstag*, 509—25. Tübingen: J C B Mohr (Paul Siebeck); Göttingen: Vandenhoeck & Ruprecht.

--- 1992. *Biblische Theologie des Neuen Testaments, Band 1. Grundlegung von Jesus zu Paulus.* Göttingen: Vandenhoeck & Ruprecht.

Sundermann, H-G 1996. *Der schwache Apostel und die Kraft der Rede. Eine rhetorische Analyse von 2 Kor 10—13.* Frankfurt am Main: Peter Lang. (Europäische Hochschulschriften, Reihe XXIII, Bd. 575.)

Talbert, C H 1987. *Reading Corinthians: A Literary and Theological Commentary on 1 and 2 Corinthians.* New York: Crossroad.

Tannehill, R C 1967. *Dying and Rising with Christ: A study in Pauline Theology.* Berlin: Töpelmann. (ZNW Beiheft 32.)

Theobald, M 1982. *Die überströmende Gnade: Studien zu einem paulinischen Motivfeld.* Würzburg: Echter Verlag. (FzB 22.)

Thrall, M E 1962. *Greek Particles in the New Testament.* Leiden: Brill. (NTTS 3.)

Thrall, M E 1994. *The Second Epistle to the Corinthians*. Two Vols. Cambridge: T & T Clark. (ICC.)

--- 1996. Paul's Journey to Paradise. Some Exegetical Issues in 2 Cor 12,2—4, in Bieringer 1996:347—63.

Turner, M 1996. *Power from on High. The Spirit in Israel's Restoration and Witness in Luke-Acts*. Sheffield: Sheffield Academic Press. (JPT Supplement Series 9.)

Van der Minde, H J 1980. Theologia Crucis und Pneumaaussagen bei Paulus. *Catholica* 34, 128—45.

Van Unnik, W C 1963. "With unveiled face", an exegesis of 2 Corinthians III, 12—18. *NT* 6, 153—69.

Vermes, G 1975. *The Dead Sea Scrolls in English*. 2nd ed. Middlesex: Penguin Books. (Pelican Books.)

Versteeg, J P 1971. *Christus en de Geest: Een exegetisch onderzoek naar de verhouding van de opgestane Christus en de Geest van God volgens de brieven van Paulus*. Kampen: Kok.

Von Dobschütz, E 1974. *Die Thessalonicher-Briefe*. Mit einem Literaturverzeichnis von Otto Merk, herausgegeben von Ferdinand Hahn. Göttingen: Vandenhoeck & Ruprecht. (KEK.)

Vorster, W S 1969. 2 Kor. 3:17: Eksegese en toeligting. *Neotestamentica* 3, 37—44.

--- (ed) 1980. *The Spirit in Biblical Perspective: Proceedings of the Fourth Symposium of the Institute for Theological Research (UNISA) Held at the University of South Africa in Pretoria on the 10th and 11th September 1980*. Pretoria: University of South Africa. (Miscellanea Congregalia 14.)

Vos, C J A 1984. Die Heilige Gees as kosmies-eskatologiese gawe — 'n Eksegeties-dogmatiese studie. DD verhandeling, Universiteit van Pretoria.

Vos, J S 1973. *Traditionsgeschictliche Untersuchungen zur paulinischen Pneumatologie*. Assen: Van Gorcum. (GTB 47.)

Vosloo, W 1983. Rûah/gees in die Ou Testament. *Skrif en Kerk* 4(2), 40—63.

Wacker, M T 1985. Reich Gottes, in Eicher, P (Hrsg), *Neues Handbuch theologischer Grundbegriffe*. Band 4, 43ff. München: Kösel Verlag.

Wanamaker, C A 1990. *The Epistles to the Thessalonians. A Commentary on the Greek Text*. Grand Rapids: Eerdmans; Exeter: Paternoster. (NIGTC.)

Watson, N M 1996. "Physician, Heal Thyself"? Paul's Character as Revealed in 2 Corinthians, in Bieringer 1996:671—8.

Weiss, J [1910] 1970. *Der erste Korintherbrief.* Nachdruck. Göttingen: Vandenhoeck & Ruprecht. (KEK 5.)

Wendland, H-D 1952. Das Wirken des Heiligen Geistes in den Gläubigen nach Paulus. *ThLZ* 78, 457—70.

Wengst, K 1972. *Christologische Formeln und Lieder des Urchristentums*. Gütersloh: Gerd Mohn. (StNT 7.)

Westermann, C 1981. Geist im Alten Testament. *EvTh* 41, 223—30.

Wiencke, G 1939. *Paulus über Jesu Tod: Die Deutung des Todes Jesu bei Paulus und ihre Herkunft*. Gütersloh: Bertelsmann.

Wilckens, U 1957. Kreuz und Weisheit. *KuD* 3, 77—108.

--- 1959. *Weisheit und Torheit: Eine exegetisch-religionsgeschichtliche Untersuchung zu 1. Kor 1 und 2*. Tübingen: J C B Mohr (Paul Siebeck). (BHTh.)

--- 1978. *Der Brief an die Römer*, 1. Teilband. Zürich: Benziger; Neukirchen-Vluyn: Neukirchener Verlag. (EKK 6/1.)

Wilckens, U 1980. *Der Brief an die Römer, 2. Teilband*. Zürich: Benziger; Neukirchen-Vluyn: Neukirchener Verlag. (EKK 6/2.)

--- 1982. *Der Brief an die Römer, 3. Teilband*. Zürich: Benziger; Neukirchen-Vluyn: Neukirchener Verlag. (EKK 6/3.)

Windisch, H 1934. *Paulus und Christus: Ein biblisch-religionsgeschichtlicher Vergleich*. Leipzig: J C Hinrichs'sche Buchhandlung. (UNT 24.)

--- [1924] 1970. *Der zweite Korintherbrief*, hrsg von Georg Strecker. Neudruck. Göttingen: Vandenhoeck & Ruprecht.

Winston, D 1979. *The Wisdom of Solomon: A New Translation with Introduction and Commentary*. Garden City: Doubleday. (AnCB.A 43.)

Witherington, B 1998. *The Acts of the Apostles. A Socio-Rhetorical Commentary*. Grand Rapids: Eerdmans; Carlisle: Paternoster.

Wolff, C 1982. *Der erste Brief des Paulus an die Korinther. Zweiter Teil: Auslegung der Kapitel 8—16*. Berlin: Evangelische Verlagsanstalt. (ThHK.)

--- 1996. *Der erste Brief des Paulus an die Korinther*. Leipzig: Evangelische Verlagsanstalt. (ThHK 7.)

Wolff, H W 1969. *Dodekapropheton 2: Joel und Amos*. Neukirchen-Vluyn: Neukirchener Verlag. (BKAT XIV/2.)

--- 1973. *Anthropologie des Alten Testaments*. München: Kaiser.

Wong, E 1985. The Lord is the Spirit (2 Cor 3,17a). *EThL* 61, 48—72.

Young, F & Ford, D F 1987. *Meaning and Truth in 2 Corinthians*. London: SPCK. (Biblical Foundations in Theology.)

Zeller, D 1985. *Der Brief an die Römer*. Regensburg: Friedrich Pustet. (RNT.)

Zerwick, M & Grosvenor, M 1979. *A Grammatical Analysis of the Greek New Testament*, 2 Vols. Rome: Biblical Institute Press.

Zmijewski, J 1978. *Der Stil der paulinischen "Narrenrede": Analyse der Sprachgestaltung in 2 Kor 11,1—12,10 als Beitrag zur Methodik von Stiluntersuchungen neutestamentlicher Texte*. Köln: Peter Hanstein. (BBB.)

Index of References

1. Old Testament

3. Early Christian Literature

Apostolic Fathers

Hermas

— Sim

8,6,4	176
9,21,3	176

Wisdom of Solomon

13	188
13,1—9	187
13,4	186
14	71

TestLev

18,11	164

4. Early Jewish Literature

Bar

2,11	19

2 Bar

4,3	107
48,50	105
54,17—19	186

2 Esdras

10,40—57	107
10,53—55	107
11,10	19

4 Esdras

6,6	28

1 En

39.4	107
41.2	107
103.9—15	98

2 En

4.1	235
66.6	98, 124

Judith

9,8	19
13,11	19

Wisdom of Solomon

7,25 ff	31
7,25	18
9,9	56
12,15	18
12,17	18

Qumran Writings

— 4 QTLevi

3,8	235
18,11	164

— Hodajoth

III,6—12	33
III,9 f	33
IV,31 f	34
IX,25—27	34
XI,13 f	33

— 1 QH

2,23—25	99
5,18—19	99
5,25	99
7,17	221
7,19	221
9,3 ff	98
9,6—7	98
9,13	98
9,25—26	98
12,35	221

— 1 QM

10.5	221

— 1 QS

4,3	34
11,5	34

Philo

— ConfLing

136	32
172	32

Index of Authors

Index of Subjects

Wissenschaftliche Untersuchungen zum Neuen Testament

Alphabetical Index of the First and Second Series

Du Toit, David S.: Theios Anthropos. 1997.
Volume II/91

Dunn, James D.G. (Ed.): Jews and Christians.
1992. *Volume 66.*
– Paul and the Mosaic Law. 1996. *Volume 89.*

Dunn, James D.G., Hans Klein, Ulrich Luz and
Vasile Mihoc (Ed.): Auslegung der Bibel in
orthodoxer und westlicher Perspektive. 2000.
Volume 130.

Ebertz, Michael N.: Das Charisma des
Gekreuzigten. 1987. *Volume 45.*

Eckstein, Hans-Joachim: Der Begriff Syneidesis
bei Paulus. 1983. *Volume II/10.*
– Verheißung und Gesetz. 1996. *Volume 86.*

Ego, Beate: Im Himmel wie auf Erden. 1989.
Volume II/34

Ego, Beate und *Lange, Armin* sowie *Pilhofer,
Peter (Ed.):* Gemeinde ohne Tempel –
Community without Temple. 1999.
Volume 118.

Eisen, Ute E.: see *Paulsen, Henning.*

Ellis, E. Earle: Prophecy and Hermeneutic in
Early Christianity. 1978. *Volume 18.*
– The Old Testament in Early Christianity.
1991. *Volume 54.*

Ennulat, Andreas: Die ‚Minor Agreements‘.
1994. *Volume II/62.*

Ensor, Peter W.: Jesus and His 'Works'. 1996.
Volume II/85.

Eskola, Timo: Theodicy and Predestination in
Pauline Soteriology. 1998. *Volume II/100.*

Feldmeier, Reinhard: Die Krisis des Gottessohnes. 1987. *Volume II/21.*
– Die Christen als Fremde. 1992. *Volume 64.*

Feldmeier, Reinhard und *Ulrich Heckel* (Ed.):
Die Heiden. 1994. *Volume 70.*

Fletcher-Louis, Crispin H.T.: Luke-Acts: Angels,
Christology and Soteriology. 1997.
Volume II/94.

Förster, Niclas: Marcus Magus. 1999.
Volume 114.

Forbes, Christopher Brian: Prophecy and
Inspired Speech in Early Christianity and its
Hellenistic
Environment. 1995. *Volume II/75.*

Fornberg, Tord: see *Fridrichsen, Anton.*

Fossum, Jarl E.: The Name of God and the
Angel of the Lord. 1985. *Volume 36.*

Frenschkowski, Marco: Offenbarung und
Epiphanie. Volume 1 1995. *Volume II/79 –*
Volume 2 1997. *Volume II/80.*

Frey, Jörg: Eugen Drewermann und die
biblische Exegese. 1995. *Volume II/71.*
– Die johanneische Eschatologie. Band I. 1997.
Volume 96. – Band II. 1998. *Volume 110. –*
Band III. 2000. *Volume 117.*

Freyne, Sean: Galilee and Gospel. 2000.
Volume 125.

Fridrichsen, Anton: Exegetical Writings. Ed. von
C.C. Caragounis und T. Fornberg. 1994.
Volume 76.

Garlington, Don B.: ‚The Obedience of Faith‘.
1991. *Volume II/38.*
– Faith, Obedience, and Perseverance. 1994.
Volume 79.

Garnet, Paul: Salvation and Atonement in the
Qumran Scrolls. 1977. *Volume II/3.*

Gese, Michael: Das Vermächtnis des Apostels.
1997. *Volume II/99.*

Gräbe, Petrus J.: The Power of God in Paul's
Letters. 2000. *Volume II/123.*

Gräßer, Erich: Der Alte Bund im Neuen. 1985.
Volume 35.

Green, Joel B.: The Death of Jesus. 1988.
Volume II/33.

Gundry Volf, Judith M.: Paul and Perseverance.
1990. *Volume II/37.*

Hafemann, Scott J.: Suffering and the Spirit.
1986. *Volume II/19.*
– Paul, Moses, and the History of Israel. 1995.
Volume 81.

Hamid-Khani, Saeed: Relevation and
Concealment of Christ. 2000. *Volume II/120.*

Hannah, Darrel D.: Michael and Christ. 1999.
Volume II/109.

Hartman, Lars: Text-Centered New Testament
Studies. Ed. by D. Hellholm. 1997.
Volume 102.

Heckel, Theo K.: Der Innere Mensch. 1993.
Volume II/53.
– Vom Evangelium des Markus zum
viergestaltigen Evangelium. 1999.
Volume 120.

Heckel, Ulrich: Kraft in Schwachheit. 1993.
Volume II/56.
– see *Feldmeier, Reinhard.*
– see *Hengel, Martin.*

Heiligenthal, Roman: Werke als Zeichen. 1983.
Volume II/9.

Hellholm, D.: see *Hartman, Lars.*

Hemer, Colin J.: The Book of Acts in the Setting
of Hellenistic History. 1989. *Volume 49.*

Hengel, Martin: Judentum und Hellenismus.
1969, ³1988. *Volume 10.*
– Die johanneische Frage. 1993. *Volume 67.*
– Judaica et Hellenistica. Band 1. 1996.
Volume 90. – Band 2. 1999. *Volume 109.*

Hengel, Martin and *Ulrich Heckel* (Ed.): Paulus
und das antike Judentum. 1991. *Volume 58.*

Hengel, Martin und *Hermut Löhr* (Ed.):
Schriftauslegung im antiken Judentum und
im Urchristentum. 1994. *Volume 73.*

Hengel, Martin and *Anna Maria Schwemer:*
Paulus zwischen Damaskus und Antiochien.
1998. *Volume 108.*

Hengel, Martin and *Anna Maria Schwemer*
(Ed.): Königsherrschaft Gottes und
himmlischer Kult. 1991. *Volume 55.*

– Die Septuaginta. 1994. *Volume 72.*

Herrenbrück, Fritz: Jesus und die Zöllner. 1990.
Volume II/41.

Herzer, Jens: Paulus oder Petrus? 1998.
Volume 103.

Hoegen-Rohls, Christina: Der nachösterliche
Johannes. 1996. *Volume II/84.*

Hofius, Otfried: Katapausis. 1970. *Volume 11.*

– Der Vorhang vor dem Thron Gottes. 1972.
Volume 14.

– Der Christushymnus Philipper 2,6-11. 1976,
[2]1991. *Volume 17.*

– Paulusstudien. 1989, [2]1994. *Volume 51.*

Hofius, Otfried und *Hans-Christian Kammler:*
Johannesstudien. 1996. *Volume 88.*

Holtz, Traugott: Geschichte und Theologie des
Urchristentums. 1991. *Volume 57.*

Hommel, Hildebrecht: Sebasmata. Band 1 1983.
Volume 31 – Band 2 1984. *Volume 32.*

Hvalvik, Reidar: The Struggle for Scripture and
Covenant. 1996. *Volume II/82.*

Joubert, Stephan: Paul as Benefactor. 2000.
Volume II/124.

Kähler, Christoph: Jesu Gleichnisse als Poesie
und Therapie. 1995. *Volume 78.*

Kamlah, Ehrhard: Die Form der katalogischen
Paränese im Neuen Testament. 1964.
Volume 7.

Kammler, Hans-Christian: Christologie und
Eschatologie. 2000. *Volume 126.*

– see *Hofius, Otfried.*

Kelhoffer, James A.: Miracle and Mission. 1999.
Volume II/112.

Klein, Hans: see *Dunn, James D.G..*

Kieffer, René and *Jan Bergman (Ed.):* La Main
de Dieu / Die Hand Gottes. 1997. *Volume 94.*

Kim, Seyoon: The Origin of Paul's Gospel. 1981,
[2]1984. *Volume II/4.*

– „The ,Son of Man'" as the Son of God. 1983.
Volume 30.

Kleinknecht, Karl Th.: Der leidende Gerechtfertigte. 1984, [2]1988. *Volume II/13.*

Klinghardt, Matthias: Gesetz und Volk Gottes.
1988. *Volume II/32.*

Köhler, Wolf-Dietrich: Rezeption des Matthäusevangeliums in der Zeit vor Irenäus. 1987.
Volume II/24.

Korn, Manfred: Die Geschichte Jesu in
veränderter Zeit. 1993. *Volume II/51.*

Koskenniemi, Erkki: Apollonios von Tyana in
der neutestamentlichen Exegese. 1994.
Volume II/61.

Kraus, Wolfgang: Das Volk Gottes. 1996.
Volume 85.

– see *Walter, Nikolaus.*

Kuhn, Karl G.: Achtzehngebet und Vaterunser
und der Reim. 1950. *Volume 1.*

Kvalbein, Hans: see *Ådna, Jostein.*

Laansma, Jon: I Will Give You Rest. 1997.
Volume II/98.

Labahn, Michael: Offenbarung in Zeichen und
Wort. 2000. *Volume II/117.*

Lange, Armin: see *Ego, Beate.*

Lampe, Peter: Die stadtrömischen Christen in
den ersten beiden Jahrhunderten. 1987,
[2]1989. *Volume II/18.*

Landmesser, Christof: Wahrheit als Grundbe-
griff neutestamentlicher Wissenschaft. 1999.
Volume 113.

Lau, Andrew: Manifest in Flesh. 1996.
Volume II/86.

Lichtenberger, Hermann: see *Avemarie,
Friedrich.*

Lieu, Samuel N.C.: Manichaeism in the Later
Roman Empire and Medieval China. [2]1992.
Volume 63.

Loader, William R.G.: Jesus' Attitude Towards
the Law. 1997. *Volume II/97.*

Löhr, Gebhard: Verherrlichung Gottes durch
Philosophie. 1997. *Volume 97.*

Löhr, Hermut: see *Hengel, Martin.*

Löhr, Winrich Alfried: Basilides und seine
Schule. 1995. *Volume 83.*

Luomanen, Petri: Entering the Kingdom of
Heaven. 1998. *Volume II/101.*

Luz, Ulrich: see *Dunn, James D.G..*

Maier, Gerhard: Mensch und freier Wille. 1971.
Volume 12.

– Die Johannesoffenbarung und die Kirche.
1981. *Volume 25.*

Markschies, Christoph: Valentinus Gnosticus?
1992. *Volume 65.*

Marshall, Peter: Enmity in Corinth: Social
Conventions in Paul's Relations with the
Corinthians. 1987. *Volume II/23.*

McDonough, Sean M.: YHWH at Patmos: Rev.
1:4 in its Hellenistic and Early Jewish
Setting. 1999. *Volume II/107.*

Meade, David G.: Pseudonymity and Canon.
1986. *Volume 39.*

Meadors, Edward P.: Jesus the Messianic
Herald of Salvation. 1995. *Volume II/72.*

Meißner, Stefan: Die Heimholung des Ketzers.
1996. *Volume II/87.*

Mell, Ulrich: Die „anderen" Winzer. 1994.
Volume 77.

Mengel, Berthold: Studien zum Philipperbrief. 1982. *Volume II/8.*

Merkel, Helmut: Die Widersprüche zwischen den Evangelien. 1971. *Volume 13.*

Merklein, Helmut: Studien zu Jesus und Paulus. Volume 1 1987. *Volume 43.* – Volume 2 1998. *Volume 105.*

Metzler, Karin: Der griechische Begriff des Verzeihens. 1991. *Volume II/44.*

Metzner, Rainer: Die Rezeption des Matthäusevangeliums im 1. Petrusbrief. 1995. *Volume II/74.*

– Das Verständnis der Sünde im Johannesevangelium. 2000. *Volume 122.*

Mihoc, Vasile: see *Dunn, James D.G..*

Mittmann-Richert, Ulrike: Magnifikat und Benediktus. 1996. *Volume II/90.*

Mußner, Franz: Jesus von Nazareth im Umfeld Israels und der Urkirche. Ed. by M. Theobald. 1998. *Volume 111.*

Niebuhr, Karl-Wilhelm: Gesetz und Paränese. 1987. *Volume II/28.*

– Heidenapostel aus Israel. 1992. *Volume 62.*

Nielsen, Anders E.: "Until it is Fullfilled". 2000. *Volume II/126.*

Nissen, Andreas: Gott und der Nächste im antiken Judentum. 1974. *Volume 15.*

Noack, Christian: Gottesbewußtsein. 2000. *Volume II/116.*

Noormann, Rolf: Irenäus als Paulusinterpret. 1994. *Volume II/66.*

Obermann, Andreas: Die christologische Erfüllung der Schrift im Johannesevangelium. 1996. *Volume II/83.*

Okure, Teresa: The Johannine Approach to Mission. 1988. *Volume II/31.*

Oropeza, B. J.: Paul and Apostasy. 2000. *Volume II/115.*

Ostmeyer, Karl-Heinrich: Taufe und Typos. 2000. *Volume II/118.*

Paulsen, Henning: Studien zur Literatur und Geschichte des frühen Christentums. Ed. von Ute E. Eisen. 1997. *Volume 99.*

Pao, David W.: Acts and the Isaianic New Exodus. 2000. *Volume II/130.*

Park, Eung Chun: The Mission Discourse in Matthew's Interpretation. 1995. *Volume II/81.*

Park, Joseph S.: Conceptions of Afterlife in Jewish Insriptions. 2000. *Volume II/121.*

Pate, C. Marvin: The Reverse of the Curse. 2000. *Volume II/114.*

Philonenko, Marc (Ed.): Le Trône de Dieu. 1993. *Volume 69.*

Pilhofer, Peter: Presbyteron Kreitton. 1990. *Volume II/39.*

– Philippi. Volume 1 1995. *Volume 87.*

– see *Ego, Beate.*

Pöhlmann, Wolfgang: Der Verlorene Sohn und das Haus. 1993. *Volume 68.*

Pokorný, Petr und *Josef B. Souček:* Bibelauslegung als Theologie. 1997. *Volume 100.*

Porter, Stanley E.: The Paul of Acts. 1999. *Volume 115.*

Prieur, Alexander: Die Verkündigung der Gottesherrschaft. 1996. *Volume II/89.*

Probst, Hermann: Paulus und der Brief. 1991. *Volume II/45.*

Räisänen, Heikki: Paul and the Law. 1983, [2]1987. *Volume 29.*

Rehkopf, Friedrich: Die lukanische Sonderquelle. 1959. *Volume 5.*

Rein, Matthias: Die Heilung des Blindgeborenen (Joh 9). 1995. *Volume II/73.*

Reinmuth, Eckart: Pseudo-Philo und Lukas. 1994. *Volume 74.*

Reiser, Marius: Syntax und Stil des Markusevangeliums. 1984. *Volume II/11.*

Richards, E. Randolph: The Secretary in the Letters of Paul. 1991. *Volume II/42.*

Riesner, Rainer: Jesus als Lehrer. 1981, [3]1988. *Volume II/7.*

– Die Frühzeit des Apostels Paulus. 1994. *Volume 71.*

Rissi, Mathias: Die Theologie des Hebräerbriefs. 1987. *Volume 41.*

Röhser, Günter: Metaphorik und Personifikation der Sünde. 1987. *Volume II/25.*

Rose, Christian: Die Wolke der Zeugen. 1994. *Volume II/60.*

Rüger, Hans Peter: Die Weisheitsschrift aus der Kairoer Geniza. 1991. *Volume 53.*

Sänger, Dieter: Antikes Judentum und die Mysterien. 1980. *Volume II/5.*

– Die Verkündigung des Gekreuzigten und Israel. 1994. *Volume 75.*

– see *Burchard, Christoph*

Salzmann, Jorg Christian: Lehren und Ermahnen. 1994. *Volume II/59.*

Sandnes, Karl Olav: Paul – One of the Prophets? 1991. *Volume II/43.*

Sato, Migaku: Q und Prophetie. 1988. *Volume II/29.*

Schaper, Joachim: Eschatology in the Greek Psalter. 1995. *Volume II/76.*

Schimanowski, Gottfried: Weisheit und Messias. 1985. *Volume II/17.*

Schlichting, Günter: Ein jüdisches Leben Jesu. 1982. *Volume 24.*

Schnabel, Eckhard J.: Law and Wisdom from Ben Sira to Paul. 1985. *Volume II/16.*

Schutter, William L.: Hermeneutic and Composition in I Peter. 1989. *Volume II/30.*

Schwartz, Daniel R.: Studies in the Jewish Background of Christianity. 1992. *Volume 60.*

Schwemer, Anna Maria: see *Hengel, Martin*

Scott, James M.: Adoption as Sons of God. 1992.
Volume II/48.
– Paul and the Nations. 1995. *Volume 84.*
Siegert, Folker: Drei hellenistisch-jüdische
Predigten. Teil I 1980. *Volume 20* – Teil II
1992. *Volume 61.*
– Nag-Hammadi-Register. 1982. *Volume 26.*
– Argumentation bei Paulus. 1985. *Volume 34.*
– Philon von Alexandrien. 1988. *Volume 46.*
Simon, Marcel: Le christianisme antique et son
contexte religieux I/II. 1981. *Volume 23.*
Snodgrass, Klyne: The Parable of the Wicked
Tenants. 1983. *Volume 27.*
Söding, Thomas: Das Wort vom Kreuz. 1997.
Volume 93.
– see *Thüsing, Wilhelm.*
Sommer, Urs: Die Passionsgeschichte des
Markusevangeliums. 1993. *Volume II/58.*
Souček, Josef B.: see *Pokorný, Petr.*
Spangenberg, Volker: Herrlichkeit des Neuen
Bundes. 1993. *Volume II/55.*
Spanje, T.E. van: Inconsistency in Paul?. 1999.
Volume II/110.
Speyer, Wolfgang: Frühes Christentum im
antiken Strahlungsfeld. Band I: 1989.
Volume 50. – Band II: 1999. *Volume 116.*
Stadelmann, Helge: Ben Sira als Schriftgelehr-
ter. 1980. *Volume II/6.*
Stenschke, Christoph W.: Luke's Portrait of
Gentiles Prior to Their Coming to Faith.
Volume II/108.
Stettler, Christian: Der Kolosserhymnus. 2000.
Volume II/131.
Stettler, Hanna: Die Christologie der Pastoral-
briefe. 1998. *Volume II/105.*
Strobel, August: Die Stunde der Wahrheit. 1980.
Volume 21.
Stroumsa, Guy G.: Barbarian Philosophy. 1999.
Volume 112.
Stuckenbruck, Loren T.: Angel Veneration and
Christology. 1995. *Volume II/70.*
Stuhlmacher, Peter (Ed.): Das Evangelium und
die Evangelien. 1983. *Volume 28.*
Sung, Chong-Hyon: Vergebung der Sünden.
1993. *Volume II/57.*
Tajra, Harry W.: The Trial of St. Paul. 1989.
Volume II/35.
– The Martyrdom of St.Paul. 1994.
Volume II/67.

Theißen, Gerd: Studien zur Soziologie des
Urchristentums. 1979, [3]1989. *Volume 19.*
Theobald, Michael: see *Mußner, Franz.*
Thornton, Claus-Jürgen: Der Zeuge des
Zeugen. 1991. *Volume 56.*
Thüsing, Wilhelm: Studien zur neutestamentli-
chen Theologie. Ed. von Thomas Söding.
1995. *Volume 82.*
Thurén, Lauri: Derhetorizing Paul. 2000.
Volume 124.
Treloar, Geoffrey R.: Lightfoot the Historian.
1998. *Volume II/103.*
Tsuji, Manabu: Glaube zwischen Vollkommen-
heit und Verweltlichung. 1997. *Volume II/93*
Twelftree, Graham H.: Jesus the Exorcist. 1993.
Volume II/54.
Visotzky, Burton L.: Fathers of the World. 1995.
Volume 80.
Wagener, Ulrike: Die Ordnung des „Hauses
Gottes". 1994. *Volume II/65.*
Walter, Nikolaus: Praeparatio Evangelica. Ed.
by Wolfgang Kraus und Florian Wilk. 1997.
Volume 98.
Wander, Bernd: Gottesfürchtige und Sympathi-
santen. 1998. *Volume 104.*
Watts, Rikki: Isaiah's New Exodus and Mark.
1997. *Volume II/88.*
Wedderburn, A.J.M.: Baptism and Resurrection.
1987. *Volume 44.*
Wegner, Uwe: Der Hauptmann von Kafarnaum.
1985. *Volume II/14.*
Welck, Christian: Erzählte ‚Zeichen'. 1994.
Volume II/69.
Wiarda, Timothy: Peter in the Gospels . 2000.
Volume II/127.
Wilk, Florian: see *Walter, Nikolaus.*
Williams, Catrin H.: I am He. 2000.
Volume II/113.
Wilson, Walter T.: Love without Pretense. 1991.
Volume II/46.
Zimmermann, Alfred E.: Die urchristlichen
Lehrer. 1984, [2]1988. *Volume II/12.*
Zimmermann, Johannes: Messianische Texte
aus Qumran. 1998. *Volume II/104.*
Zimmermann, Ruben: Geschlechtermetaphorik
und Geschlechterverhältnis. 2000.
Volume II/122.

For a complete catalogue please write to the publisher
Mohr Siebeck · Postfach 2030 · D–72010 Tübingen.
Up-to-date information on the internet at http://www.mohr.de